Horrifying Sex

ALSO BY RUTH BIENSTOCK ANOLIK

The Gothic Other: Racial and Social Constructions in the Literary Imagination (McFarland, 2003)

Horrifying Sex

*Essays on Sexual Difference
in Gothic Literature*

Edited by RUTH BIENSTOCK ANOLIK

McFarland & Company, Inc., Publishers
Jefferson, North Carolina, and London

LIBRARY OF CONGRESS CATALOGUING-IN-PUBLICATION DATA

Anolik, Ruth Bienstock
    Horrifying sex : essays on sexual difference in Gothic literature / edited by Ruth Bienstock Anolik.
      p.   cm.
    Includes bibliographical references and index.

    ISBN-13: 978-0-7864-3014-7
    (softcover : 50# alkaline paper) ∞

    1. English literature—19th century—History and criticism. 2. Sex differences (Psychology) in literature. 3. English literature—20th century—History and criticism. 4. American literature—19th century—History and criticism. 5. American literature—20th century—History and criticism. 6. Horror tales, English—History and criticism. 7. Horror tales, American—History and criticism. 8. Gothic revival (Literature)—Great Britain. 9. Gothic revival (Literature)—United States. 10. Sex role in literature. I. Anolik, Ruth Bienstock, 1952–
PR468.S48H67   2007
820.9'353—dc22   2007015389

British Library cataloguing data are available

©2007 Ruth Bienstock Anolik. All rights reserved

No part of this book may be reproduced or transmitted in any form or by any means, electronic or mechanical, including photocopying or recording, or by any information storage and retrieval system, without permission in writing from the publisher.

Cover image ©2007 Thinkstock

Manufactured in the United States of America

McFarland & Company, Inc., Publishers
  Box 611, Jefferson, North Carolina 28640
    www.mcfarlandpub.com

In memory of Herbert Bienstock
and in honor of June Klein Bienstock,
my parents, who taught me
by example that human difference is cause
for celebration, not horror.

Acknowledgments

To Bob, Jonathan, Rachel and Sarah, my reluctant muses. To Doug Howard, my partner in *The Gothic Other*. To my friends whose celebration of my earlier effort continues to encourage me: Debby and Joe Foster, Sharon Pollack, Barbie Zelizer and Carol Gantman.

An earlier version of Dawn Fulton's essay appeared in *Emerging Perspectives on Maryse Condé: A Writer of Her Own*, edited by Sarah Barbour and Gerise Herndon (Trenton, NJ: Africa World Press, 2006).

An earlier version of Paulina Palmer's essay appeared in her book, *Lesbian Gothic: Transgressive Fictions* (London: Cassell/ Continuum 1999).

Contents

Acknowledgments   vi

Introduction. Sexual Horror: Fears of the Sexual Other
(Ruth Bienstock Anolik)   1

PART I. THE FATAL WOMAN

1. Life-in-Death: The Monstrous Female and the Gothic Labyrinth in *Aliens* and "Ligeia" *(Katherine Henry)*   27

2. Morbid Mothers: Gothic Heredity in Florence Marryat's *The Blood of the Vampire* *(Octavia Davis)*   40

3. The Unbearable Hybridity of Female Sexuality: Racial Ambiguity and the Gothic in Rider Haggard's *She* *(Tamar Heller)*   55

4. Frankenstein's Other: The Monstrous Feminine in Maryse Condé's *Célanire cou-coupé* *(Dawn Fulton)*   67

PART II. THE SATANIC MALE

5. "There Was a Man": Dangerous Husbands and Fathers in *The Winter's Tale, A Sicilian Romance* and *Linden Hills* *(Ruth Bienstock Anolik)*   83

6. Sexual or Supernatural: Threats in Radcliffe's *The Italian* *(Elizabeth Harlan)*   102

7. Investigating the Third Story: "Bluebeard" and "Cinderella" in *Jane Eyre* *(Victoria Anderson)*   111

8. Monstrous Men: Violence and Masculinity in Robert Browning's *The Ring and the Book* *(Michael Ackerman)*   122

9. "I Am God": The Domineering Patriarch in Shirley Jackson's Gothic Fiction *(Bernice M. Murphy)*   135

Part III. Homosexual Horror

10. Other Love: Le Fanu's *Carmilla* as Lesbian Gothic
    (*Adrienne Antrim Major*) — 151

11. Preying on the Pervert: The Uses of Homosexual Panic
    in Bram Stoker's *Dracula* (*Damion Clark*) — 167

12. Horror and Homosexuality in Christopher Isherwood's
    Mr. Norris Changes Trains (*Brian Whaley*) — 177

13. Invasion of the Husband Snatchers: Masculine Crisis and
    the Lavender Menace in *I Married a Monster from Outer
    Space* (*Andrew Scahill*) — 188

Part IV. *Vive la Différence*: Celebrating the Sexual Other

14. The Lesbian Vampire: Transgressive Sexuality
    (*Paulina Palmer*) — 203

15. Another "Gendered Other"? The Female Monster-Hero
    (*Julie Miess*) — 233

16. Imagineer: Clive Barker's Queering of the Conservative
    Bent of Horror Literature (*K.A. Laity*) — 248

Contributors — 259

Index — 263

Introduction

Sexual Horror: Fears of the Sexual Other
RUTH BIENSTOCK ANOLIK

Although it is always dangerous to attempt to define the generically slippery Gothic mode, one theme that typically emerges in any text aligned with the Gothic tradition is the encounter with the unknown. This theme informs most of the tropes that conventionally identify the Gothic: the dark and labyrinthine castle that resists apprehension by the hapless characters who invariably get lost in its depths; the equally dark and labyrinthine text that resists readerly comprehension; the ghosts and other supernatural beings who resist human understanding; the tendency of the Gothic text to open in a belated moment, ensuring that neither reader nor characters understand the situation in which they find themselves. Perhaps the motif that best emblematizes the power of the unknown in the Gothic text is the construction of the many walls and barriers that invariably arise to block the movement of the Gothic subject. While these walls are correctly interpreted as articulating the constraints imposed upon the Gothic body, particularly that of the young woman, it is important to recognize that these walls also represent epistemological resistance: the subject cannot know what lies beyond.

In *The Gothic Text* Marshall Brown delineates the epistemological significance of the Gothic barrier, as well as contextualizing the Gothic moment within the age of the Enlightenment. Brown proposes an analogue between the paradigms of consciousness posited by the Gothic and by Kant. Both present a model in which transcendent mysteries lie beyond the boundaries of that which is available to human comprehension: the known lies within the bounds accessible to Enlightenment reason and the unknown lurks beyond these boundaries. Brown suggests that the Gothic fascination with this unknown is a reflection of the Enlightenment response to the limits of reason. Brown's thinking is clearly indebted to Terry Castle, who contextualizes the development of an anxious response to the unknown and the incomprehensible within the Enlightenment in

The Female Thermometer; Castle makes a compelling case for the necessity of the Enlightenment as a precondition for the sense of the uncanny that informs the Gothic text. Castle thus expands the metaphor of the Enlightenment: the presence of light is what allows for the casting of frightening dark shadows. The place of dark shadows that is created by the light of the Enlightenment, the dark recesses of the human psyche inaccessible to reason, is the locus of the Gothic.[1]

Traditionally, the emblem of the unknown that lurks behind the Gothic wall is the supernatural, the monstrous, the inhuman: the gigantic ghost of the deposed Alfonso in Horace Walpole's *The Castle of Otranto* (1764); the horrifying ghost of the Bleeding Nun in Matthew Lewis's *The Monk* (1796); Satan himself in Charlotte Dacre's *Zofloya* (1806). Yet there is an equally powerful Gothic tendency to locate horror upon the human Other who becomes the emblem of unknown danger. The human being who lies beyond the barrier of epistemological apprehension by virtue of being different from the subject then takes the place of the ghost or monster as the source of Gothic horror. As Patrick Brantlinger suggests in *The Reading Lesson*, the shift from a supernatural source of horror to a human source makes great sense during the time of the Enlightenment. In discussing Smollett's *Ferdinand Count Fathom* (1753) as a forerunner of the Gothic, Brantlinger observes: "*Fathom* does not depend on supernatural machinery; and anyway, in an enlightened age, who could be so credulous as to believe in phantoms and necromancy?" (31). As the power of ghosts to impose fear wanes, the mysterious power of the human Other increases. As Terry Castle suggests in her essay "The Spectralization of the Other in *The Mysteries of Udolpho*," the Enlightenment focus on the thinking of the self, and the Romantic and Gothic emphasis on the feeling of the self converge in an amplified sense of the inner self and a complementary diminished awareness of the Other, who is reduced to the status of a ghost, not quite real. Thus with the spectralization of others, and the awareness that some parts of the human psyche are inaccessible even to the self, the locus of the truly mysterious unknown becomes the human mind rather than the haunted house.

David Frankfurter traces the progression of the construction of the Other as inhumanly unknowable to the construction of the Other as the dangerous and horrifying source of evil. His work *Evil Incarnate* provides a useful overview of the tendency to incarnate transcendent evil in the human Other, the person who is the unknowable member of a mysterious nonnormative group, perceived as evil because of the markers of difference that designate the Other. Frankfurter provides examples of this tendency: the configuring of women as witches, the accusations of Jews in the blood libel and more recent accusations of Satanic rituals in day-care centers. He also explains how this tendency is abused by leaders who demonize the Other for political ends. Thus in Frankfurter's view, the notion of evil is a myth, a cultural construct, the result of objectification, of failing to see the Other as a subject. Viewed through this prism, the central Gothic struggle between Good and Evil is humanized; the struggle is not between transcendent Good and Evil but between the human Self and the equally human but seemingly inhuman and dangerous Other. This reading of the Gothic struggle suggests a useful distinguishing quality of the Gothic, a way of recognizing the Gothic novel (and other Gothic texts as well). In *Reading the Other* Carol de Dobay Rifelj argues that the project of "the novel" is to know the Other: "the province of the novel is that of intersubjectivity" (viii). Rifelj examines a number of novels that she thinks address the mystery of "the mental life of other people [to] engage the problem of other minds from difference angles" (viii). It is not surprising to note that none of the novels that Rifelj examines fall within the Gothic tradition. For the Gothic novel transgresses the boundaries of this attempt at generic definition; the project of the Gothic is the reverse of that which Rifelj identifies within that monolithic entity "the novel." Indeed, the Gothic text, including the Gothic novel, focuses unremittingly on the subjectivity of the Self; in encountering the incomprehensible (and therefore dangerously evil) Other, the Gothic self acquires only self-knowledge.

The encounter of the Gothic self with the unknown human Other characterized by difference in race, religion or class is the concern of *The Gothic Other: Racial and Social Constructions in the Literary Imagination*, which I edited with Douglas Howard. That collection focuses on moments in which the Gothic encounter with the unknown is figured as the encounter with the dark and mysterious human Other, who is rendered preternaturally inhuman because of differences in race, religion or class.[2] The earlier collection thus argues for congruence between the Gothic fear of physical darkness, which presents an epistemological barrier to perception, and the fear of racial darkness and other social markers of difference, which present a psychological barrier to social understanding. As *The Gothic Other* suggests, increased encounters between various social groups that accompanied eighteenth century exploration and commercialization ensured that since the time of the emergence of the Gothic, the racial, cultural and religious human Other is a more visible and credible threat than any supernatural ghost.

Unlike the Other who comes from beyond the containing boundaries of race, social class or religion, usually bearing markers of difference, the sexual Other — the figure that haunts this collection, *Horrifying Sex* — is always present. For although the sexual Other is mysterious, threatening and different, lurking on the other side of the sexual divide, no national barriers or cultural or social markers separate the sexual Other from the Self. The sexual Other is thus particularly and unavoidably dangerous, infiltrating the home and even the bed of the threatened Self. Moreover, as Simone de Beauvoir observes in *The Second Sex,* "Eroticism is a movement toward the *Other*" (446)—there is a strong human impulse to encounter, rather than to avoid, the sexual Other. Additionally, as Beauvoir suggests in her introduction to *The Second Sex,* since the attraction is mutual, the sexual Other cannot avoid this bond either. The statement she makes regarding the figure of the woman is applicable to others who are marked by sexual difference, the man, the homosexual, the lesbian: "The bond that unites her to her oppressor is not comparable to any other [...] the cleavage of society along the line of sex is impossible" (xxv). Thus the Self and the sexual Other are inextricably linked, irrevocably forced into tense and frightening encounters with the unknown. The Gothic text repeatedly reminds its readers that there is no escape from the dangers of the sexual Other. Even the cloister, a favorite Gothic locus, is not safe: nuns and monks, like Agnes and Ambrosio in Lewis's *The Monk,* are also subject to the depredations of the sexual Other. As in the case of Lewis's novel, the encounter with the human Other who is paradoxically similar (sharing the markers of the normative) but different (marked by sexual difference) generates the anxiety that drives the texts discussed in the essays in this collection.

The observation that the Gothic text is haunted by sexual anxiety is, of course, not particularly startling.[3] But this collection amplifies that observation to assert that Gothic anxieties regarding sex and sexuality are a manifestation of the fear of the unknown; the anxiety is not generated by some generalized fear of sex but is an anxious response to the difference of the sexual Other—male, female or homosexual—who resists epistemological apprehension and who is as unknowable and therefore as mysterious and frightening as the supernatural. And indeed, it is possible to see the fear of the unknown supernatural and the fear of the unknowable sexual Other co-existing from the earliest moment of the English Gothic,[4] the period of the high Gothic beginning with Horace Walpole's *Castle of Otranto* (1764) and ending with Charles Maturin's *Melmoth the Wanderer* (1820). While the early Gothic texts obligingly feature an array of classical supernatural manifestations, each also presents an equally unsettling human figure who is dangerous not because of supernatural powers but because of sexual difference: Walpole's iconic villain Manfred who attempts to rape the innocent Isabella to perpetuate his corrupt dynasty; Lewis's monk, Ambrosio, who poses a fatal sexual danger to the virginal Antonia (who is, coincidentally and unknown to him, his sister), and Lewis's seductive Matilda, whose sexuality first leads Ambrosio astray; Maturin's Melmoth, who seduces the innocent

Immalee — he is the serpent in her paradise, the "tempter" (291) who leads her astray. The temptation he poses is sexual and his demonic possession of her is figured as a marriage: "Wed me ... *and you shall be mine for ever and ever*" (324, italics Maturin's).

As these examples indicate, there is usually slippage between sexual danger and supernatural danger in the Gothic text. For in each case the danger posed by the sexual Other is informed by supernatural danger. Matilda aligns herself squarely with the supernatural by selling her soul to the Devil; Melmoth is a Satan-like creature, living eternally and damning souls; even the mundane Manfred has a supernatural counterpart, the ghost of his grandfather who steps down from a picture as Manfred tries to rape Isabella. Thus in each of these texts the sexual Other takes on the aura of dangerous power from the supernatural, suggesting that the sexual Other is, like the ghostly manifestation, preternaturally dangerous. This slippage works both ways: sometimes a supernatural manifestation will take on the aura of sexual danger as in the case of Lewis's Bleeding Nun, whose epithet suggests the dangers posed by the menstruating woman (a perceived danger that is discussed in the essays of Octavia Davis and Julie Miess in this collection). As the essays of Adrienne Antrim Major, Damion Clark, and Andrew Scahill suggest, in the case of the homosexual Other, the sexual danger is so frighteningly inexpressible that it can be articulated only through a relocation onto a figure of supernatural horror.

In *Making Sex*, Thomas Laquer explains why the singular fear of the sexual Other and sexual difference might emerge in the Gothic text during the time of the Enlightenment, to supplement other fears of human difference. Laquer argues that one of the many conceptual boundaries developed by Enlightenment epistemology was the distinct boundary between the sexes. While this boundary certainly also has an economic basis, Laquer shows how, as labor became gendered once economic activity moved from the farm to the factory, economic divisions were supported by epistemological divisions. He cites the pre-Enlightenment notion of the woman as a variation of the male, rather than as a distinct type: "The record on which I have relied bears witness to the fundamental incoherence of stable, fixed categories of sexual dimorphism, of male and/or female" (22). This paradigm, however, changed during the Enlightenment: "in or about the late eighteenth [century], to use Virginia Woolf's device, human sexual nature changed.... By around 1800, writers of all sorts were determined to base what they insisted were fundamental differences between the male and female sexes ... on discoverable biological distinctions" (5). This, as Laquer notes, produced a "shift" in the "social order," as writers made determinations about the "political, economic, and cultural lives of men and women, their gender roles" (6),[5] resulting in a rigid binary structure of two mutually exclusive sexual categories.[6] In creating this structure, the Enlightenment creates the space of the other gender, an unknown territory that is the locus of the Gothic. Of course another binary that thus developed was the heterosexual/homosexual, or normative/nonnormative binary. As the gender roles solidified, the homosexual who did not fit neatly into the male/female binary was excluded completely, consigned to the realm of the unspoken and the unknown. In writing of the *fin-de-siècle* in *Sexual Anarchy*, Elaine Showalter notes a later development of this tendency, as well as its relation to constructions of other models of the human Other: "In periods of cultural insecurity, when there are fears of regression and degeneration, the longing for strict border controls around the definition of gender, as well as race, class and nationality, becomes especially intense" (4). The essays in *Horrifying Sex* explore the cultural work performed by the Gothic that both concretizes and interrogates the borders that demarcate sexuality, through representations of the horrifying Other who lurks on the other side of the sexual border.

The nature of Gothic representation explains why the response (of both subject and reader) to the sexual Other, shunted by Enlightenment categorization to the other side of the epistemological divide, is best described as "horror," and not as "terror," horror's tamer relative. The distinction between the two is established early in the history of Gothic criticism by Ann Radcliffe in "On the Supernatural in Poetry," published in 1826:

> Terror and horror are so far opposite, that the first expands the soul and awakens the faculties to a high degree of life; the other contracts, freezes, and nearly annihilates them ... and where lies the great difference between horror and terror, but in the uncertainty and obscurity, that accompany the first, respecting the dreaded evil? [168].

Thus in Radcliffe's still-influential formulation, terror is wrapped up in suspense and dread; it is the fear that has not yet been realized, the fear generated by the danger that has not yet been encountered, and is thus closer to the sense of the infinite sublime because the possibilities for terror are infinite. Horror, on the other hand, is the fear that has been realized; the danger having been encountered, nothing remains for the imagination. The *frisson* of suspense is drained from this emotion as the subject's fully explicit encounter with dangerous evil lacks all "uncertainty" or "obscurity."

An analogy may be made between these two responses and the two approaches deployed by the Gothic text in representing the human Other: spectralization and demonization. In the case of spectralization, as described by Castle in "The Spectralization of the Other," the other is reduced to a marginal, ghostlike presence; spectralization represents a social and psychological repression. Thus, for example, the many absent and abject mothers who silently and invisibly haunt the Gothic text.[7] But since these specters are notable for their absence, they evoke at most a vague terror. Horror is evoked when the second Gothic strategy, demonization of the Other, is deployed. In this case the incarnation of evil, including the returning repressed specter, is fully present and visible. Since the often-alluring sexual Other is inevitably encountered in the everyday world and since the Gothic text cannot resist the encounter with the frightening unknown, the horrified response typically characterizes the Gothic encounter with the sexual Other.

The second term of the title of this collection also requires some explication. For certainly horror is evoked not only by the biological distinction of "sex" but by the social, cultural and psychological distinction of "gender." In subsuming both concepts under the rubric "sex," I invoke Laquer's argument for an erasure of the linguistic boundary between the two terms: "sex" and "gender." Laquer makes a compelling case for this erasure: "on the basis of historical evidence ... almost everything one wants to *say* about sex—however sex is understood—already has in it a claim about gender. Sex ... is explicable only within this context of battles over gender and power" (11). In "Derrida and Gender," Peggy Kamuf makes a similar argument, observing that "the distinction often made in English between sex and gender" (83) does not exist in French. Kamuf turns to Judith Butler to argue that there is a "continuity in the place of the supposed 'radical discontinuity' between the two terms" (83). Kamuf quotes Butler's *Gender Trouble* (7): "Perhaps this construct called 'sex' is as culturally constructed as gender; indeed, perhaps it was always already gender, with the consequence that the distinction between sex and gender turns out to be no distinction at all" (qtd. in Kamuf 84). That approach is also taken in this collection in which it is to be understood that all statements about "sex" are made in a historical and cultural context and thus are linked to the idea of "gender."

As the essays in *Horrifying Sex* reveal, the strategy of turning to the sexual Other to generate Gothic fear does not end with the Enlightenment, nor is it confined to the "canonical" Anglo-American Gothic texts produced during the period of the high Gothic. In fact, this collection contests the notion that the Gothic begins in 1764 with the publication of Walpole's *The Castle of Otranto* and ends with the publication of *Melmoth* in 1820; the range of the essays in *Horrifying Sex* also disputes the notion that the Gothic is confined to the genre of prose fiction. For the texts covered in this collection span the centuries — from pre-Enlightenment through the twentieth century—and the continents. Many genres of literature are considered here: drama, poetry, folktale and film, in addition to the more conventional Gothic novel and short story. What brings this disparate group of texts together is their horrified response to the unknown sexual Other; this collection thus asserts that this particular trope, whenever or wherever it appears, links the text to the Gothic tradition. The variety of texts that thereby find their way into the Gothic tradition and into this collection attests to the transgressive resistance of the ever-evolving, yet ever-repeating Gothic mode to the containment of chronological, generic and national categories.

    The essays in *Horrifying Sex* are organized by the type of sexual Other who haunts the Gothic text. The first three parts of the collection correspond to three recurring types: the female sexual Other in "The Fatal Woman"; the male sexual Other in "The Satanic Male"; the homosexual Other in "Homosexual Horror." The fourth part of the collection, "*Vive la Différence:* Celebrating the Sexual Other," marks the reversal of the conventional tendency to demonize the sexual Other that is traced by the essays in the first three sections; the texts discussed in this last section promote a celebration of the sexual Other and an interrogation of the systems that construct the nonnormative person as an Other.

    Part I of *Horrifying Sex* reflects the primacy of the construction of the female Other by male hegemony identified by Simone de Beauvoir in *The Second Sex*. The title of this section, "The Fatal Woman," a translation of the French *femme fatale*, is meant to indicate an expansion of the meaning of the French term: as the essays in this section reveal, all women, not just the dangerously alluring, are subject to being represented as the demonized Other. Beauvoir demonstrates that the patriarchy figures the male as the Self, the subject who is knowable and human, and the female as the Other, not fully human nor fully comprehensible, object rather than subject. Laquer extends Beauvoir's insights; he notes that the female body, too, is construed as different and incomprehensible: the "unstable female body ... is either a version of or wholly different from a generally unproblematic, stable male body" (22). The male body thus represents the fixed norm against which the mysteriously abnormal female body, with its mysteriously invisible reproductive apparatus, is measured. Showalter notes the representation of women in the *fin de siècle* as "figures of disorder.... Women's social or cultural marginality seems to place them on the borderlines of the symbolic order" (8). Citing Laqueur's work, Showalter remarks that while the modern age works to "shore up" (8) the boundaries between genders, "the sexual borderline between the masculine and the feminine represented the dangerous vanishing point of sexual difference" (8).[8] The horrified response to these disruptive women is traced by Julia Kristeva and Judith Halberstam. In *Powers of Horror*, Kristeva marks the shift from repulsion to horror. Since cultural borders provide a sense of security, "a border that has encroached upon everything" (3) is cause for horror: "It is thus not lack of cleanliness or health that causes abjection but what disturbs identity, system, order" (4). In *Skin Shows,* Judith Halberstam adds that the monstrous body is repulsive and horrifying because it resists stable, normative categories. In transgressing the model of the normative male body, the female body is construed as monstrous by the horrified gaze of the patriarchy.[9] As we shall see in the essays in "The Fatal Woman," the cultural horror[10] generated by the monstrous, non-normative, transgressive and powerful woman readily translates to Gothic horror in response to the inhumanly different female constructed by the Gothic text. Of course the Gothic does not invent this figure—and indeed one of the recurring themes of *Horrifying Sex* is that most tropes regarded as Gothic predate the "invention" of the Gothic in the eighteenth century.[11] In fact, the Gothic does not create cultural anxieties so much as it identifies them and gives them a voice and a face.

The monstrous woman is given a quite monstrous face in the texts discussed by Katherine Henry in "Life-in-Death: The Monstrous Female and the Gothic Labyrinth in *Aliens* and 'Ligeia.'" Henry traces the construction of the trope of the supernaturally and monstrously dangerous female Other in a twentieth century film and in a canonical nineteenth century Gothic story by Poe. Both texts present the female body as the dark and labyrinthine site of the unknown. Building on Beauvoir's notions of the female body as posing conflicting possibilities of liberating transcendence and engulfing immanence to the male subject, Henry asserts that each text represents this troubling paradox through horrifying representations of a female body that ultimately engulfs the questing male subject defeating his dream of transcendence. Henry's reading further suggests that the monster of *Aliens* is particularly monstrous because of her preternatural maternal power.

In "Morbid Mothers: Gothic Heredity in Florence Marryat's *The Blood of the Vampire*," Octavia Davis considers another anxious response to the threatening power of the procreating female body, also projected onto the figure of the unnatural, monstrous woman. Marryat's novel constructs the image of the female vampire who embodies the cultural fears of Victorian England regarding the procreating (menstruating and sexually active) woman. Davis demonstrates that such women were figured in contemporary medical writing as being blood-deprived and therefore parasitic, cannibalistic and vampiric, drawing energy from those around them to replenish the resources lost in menstruation and childbirth. In tracing Marryat's amplification of the representation of the woman in the scientific literature, Davis uncovers misogyny disguised as science in the nineteenth century and demonstrates how irrational anxieties may inform contemporary truisms. Davis also demonstrates the tendency of the female writer to internalize the message of the dominant culture that figures her as monstrous and dangerous.

In addition to posing a sexual danger, the female vampire in *The Blood of the Vampire*, whose lineage is biracial, represents the hybridized racial Other. The undying, dangerously voracious woman that Tamar Heller discusses in "The Unbearable Hybridity of Female Sexuality: Racial Ambiguity and the Gothic in Rider Haggard's *She*," also explores the double threat presented by racial and sexual Otherness to the Victorian imagination. Heller asserts that this threat indicates the intersection of anxieties about imperial power and masculine power; the figure of Ayesha endangers British manliness on a political and sexual level. Moreover, Heller argues, the dangers posed by Ayesha are even more unsettling because of the sense that the proper white woman is potentially as dangerous as the racial Other because of their shared sexuality.

The anxieties that occur at the crossroads of sex, race and empire also appear in the text discussed by Dawn Fulton in "Frankenstein's Other: The Monstrous Feminine in Maryse Condé's *Célanire cou-coupé*." In studying Condé, a contemporary West Indian who writes in French, Fulton discovers another instance of a feminized Gothic icon of monstrous Otherness: Condé's female version of Frankenstein's monster. Fulton argues that Condé's creature is monstrous not only because of her unknown origins, unnatural re-creation and ambiguous inscrutability, but also because she represents sexual and racial transgression. Here too the anxious representation of the woman betrays concerns regarding maternal power—the fear that the monstrous mother will produce a monstrous child. Fulton draws connections between the figure of the monstrous woman—subject to multiple interpretations but resistant to a single confining interpretation—and the monstrously fantastic text, equally resistant to a defining hermeneutic, especially as it is located within a multicultural network with a number of different and competing interpretative perspectives.

The writers of the essays that appear in Part II, "The Satanic Male," consider texts that invert the hegemonic male perspective revealed in the previous section: these texts construct the Self as female, gazing with horror at the male Other. As Beauvoir recognizes: "To be sure, each sex incarnates the Other in the eyes of the opposite sex" (230). And indeed the subjectivity of the woman is unique in enfolding the sense of Otherness: "to be a woman would mean to be the object, the Other ... the Other nevertheless remains subject in the midst of her resignation" (Beauvoir 51). Beauvoir further qualifies her definition of female subjectivity: "but in man's eyes woman often appears in spite of everything as an *absolute other*" (230). Thus in taking the perspective of the female object, the texts discussed in this essay align themselves with the mode of the

Female Gothic, which is inherently subversive in operating from the perspective that displaces the perspective of the patriarchy.

The category of Gothic first noted and designated as "female Gothic" by Moers in *Literary Women* (1976) typically expresses female concerns using female strategies; Female Gothic is written from and to the female perspective, focusing on concerns of women. As indicated in the collection of essays *The Female Gothic*, edited by Juliann Fleenor, the Gothic written from the female point of view typically features a fearful representation of a male, who is so cruelly dangerous as to appear inhuman. Hence Joanna Russ's wonderfully titled essay in that collection: "Somebody's Trying to Kill Me and I Think It's My Husband: The Modern Gothic." Yet despite this evocative title, Russ misses an important point: the coherence that connects the various strains of the Gothic. She writes that texts which are "modern Gothic ... bear no resemblance to the literary definition of 'Gothic.' They are not related to the works of Monk Lewis or Mrs. Radcliffe, whose real descendants are known today as Horror Stories. The Modern Gothic resembles instead, a crossbreed of *Jane Eyre* and Daphne Du Maurier's *Rebecca*" (34). The texts covered by the essays in "The Satanic Male" indicate that attempts like Russ's to construct generic boundaries around the Gothic are always subject to deconstruction. Although a number of the texts examined do not fit into Russ's generic category, or indeed, into any canonically pure definition of the Gothic, each displays the sensibility of the Female Gothic; even those texts authored by male writers demonstrate the horror evoked by the male Other, the type that haunts the Gothic, beginning with Walpole's Manfred, chasing the innocent Isabella through the labyrinths of the haunted Castle of Otranto in an attempt to rape her.[12]

Yet, as the story of Manfred suggests, there is a motivation other than sexual for the inhuman malevolence and danger posed to the woman by the male sexual Other. For Manfred's primary desire is not sexual but dynastic; his desire for Isabella's body is motivated by his desire to engender an heir so that he can perpetuate his dynasty and consolidate his property ownership. And, as the essays in this section indicate, this is typical of the male Other. Although the occasional villain, like Lewis's monk Ambrosio, is motivated mainly by lust, greed motivates most of his cohorts, including the iconic Montoni in Radcliffe's *The Mysteries of Udolpho*. Thus, whereas the female is construed as monstrous in the Gothic because of psycho-sexual anxieties of the male in response to the mysterious, non-normative female body and mind, the horrifying male Other expresses anxieties that have as much to do with the body politic as with the sexual body. The fear of the male or of male sexuality is a symptom of the anxious response to unbridled power (including sexual power) that social structures grant the heterosexual male. Thus, to return briefly to the distinction discredited above, the fears generated by the male sexual Other are attributable more to gender than to sex; the expression of sexual fears is a code for fears determined by gender differences. This argument extends the perception articulated by Judith Halberstam, who points out (as quoted by Michael Ackerman in this collection) that often within the Gothic "rape ... is not the sexual enactment of violence ... it is violence enacted with bodily or fleshly weapons. *Sex is a metaphor for violence,* not the other way around" (156).[13] In fact, the violence that is encoded in the Gothic by the danger of rape is not only physical. As the essays in this collection show, the violence posed by men in the material world of law and culture can take psychological and legal forms that are no less damaging for not being physical. Thus while the effects of the powerful male may be all too visible, he too is encoded as a mysterious Other, inscrutably and inhumanly destructive.

Perhaps the best evidence for the argument that the Gothic male sexual Other is still a mysterious and inhuman cipher even though his effects are explicitly clear is to be found in the conventional description of the male sexual Other, almost always described as dark-complexioned; Alice Moore captures the essence of this male figure in the title of her work: "'Dark, Irate and Piercing': Male Heroes of Female Authored Gothic Novels." In fact, the conventional darkness of the male sexual Other emblematizes not just his moral darkness but the epistemological darkness he imposes, his inhuman resistance to apprehension and empathy. Most of the inhumanly menacing men discussed by the essays in this section exhibit this physical darkness, including the dark Italians of Radcliffe, Shakespeare, and Browning, the dark Mr. Rochester, and Gloria Naylor's revision of this trope, the dark-complexioned and Satanic African-American, Luther Nedeed.

These physically and morally dark, unfathomable men populate all three of the texts discussed by my essay, "'There Was a Man': Dangerous Husbands and Fathers in *The Winter's Tale, A Sicilian Romance* and *Linden Hills.*" The essay traces the development of a particular variety of darkly dangerous male Other, the male relative. In arguing for a direct textual link between the texts of Shakespeare, Radcliffe and Naylor, I assert that in each case the preternaturally dangerous male encodes the real dangers posed by the fathers and husbands to women and children in the material world, the danger posed by unchecked tyranny both in the political and domestic arenas.

In "Sexual or Supernatural: Threats in Radcliffe's *The Italian,*" Elizabeth Harlan narrows the focus of my paper to look more closely at a more infamous Radcliffean example of the male sexual Other, the eponymous villain of Radcliffe's novel. Harlan argues that *The Italian* discounts supernatural dangers—including the danger posed by the Catholic Church

—unveiling rape as a central threat to Radcliffe's contemporary readers. Here too Harlan presents a legal subtext: in Radcliffe's time the rape and subsequent forced marriage of a woman was one way to acquire her property.

Victoria Anderson focuses on the figure of yet another dark man, Mr. Rochester, in "Investigating the Third Story: 'Bluebeard' and 'Cinderella' in *Jane Eyre*." The play on words in Anderson's title indicates that just as the third story in Mr. Rochester's house contains a secret relevant to Jane Eyre's situation, so do the folk stories that hover around Brontë's text. Anderson locates the textual precursors to Mr. Rochester in the dangerous lovers, husbands and fathers of the "Bluebeard" and "Cinderella" tales, thus uncovering a subtext that amplifies the dangers presented to Jane by Mr. Rochester. Anderson argues that in ignoring the textual clues that link her to her hapless precursors, Jane reveals a blindness that mirrors the blindness of Mr. Rochester.

In "Monstrous Men: Violence and Masculinity in Robert Browning's *The Ring and the Book*, Michael Ackerman makes a compelling case for the positioning of Browning's long Victorian poem within the Gothic tradition. Although it is not a work of prose, and not written by a woman, *The Ring and the Book* evinces a key trait of the Female Gothic: the tyrannical and monstrously inhuman husband is the source of the horror for the woman, whose perspective unfolds during the course of the narrative. Ackerman argues that Browning moves beyond an indictment of the horrifying patriarch, to condemn additionally the church and state that support the brutal patriarch and that punish the patriarch only for revealing the horrifying underpinnings of society through his crime.

The essay "'I Am God': The Domineering Patriarch in Shirley Jackson's Gothic Fiction" by Bernice M. Murphy traces a twentieth century American incarnation of the brutal patriarch. Murphy argues that despite Jackson's association with the supernatural, largely based on the popularity of *The Haunting of Hill House*, all of her *oeuvre*, including *Hill House*, posits the source of danger as the malevolently dangerous, preternaturally powerful "God-like" father. Like the other writers considered in this section, Jackson responds to the realities of her own time and place, specifically the post-war pressure placed upon young women to return to their subordinate place in the patriarchy. Murphy notes that it is fitting indeed that in Jackson's final novel, *We Have Always Lived in the Castle*, the two young women exile the patriarchal men; the end of the novel finds the women choosing to spectralize themselves, to appropriate the role of the ghost in possession of the domestic space. And as Virginia Woolf's *A Room of One's Own* suggests, choice is all that distinguishes a woman's sanctuary from her prison.

As the essays in "The Satanic Male" indicate, frequently in the

Gothic text it is the innocent woman who is besieged by the demonic heterosexual male. Yet there is another possible reading of this Gothic icon, as illustrated by his first English incarnation, Walpole's Manfred. Tim Mowl asserts that Horace Walpole deployed the tropes of *The Castle of Otranto* in eighteenth century England to address anxieties associated with his homosexuality after being "outed" (185) in the letter of an enemy. Mowl argues that in the narrative of *Otranto*, the story of the return of past guilt and of the lustful (albeit heterosexual) man exposed and stripped of family and property, it is possible to see an expression of Walpole's homosexual anxieties. Mowl writes of Walpole, "He might well have considered it expedient after being described as a hermaphrodite to bring out a rip-roaring redblooded romance that included threats of rape in gloomy cellars and portrayed normally sexed young men falling in love normally, with beautiful high-born maidens in distress" (186). Thus Mowl reads the rampantly heterosexual Manfred, insecure and at risk because of the buried secrets of his past, as an evocation of the even more "dangerous" and secretive homosexual, an expression of Walpole's internalization of the homophobia of his time. Patrick Brantlinger develops this reading of the homosexual male Other, arguing that a variant of the Gothic theme of the villain sexually besieging a woman is the villain chasing after another man. He identifies "both homosexuality and homophobia" at work in the romance that "rather than hinging upon the villain's pursuit or persecution of an innocent heroine ... involves the pursuit or persecution of one male character by another" (40). Brantlinger cites *Caleb Williams* and *Frankenstein* as examples of this variation and reads Ambrosio's rape of Antonia in Lewis's *The Monk* as encoded homosexual rape because Antonia is generally described in androgynous terms: the description of the rape "could also be one of a homosexual rather than heterosexual violation" (41).[14]

Part III of *Horrifying Sex*, "Homosexual Horror," focuses on instances in which the homosexual Other is represented as the inhuman Other, moments in which the fear of the homosexual figure is coded as fear of an inhuman creature[15]; the range of the essays in this section reveal that fear of the homosexual Other, too, is a recurrent trope in the Gothic. As the example of Manfred illustrates, this anxiety is typically presented in code, because this is a fear for which no more explicit language exists. After all, even more than the woman, the homosexual is spectralized by early modern culture, the invisible and unnameable ghost. In *Between Men*, in which Eve Kovotsky Sedgwick articulates the congruence of social attitudes with Gothic tropes, she notes "One of the most distinctive of Gothic tropes, the 'unspeakable,'" is aligned by the long cultural silence regarding homosexuality: "sexuality between men had, throughout the Judaeo-Christian tradition, been famous among those who knew about it at all precisely for having no name" (94). Given Laquer's observations of the sexual binary imposed by Enlightenment thinking, it is possible to see that the figure of the homosexual is particularly troubling as it disables the central binary of sexuality: male/female. The invisibility and silence of the homosexual, the spectralization of this troubling figure, derives from the inability of the binary to accommodate the homosexual. Yet, as Castle indicates in *The Apparitional Lesbian,* this Gothicized specter, erased, silenced and repressed by Western culture, manifests a singular haunting power. Indeed, besides exhibiting the power of that which hovers unspoken around the margins of a culture, as the essays of this section demonstrate, the repressed figure of the homosexual returns in the Gothic text in the form of the demonized monster—the vampire, the alien from outer space—incarnate and even more horrifying than ever.

In "Other Love: Le Fanu's *Carmilla* as Lesbian Gothic," Adrienne Antrim Major reads the female vampire as a code for lesbian danger, and for all dangerously subversive female power. Major argues that *Carmilla* is an especially horrifying lesbian because she is able to penetrate the safe domestic space that is protected by the patriarch; Le Fanu anxiously reveals to his reader that any proper Victorian girl may, in fact, become a lesbian. Major also persuasively argues that the encoded lesbian vampire reveals an even deeper male fear: the fear of intellectual intercourse between women, in which women find pleasure without male intervention. Major's reading argues, then, that the lesbian vampire becomes a code for the dangerous literary tradition of the Female Gothic.

In "Preying on the Pervert: The Uses of Homosexual Panic in Bram Stoker's *Dracula,*" Damion Clark provides a compelling explanation for Stoker's deployment of the vampire as a code for the homosexual. Clark observes that *Dracula* was written in response to the trial of Oscar Wilde who was, like Stoker, an Irishman. Clark asserts that in Dracula Stoker plays up Dracula's sexual danger and diminishes his cultural danger. By demonizing the homosexual Other and promoting the sexual norm, Stoker locates himself within the norm and tells his readers that they do not need to fear him as an Irishman because he is also a heterosexual.

In "Horror and Homosexuality in Christopher Isherwood's *Mr. Norris Changes Trains,*" Brian Whaley also explores the political implications of the demonization of the homosexual Other. Whaley discusses Isherwood's character, Kuno Pregnitz, living in Germany during the time of Hitler's rise; Whaley argues that although the homosexual Pregnitz appears to be inhumanly Other, the movement of the text is to show that this gay man is not really a threat to anyone—except maybe himself. The real danger in Isherwood's novel emanates from Nazi culture and ideology that works by perpetuating the notions of the human Other as demonic, constructing the gay man as a monster who must be eliminated.

Whaley further notes that in Nazi ideology, gays were figured as "alien to the species."

In "Invasion of the Husband Snatchers: Masculine Crisis and the Lavender Menace in *I Married a Monster from Outer Space*," Andrew Scahill discusses a text that literalizes this metaphor—a 1950s film in which the gay man is figured as a creature from outer space, truly alien to the human species. Scahill asserts that alien invaders disguising themselves as heterosexual males stand in for the invisibly infiltrating gay man who seeks his own kind and who must be distinguished and eradicated from "normal" society. Scahill contextualizes this fearful representation of the homosexual male, the "lavender scare," with the "red scare" in which the Communist was also construed as an invisible threat to the norms of postwar heterosexual suburbia.

In her essay on Clive Barker that appears in Part IV of *Horrifying Sex*, K.A. Laity argues that the tendency of the Gothic to demonize the Other reveals a conservative tendency: the use of horror to encourage readers to stay on the normative path, showing readers the dangers that await those who deviate from the norm. Laity's argument is compelling, and the many instances of demonization of the Other explored in *Horrifying Sex* do suggest that this tendency of the Gothic is a conservative one. And yet, there is a subtext to many of the essays in the first three sections of this collection: within the Gothic texts they discuss, a number of the writers identify a horrified response to a culture that figures human beings as monsters. Thus if one reads between the lines of the indeterminate Gothic text, it is sometimes possible to discern an indictment of inhumanly cruel social structures and a grudging sympathy for the monsters they create. Indeed, many of the monsters discussed in the earlier essays are interestingly ambiguous, dangerous but also attractive in their excessive, exuberant, monstrous vitality. By giving so much narrative energy to the monstrous Other, the Gothic author recalls Blake's comment that Milton was of the Devil's party without knowing it. Here too the pattern is set by Walpole's Manfred, who is "not one of those savage tyrants who wanton in cruelty unprovoked. The circumstances of his fortune had given an asperity to his temper, which was naturally humane" (30). Manfred is thus a victim of the system of tyranny that makes him monstrous. Similarly, the texts discussed in my essay, "'There Was a Man,'" develop an indictment of patriarchy. Michael Ackerman argues that Browning's poem also indicts the patriarchy as well as the church and state that support it and Brian Whaley asserts that Nazi ideology is the ultimate monster of Isherwood's text.

The writers of the texts considered in the concluding section of this book, "*Vive la Différence*: Celebrating the Sexual Other," move beyond secret admiration or sympathy for the sexual Other to a celebratory embrace of the sexual Other and an explicit indictment of the culture that spectralizes and demonizes difference. The works discussed in this section explicitly respond to the conventional demonization discussed in the first three sections, refuting and rebuking the strategy of demonization. Not surprisingly, each of these texts is contemporary, expressing the relative acceptance in contemporary culture of the sexual Other: the female, the lesbian and the gay man.[16] The writers of the texts discussed in this section look at the monster from the inside, thus heeding the exhortation of Jessica Benjamin: "To halt this cycle of domination ... women must claim their subjectivity.... They must offer men a new possibility ... of an equal other" (221). These writers also recall Hélène Cixous's exhortation in "The Laugh of the Medusa": "You only have to look at the Medusa straight on to see her. And she's not deadly. She's beautiful and she's laughing" (885). In disrupting the conventions of culture and of the Gothic, these writers fulfill what Kristeva asserts is a function of literature: "not an ultimate resistance to but an unveiling of the abject ... a hollowing out of abjection" (208). The writer "has to engage with what he calls demonic only to call attention to it as the inseparable obverse of his very being, of the other (sex) that torments and possesses him" (208). The writers discussed in "*Vive la Différence*" thus perform the cultural work of literature, unsettling the boundaries that maintain quietude "under the cunning, orderly surface of civilization" (Kristeva 210): they celebrate the Other and interrogate the system of creating a binary that excludes the Other.

In her essay, "The Lesbian Vampire: Transgressive Sexuality," Paulina Palmer provides a comprehensive overview of the subversive cultural uses of the lesbian vampire. She notes that contemporary writers deploy the joyous lesbian vampire to respond to the earlier use of the lesbian vampire as an emblem of sexual horror. The writers that Palmer discusses appropriate and rework the trope as it is found in classic vampire narrative. By taking the perspective of the monstrous Other, the lesbian vampire who addresses the reader directly, the texts that Palmer reads interrogate the conventional demonization and spectralization of the Other. Palmer's writers also anticipate the erasure of the boundaries that separate the Other from the self, the recognition that the Other, too, bears an empathetic subjectivity. Rather than normalize the Other, Palmer asserts, these writers celebrate difference, recognizing the joys of female power and erotic pleasure. Perhaps the most remarkable, or celebratory, quality of the works that Palmer discusses is their humor. Far different in tone from the conventionally lugubrious Gothic, these works joyously immerse themselves in a playful approach to the conventions.

Julie Miess also considers the joyful possibilities of the female vampire—as well as the potential humor in the Medusa, the Lamia and the female werewolf—in her essay, "Another 'Gendered Other'? The Female Monster-Hero." Miess traces the development of the joyously Female Monster-Hero in a play by Elfriede Jelinek, the Austrian Nobel Prize winner, in a short story by the African American writer Toni Brown, and in a story by Suzy Charnas and the film it inspired. Miess asserts that the Female Monster-Hero, the woman who revels in her monstrous power, is a direct response to texts like *Aliens* and *Carmilla*, texts that she argues demonize the figure of the powerful woman; Miess thus traces a direct response to the strategies identified in the essays of Katherine Henry and Adrienne Antrim Major. In her observation of the celebration of the powers of menstruation in the story "Boobs" by Suzy Charnas, Miess identifies a rebuttal to the kind of demonization of the menstruating women observed in Octavia Davis's essay (and by Kristeva in *Powers of Horror*). The Female Monster-Heroes in the texts that Miess discusses celebrate and rejoice in their power and welcome the opportunity to be free of the constricting bounds of normative society.

K.A. Laity also observes the celebratory embrace of monstrosity in "Imagineer: Clive Barker's Queering of the Conservative Bent of Horror Literature." Laity asserts that in inverting and contesting the binary of normal/monstrous, Barker draws upon the subversive transgressiveness of queer theory. Barker not only celebrates the monster, especially the gay "monster," he questions the construction of monstrosity and indicts the social order that construes the Other as monstrous. Thus Laity identifies in Barker's writing a movement toward an embrace of the monster and a union with the monster, rather than the rejection of the monster that the conventions dictate.

Although the divisions of *Horrifying Sex* are determined by the type of sexual difference that is demonized and spectralized in the Gothic mode, other connections emerge to link various essays, thereby transgressing the boundaries of my primary categorization, as appropriate for any work that touches on the Gothic. One intertextual conversation that emerges between the essays in this collection involves the Gothic filmic text. Katherine Henry, Julie Miess and Andrew Scahill each explore the translation of Gothic tropes to film. In *Framing Monsters*, Joshua David Bellin makes some observations that are relevant to their discussions. Bellin notes that the fantasy film often "takes part in the processes of ensuring the authority of dominant social groups by demonizing the outcast and disempowered" (2). He argues that the "biologically engineered *Tyrannosaurus regina* of *Jurassic Park* (1993) was [one of] a slew of monstrous women who ruled the nation's movie screens in the 1980s and 1990s" (107), including "the rapacious queen of *Aliens* (1986)" (107) that Katherine Henry discusses. In fact, as Andrew Williams demonstrates in his work on the sexual Other in two early films, *Nosferatu* (1922) and *The Phantom of the Opera* (1925), there is a long tradition of figuring the sexual Other as monstrous in film. Williams reminds us that the term used to describe the sexually alluring Theda Bara character was "The Vamp," derived from the word vampire. She was "far from supernatural but nevertheless a threat to social stability." Williams notes that, as in the case of the Vamp, the danger of the sexual Other lies in part with the exotic allure of the Other, the abnormal "inhuman sexuality" (3), that threatens to destabilize the norm. Williams also notes that more recent films like the screen version of Andrew Lloyd Webber's *Phantom of the Opera* and the Francis Ford Coppola remake of *Dracula* move toward the kind of interrogation of and resistance to the demonization of the sexual Other that is explored in the last section of this collection.

A number of essays in *Horrifying Sex* trace the conflation of sexual anxiety with racial anxiety—the amplification of the dangers of the sexual Other who is defined as being the racial, social or religious Other as well.[16] This convergence is observed by Showalter in her examination of the popular figure of Salome in *Sexual Anarchy*. Showalter notes that a 1908 performance "precipitated an outburst of Orientalist, anti-Semitic, and misogynist horror" (159). As Deirdre Bair notes in her introduction to the Vintage edition of *The Second Sex*, Beauvoir, too, was struck by the parallels between the construction of the racial Other and of the sexual Other; she recognized "that white men had succeeded in relegating both black men and all women into positions of 'alterity' or 'otherness'" (xii). In *Horrifying Sex*, the essays of Victoria Anderson, Damion Clark, Octavia Davis, Elizabeth Harlan, Tamar Heller, Julie Miess, Paulina Palmer, Brian Whaley and myself all consider texts in which racial, social or religious anxieties intersect with the sexual anxiety evoked by the sexual Other.[17]

A number of essays in *Horrifying Sex* consider the way in which icons of monstrosity are revisited and revised in the Gothic text to encode sexual horror. Dawn Fulton's essay examines a feminized Frankenstein's monster relocated to the West Indies. The alien from outer space figures in the texts discussed by Katherine Henry, Paulina Palmer and Andrew Scahill. A related concept, that of the political alien, the dangerous foreigner, emerges in the texts discussed by Brian Whaley and Damion Clark. The undying figure of the vampire returns in texts discussed by Damion Clark, Octavia Davis, Adrienne Antrim Major, Julie Miess, Paulina Palmer and Brian Whaley to express and to refute anxieties generated by women, men and homosexuals. That this overdetermined figure is used by writers to both promote and subvert social norms is an indication of its flexibility, demonstrating why the vampire continues to haunt the Gothic imagination.[18] The flexibility of the vampire figure points toward another overarching theme of *Horrifying Sex*: the endurance and flexibility of the Gothic mode that uses, reuses and transforms its conventions, evolving to reflect the evolution of cultural concerns and anxieties.

Notes

1. In *Powers of Horror*, Kristeva argues that it is not only the Gothic that is interested in these dark spaces that lie outside the borders of the known: "all literature is probably a version of the apocalypse that seems to me rooted ... on the fragile border ... where identities ... do not exist or only barely so" (206).

2. For an additional discussion of this topic, see Robert Miles's "Europhobia: The Catholic Other in Horace Walpole and Charles Maturin."

3. In 1927, Railo notes "the importance of the part played by a love-theme of terror, such as incest, in the work of the English Romanticists" and condemns the "abnormality" of Romantic eros. Railo does, in fact, recognize that, at least in the case of Lewis, sexual "abnormality" is accompanied by epistemological confusion—Lewis depicts "an eroticism bordering on bestiality in circumstances of secrecy and night" (279–281). Another early and influential critic of the Gothic, Mario Praz, also focuses on sexuality as a fundamental preoccupation of the Gothic in *The Romantic Agony*. Praz asserts that one of the "most characteristic aspects" and the "mainspring" of "Romantic literature" is "erotic sensibility" (preface to 1st edition, xv). Among the "sexual idiosyncracies" (xv) that Praz observes are two types that furnish the titles for two of the sections in this collection: the Satanic Male and the *Femme Fatale*. Praz asserts that the Satanic Male metamorphoses from "Milton's type of Satan" (63) to Radcliffe's Schedoni and Montoni, Lewis's monk, Maturin's Melmoth, the Byronic "Fatal Man" (80) and hence to the vampire. In his discussion of "La Belle Dame Sans Merci" (the "Fatal Woman") (201), including Matilda in *The Monk*, whom Praz locates "at the head of the line" (201), Praz notes that these women are in the tradition of the Medusa, an iconic figure that melds the associations of "beauty" and erotic attraction with "horror" (27). Yet while Railo and Praz identify the sexual anxiety of the Gothic text, they do not identify its source in the sexual Other. Even a contemporary critic, John Nicholson, who focuses in "On Sex and Horror" on the horror evoked by sex in contemporary horror films, fails to note the significance of the construction of the sexual Other as a source of horror. For him, such films as *The Exorcist* and *Carrie* deploy horror as a way to present sex and to excuse the "aberration" of childhood sexuality. Thus the devil in *The Exorcist* provides a "Satanic excuse for childish sexuality" (254). Girls acting out sexually "were therefore possessed since no girl in her right mind would do any of these things" (250). But there is more to this: the horror of these films and the other Gothic texts is not just the horror of sexuality, or the horror of children's sexuality. It is also the horror evoked by that which is unknown, unfamiliar, the aspect of sexuality that lies beyond comprehension, that does not fit into the normative binary.

4. Patrick Brantlinger notes the connection between the supernatural and sexual anxiety (without explicitly linking that anxiety to sexual difference) in *The Reading Lesson*: "As in Freud's treatment of the uncanny, the repressed that returns in Gothic romances, far more vividly than in most realistic novels, is simultaneously supernatural and sexual (for Freud, of course, the supernatural is a manifestation of the sexual)" (29). In fact, Freud recognizes other psychological causes for fear of the supernatural in *Totem and Taboo,* including the fear of being associated with death and the dead, displaced anger at the dead and a sense of unresolved guilt toward the dead. Brantlinger observes the post-Enlightenment translation of fears of the supernatural unknown to fears of the more realistic, and more realistically dangerous, sexual unknown: "Rather than rejecting Gothic conventions, these [later, more realistic writers] all make use of them ... in a more realistic register" (29). He adds: "The supernatural in Gothic tends to function like an aspect of dreamwork, partially—but

only partially—displacing or disguising the sexual energies that lie at the heart of its nightmarish fantasies" (35).

5. Kamuf notes that Butler's reversal of the "sex/gender" distinction "repeats a recognizable procedure of deconstruction that Derrida worked out.... [T]he hierarchized terms of a binary opposition are reversed, the secondary or derived term is generalized as *différance*" (87). This deconstructive practice, in fact, echoes the strategy of the Gothic's recurring insistence on breaking down all walls, including walls of distinguishing categories. Kamuf is helpful in making the connection between Derrida's notion of *différance* and the sexual/gender difference that informs the texts discussed in this collection. She argues for the "[p]ossibility that anything or everything Derrida has written can be taken to refer its reader somewhere or somehow to [a] sexual difference" (88). In discussing Derrida's essay *"Geschlecht*: Sexual Difference, Ontological Difference," a reading of Heidegger on sexual difference, Kamuf notes Derrida's argument that "it is the binary of sexual difference and not sexuality as such that for Heidegger must be neutralized" (91). Thus in seeking the neutrality of *Dasein*, "Heidegger thinks first of sexual neutrality" (91). This fear of difference echoes the Gothic fear of difference, of the Other. In this, Kamuf argues, Derrida notes that Heidegger "reproduces one of the olderst gestures of ... philosophical discourse" (93), working to neutralize sexuality and the sexual binary, resulting, as Kamuf argues, in "the enforced subordination of one sex to the other" (93) since neutrality refuses the existence of that other second sex.

6. As recent discussions of the biological condition of "intersexuality" indicate, even in the realm of biology, of chromosomes and of genitalia, the sexual binary is not as clearly distinct as Enlightenment thinking might indicate and desire.

7. I discuss the absent, spectralized mother in "The Missing Mother." Lynette Carpenter and Wendy K. Kolmar note the spectralizaton of the female writer in *Haunting the House of Fiction*.

8. As Kristeva notes, in the biblical patriarchy the figure of the woman destabilizes the notion of a patriarchal god, who denotes male power. The biblical abjection of the woman and the female body is a means "of separating oneself from the phantasmatic power of the mother, that archaic Mother Goddess who actually haunted the imagination of a nation at war with the surrounding polytheism" (100). In this it is possible to see the relationship between spectralization and demonization. In response to the terror of the lingering spectralized goddess, the patriarchy demonizes the woman, thereby creating a visible danger that may be readily encountered and defeated. The image of the goddess, the powerful female, also needs to be eradicated because it transgresses the notion of the woman as passive object.

9. As William Safire helpfully adds in providing his description of a *chimera* ("best known as a fire-breathing she-monster mixing a lion's head, a goat's body and a serpent's tail that gave ancient Greek children nightmares), ... [i]t's always described as a 'she-monster': you never hear about chimerical 'he-monsters'" (22).

10. Indeed, it is possible to see that the cultural response is Gothicized in that it draws upon conceptions of the supernatural to portray female power that can only be imagined as preternatural. Developing her discussion of the early female goddess, the avatar of female maternal power, Beauvoir remarks: "Perhaps the myth of woman will some day be extinguished; the more women assert themselves as human beings, the more the marvelous quality of the Other will die out in them" (142). Beauvoir continues: "The source of these terrors lies in the fact that in the Other, quite beyond reach, alterity, otherness, abides. In patriarchal societies woman retains many of the disquieting powers she possessed in primitive societies" (169).

11. The figure of the Medusa, rehabilitated by Hélène Cixous, whose work is discussed later in this collection, is an iconic example of the horrifyingly transgressive female monster. In the figure of Eve, too, it is possible to see an early and influential presence of the dangerous female tinged with the aura of supernatural evil. Although Eve is human, indeed is every-woman, she is the agent of Satan, the font of absolute and supernaturally inhuman evil and, like the figure of the witch who

succeeds her, is closely aligned with the Devil in the Christian imagination. The continuing impact of this strategy of demonic association, and its relationship to the construction of the cultural Other, is examined by Joan Gregg in *Devils, Women, and Jews: Reflection of the Other in Medieval Sermon Stories*. In fact, the Jewish tradition provides a variation of the theme of the monstrous female Other. Although the serpent is not aligned with the transcendentally evil Satan, that role is conveniently filled by Eve's double, the female demon Lilith, who is supposedly Adam's first wife, cast off because she refused to be subordinate to him, and doomed to wander the world, a constant danger to newborn children. Susan Staub records a more recent instance of the inhumanly dangerous woman in *Nature's Cruel Stepdames: Murderous Women in the Street Literature of Seventeenth Century England*, a study of popular seventeenth century pamphlets that depicted female criminals, including child- and husband-killers. In fact a recent book by the legal scholar Catherine A. MacKinnon, which examines the contemporary state of international women's rights, identifies the enduring question of the categorical placement of the female in its title: *Are Women Human?*

12. The Marquis de Sade, whose life (1740–1814) was synchronized with the development of the Gothic novel, deserves a place in the discussion of the construction of the malevolent, narcissistic male. De Sade, however, tended to minimize the sexual politics of his novels and of the Gothic. Writing of Radcliffe and Lewis, whom he admired, he writes of the Gothic that "twas the inevitable result of the revolutionary shocks which all of Europe has suffered" (109). Beauvoir, however, notes the spectralization of the women deployed by de Sade and his male constructions: "The Marquis de Sade and Sacher-Masoch satisfy upon women the desires that haunt them" (194).

13. This view, then, reflecting more contemporary notions of rape, is in opposition to Railo, who in the early twentieth century asserts: "The persecution of the heroine is ... at bottom an erotic feature, and reflects, no matter what the type of literature in the period may be, the active love-instinct of the male and the passivity of the female" (280).

14. Brantlinger adds that Gothic texts written by gay writers—including Walpole, Beckford and Lewis—"manage to speak the unspeakable, expressing the anxiety and terror of their authors' 'private obsessions' that could not otherwise be publicly expressed" (41). In a recent issue of *Gothic Studies* dedicated to *Queering Gothic Films*, the guest editor Michael Eberle-Sinatra develops this point in his introductory essay, "Exploring Gothic Sexuality." He asserts that most Gothic texts are "'queer' ... for the Gothic has long been associated with different sexualities" (124). A recent contribution to this discussion may be found in George Haggerty's *Queer Gothic*.

15. The absence of a celebration of the male Other may not be as remarkable as it appears. Although male sexual power is demonized in the Female Gothic, the celebration of male power still permeates our culture—there would be little Gothic irony and subversiveness in a text perpetuating that message.

16. My earlier collection, *The Gothic Other*, considers moments in which the dangers of the racial, social and religious Other is amplified by sexual difference, another example of slippage in the Gothic text that resists categorization.

17. A variation of this convergence is explored by Glajar and Radulescu in *Vampirettes, Wretches, and Amazons: Western Representations of East European Women*, which explores the stereotypical representation of Eastern European women in literature, film and popular culture of the West.

18. Showalter articulates the useful transgressiveness of Stoker's *Dracula*: "The novel is also about the thrills and terrors of blurred sexual, psychological, and scientific boundaries ... [between] the states of living, dead, and undead, or of masculinity, femininity, and bisexuality" (179).

Works Cited

Anolik, Ruth Bienstock. Introduction. "The Dark Unknown." In *The Gothic Other: Racial and Social Constructions in the Literary Imagination*, 1–14, ed. Ruth Bienstock Anolik and Douglas L. Howard. Jefferson, NC: McFarland, 2004.
_____. "The Missing Mother: The Meanings of Maternal Absence in the Gothic." *Modern Language Studies* 33 (Spring/Fall 2003): 24–43.
_____, and Douglas L. Howard. *The Gothic Other: Racial and Social Constructions in the Literary Imagination*. Jefferson, NC: McFarland, 2004.
Bair, Deidre. Introduction to *The Second Sex,* by Simone de Beauvoir, vii–xviii. Trans. and ed. H.M. Parshley. New York: Vintage, 1989.
Beauvoir, Simone de. *The Second Sex*. Trans. and ed. H.M. Parshley. Introduction by Deirdre Bair. New York: Vintage, 1989.
Bellin, Joshua David. *Framing Monsters: Fantasy Film and Social Alienation*. Carbondale: Southern Illinois University Press, 2005.
Benjamin, Jessica. *The Bonds of Love: Psychoanalysis, Feminism, and the Problem of Domination*. New York: Pantheon, 1988.
Brantlinger, Patrick. *The Reading Lesson: The Threat of Mass Literacy in Nineteenth-Century British Fiction*. Indiana University Press, 1998.
Brown, Marshall. *The Gothic Text*. Stanford: Stanford University Press, 2005.
Carpenter, Lynette and Wendy K. Kolmar, eds. *Haunting the House of Fiction: Feminist Perspectives on Ghost Stories by American Women*. Knoxville: The University of Tennessee Press, 1991.
Castle, Terry. *The Apparitional Lesbian: Female Homosexuality and Modern Culture*. New York: Columbia University Press, 1994.
_____. *The Female Thermometer: Eighteenth Century Culture and the Invention of the Uncanny*. New York: Oxford University Press, 1995.
_____. "The Spectralization of the Other in *The Mysteries of Udolpho*." In *The Female Thermometer*, 120–139. New York: Oxford, 1995.
Cixous, Hélène. "The Laugh of the Medusa." *Signs* 11 (1976): 875–893.
Eberle-Sinatra, Michael. "Exploring Gothic Sexuality." *Gothic Studies*: Queering Gothic Films 7.2 (Nov 2005): 123–6.
Fleenor, Juliann E., ed. *The Female Gothic*. Montreal: Eden Press, 1983.
Frankfurter, David. *Evil Incarnate: Rumors of Demonic Conspiracy and Satanic Abuse in History*. Princeton: Princeton University Press, 2006.
Glajar, Valentina, and Domnica Radulescu, eds. *Vampirettes, Wretches, and Amazons: Western Representations of East European Women*. East European Monographs. Distributed by Columbia University Press, 2004.
Gregg, Joan Young. *Devils, Women and Jews: Reflections of the Other in Medieval Sermon Stories*. Albany: State University of New York Press, 1997.
Haggerty, George. *Queer Gothic*. Urbana: University of Illinois Press, 2006.
Halberstam, Judith. *Skin Shows: Gothic Horror and the Technology of Monsters*. Durham, NC: Duke University Press, 1995.
Kamuf, Peggy. "Derrida and Gender: The Other Sexual Difference." In *Jacques Derrida and the Humanities: A Critical Reader,* ed. Tom Cohen, 82–107. Cambridge: Cambridge University Press, 2001.
Kristeva, Julia. *Powers of Horror: An Essay in Abjection*. New York: Columbia University Press, 1982.
Laquer, Thomas. *Making Sex: Body and Gender from the Greeks to Freud*. Cambridge: Harvard University Press, 1992.
Maturin, Charles. *Melmoth the Wanderer*. Oxford: Oxford University Press, 1989.
Miles, Robert. "Europhobia: The Catholic Other in Horace Walpole and Charles Maturin." In *European Gothic: A Spirited Exchange, 1760–1960*, ed. Avril Horner, 84–103. Manchester: Manchester University Press, 2002.
Moers, Ellen. *Literary Women: The Great Writers*. New York: Doubleday, 1976.

Moore, Alice. "'Dark, Irate and Piercing': Male Heroes of Female Authored Gothic Novels." *DAI* 53 (Dec. 1992): DA9233112.
Mowl, Tim. *Horace Walpole: The Great Outsider*. London: Murray, 1996.
Nicholson, John. "On Sex and Horror." In *Gothic Horror: A Reader's Guide from Poe to King and Beyond*, ed. Clive Bloom, 249–277. New York: St. Martin's Press, 1998.
Praz, Mario. *The Romantic Agony*. 1933. Trans. by Angus Davidson. 2nd ed. London: Oxford University Press, 1970.
Radcliffe, Ann. "On the Supernatural in Poetry." In *Gothic Documents: A Sourcebook, 1700–1820,* ed. E.J. Clery and Robert Miles, 163–172. Manchester: Manchester University Press, 2000.
Railo, Eino. *The Haunted Castle: A Study of the Elements of English Romanticism*. London: Routledge, 1927.
Rifelj, Carol de Dobay. *Reading the Other: Novels and the Problem of Other Minds*. Ann Arbor: University of Michigan Press, 1992.
Russ, Joanna. "Somebody's Trying to Kill Me and I Think It's My Husband: The Modern Gothic." In *The Female Gothic*, ed. Juliann E. Fleenor, 31–56. Montreal: Eden Press, 1983.
Sade, Marquis de. "Reflections on the Novel." 1800. *The 120 Days of Sodom and Other Writings,* 97–116, ed. and trans. Austryn Wainhouse and Richard Seaver. New York: Grove Weidenfeld, 1996.
Safire, William. "On Language: Chimera." *New York Times Magazine,* 22 May 2005, 22.
Sedgwick, Eve Kovotsky. *Between Men: English Literature and Male Homosocial Desire*. New York: Columbia University Press, 1985.
Showalter, Elaine. *Sexual Anarchy: Gender and Culture at the Fin de Siècle*. New York: Viking, 1990.
Staub, Susan. *Nature's Cruel Stepdames: Murderous Women in the Street Literature of Seventeenth Century England*. Pittsburgh: Duquesne University Press, 2006.
Walpole, Horace. *The Castle of Otranto*. New York: Oxford University Press, 1982.
Williams, Andrew P. "The Silent Threat: A Re(viewing) of the 'Sexual Other' in *The Phantom of the Opera* and *Nosferatu*." *The Midwest Quarterly* 38 (Autumn 1996): 90–102, http://proquest.umi.com.ps2, 1–5.

Part I
The Fatal Woman

1
Life-in-Death: The Monstrous Female and the Gothic Labyrinth *in* Aliens *and* "Ligeia"

KATHERINE HENRY

After an agonizingly long calm with no fresh water, Coleridge's Ancient Mariner sees Life-in-Death, a red-lipped, golden-haired woman, with skin "white as leprosy," who rolls dice with Death for the ship's crew, and wins the Mariner alone. The scenes that follow resemble, among other things, a ghastly trip to the underworld, the Mariner surrounded by the animated corpses of his fellow seamen, and finally rescued by a Charon-like "Pilot" who ferries him back to the world of the living. It is "life-in-death" for the Mariner in two respects: not only is he the only living human being on a ship of the dead; his living soul, too, ridden with guilt and unable to look upward and pray for forgiveness, is enduring a kind of spiritual death. Moreover, that the Mariner's life-in-death is brought on by an encounter with a monstrous and disconcertingly sexualized woman suggests the dark counterpart to woman as mother and life-giver. Life-in-Death belongs to a long line of death-bringing women and *femmes fatales*, from Circe and Eve to Charlotte Brontë's Bertha Mason and Orson Welles's Lady from Shanghai. But what is of particular importance is that her name constitutes a figure of immanence. It does not situate life and death in binary opposition; rather, it represents a region of death within which life is entrapped and engulfed, life that has been swallowed up by death. This figure of immanence evokes the interior of a woman's body, not as nurturing womb, but as dark, suffocating cavity: Jonah in the whale's belly, the mother who eats her young.

This essay examines two Gothic texts that assemble a similar constellation of elements and images: James Cameron's 1986 film *Aliens*, and Edgar Allan Poe's "Ligeia." Both texts involve a terrifying encounter with the monstrous female, and both involve a passage into a dark, disorienting underworld, an interior space that radiates a power simultaneously life-draining and hideously life-giving. In both cases the descent into the labyrinthine darkness indicates a particular variation on the Self-Other relationship. In the Hegelian model, the Other exists independently of the Self: it is the Other's independent existence that both affirms the Self's identity and challenges its mastery.[1] The Gothic Other, by contrast, has been read as the return of the Self's own repressed fears and desires, a terrifying mirror image of the Self.[2] Still, it is the Gothic Other's existence outside and apart from the Self that allows it to function as an objective representation of psychological distress, as the focal point of terror. In these two texts, however, the descent into the Gothic labyrinth can be read as the immersion of Self in Otherness, specifically the Otherness of the female. In these scenes, the Other is not so much an object as it is a suffocating atmosphere—a dank, cramped, womb-like space, a chamber in a decaying abbey, a winding, miasmal tunnel. The terror is magnified precisely because its source cannot be pinpointed; it could be anywhere or everywhere. And it is not until the sexual Other again assumes an objective form that the narrative can in each case be resolved. If, as Eve Kosofsky Sedgwick has suggested, the Gothic is characterized by a disruption or blurring of the boundary that separates inside from outside, then we might well read these scenes as representing Gothic horror at its most extreme.[3] Here the very concepts of inside and outside have been transformed, insideness now a quality of the Other rather than of the Self, and the boundary that formerly separated the two turned into a well that engulfs.

A key moment in *Aliens* occurs when the contingent of Marines sent to rescue the colonists on LV-426 first descends into what they will later learn is the alien queen's nest, a dripping, slime-coated maze of passages strewn with the cocooned bodies of the dead and dying colonists. Using a tracking device to detect motion, they search for signs of life, as video transmitters attached to their helmets send fuzzy images back to Ripley, Burke and Gorman in the mobile command center. Immediately we get a sense of entering the body of a giant vertebrate: a spine-like ridge appearing overhead, with arching ribs and sinews forming the walls of the orifice through which the Marines must proceed.[4] As the scene continues, the Marines learn in graphic detail what Ripley already knows, that the alien mother deposits her embryos inside living human beings, who then function as hosts until the gestation period ends in a horrifically bloody birth that kills the host. A few moments later Hudson, the tough-talking coward, gets a reading on his tracking device, although he cannot lock in on the source of the motion: "Multiple signals," he tells Apone, with increasing anxiety; "they're closing!" We are shown glimpses of movement in the walls of the tunnel, the twisted cords that before had seemed rigid and bone-like suddenly squirming to life. As the team proceeds deeper into the nest, the readings on Hudson's tracker get increasingly erratic, and Hudson panics: "They're all around us, man," he wails. "They're coming out of the goddamn walls!"

The labyrinth—the maze of secret passages and trap doors beneath the castle, for example, or in the convent or the haunted house—is a recurring figure in Gothic literature, associated with a loss of orientation, the failure of the sense of sight, and the elevation of lower-order senses. It has been read as a journey into the Freudian unconscious, a burrowing down into the deeper recesses of the mind, the failure of vision signifying the hero's loss of enlightened, rational control and his terrifying encounter with his own repressed demons and desires.[5] Clearly the scene in the alien nest can comport with such a reading.[6] The disintegrating contact between the command center and the rescue crew; the latter's grudging compliance and, later, its refusal to obey orders; the break-up of video transmission and the growing sense of panic—all this neatly suggests a rational mind losing control over its unconscious. Furthermore, the system's electronic blueprints, which the command center uses to locate the position of the rescue crew and guide them through, offer a striking illustration of the labyrinth. Their bird's-eye view gives the command center a perspective—and thus a capacity to navigate—that is not available to the Marines inside: Gorman and the others can, in effect, see around corners and beyond walls, while the other Marines' vision is limited to what is immediately in front of them, and even that is severely limited by the darkness.

The terrifying descent into darkness has also often been associated with anxieties generated by the feminine and by the maternal. Leslie Fiedler writes, "beneath the haunted castle lies the dungeon keep: the womb from whose darkness the ego first emerged, the tomb to which it knows it must return at last. Beneath the crumbling shell of paternal authority, lies the maternal blackness, imagined by the gothic writer as a prison, a torture chamber" (132). Nina Auerbach traces in the Victorian imagination what she calls "the self-transforming power surging beneath [woman's] apparent victimization," the "angelic demon ... source of all creative and shaping power" (34, 185), who threatens the established order and thus requires repressive containment. She sees such mythic power as the central concern of a wide range of popular, literary, artistic, and scientific texts: a Gothic text like Bram Stoker's *The Lair of the White Worm*, whose female Dracula-figure lives "at the bottom of a deep and fetid well that crawls with the repulsive vitality of vermin, insects, and worms," her "metamorphic power ... darkly intrinsic to womanhood itself"; Freud's "talking cure" for hysteria, which she reads as an effort to harness "the female capacity for metamorphosis without which male magic has no meaning" (25, 29). While Auerbach finds an encounter with a mythologized womanhood in Freudian psychoanalysis, Claire Kahane examines the remarkable capacity of Gothic forms both to engage and to represent the female psyche, in particular the encounter with the maternal. She describes the "secret center of the Gothic labyrinth" as a site "where boundaries break down, where life and death become confused and identities unclear, where the felt presence of a spectral mother—though typically dead or absent, exerts an uncanny force" (243). Kahane's account is particularly useful in examining the Gothic labyrinth in *Aliens* because it suggests another dimension to this horrific, feminized, interior landscape, a way of reading it as something other than just psychic space. Her description of the Gothic labyrinth as a place "where boundaries break down ... and identities [become] unclear" suggests that it also has metaphysical significance in its radical repositioning of the subject inside—rather than opposite—the object.

It is this metaphysics that interests Simone de Beauvoir in *The Second Sex*, her account of the male subject's metaphysical journey toward self-transcendence and its inevitable unfolding in gendered terms. Although she draws heavily on the Hegelian model of the Self-Other dialectic, her account is suggestive in its linkage of the desire to transcend the self and the inwardness that is associated with femininity, thus meriting closer attention here. According to Beauvoir, man has established woman as the Other through which he can achieve self-transcendence. But the project is doomed at the outset to failure, because to define woman as Other is to construct her as ultimately unknowable, as forever eluding man's grasp and therefore frustrating his dream of possession. And so woman has come to embody a series of contradictory principles—principles that express her promise of abundance and spiritual fulfillment as well as her necessary part in ultimately thwarting its realization. "There is no figurative image of woman which does not call up at once its opposite," writes Beauvoir: "she is Life and Death, Nature and Artifice, Daylight and Night. Under whatever aspect we consider her, we always find the same shifting back and forth.... In the figures of the Virgin Mary and Beatrice, Eve and Circe still exist"[7] (186). One of the pairs of opposing figures that Beauvoir traces—the clear or starry sky and the pool of water—represent the feminine qualities of transcendence and immanence; that is, woman's capacity to elevate the masculine subject out of a mere bodily life and into the spiritual realm, as well as her persistent association with the prison of bodily existence and the inevitability of decay and death. It is this latter quality of the feminine

1. *Life-in-Death* (Katherine Henry)

Other that lends itself to Gothic modes of representation; indeed, Beauvoir herself often relies on language and imagery that seems drawn from that of Gothic horror in her account of the feminine quality of immanence. Man "aspires to the sky," she writes, "to the light, to the sunny summits, to the pure and crystalline frigidity of the blue sky; and under his feet there is a moist, warm, and darkling gulf ready to draw him down" (147). This "darkling gulf" is also the "maternal shadows," a "cave, [the] abyss, hell." It is associated with the interiority of a woman's body and, of course, the womb: "that warm, peaceful, and safe retreat, [that has become] a pulp of humors, a carnivorous plant, a dark, contractile gulf, where dwells a serpent that insatiably swallows up the strength of the male" (147, 191). Thus has mother become monster, sanctuary become torture chamber, the life-giving become the deadly.

The image of the emasculating serpent that dwells in the "darkling gulf," recalling Stoker's White Worm, could easily describe the monster queen mother of *Aliens*. As the scene described above opens, Ripley has just realized that the Marines are in close proximity to the fusion reactor that powers the colony's primary heat exchange, and Gorman must order them to give up the ammunition for their pulse rifles—a restriction that the rescue crew reads as emasculating. The command Apone repeats as he disarms them is "pull 'em out"—a command that is echoed later by Ripley, as she shouts to a frantic Gorman to "pull your team out!" The aliens effectively render Hudson a blubbering coward, and Gorman utterly impotent as a commander. Moreover, this progressive "swallowing up" of the strength of the male corresponds to their literally being swallowed up in the hot, wet tunnels of the alien queen's nest. The narrative, in other words, enacts precisely the dialectic that Beauvoir describes: the masculine project of space travel and colonization gets swallowed up in its antithesis, the "dark, contractile gulf" of reproductive sexuality, decay, and death; the promise of transcendence lost in the reality of the female's immanence. What is especially striking about this narrative is its radical destabilization of the categories of inside and outside, subject and object. The infinite outside of outer space turns into a suffocating inside; escape turns into imprisonment and burial. Likewise, the pursuit of the distant, desired object becomes entry into the object; indeed, the very notion of object loses its applicability to something formless, something that cannot be pinpointed, that is, as Hudson says, "all around us, man!" The story, then, involves more than just a confrontation with a monstrous female; it entails the temporary collapse of the fundamental categories of metaphysical thinking.

Other critics of *Aliens* have commented on Ripley as the film's hero, on her transformation from the mission's pale, reluctant participant, whom Vasquez calls "Snow White," into an armed and armored warrior who herself takes on characteristics of the alien queen.[8] In fact, Ripley is particularly suited to resolve the film's plot and restore stability to the concepts with which we order our world. It is, after all, in the confrontation with Ripley that the alien queen assumes an objective form—a development that we might read figuratively as marking our exit from the object's interior, our release from the belly of the beast. At first glance it may seem odd that a woman is the one to defend a fundamentally masculine order against an out-of-control reproductivity. But, to draw again on Beauvoir's account, it is woman—not man—onto whom man's metaphysical aspirations are projected. In other words, the dialectic of desire, frustration and repulsion that man's project of self-transcendence initiates is played out as a conflict between two versions of femininity. Against the alien queen's darkness, the "contractile gulf" of her nest, and the repulsiveness of her reproductive processes, we have Ripley's whiteness and aloof intelligence, and her adoptive rather than biological motherhood; and yet in other equally important ways they are mirror images of each other. This drama of contradictory principles, both feminized, enacting a master narrative of yearning for "the light, ... the sunny summits, ... the pure and crystalline frigidity of the blue sky," is at the heart of the story told in *Aliens*.

The drama, and horror, of contradictory female principles also lies at the center of an earlier, more canonical, Gothic text: Edgar Allan Poe's "Ligeia."[9] It is difficult to imagine a more precise literary rendering of the transformation of feminine Other described by Beauvoir—from the promise of transcendence to the horror of the "darkling gulf"—than Poe's story. The title character is the narrator's first wife, and the story recounts her brief life, her death, and her final return in the revivified corpse of his second wife, the lady Rowena. Repeatedly Ligeia is described in the very terms Beauvoir identifies as representative of this dialectic of transcendence and immanence: her forehead is "divine," her "sweet mouth" is "the triumph of all things heavenly, ray[s] of the holy light" fall upon her brilliant teeth (480). Her eyes, the "twin stars of Leda," contain "something more profound than the well of Democritus," something that the narrator would "struggle to fathom" "through the whole of a midsummer night," whose closest analogies are "a stream of running water," "the ocean," "the falling of a meteor," and "one or two stars in heaven" (481, 82). A scholar of "rare learning," she is seen by the narrator as his guide to self-transcendence:

> With how vast a triumph [he exclaims]—with how vivid a delight—with how much of all that is ethereal in hope—did I *feel*, as she bent over me in studies but little sought for—but less known, that delicious vista by slow but very perceptible degrees expanding before me, down whose long, gorgeous,

and all untrodden path I might at length pass onward to the goal of a wisdom too divinely precious not to be forbidden! [483].

It is woman's persistent duality that animates such passages; just as the imagery of starry heavens cannot appear without its complementary images of profound wells and watery deeps, here the narrator's rapturous pursuit of "metaphysical" truth is imagined as a journey *down*ward. The "shifting back and forth," to apply Beauvoir's phrase, is between soaring and sinking, uplift and immersion, ascension and burial. And a few lines later, the narrator tellingly mixes metaphors: Ligeia "rendered vividly luminous," he says, "the transcendentalism in which we were immersed" (483).

As Ligeia's death approaches, the possibility of transcendence is increasingly obviated by the frustration that Beauvoir claims is its inevitable counterpart—a shift that is marked in two ways. First, Ligeia's passion for the narrator intensifies to a "wild longing," an uncontrollable desire that the narrator claims he "[has] no power to portray—no utterance capable of expressing" (484). Her passion had always simultaneously "delighted and appalled" him; now, he says, her "more than womanly abandonment to a love ... all unworthily bestowed ... amounted to idolatry" (482, 484). The narrator's discomfort with his new god-like status in Ligeia's eyes actually masks a deeper anxiety over the intensity of her appetite—a fear of being consumed by the force of her uncontrollable passion.[10] Where earlier the narrative had highlighted the narrator's pursuit of his object, here the narrator has himself become the object of Ligeia's fierce desire, her adored "idol"; he has changed from the worshiper into the one who is worshiped. Moreover, that it defies his capacity of expression further identifies Ligeia's passion as a threat to the narrator's pursuit of self-transcendence through knowledge; if we understand language as the medium through which man orders and contains the world around him, then this is a love that resists containment. The narrator's project of self-transcendence is turning dialectically into a confirmation of his powerlessness and a terrifying, suffocating possession by the Other.

The second mark of this dialectical turn into the "darkling gulf" is the increasingly pervasive imagery of decay and bodily decomposition, particularly evident in the poem Ligeia composes on her deathbed (484–5): "The Conqueror Worm" offers a hellish account of a perverse theatrical event that ends in the bloody massacre of the performers. In what could well describe the alien queen's nest, the "scenic solitude" of the stage set produces "a crawling shape," a "blood-red thing" with "vermin fangs / In human gore imbued." As "haggard and wan" seraphs look on, the conqueror worm feeds on the performers in the "motley drama," the "dying forms" of which are shrouded by the falling curtain. The worm—itself a conventional metonym for what happens to the human body after death—is here the conquering "hero" of "the tragedy, 'Man,'" suggesting the inevitable triumph of the grave's immanence over the soul's transcendence. Gone is any hint of Ligeia's association with the stars in heaven. And the poem's evocative image of a "Phantom chased for evermore / By a crowd that seize it not" suggests the utter futility of any pursuit of a transcendent truth. Significantly, the lights go out in the final stanza, indicating the descent into the abyss, the realm of decomposition and death—of the conqueror worm—imprisonment in a decaying body without any hope of escape.

After Ligeia's death, the narrator moves into a crumbling abbey and marries—or, rather, purchases—the "fair-haired and blue-eyed lady Rowena Trevanion." Much of the remainder of the narrative is given over to describing, in minute detail, the "accursed" bridal chamber, an isolated apartment, featuring a gold censer suspended by a long chain from the vaulted ceiling and walls hung with lush Arabesque tapestries, all of which endow the chamber with "a hideous and uneasy vitality" (486, 487). Within two months the lady Rowena is on her deathbed, and the bridal chamber is thus transformed into what it all along seemed meant to be: a death chamber. The narrative has turned from light to darkness, from promise to terror, from soaring to being engulfed, from the life-giving to the life-draining, and its figurative descent into the Gothic labyrinth is complete. Wandering in a maze of opium-induced visions, the narrator loses the capacity to distinguish between imagination and reality, and the chamber becomes the scene of his paranoid "phantasy" (487). We get recurring images of confinement and bondage: the "gigantic sarcophagus of black granite" that stands in each of the chamber's angles, visions of the "entombed" Ligeia, the "iron shackles" of the narrator's opium addiction, which has turned him into a "bounden slave" (487, 486). As he becomes aware of signs of life in the lady Rowena's corpse, the narrator's sense of sight grows increasingly unreliable. He hears a faint sob, and *feels* that it is issuing from "the bed of ebony—the bed of death (489). But, despite "strain[ing his] vision," he perceives nothing at first (490). Eventually the sound comes again and, as if to convince himself by repetition, he claims: "I saw—distinctly saw—a tremor upon the lips" (490). Then his "vision [grows] dim," and he "[sinks] into visions of Ligeia" (490, 491).

Moreover, just as in *Aliens*, this descent into the Gothic labyrinth corresponds with the dialectical transformation of the feminine Other from transcendence to immanence. The bridal-chamber-turned-death-chamber resembles a giant female reproductive tract in a few suggestive details: in the "vast folds" of the tapestries that line its walls; in its "hideous and uneasy vitality"; in the "three or four large drops of a brilliant and ruby coloured fluid," which appear "as if from some invisible spring in the atmosphere of the room" (487, 489). The long chain and censer feature "perforations so contrived that there writhed in and out of them, as if endued with a serpent vitality, a continual succession of parti-coloured fires" (486); like the alien queen's nest, this gloomy chamber with the serpent-like censer hanging from the ceiling recalls Beauvoir's description of woman's terrifying interior as the "dark, contractile gulf, where dwells a serpent that insatiably swallows up the strength of the male" (191). More generally, the narrative after Ligeia's death creates not only a claustrophobic sense of insideness, but also a sense of Ligeia's invisible, surrounding presence. Her objective presence, in other words, has given way to a kind of possession of the narrator's very being, his "spirit fully and freely burn[ing] with more than all the fires of her own" (487). He rhapsodizes "the wild eagerness, the solemn passion, the consuming intensity of [his] longing for the departed Ligeia," and fantasizes that he "could restore her to the pathways she had abandoned upon earth" (487–488). He feels "some palpable although invisible object [passing] lightly by [his] person," and sees—or hallucinates—a "faint, indefinite shadow ... in the very middle of the rich luster thrown from the censer" (488–489). And, suggesting that the chamber itself is a living creature, the wind in the tapestries seems to the narrator like "faint, almost articulate breathings" (488).

When Ligeia does assume an objective form again, in the re-animated corpse of the lady Rowena, what had previously been marks of beauty have been transformed into incitements to terror. With "huge masses of long and disheveled hair" and "full ... black ... wild eyes," she is both threatening and disturbingly sexualized, the archetypal female monster.[11] She is "life-in-death," a perverse life-giver who robs the lady Rowena of a peaceful death, the demonic author of what the narrator calls "this hideous drama of revivification" (491). Thus "Ligeia" traces the same narrative pattern evident in *Aliens*: what begins as an ambitious pursuit of the stars turns out to be immersion in the abyss, and the trajectory cannot be resolved until the female Other assumes an objective form. In *Aliens* the project of space colonization ends up deep in the slime-coated tunnels of the alien queen's nest. The representation of the alien queen herself changes from an all-encompassing source of dread whose locus is impossible to pinpoint into an objectively-defined monster with whom Ripley can do battle. In "Ligeia" the narrator's transcendent "metaphysical investigations" end up in drug-induced paranoia, in a menacing interior where Ligeia seems a living but invisible presence, and it is only when Ligeia reappears that the plot can achieve its climax and the story can come to an end. This narrative pattern enacts the nightmare of being both possessed from within and swallowed up by the female Other, where the Other no longer functions as the object against which the Self is defined and its identity constituted, but rather as infestation, or as the suffocating space within which the Self must endure a kind of living death. It asks us to imagine, with horror, what it would mean for this most basic dualistic structure of Western metaphysics to collapse.

The identification of this particular narrative pattern in the Gothic is significant in other ways. In *Torture and Truth*, Page DuBois reads the trope of the classical hero's descent into the underworld as the pursuit of a secret truth through his immersion in a realm that is marked by its Otherness and associated with "the interiority of the woman's body" (105). The woman's body, she explains, "was seen as analogous to the earth, with its caves, crevasses, openings into an invisible world from which the living emerged, into which the dead departed" (78). It is tempting, then, to read the descent into the Gothic labyrinth as a Romantic version of this classical trope, as the passage "between life and death, from open, exterior space to enclosed, contained space" (82). But DuBois reminds us that the ultimate goal of the descent into the realm of the dead is the acquisition of a secret truth: the underworld, she writes, is "the elsewhere toward which truth is always slipping"; it is constructed "as other and as *therefore* in possession of the truth" (105, italics DuBois's). In other words, it represents not the frustration and obviation of the pursuit of transcendent truth so much as its culmination. The descent into the Gothic labyrinth, however, rehearses an anxiety peculiar to modernity: it is specifically subject-centered epistemologies that engage the Other in the task of identity formation and therefore generate such intense anxiety over separateness.

More relevant to the study of this trope in the Gothic is Susan Wolstenholme's study of similar narrative patterns in woman-authored texts. Wolstenholme argues that it is precisely this capacity of the Gothic to disrupt the unitary gaze—the gaze that establishes woman as object—that women writers have found so productive. Thus the menacing disappearance of the Other—her diffusion into the surrounding atmosphere—appears to Wolstenholme, from a feminist perspective, as the distinctive ability of Gothic narrative to assume "diffuse, de-centered, moving" vantage points (11). Moreover, Wolstenholme associates this tendency with the maternal, with the interiority of the womb and the creation of external, subjective existence in childbirth, and with the radical unsettling of subject and object, interior and exterior, that motherhood invokes. In what she calls "mother texts"—texts that are centered around an "absence ... hiding from sight and revealing become indistinguishable from one another" (12–13). And so, while *Aliens* and "Ligeia" are driven toward restoring the feminine Other to her horrific objectivity, the woman-authored texts that Wolstenholme reads, maintaining the absence at their center, have no such requirement. It is, in the end, testament to the remarkable richness of Gothic forms that this motif of object-become-space can embrace not only opposing perspectives, but opposing politics as well.[12]

Notes

1. See Hegel's analysis in "Lordship and Bondage."
2. See, for example, William Patrick Day, *In the Circles of Fear and Desire,* and Rosemary Jackson, *Fantasy: The Literature of Subversion.*
3. See also Eugenia C. DeLamotte, *Perils of the Night* (25–28).
4. Thomas Doherty writes: "the architectural motif might be described as 'abstract genital,' a style that is alternately penile and uterine, all sharp tumescent shafts, vaginal entrances, and fallopian interiors" (196).
5. In his reading of the Gothic labyrinth, Fred Botting draws an analogy between the descent into the labyrinth and the reader's immersion in the tale of horror, focusing on precisely the loss of reason:

> What counts is the play of light and dark, reason and imagination, virtue and vice, a play which characterizes the horrible attraction of Gothic fiction in that it involves readers, like its heroines, in the pleasurable and terrible loss of rational understanding to imaginative excess, a suspension of mastery or knowing subjectivity in an abandonment to the vicissitudes and uncertainties of the narrative, which, by means of the guiding hand of the author, eventually explains the mysteries and returns one to one's proper, moral place [255].

Botting's essay goes beyond a narrow interpretation of the labyrinth as psychic space, however, applying Foucault's concept of heterotopia, as well as his account of visibility and the mechanisms of power.

6. Dennis Patrick Slattery offers such a reading, identifying the "underworld" of the alien queen's nest as "the realm of the unconscious ... psychic geography, archetypal in structure" (33). Both Slattery and Lynda Bundtzen, moreover, draw connections between *Aliens* and the myth of Demeter and Persephone, and thus between the alien queen's nest and Hades.
7. Without citing Beauvoir, Leslie Fiedler reads this splitting of the feminine into opposites as similarly symptomatic of the male subject's "doomed" choice: "If the most husbandly embrace converts the Fair Maiden into her Dark opposite, reveals Clarissa as Circe—then man is doomed forever to choose between the blasphemous pursuit of an unattainable ideal and the self-destructive plunge into the gulf of sensuality" (310). Auerbach emphasizes the connection between these apparent opposites: "'So like, and yet so unlike' are the female angel and the demon," she writes. "It requires only the fire of an altered palette to bring out the contours of the one in the face of the other" (107).
8. In her account of the rise of the female action hero, Sherrie Inness notes the pivotal position of Ripley: "As an action figure, she revealed a new image of womanhood. Tough, muscular, heroic, she showed that women could handle the heroic roles long dominated by men" ("'It's a Girl Thing'" 84). See also Sherrie A. Inness's *Tough Girls: Women Warriors and Wonder Women in Popular Culture.*
9. In "'Ligeia' and the Problem of the Dying Woman," J. Gerald Kennedy also notices the applicability of Beauvoir's account to Poe's story, but with a different emphasis, focusing instead on her discussion of the idealized woman in the poetry of André Breton (114–116). And, without citing Beauvoir specifically, David Punter's reading of "Ligeia" identifies a strikingly similar narrative trajectory:

Behind these *ambiviolences* [is] the threat of the mother, the fear of undifferentiation, conceived to be cast down, "set up," in all senses, in order to demonstrate a weakness, with the aim of confirming the (masculine) ego in its upward trajectory towards the realm of light, beneath which lies buried, under the sign—which can never be a signature—of the female, the figure of the sailor's wife (for example) waiting and waving—or drowning—while the masculine sails off to brave new worlds [216].

10. In "Amorous Bondage" Joan Dyan offers an excellent reading of what she calls "the all-consuming etiology of possession" in Poe's fictional representations of women, including Ligeia, and his review of Paulding's *Slavery in the United States*. She notes that Poe's "To—," written to Marie Louise Shew in 1848, enacts the fantasy of "being swallowed up by the object of his affections," thereby "articulat[ing] a specific relation of domination, where the speaker who had defined himself as possessor is in turn defined by his possession" (246, 247).

11. Dyan notes that Ligeia "might well be Poe's rendition of the favorite fiction of white readers: the 'tragic mulatta' or 'octoroon mistress'" (260).

12. Auerbach also comments on the conflicted politics of the tropes and images she discusses: "in the nineteenth century the dialectic between womanhood and power was so central and general a concern," she writes, "one so fundamental to the literature, art, and social thought of the period, that it is misleading to pigeonhole it as 'feminist' as though it were the concern of one interest group alone" (188). The very elements that gave rise to the figure of the "angelic demon," she suggests, also gave woman "imaginative centrality in a culture increasingly alienated from itself. Powerful images of oppression became images of barely suppressed power" (188).

Works Cited

Aliens. Dir. James Cameron. Perf. Sigourney Weaver, Carrie Henn, Michael Biehn, Lance Henriksen, Paul Reiser, Bill Paxton, and William Hope. 1986. DVD. Twentieth Century Fox Home Entertainment, Inc., 1999.

Auerbach, Nina. *Woman and the Demon: The Life of a Victorian Myth*. Cambridge: Harvard University Press, 1982.

Beauvoir, Simone de. *The Second Sex*. Trans. H.M. Parshley. New York: Vintage Books, 1989.

Botting, Fred. "Power in the Darkness: Heterotopias, Literature, and Gothic Labyrinths." *Genre* 26.2-3 (1993): 253-282.

Bundtzen, Lynda K. "Monstrous Mothers: Medusa, Grendel, and Now Alien." *Film Quarterly* 40.3 (1987): 11-17.

Coleridge, Samuel Taylor. "The Rime of the Ancient Mariner." In *The Oxford Authors: Samuel Taylor Coleridge*, ed. H.J. Jackson, 46-65. Oxford and New York: Oxford University Press, 1985.

Day, William Patrick. *In the Circles of Fear and Desire: A Study of Gothic Fantasy*. Chicago: University of Chicago Press, 1985.

DeLamotte, Eugenia C. *Perils of the Night: A Feminist Study of Nineteenth-Century Gothic*. New York: Oxford University Press, 1990.

Doherty, Thomas. "Genre, Gender, and the *Aliens* Trilogy." In *The Dread of Difference: Gender and the Horror Film*, ed. Barry Keith Grant, 181-199. Austin: University of Texas Press, 1996.

DuBois, Page. *Torture and Truth*. New York and London: Routledge, 1991.

Dyan, Joan. "Amorous Bondage: Poe, Ladies, and Slaves." *American Literature* 66.2 (June 1994): 239-273.

Fiedler, Leslie A. *Love and Death in the American Novel*. 1960. Normal, IL: Dalkey Archive Press, 1997.

Hegel, G.W.F. "Lordship and Bondage." In *Phenomenology of Spirit*, trans. A.V. Miller, 111-119. Oxford: Oxford University Press, 1977.

Inness, Sherrie A. "'It's a Girl Thing': Tough Female Action Figures in the Toy Store."

In *Action Chicks: New Images of Tough Women in Popular Culture,* ed. Sherrie A. Inness, 75–94. New York: Palgrave, 2004.

_____. *Tough Girls: Women Warriors and Wonder Women in Popular Culture.* Philadelphia: University of Pennsylvania Press, 1999.

Jackson, Rosemary. *Fantasy: The Literature of Subversion.* London: Methuen, 1981.

Kahane, Claire. "The Maternal Legacy: The Grotesque Tradition in Flannery O'Connor's Female Gothic." In *The Female Gothic,* ed. Juliann E. Fleenor, 242–256. Montreal: Eden Press, 1983.

Kennedy, J. Gerald. "Poe, 'Ligeia,' and the Problem of Dying Women." In *New Essays on Poe's Major Tales,* ed. Kenneth Silverman, 113–129. Cambridge: Cambridge University Press, 1993.

Poe, Edgar Allan. "Ligeia." In *The Unabridged Edgar Allan Poe,* ed. Tam Mossman, 479–492. Philadelphia: Running Press, 1983.

Punter, David. "Death, Femininity and Identification: A Recourse to 'Ligeia.'" *Women's Writing* 1.2 (1994): 215–228.

Sedgwick, Eve Kosofsky. *The Coherence of Gothic Conventions.* New York: Methuen, 1980.

Slattery, Dennis Patrick. "Demeter-Persephone and the *Alien*(s) Cultural Body." *New Orleans Review* 19.1 (1992): 30–35.

Wolstenholme, Susan. *Gothic (Re)visions: Writing Women as Readers.* Albany: State University of New York Press, 1993.

2

Morbid Mothers: Gothic Heredity in Florence Marryat's The Blood of the Vampire

OCTAVIA DAVIS

Florence Marryat was widely known during the Victorian period in her native England and the United States as a popular novelist and commentator on the Spiritualist movement.[1] In 1897, the same year that *Dracula* appeared, Marryat published *The Blood of the Vampire*, a novel about a young woman who involuntarily sucks the life from her acquaintances.[2] Marryat's novel, far more insistently than *Dracula*, associates blood with heredity, and heredity with the female body. While *Dracula* carries the name of the eponymous monster, for example, *The Blood of the Vampire* refers to the breeding of the vampire Harriet Brandt, to the terrifying legacy and potentiality of her *blood*, rather than to her name. Marryat's novel, read in the context of her semi-autobiographical accounts of Spiritualism, offers valuable insight into contemporary popular and scientific understandings of heredity and sexuality, which constructed the sexually mature female body as dangerous and in need of control.

The female body made a logical target for control in late nineteenth century British scientific discourses because the natural world had long been conceived as the feminine, imperfect creation of a masculine God. Though mainstream scientific discourses embraced the notion of evolution, many retained teleological conceptions of the earth in which feminine Nature necessarily evolved toward the perfection of God, becoming an increasingly well-suited home for increasingly evolved "man."[3] Theories of global cooling, for example, intersected with teleological conceptions of the earth to posit the distant tropics and their denizens as living histories of Europe's primeval past, thus constructing "native" bodies as perpetually immature, bestial, and feminine, the anachronistic opposite of the "highly evolved" white British male scientist. Despite the persistence of teleological notions of change, however, nineteenth century science embraced the theory of degeneration, the idea that species can regress as well as progress on an evolutionary continuum.

In an effort to prevent a slippage of the empire into the degenerate past, late nineteenth century British science sought to control Nature and "her" processes abroad and in England, commonly referred to as the "mother country." The analogues of earth and body, Nature and woman, "mother country" and mother, made British women a locus of anxiety about the primeval past and uncontrollable future.[4] Eugenics and other turn-of-the-century practices, such as social reform and criminology, worked to recruit the general population to white middle-class imperial purposes, but located the environment of evolutionary change more squarely in the bodies of women, imagined to be more "natural" than those of men. In *The City of Dreadful Delight*, for example, Judith Walkowitz notes the tendency of nineteenth century reformers to imagine poor Londoners as "actively and perniciously female" and to "blame 'bad mothers' for the degenerate conditions of the slums and the physical degeneracy of the slum-dwellers" (119–20). Not only were "bad mothers" blamed for the decay of the poor, but girls were defined primarily as potential mothers in whose hands lay the evolutionary fates of future English citizens. George Sims in *How the Poor Live* (1883), for example, urged social reformers to help poor girls extricate themselves from poverty so they could become "mothers of a better and useful class" (49). Controlling female bodies, Sims suggested, would avert evolutionary disaster and secure a bright future for London.

As scholars of late nineteenth century literature note, scientific and social theories about evolution and degeneration created new possibilities for fictional representation in the Gothic mode because of the slippage in time, place, and social categories inherent to them. Robert Mighall, for example, demonstrates not only that Gothic fiction frequently utilized the taxonomic categories of contemporary science in the creation of the Gothic Other, but also that nineteenth century science relied upon the discursive practices of Gothic fiction (132). *How the Poor Live* offers an example of the discursive intersections Mighall describes: Sims introduced his text as a "book of travel" into the "dark continent" of the "benighted" urban poor. Given gendered assumptions about Nature, however, the female body emerged in nineteenth century science and fiction as a particularly dangerous Gothic Other, as *The Blood of the Vampire* demonstrates. Moreover, the novel and Marryat's other discussions of motherhood, female vampirism, and science suggest that some nineteenth century women actually believed themselves to manifest the horrific traits imagined in the fictional Gothic Other. Marryat endows her fictional vampire with the same destructive characteristics she attributes to herself and to other women, indicating that she had incorporated and internalized claims that white middle-class British women exhibited vampiric tendencies similar to those of the degenerate Other. The fictional destruction of the female vampire illustrates the consequences for living women of scientific theories that defined them in terms of an evolutionary continuum as *abnormal* people, even if they were "normal" as women.

Scientific theories about heredity and human behavior abounded at the end of the nineteenth century, and central to many of them were assumptions about blood. Darwin's theory of pangenesis, the belief that all cells of the body carry "gemmules," transmitters of inheritable properties, and the popular use of blood as a metaphor for heredity, yielded the common belief that inheritable properties were carried in the blood. Further, Francis Galton based eugenics on the idea that the struggle for survival of the fittest occurred among gemmules in the bloodstream. In *Hereditary Genius* (1892), Galton argued that "the character of a man is wholly formed through the gemmules that have succeeded" against "other antagonistic gemmules" (353). By using eugenic principles to control the reproductive choices of potential parents, Galton hoped to insure that "pure blood" would vanquish "mongrel alliances" in the individual and social body, thereby creating a race of "better" people (Galton 353–54). At the same time that blood operates as a metaphor for character in eugenics, it also operates as a metaphor for what hides beneath the surface. Galton states that "gemmules of innumerable qualities, derived from ancestral sources, circulate in the blood," only some of which are visible on the body. Lurking below the surface, however, "there is a vastly larger number of capabilities ... and for every *patent* element there are countless *latent* ones" (353, italics Galton's). Thus, blood functions simultaneously as a metaphor for static and dynamic conceptions of the self, for what is visible and subject to interpretation, and for what is latent, invisible, and uncontrollable.

Such scientific conceptions of blood coincided with Gothic and Romantic concerns with the troubled and potentially dangerous relationships between surface and essence, the present and the ancestral past. Marryat's *The Blood of the Vampire* explores the terrifying threat to "civilized" society posed by a young woman who on the surface appears to be a desirable catch for an upper-class gentleman but whose bloodstream conceals the invisible latencies of a monstrous past. The novel conforms to the assumption of eugenics that blood may conceal latent characteristics derived from the geographical conditions exerted upon the parents; the novel, in fact, seems preoccupied with dramatizing scientific theories in vogue at the time of its publication. Because the novel is long out of print and difficult to obtain, a summary might be helpful.

Just of age, the heiress Harriet Brandt appears at a Belgian resort amid speculations about her origins. Harriet, who is only vaguely aware of her parentage, attaches herself to the young mother Margaret Pullen, who immediately shows signs of exhaustion. Harriet attracts the attentions of Margaret's engaged brother-in-law, Ralph Pullen, and, although his fiancée Elinor Leyton is jealous, Elinor is too cold and controlled to let her feelings show. Harriet's new friends decline in health, except the Baroness Gobelli, who is of "low origin." Doctor Phillips arrives to examine Margaret's dying baby and reveals to Margaret that Harriet, the illegitimate daughter of a mad English scientist and a bloodthirsty Jamaican "half-caste," is killing the child with her presence. After the baby's death, Harriet returns to London with the Gobelli family, but she continues to pursue Ralph Pullen. Doctor Phillips sends Anthony Pennel to prevent Harriet from destroying Ralph and Elinor's engagement. Pennel, though forewarned about Harriet's deadly charms, falls in love with Harriet and dreams of inspiring her to use her intellect for good works. Harriet responds to his sincere regard and manly frame by falling in love. They marry and Pennel soon dies. Harriet kills herself on his deathbed, leaving a note that explains she has escaped the "curse of heredity" in death.

Harriet Brandt, like that other more famous literary female monster, Bertha Mason, comes from Jamaica. Like Bertha Mason, Harriet Brandt threatens the stability of the middle-class British family because her "Creole" body and overly emotional mind make her unfit for marriage.[5] While Bertha Mason's imprisonment in marriage and in the attic removes her from reproductive circulation, Harriet Brandt, like one of Galton's hemoglobinous "antagonistic gemmules," comes to Europe unchaperoned, unmarried, and in search of "mongrel alliance." That Harriet has survived her childhood in the tropical colony, defined as distant both geographically and temporally, proves that her primeval blood endows her with a pathological hardiness. As Harriet reports, while "so few English children live to grow up in Jamaica," she thrives in the tropical sun (21). From her mother's side, the novel indicates, Harriet carries the earthy, "unrefined" blood of African slaves, which allows her to endure the primeval miasma of the tropical West Indies.

According to Doctor Phillips, whose professional opinion the novel endorses, Harriet Brandt's blood carries elements that span the evolutionary continuum, from tropical rodent to white British male. Harriet Brandt's maternal grandmother, for example, was a slave who, while pregnant with Harriet's mother, "was bitten by a Vampire bat" (122). According to Doctor Phillips, the blood of the vampire bat allied with the unevolved blood of the pregnant slave to make of Harriet's mother an inhuman amalgam of animal and degenerate human traits. In Harriet Brandt's fiendish mother, animal appetites dominate to such an extent that she exceeds even the degeneracy attributed by contemporary science to the "lower" races. As bad as Harriet's mother may have been, she made, according to Doctor Phillips, "a fitting match" for Harriet's father (121). While Harriet believes her father to have been a British doctor and scientist, a worthy source of blood in contemporary estimations, Doctor Phillips reveals that Brandt was a murderous vivisectionist who tortured and killed animal and human alike in the practice of his scientific experiments (120–121).[6]

Like her parents, Harriet carries degenerate blood. For example, the narrator describes her repeatedly as bestial in her movements and sensual appetites. Harriet's sensuality exceeds human bounds; the mere touch of Ralph Pullen's hand against hers "seemed to rouse all the animal in Harriet Brandt's blood" (109). Harriet's bestial movements and sensuality, which escape surface appraisals of her body, manifest the pollution of her blood, as do her kinship with the "savages" of Jamaica, the traces of which are also quite nearly absent from the surface of her body. Harriet's relation to "negro servants" compounds her taxonomic dissonance in terms of both race and class. Though her father was a wealthy English scientist and her grandfather was a justice of "Barbadoes," Harriet's mother and grandmother were slaves. The hotel proprietor, however, identifies nothing low-class about Harriet, whom she takes for a "German Princess." Though her blood transgresses social and racial categories, Harriet appears refined, and her skin is "colourless but clear" (3), devoid of the most obvious sign of race. Despite Doctor Phillips's claim that he could identify Harriet as a "quadroon" at a single glance, the novel suggests that he would never suspect the extent of Harriet's degenerate complexity if he were not privy to the history of the Brandt family.

The surface of Harriet's body exhibits conventional white middle-class feminine delicacy that belies not only the racial and social origins of the "primitive" Other, but also the latent sexual tendencies that contemporary science defined as regressive. Based on Doctor Phillips's description of Harriet, Anthony Pennell expects to meet a masculine woman, "a juvenile virago," but finds instead a "lovely girl" whom he fails to recognize as the infamous West Indian heiress (250, 236). Though Harriet appears to both male and female characters to meet prevailing definitions of femininity, she frightens Margaret Pullen with her aggressive affection. Margaret later describes Harriet's semi-clad body as a "slight boyish figure"; however, it is Harriet's behavior, *not her body*, that causes Margaret Pullen to fear that Harriet may be one of the "unsophisticated girls" who develop "unaccountable affections for one of their own sex" (38, 93). In fact, the novel's emphasis on the degeneracy of Harriet's blood suggests that her overt desire for Margaret's affection illustrates what contemporary science termed primitive bisexuality.

According to contemporary theories of sexual dimorphism, Harriet Brandt's hungry desire for Margaret betrays her reversion from "true" femininity to "primitive" hermaphroditism. In *The Descent of Man*, Darwin asserted that vertebrates descended from a remote "hermaphrodite or androgynous" ancestor (qtd. in Dijkstra, *Idols of Perversity* 170). Darwin and numerous writers who followed him claimed that male and female were two divergent lines of development, with the male tending toward greater individuality and strength in mind and body, and the female tending toward imitation and emotion.[7] Any behaviors inconsistent with these definitions of sexual dimorphism were interpreted as reversions to a more primitive state. Thus, Harriet's desire for Margaret, as well as her deadly physical strength, evidence her regression toward the ancestral sexual and racial past.

While Harriet's mixed-race blood occasions "primitive" sexuality, according to the novel, it also operates in accordance with contemporary understandings of female sexuality that defined the woman of childbearing age as dependent upon her environment for energy. Patrick Geddes and J. Arthur Thomson, whose book *The Evolution of Sex* appeared in 1889, describe reproduction in terms of two variable forces, defined as male and female uses of energy. The "forces preservative of race," Geddes and Thomson explained, are split between male katabolic expenditure of energy and female anabolic absorption of energy. Katabolism is the "power to sustain individual life (individuation); anabolism is the power to produce new individuals (genesis)" (263). Female anabolism *continues* the species by absorbing energy from the parent organism; male katabolism gives active, combative energy and creates species *change*. These two opposing forces operate within the body of every person, but in men katabolism dominates, while in women anabolism prevails. However, if a woman expends energy in a katabolic, "masculine" manner in pursuit of her own development or desires (individuation), she robs her body of the energy needed to reproduce successfully:

> genesis in all its forms is a process of *disintegration*, and thus opposed to that process of integration which is one element of individual evolution. The matter and energy supplied for the young organism represent so much loss for the parent; while, conversely, the larger the amount of matter and energy consumed by the functional actions of the parent, the less must be the amount remaining for those of the offspring [Geddes and Thomson 263].

To prevent race degeneration, according to this widespread conception of human reproduction, women must avoid katabolic (male) expenditures of energy so that they preserve their bodies as the best environments possible for the creation of future children.

However, even if a woman could avoid squandering her energy in the pursuit of her own development to the detriment of her future children and the race, she would nonetheless continue to operate at an energy deficit because of her female sexuality. According to numerous late nineteenth century scientific texts, blood carries not only inheritable qualities, but also vital essence, understood to be cerebral and sexual energy. The theory of vital essence buttressed racist and sexist understandings about the fundamental differences between white males and people defined as less highly evolved. According to the theory, the "lower" races and women are more sexual than their cerebral white male counterparts; therefore, they waste the energy needed to further their intellectual and moral progress. With the onset of puberty, women and the "lower" races cease to develop, unlike white men, who continue to evolve. As brain specialist Harry Campbell explained in 1891, the mental traits of the "child characterize also primitive man," and "women remain throughout life children" (159, 161). Menstruation arrests cerebral development by draining energy contained in menstrual blood, making a woman passive, imitative, and dependent. Childbearing is particularly devastating: "constant confinement, together with exhausting effects of child-bearing, nursing, and the continual irritation of household worries, tells profoundly on the woman's health; so that after a few years of married life the blooming girl is but too often changed into a haggard bloodless woman" (Campbell 122–23). Menopause, on the other hand, restores a modicum of energy and intellect: "She becomes more active, less a creature of feeling, more intellectual" (Campbell 153, 176). The loss of blood through menstruation, childbearing, or any other form of depletion, was thus understood to consume energy, strength, and intellectual function; the tendency to incur such loss was believed to distinguish the "lower" races and women from more continent, civilized men. Thus, blood operated at the *fin-de-siècle* as a metaphor for both heredity and energy, sexual and mental.

According to science popular at the time, because women lose blood and vitality through menstruation, pregnancy, childbirth, and rearing children, they must compensate for this loss by drawing energy from their environments (Campbell 122–23). In order to compensate for the innate scarcity of energy in the female, Geddes and Thomson argued, the "constitutional bias of the (female) sex" (15) is parasitic. From the level of insects to human beings, the female was seen as essentially anabolic, or energy-absorbing, in relation to her environment. Females, Geddes and Thomson reasoned, "live at a profit," taking more in than they expend, "whence the capacity to bear offspring" (22). Predictably, they argued, females appear in greater numbers where the pickings are plentiful: "In towns and in prosperous families, there seem to be more females, while boys are numerous in the country and among the poor" (Geddes and Thomson 41–42). Though the maternal function renders a woman "bloodless," her anabolic system works to revitalize her by absorbing vital essence from the environment and people around her. Hence, late nineteenth century scientists such as Havelock Ellis reported that "weak and anemic girls so often become full-blooded and robust after marriage."[8] Using similar logic, Geddes and Thomson cautioned against using withdrawal as a method of contraception because it deprives women of the energy they derive from the vital infusion of their partners: "such a practice is maintained by some to be injurious to the male, and *yet more to the female*" (271, italics mine). Thus, according to mainstream contemporary science, women lose blood and energy because of their sexuality, but female anabolism revitalizes them at the expense of the world and people around them.

In congruence with contemporary theories of female sexuality, *The Blood of the Vampire* depicts every significant female character, from Harriet's beastly mother to the ideally feminine Margaret Pullen, in anabolic relation to her environment. The Baroness Gobelli, for example, representing the lower-class European double of Harriet Brandt's vampiric mother, confirms that both the "lower" races and classes drain the energies of groups thought to be more highly advanced. Like Harriet's Jamaican mother, Baroness Gobelli comes from lowly origins. The baroness, who often expresses "bloodthirsty sentiments," jokes about infanticide and suggests that she should have murdered her son, Bobby (Marryat, *The Blood of the Vampire* 53, 10). Not surprisingly, Bobby is blood-deprived, "half-witted and very weakly," "an anaemic young fellow and very delicate" (33, 149). Indiscriminate in her parasitism, the baroness fleeces lords and ladies by falsely claiming to be a spirit medium. The baroness is a sort of social and financial "half-caste," voracious in her appetites, and cruelly parasitic in her dealings with everyone she encounters.

Elinor Leyton, on the other hand, boasts impeccable racial and social breeding. The daughter of an aristocratic English lord, Elinor represents the perversion of the dimorphically evolved woman, the New Woman who is cold, unemotional, and ultimately unproductive because she squanders energy in the katabolic pursuit of her own interests, rather than conserving it for her future children. In the words of contemporary social critic Arthur Laidlaw, a woman "whose maternal instinct is suppressed and her sexual impulse unsatisfied is liable to be extremely callous." The narrator describes Elinor in terms consistent with the stereotypically cold New Woman; she has no patience for children and makes fun of Margaret's concern for her sick baby; when the baby dies, Elinor "spoke sympathetically, but there were no tears in her eyes, and she did not caress, nor attempt to console her friend" (144–45). Not only lacking the maternal instinct, Elinor also expresses no affection for her fiancé and asserts, "I'm afraid the man was not born yet for whose convenience I was made" (95). While lust and sensuality are pathological conditions for a woman in *The Blood of the Vampire*, so is the lack of other-directedness and altruism. The novel clearly indicates that Elinor Leyton's lack of emotion drives Ralph Pullen to near-perdition in Harriet's embrace. Not only does a cold woman drive a man to sin, but as her fiancé predicts in the words of contemporary wisdom about the atavistic New Woman: "The woman who commences by pursing her mouth up at everything, ends by opening it wider than anybody else!" (108). By refusing to engage in the dependence of anabolic exchange, the novel suggests, the cold woman deprives herself, merely postponing and amplifying her biologically determined need.

Even Margaret Pullen, the ideal woman and mother in the text, is not free of morbid anabolism. Though in her "quiet plainness" and "quiescent passivity," Margaret shrinks from all anti-maternal uses of energy, she nonetheless lacks control of her emotions.[9] While pregnant, according to the narrator, Margaret suffers "a terrible blow" when her husband must leave her in England and sail to India. Already prone to depression, she falls prey to "morbid" thoughts about the death of her daughter and herself (10–11). In her autobiographical work on Spiritualism, *There Is No Death*, Florence Marryat described herself in a situation almost identical to the one she later fictionalized in *The Blood of the Vampire*. Like her character Margaret Pullen, Marryat was forced to separate from her husband while pregnant, though she sailed to England from India. She relates that the voyage home "was a terrible affair. I was suffering mentally and physically, to such a degree that I cannot think of the time without a shudder" (64). Shortly after landing, Florence Marryat delivered a baby with a birth defect so severe that ten days later, it died. The attending doctors found the mother guilty of causing the infant's fatal deformity: "I was closely catechized as to whether I had suffered any physical or mental shock, that should account for the injury to my child, and it was decided that the trouble I had experienced was sufficient to produce it" (Marryat, *There Is No Death* 73). While *The Blood of the Vampire* indisputably identifies Harriet Brandt as the killer of Margaret's baby, Florence Marryat's assumption of guilt in *There Is No Death* suggests that Margaret, by virtue of her emotional state during and after pregnancy, may have unintentionally deprived her infant by succumbing to "morbid" emotion. In imposing this culpability upon Margaret, Marryat illustrates her internalization of the message of her own doctors.

In *The Spirit World*, another book about Spiritualism, Marryat reports a more complex case of feminine anabolism that constructs white middle-class female bodies as radically vulnerable to and productive of blood depletion and pollution. Shortly after her own daughter Eva suffered from "blood-poisoning" and died while giving birth, Marryat spent a few days with a pregnant friend named Bessie, who made her living as a medium who could materialize the spirits of the dead. Marryat describes materialization as a vampiric process in which the dead spirit renders its body visible by "detach(ing) certain particles from (the medium's) organism" (Marryat, *The Spirit World* 153–4). During Marryat's stay, her dead daughter Eva materialized every night from the body of the pregnant medium Bessie. The materialization of Eva weakened Bessie's pregnant body to the extent that Marryat had to cut her visit short. However, it was not so much the vampiric materialization that threatened Bessie as the proximity of Eva's poisoned blood: "if I remained, Bessie might suffer in her coming trial, as Eva did, from blood-poisoning, which (as everyone knows) is most contagious, especially for women in the same condition" (237). According to Marryat, the pregnant body, "as everyone knows," contracts blood peculiarities, such as poisoning, from the mere presence of another body, particularly one that is also pregnant. Even though her physical body is dead, Eva's blood-poisoned spirit body threatens to pollute the anabolic body of the pregnant mother. To make matters worse, Marryat suffered from nervousness during her visit, which, she reported, Bessie also absorbed (237–38). Bessie, her pregnant body in vampiric need of energy from her environment, suffers from the proximity of Florence Marryat's nervous body and her dead, blood-poisoned daughter.

Given the prevailing scientific definition of the normal female as anabolic, the proliferation of vampiric female characters in the novel, and Marryat's own belief that she parasitically destroyed her infant, Doctor Phillips's diagnosis of Harriet as a vampire seems hardly as startling as the presence of her "mongrel" Creole blood. Doctor Phillips discloses to Harriet:

> You will always exert a weakening and debilitating effect upon [your friends], so that after a while, having sapped their brains, and lowered the tone of their bodies, you will find their affection, or friendship for you visibly decrease. You will have, in fact, *sucked them dry* [298, italics Marryat's].

Doctor Phillips explains to Harriet that she sucks the vitality from the brains and bodies of the people with whom she associates because she has a "drawing" temperament. As part of Harriet's anabolic parasitism, she depletes people not only of energy, but also of their affection for her, so that she constantly needs emotional sustenance.

Harriet's medical diagnosis parallels the psychic reading that Florence Marryat reports in *There Is No Death*, a reading Marryat finds so accurate that she is "struck dumb" by the ability of a complete stranger to "intimately penetrate my inner life," to reveal "truths concerning myself which I had not recognized" (Marryat, *There is No Death*, 173–74). The medium reveals the following:

> You are one of the world's magnets.... You draw people to you, and live upon their life; and they have no more to give, nor you to demand, the liking fades on both sides. It must be so, because the spirit requires food the same as the body; and when the store is exhausted, the affection is starved out, and the persons pass out of your life.... Constant intercourse may be fatal to your dearest affections. You draw so much on others, you *empty* them, and they have nothing more to give you [174–75 italics Marryat's].

Marryat reports in this passage that she lives parasitically on her acquaintances, using them until they no longer please her. Woe to friends she cares for, however, because like Harriet, Marryat "may be fatal" to people she loves. Her anabolic force, according to *There Is No Death*, draws upon the physical environment, as well. The medium cautions, "you would soon die" if confined to one place: "after you have lived in place a little while, you become sad, weary, and ill—not physically ill, but mentally so—and you feel as if you *must* leave it, and go to another place.... It is because your nature has exhausted all it can draw from its surroundings" (175). According to *There Is No Death*, the words of the medium catalyze Marryat's self-understanding, indicating that she already believed prevalent understandings about deadly female anabolism. Furthermore, Marryat accepts without comment the medium's assertion that "Woman cannot draw spiritual life from women only. She must take it from men" (178). Thus, Marryat indicates in *There Is No Death* that she considers female anabolism, though potentially deadly, to be normal in women.

Despite Marryat's apparent acceptance of her parasitic nature, she nonetheless grieves in *There Is No Death* that her lack of control and failure to dominate her emotions for the sake of her unborn child not only deformed and killed it, but doomed it to a despondent purgatory. She writes:

> I knew before that my uncontrolled grief had been the cause of the untimely death of her body, but it never struck me that her spirit would carry the effects of it into the unseen world. It was a warning to me (as it should be to all mothers) not to take the solemn responsibility of maternity upon themselves without being prepared to sacrifice their own feelings for the sake of their children [80].

In her confession and warning to "all mothers," Florence Marryat locates in the body of the mother the responsibility to prevent every departure from perfect health in the child; she must be willing to "sacrifice" herself for the sake of her unborn children's health. In writing these passages, the author disciplines herself in accordance with the dictates of science and participates in their dissemination by warning other mothers to take as "solemn responsibility" the need to sacrifice themselves in order to avoid destroying their children.

In its depiction of Harriet's suicide, *The Blood of the Vampire* confirms that women must act first and foremost as mothers of the race, even if it means sacrificing their own lives. Harriet explains in a suicide note written upon the death of her husband that she must kill herself in order to extinguish her bloodline: "My parents made me unfit to live. Let me go to a world where the curse of heredity which they laid upon me may be mercifully wiped out" (345). According to the novel, despite her many conventionally "good" qualities and sincere desire to put them to use, Harriet is both "unfit to live" and "unfit" to produce the child she most likely carries. She must kill herself, therefore, for the good of others and to prevent the birth of future monstrosity. Harriet Brandt's suicide further confirms that the contemporary scientific emphasis on producing the ideal maternal and racial bodies coexisted with a contradictory imperative for feminine characteristics to disappear from the human organism altogether. Though science professed a belief in sexual dimorphism, two separate lines of evolutionary development, the differences between men and women were nonetheless imagined in hierarchical terms. By defining all human bodies as more or less "natural" or "primitive," and, thus, feminine and in need of control or eradication, mainstream contemporary science tightened in the disciplinary reins on women and, by analogy, on all bodies defined as relatively feminine.

Mainstream nineteenth century scientific theories constructed women of child-bearing age as living at the expense of others; Harriet is a monster not because she lives anabolically on her environment, but because her tainted blood exacerbates the anabolic process. By depicting female anabolism as a common female trait, *The Blood of the Vampire* profoundly reinforces the threat of degeneracy due to the combination of race and class that Harriet Brandt represents. In fact, it is not her vampirism to which Ralph Pullen refers when he explains why Harriet "is not the sort of girl that any man could marry"; it is her heredity: "One might get a piebald son and heir!" (261). H.L. Malchow points out that the "most emotive" danger in the novel is the threat of racial pollution (169). However, by depicting all its major female characters as vampiric or flawed in some way, the novel also illustrates the terrifying truth of Harriet's observation that "people drop every day like rotten sheep:— everyone might accuse himself of causing the death of his neighbor" (Marryat, *The Blood of the Vampire* 327). Harriet's entrapment in hereditary destiny is the condition of humanity, according to contemporary science and the novel, though her potently degenerate blood makes her case more horrifying. As *The Blood of the Vampire* illustrates, the evolutionary continuum defines all people, particularly women, as too close for comfort to Nature and the hereditary Other concealed inside.

Marryat's novel offers no solace and no solutions; instead, it resists contemporary science by dwelling upon the pain Harriet suffers when she unintentionally kills her beloved husband while on their honeymoon. According to contemporary beliefs, all women, blood-deprived and parasitic by nature, embody the dangerous and horrifying Other; they hover, therefore, on the brink of Harriet's cannibalistic vampirism precisely because of their sexuality, defined by late Victorian science as less highly evolved than katabolic male sexuality. *The Blood of the Vampire* and Marryat's writings on Spiritualism dramatize the terrifying notion that while most women exhibit anabolic dependence, "uncontrolled" and hereditarily tainted women exceed "normal" levels of parasitism and deprive their loved ones of vital energy. As potential mothers, women deprive their children of the energy needed to grow and evolve. Physically and morally stunted by their morbid mothers, the second generation fails to succeed, hence, according to contemporary understandings, the monstrosity of Harriet Brandt and the tragic death of Florence Marryat's own newborn baby. In an effort to preserve white middle-class hegemony from the imagined threat of racial degeneration, scientists targeted the female body as an instrument through which they might preserve the human race; the writings of Florence Marryat demonstrate the tormenting anxiety and guilt assumed by white middle-class women in accordance with these beliefs.

Notes

1. Florence Marryat (1838–99), the youngest child of popular Victorian novelist Frederick Marryat, was born in Brighton and educated by a governess. She married for the first of at least two times at sixteen to T. Ross-Church and traveled with him extensively in India. Marryat lived a relatively public life, publishing dozens of novels, working as an actress and director, and participating in the Spiritualist movement.

2. Sian McFie, author of "'They Suck Us Dry': A Study of Late Nineteenth-century Projections of Vampiric Women," in *Subjectivity and Literature from the Romantics to the Present Day*, offers the first critical study of *The Blood of the Vampire* that I have found. McFie argues that Marryat's vampires reveal her uncertainty about the physical and spiritual nature of women, particularly with regard to sexuality (66). While McFie identifies tensions in the novel, she does not locate its engagement with contemporary discussions of female anabolic sexuality. I am indebted to McFie for the reference to *There Is No Death*. In *Gothic Images of Race in Nineteenth-Century Britain*, H.L. Malchow reads *The Blood of the Vampire* as dramatizing the threat of racial pollution. I concur with this reading and suggest further that novel defines female sexuality as vampiric.

3. For a discussion of teleology in British geographical discourse, see David N. Liv-

ingstone's *The Geographical Tradition: Episodes in the History of a Contested Enterprise.*

4. In the chapter on "Laboring for Empire," in her book *Rule Britannia*, Deirdre David demonstrates that changes in the roles of women and threats to imperial hegemony at the end of the century manifested in fears of uncontrolled women who jeopardized the health of their unborn babies and, thus, threatened to weaken the empire.

5. While scholars dispute whether or not Bertha Mason is a white woman or a woman of mixed race, *The Blood of the Vampire* makes perfectly clear that Harriet carries the blood of "slaves." See Susan Meyer, *Imperialism at Home: Race and Victorian Women's Fiction* (64), for a discussion of scholarly interpretations of Bertha Mason's race.

6. Harriet's father, Henry Brandt, bears a striking resemblance to the scientist of *The Island of Dr. Moreau*, published by H.G. Wells the previous year. *The Island of Dr. Moreau*, like *The Blood of the Vampire*, questions the distinction between animal and human by showing that physical form and moral character are made "plastic" (131) through the transfer of blood. Both novels suggest that the sort of degenerate behavior Henry Brandt and Dr. Moreau practice can make an educated white man as inhuman as the animals he subjects to study.

7. For a thorough discussion of contemporary scientific interpretations of women, see Bram Dijkstra's *Idols of Perversity: Fantasies of Feminine Evil in Fin-de-Siecle Culture.*

8. See Bram Dijkstra's *Evil Sisters: The Threat of Female Sexuality in Twentieth-Century Culture* (201).

9. See Geddes and Thomson, *The Evolution of Sex* (25).

Works Cited

Campbell, Harry. *Differences in the Nervous System of Man and Woman: Physiological and Pathological.* London: H.K. Lewis, 1891.
David, Deirdre. *Rule Britannia: Women, Empire, and Victorian Writing.* Ithaca: Cornell University Press, 1995.
Dijkstra, Bram *Evil Sisters: The Threat of Female Sexuality in Twentieth-Century Culture.* New York: Henry Holt, 1996.
_____. *Idols of Perversity: Fantasies of Feminine Evil in Fin-de-Siècle Culture.* New York: Oxford University Press, 1986.
Galton, Francis. *Hereditary Genius.* London: Macmillan and Company, 1892.
Geddes, Patrick, and J. Arthur Thomson. *The Evolution of Sex.* 1889. New York: Humboldt, 1890.
Laidlaw, Arthur. "On the Artificial Characteristics of Women." *The Universal Magazine and Free Review* 8 (April–Sept 1897): 663–70.
Livingstone, David N. *The Geographical Tradition: Episodes in the History of a Contested Enterprise.* Cambridge: Blackwell Publishers, 1992.
Malchow, H.L. *Gothic Images of Race in Nineteenth Century Britain.* Stanford: Stanford University Press, 1996.
Marryat, Florence. *The Blood of the Vampire.* London: Hutchinson, 1897.
_____. *The Spirit World.* London: F.V. White, 1894.
_____. *There Is No Death.* New York: National Book, 1891.
McFie, Sian. "'They Suck Us Dry': A Study of Late Nineteenth Century Projections of Vampiric Women." In *Subjectivity and Literature from the Romantics to the Present Day*, ed. Philip Shaw and Peter Stockwell. London: Pinter Publishers, 1991.
Meyer, Susan. *Imperialism at Home: Race and Victorian Women's Fiction.* Ithaca: Cornell University Press, 1996.
Mighall, Robert. *A Geography of Victorian Gothic Fiction: Mapping History's Nightmares.* New York: Oxford University Press, 1999.
Sims, George Robert. *How the Poor Live and Horrible London.* 1883. New York: Garland Publishing, 1984.

Walkowitz, Judith R. *City of Dreadful Delight: Narratives of Sexual Danger in Late-Victorian London*. Chicago: University of Chicago University Press, 1992.
Wells, H.G. *The Island of Dr. Moreau: Seven Science Fiction Novels of H.G. Wells*. New York: Dover, 1896.

3

The Unbearable Hybridity of Female Sexuality: Racial Ambiguity and the Gothic in Rider Haggard's She

TAMAR HELLER

"At length the curtain began to move. Who could be behind it?—some naked savage queen, a languishing Oriental beauty, or a nineteenth-century young lady, drinking afternoon tea?" (141).[1] So wonders Horace Holly, the narrator of Rider Haggard's *She*, moments before meeting Ayesha, the novel's entrancing yet murderous *femme fatale*. That Holly would not be surprised if Ayesha were a racial Other—a "naked savage queen," "a languishing Oriental beauty"—or a young Englishwoman underscores the theme of ambiguous racial identity at the heart of Haggard's version of Gothic. Ayesha defines herself as Arabian "by my birth" (146), and, miraculously youthful, for several thousand years has been queen of an African tribe. Yet her body is insistently described as white, even "white as snow" (142).

A number of critics, including Nina Auerbach, Sandra Gilbert and Susan Gubar, and Rebecca Stott, have seen Ayesha as an embodiment of conservative anxieties about the New Woman in the *fin-de-siècle*.[2] In addition, a growing body of scholarship has identified Haggard's importance as an ideologue of late-Victorian empire.[3] Patrick Brantlinger includes Haggard's work in his discussion of "imperial Gothic," a genre which reflects concerns about the decline of British imperial power in the last decades of the nineteenth century (see *Rule of Darkness* 227–53). Since the ideology of imperialism was undergirded by late-Victorian ideals of manliness, threats to imperial power are equally threats to male identity. This essay will address the intersection of anxieties about imperial power and anxieties about masculine power by focusing on Ayesha's embodiment of both whiteness and non-whiteness. This hybridity registers fears not only about racial difference, but, importantly, about the threat that female sexuality, and the female power that it tropes, poses to British manliness.

Unquestionably, Ayesha is one of the Victorian period's most notable examples of a figure who combines multiple racial identities. Terence Rodgers has persuasively argued that Ayesha's depiction is heavily Orientalist, although he claims that, by giving Ayesha "Egyptian origins," Haggard makes the novel less about "the colonizing discourse of black Africa" than about the colonization of the East ("Restless Desire" 38). I prefer, though, to read Haggard's Orientalism not as deemphasizing blackness but rather as expanding the novel's representation of types of racial difference. Underscoring Ayesha's simultaneous encoding of blackness, Orientalism, and whiteness, Haggard gives her a tripartite identity suggested by Holly's linking in one sentence the terms "naked savage queen," "languishing Oriental beauty," and "nineteenth-century young lady." In this sense, Ayesha is an important late-Victorian example of how the "exotic body," in Piya Pal-Lapinski's words, "has always been inscribed ... by a kind of métissage, a racial elusiveness" (*The Exotic Woman* xv). This métissage is entwined with anxieties about female sexuality. To the extent that she is depicted as a racial Other, Ayesha is an image, as were women of color in the Victorian period, for sexual promiscuity and aggressiveness, traits that underscore her emasculating New Womanhood. Ayesha's whiteness, however, renders her sexuality even more dangerous than if she were unambiguously Other. If, underneath a surface gentility, the "nineteenth-century young lady, drinking afternoon tea" is as oversexed as a "naked savage queen" or the denizen of an Oriental harem, the boundaries that separate white and black, "pure" and sexual woman, blur and disturb the intertwined racial and sexual hierarchies defining Victorian culture.

Even the degree to which Haggard makes Ayesha a figure for sexual abstinence as well as voracity does not mitigate the threat to male power that she embodies. Rather than symbolizing the chaste sexuality of the domestic woman, which is subject to male control, Ayesha's anorexic eating habits recall the discourses of Victorian feminists who sought to make women independent of male appetite. In this sense, both Ayesha's desire and her ability to suppress it encode an autonomy that reflects the late nineteenth century climate of changing female roles. In whichever of her shifting incarnations, then—as a figure for whiteness or blackness, overpowering sexuality or its suppression—the threat that Ayesha poses to male power must be contained in order to quiet the interlinked sexual and racial anxieties she evokes.

Hybridities of the Dark Continent

Like *King Solomon's Mines* (1885), Haggard's best-selling first novel, *She* is structured by the classic imperialist ideologeme of intrepid white men exploring the dark continent. Ancient papers bequeathed to Horace Holly's young ward, Leo Vincey, trace his ancestry to Kallikrates, an Egyptian priest of Greek background slain by the queen of a savage tribe when he refused to become her lover. Travelling to Africa to determine the truth of this history, Holly and Leo enter a geography which recalls the erotically charged landscape of *King Solomon's Mines*, in which, as Norman Etherington and Anne McClintock have noted, mountains named "Sheba's breasts" are part of a symbolic female body open to male imperial penetration (Etherington xxxiv; McClintock 1–4). Symbols for the female body are similarly embedded in the African landscape of *She*, including breast-like volcanoes, vaginal chasms, and a treacherous swampy terrain that Sandra Gilbert and Susan Gubar describe as a "Freudianly female *paysage moralisé*" (Etherington xxxiv; Gilbert and Gubar 13). Signifying those subject to white British domination, this eroticized landscape is also, of course, racialized. As the travelers close in on their destination, they locate one of the landmarks they seek, a promontory called the "head of the Ethiopian," which is "shaped like a negro's head and face, whereon was stamped a most fiendish and terrifying expression. There was no doubt about it; there were the thick lips, the fat cheeks, and squat nose ... and, to complete the resemblance, there was a scrubby growth of weeds or lichen ... which ... looked for all the world like the wool on a colossal negro's head" (58).

Once the explorers reach this symbol of an unambiguous blackness, however, racial ambiguity enters the narrative. The Amahagger, the African tribe whom Ayesha rules, are themselves of indeterminate race: "[C]omparatively light in color ... they varied in their degree of darkness of skin, some being as dark as Mahomed [the Englishmen's Arab employee] and some as yellow as a Chinese" (80). Furthermore, Holly claims the women's hair was "not crisped like a negro's" (80). We later hear that the Amahagger are the "bastard brood" born of interracial union between African blacks and Arabs, a hybridity that explains the "bastard" version of Arabic the tribe speaks (77).

If the Amahagger are comparatively light-skinned, Ayesha is still fairer. At the beginning of the novel, Leo's father, entrusting to Holly the documents that relate the fate of his ancestor, describes the murderer of Kallikrates as "the mighty Queen of a savage people, a white woman of peculiar loveliness" (11), and Haggard continually emphasizes the snowy purity of Ayesha's body. As Holly approaches a curtained nook to meet her for the first time, Ayesha stretches out "a most beautiful white hand (white as snow) ... with long tapering fingers, ending in the pinkest nails" (142). In addition to being whiter than the Amahagger, Ayesha also speaks "much purer and more classical Arabic" than they do (142) and claims, because of her Yemenite origins, to be "an Arab of the Arabs" (146), or, as Holly puts it, of the "true Arab blood as distinguished from the naturalized Arabs" (146). As Norman Etherington points out, in endowing Ayesha with "a 'pure' white skin, a 'pure' Arab descent, and 'pure' Arab dialect," Haggard alludes to "notions of linguistic and racial purity that were only beginning to take hold among intellectual racists of the late Victorian era" (*Annotated She* 226 n3).

Ayesha's anti-Semitism, which echoes English attitudes of the period, serves further to distinguish her from racial Others. Telling Holly about being stoned two thousand years earlier by Jews hostile to her innovative philosophy, Ayesha recalls their "dark faces" while displaying the contrasting "milky beauty" of an arm that bears a scar from the attack (148, 149). This depiction of the Jews as dark-skinned, lawless Orientals reflects how, as Meredith Veldman has claimed, "[i]n the aggressive phase of Western imperial expansion that characterized the final decades of the nineteenth century ... 'the Jew'" stood "in opposition to English national identity" (13). In Veldman's analysis of images of Jesus in nineteenth century children's fiction, she traces how, in the *fin-de-siècle* period, Jesus, like Ayesha, was rescued from "the taint of Jewishness and Orientalism" by being described, according to one writer, as having features "paler and of a more Hellenic type" than those of the Jews surrounding him (14–15). This attempt to give a figure a classical heritage (as opposed to an Orientalized one) also governs Haggard's characterization of Leo, who, with his English father and Greek mother, is in danger of being a figure for miscegenation. Emphasizing Leo's golden curls and gorgeous face, which recall classical images of Apollo, Holly reassures the reader that the young man has "nothing of the supple form or slippery manner of the modern Greek about him" (212), a description which serves the same function of diluting racial Otherness as Haggard's careful whitening of Ayesha's skin.

That Haggard can simultaneously characterize Ayesha as white while portraying another Arab, Mahomed, as black, however, is tribute to the ambiguity surrounding the racial classification of Arabs during the Victorian period. As Etherington's remark about Haggard anticipating late-Victorian notions of racial purity suggests, systems of racial classification, while present in the late eighteenth and early nineteenth centuries, tended to be more fluid prior to the rise of the *fin-de-siècle*'s systematic racist taxonomies. The flexible categorization of Arabs is a case in point: in the nineteenth century Arabs were often labeled Caucasians, yet distinctions could also be made between types of Arabs, as in Robert Knox's

The Races of Men (1850), in which North African Arabs, whom Knox labels "pure savages," are grouped with blacks, while fairer-skinned Levantine Arabs are not.⁴ While such attempts to differentiate groups of Arabs seem to establish the purity of some, however, these distinctions can blur: in Victorian geographies the Egyptians, for example, can be classified as black or white depending on the author's bias. In fact, in making Ayesha a "white" Arab, Haggard conveniently overlooks the history of Yemenite kings, who the nineteenth century *Encyclopedia Britannica* claimed were descended from "Himyar the dusky," an African (see Etherington 226 n3). In other words, the ambiguous classification of Arabs during the Victorian period made it possible for Haggard to claim Ayesha is white, even though this very ambiguity also renders questionable her racial "purity."

One sign, indeed, that Haggard himself associates Ayesha with racial hybridity rather than with pure whiteness is the color of her eyes and hair, which are black. In contrast, many of the preserved corpses of Kôr, which populate the cave in which Ayesha lives, have fair hair, like that of one woman who combines "yellow hair" with a "bosom whiter than [her] robes" (183). In contrast to these golden locks, the "dark masses" of Ayesha's perfumed hair (291) evoke the "languishing Oriental beauty" that Holly thinks he might find when he meets the queen. Significantly, the scene in which Ayesha engages most openly in "wanton play" with Holly is one where she shakes her heavy black tresses over his forehead, rendering him "faint and weak" with desire (191). At the end of the novel, this sign of Ayesha's Otherness becomes a fetish, as Holly and Leo each detach a lock of the dead queen's hair as souvenir and trophy.⁵ Ayesha's luxuriant hair sets off her lushly objectified body in scenes which evoke the nineteenth century visual and narrative tradition of the odalisque, in which, as Piya Pal-Lapinski says, a "seductive nude or clothed woman" displays her body against an Oriental backdrop (*The Exotic Woman* xvi). Even when wrapped in mummy-like swathing, Ayesha offers tantalizing glimpses of skin and voluptuous curves, peepshows that lead to ever-more revealing stripteases, culminating in the scene at the end of the novel, when, before she steps into the pillar of fire, she casts off her clothes and exhibits herself to the men "clad in nothing but her abundant locks" (291).

Were Ayesha nothing but the objectified body of Woman-as-Other, though, She would not be nearly as terrifyingly Gothic an image of female power as she is. Not simply desirable object but desiring subject, Ayesha defines herself by the intensity of her love for the dead Kallikrates, whose body she preserves with necrophiliac zeal, and for whom she feels a passion she claims has been "eating at my heart" for two thousand years (165). Her regal, indeed tyrannical, power is linked to this passion for the "splendid animal" body of Kallikrates (6) and his apparent reincarnation, Leo, as when she kills Ustane, her rival for Leo's affections, because the young woman "stands between me and my desire" (201). The aggressive power of Ayesha's desire—in which she, rather than the male, is the initiator of sexual conquest—encodes in a larger sense her New Woman–like power to be independent of men. As Mina says disapprovingly in *Dracula*: "the New Woman won't condescend in future to accept" marriage proposals; "she will do the proposing herself. And a nice job she will make of it, too!" (87).

Significantly, Ayesha's aggressive sexuality and the independence it embodies poses a threat to traditional masculinity. In addition to her ability to obliterate men altogether—as she does when she slays Kallikrates—she has the power to obliterate their manliness; at one point Leo claims that Ayesha has him "utterly cowed, as if all the manhood had been taken out of him" (228). In one of her most emasculating actions, Ayesha deploys the full force of her sexual appeal in order to make Leo swear undying love for her over the corpse of the faithful Ustane. While loudly lamenting his inability to resist temptation, Leo cannot help but, "with the corpse of his dead love for an altar ... plight his troth to her red-handed murderess" (230). This abandonment of chivalrous British masculine behavior plunges Leo into self-disgust: "Leo groaned in shame and misery; for though he was overcome and stricken down, he was not so lost as to be unaware of the depth of the degradation to which he had sunk" (230–31).

Again, Ayesha's hybridity—her status both as white woman and racial Other—renders her powerful desire particularly disruptive of Victorian gender roles. In his essay "The Hottentot and the Prostitute," Sander Gilman examines a pattern of nineteenth century examples, such as Manet's *Olympia*, in which a black woman is paired with an eroticized white woman in order to imply the similarity between them. Indeed, according to Gilman, the black woman externalizes the white woman's transgressive sexuality; in a number of *fin-de-siècle* images, in fact, the black woman disappears and the white woman, often a prostitute, is posed like an exotic primitive. Underneath the skin, in other words, the apparently chaste white woman is inherently licentious. In *She*, we see both versions of the link between black and white female sexuality that Gilman discusses: the Amahagger, with their extraordinarily powerful and sexually aggressive women, externalize Ayesha's unconventional sexuality, while Ayesha herself, a presumably white woman who evokes stereotypes of the libidinous Other, threatens even more frighteningly to unsettle the ideal of the passionless domestic angel.

Ambiguous Appetites: Sex, Food, and Female Power

At the same time, however, Ayesha's sexuality is more complex than that of the women Gilman analyzes. Sandra Gilbert and Susan Gubar capture this complexity when they describe Ayesha as "an odd mixture of the two types—an angelically chaste woman with monstrous powers, a monstrously passionate woman with angelic charms" (6). After all, Ayesha is simultaneously a figure for sexual desire and sexual frustration; the two thousand years that she is forced to wait for Kallikrates's reincarnation is surely one of the longer stints of abstinence in history. More significantly, Ayesha preaches a philosophy of the control of appetite, disdaining the Amahaggers as "[e]aters of human flesh" (174), and criticizing the Englishmen for eating meat "like a brute beast" (262). Ayesha herself "never touched anything except cakes of flour, fruit, and water" (262), and she urges Holly to adopt this diet, claiming that fruit is the "only true food for man" (191).

In nineteenth century England, vegetarianism reflected a number of ideological perspectives. Haggard's immediate source for Ayesha's rejection of meat was Bulwer-Lytton's *The Coming Race*, in which an advanced cave-dwelling people ruled by a powerful queen profess vegetarianism. In this text, vegetarianism expresses the novel's anti-democratic and elitist vision; presumably, those who eschew meat are higher on the evolutionary scale, a characterization that recalls Ayesha's totalitarian politics and her contempt for the brutish, meat-eating masses. In the nineteenth century vegetarianism could also be associated with the control of sexuality; for instance, campaigns against masturbation recommended a meat-free diet to curb "animal passions" (Numbers, *Prophetess of Health* 153),[6] and in her history of anorexia Joan Jacobs Brumberg cites the fears of physicians that pubescent young girls who ate meat were prone to sexual license (176). Yet, while it could be entwined with conservative ideologies, in the nineteenth century vegetarianism, which counted among its disciples the radical poet Percy Bysshe Shelley, had a long-standing association with progressive and reformist movements.[7] Indeed, as James Gregory has shown, following the resurgence of vegetarianism in England in the 1860s, late-Victorian fictional representations of vegetarians frequently emphasized their connection with "advanced reform movements of the period," including socialism, anti-vivisectionism, and feminism ("Vegetarians in the 'Kingdom'" 1).[8] In fact, as Gregory notes, the late-Victorian vegetarian movement "presented itself as a cause for 'progressive' women," reflecting the degree to which discussions of food were gendered during the period (*The Vegetarian Movement* ch. 5.2; 4).[9]

I would argue, indeed, that Ayesha's vegetarianism is integral to her symbolism as a New Woman, and that the rhetoric of anti-carnality she espouses reflects anxieties about the body, or somatophobia, in late nineteenth century feminist discourses. On one hand, Ayesha's philosophy that only brutes eat meat might seem to evoke the conservative rhetoric of sexual control that, as mentioned earlier, animated a number of Victorian discourses about female appetite. On the other hand, though, not only conservative ideologues preached appetite control. As Lucy Bland argues in her aptly entitled study *Banishing the Beast*, Victorian feminists frequently recommended curbing sexual appetite—not only female appetite but, more significantly, male appetite, a strategy akin to that of the temperance and social purity movements (some of whose members were also feminists). In numerous instances, such as the campaigns against the Contagious Diseases Acts, Victorian feminists emphasized the spirituality of women and their vulnerability to male lust. While such rhetoric to some extent reinforced the ideal of the passionless Victorian angel, many feminists saw sexual abstinence as a potent weapon with which to resist men's attempts to control women. In feminist discourses of bodily control, food and sex can each represent the other, as they did most dramatically in the hunger strikes undertaken by turn-of-the-century suffragettes; refusing food, women also symbolically defied the type of male sexual control implicit in brutal, rape-like force-feedings.[10] While Ayesha does not resort to quite such spectacular feats of appetite control, her abstemiousness, like that of the suffragettes, is a sign of her autonomy. Preaching a philosophy of appetite control she urges on the men, she echoes nineteenth century feminist discourses of spiritual idealism. Such a discourse is all the more disruptive of male power because it simultaneously undercuts imperial authority; as James Gregory points out, eating meat, particularly roast beef, "remained powerfully associated with national identity" ("Vegetarians in the 'Kingdom'" 1), and Ayesha's recommendation that British men abandon meat-eating is hence yet another way of diluting their manliness.

Thus, Ayesha's avoidance of carnality does not domesticate her. Rather, just as Victorian feminism itself borrowed the image of the pure and powerful mother from domestic ideology to argue for the expansion of civic participation for women, Ayesha's intellectual and spiritual side, as Nina Auerbach says, "fuels her latent powers into political life" (37). Indeed, Ayesha's grandiose political ambitions, which involve invading England after she leaves Africa with Leo, makes her, like the female vampires in *Dracula*, a terrifying *fin-de-siècle* image of the primitive, voracious, and castrating woman. In a revealing passage in the manuscript of *She*, Haggard is particularly explicit in comparing Ayesha's imperialist plans to the aggressive and murderous female sexuality of the Amahagger, who force red-hot pots on the heads of their enemies in what Gilbert and Gubar describe as "a vivid enactment of both castration fears and birth anxieties" (14). In this manuscript passage, Holly, who like Leo has been horrified by Ayesha's desire to overthrow the English government, has a "most horrible nightmare" in which She, "dressed in a modern ball dress," supervises the "hot-potting" of the prime minister himself (*Annotated She* 235 n15). Appropriately enough, the weapon against male authority here is a cooking-pot, suggesting that the tools of feminine domesticity may be used to stifle male appetite for power.

Ayesha's humiliating death, in which she bathes in the fire that once granted her prolonged youth only to shrivel into a hideously withered corpse, begs to be read as a backlash against the power that would, as Holly says, have "revolutionised society" (293). Ayesha's transformation into a wizened being "no larger than a big monkey" (294) has been read as an image of devolution, or, as Patricia Murphy puts it, "woman's Darwinian reversion" to primitivism (764). Yet, in light of the novel's depiction of a threatening racial hybridity, it is equally significant that Ayesha's terrible end forestalls any chance that interracial romance may flourish. In his earlier romance, *King Solomon's Mines*, Haggard killed off the black woman Foulata who falls in love with the white explorer John Goode, a plot development referred to approvingly by one contemporary reviewer who congratulated Haggard on "extricat[ing]" Goode from the "difficult position" of being in love with a native ("King Solomon's Mines" 248). In *She* Ayesha's murder of Ustane (with whom Leo clearly has sex in the serial version of the novel) similarly rescues the white hero from an interracial affair. Ayesha herself is enough of a racially ambiguous figure for Haggard to ensure that she does not consummate her union with Leo. Not coincidentally, as She ages in fast-forward her skin darkens, turning from white to "dirty brown and yellow" (293)—another sign of the atavistic threat lurking under her ivory skin.

The extinction of Ayesha would seem to reinstate male power, leaving Holly and Leo able to pursue their homosocial adventures without female interference. Yet closure in Haggard's imperial Gothic is as beset by ambiguity as is Ayesha herself. Both Holly and Leo—the latter turned white-haired by witnessing Ayesha's death—continue to be haunted by memories of her, becoming male versions of the hysteric who, as Freud's colleague Breuer said, "suffers mainly from reminiscences" (Breuer and Freud 2:7). Ending with its English travelers either dead—in the case of the servant Job—or disabled and traumatized, like Holly and Leo, *She* does not end with the same purgation of female power as does its predecessor, *King Solomon's Mines*, in which Haggard kills off not only Foulata but the monstrous witch, Gagool, that novel's image for castrating femininity. Crushed beneath a gigantic boulder, Gagool is more spectacularly obliterated than Ayesha, who with her last breath promises to return to life. Indeed, in Haggard's 1905 sequel *Ayesha: The Return of She*, not only is Ayesha resurrected but so is her ability to emasculate men. Spending decades obsessively seeking a reincarnated Ayesha, Leo and Holly finally locate her in Tibet, where she is worshipped as a goddess by a religious community. Although she regains her tempting beauty once Leo reaffirms his love for her, she pointedly avoids sexual contact with him, significantly taming his appetite: "Leo lost appetite, grew thin and pale, and could not sleep" (263). As in *She*, Ayesha's emasculating power is thus located both in her carnality and her rejection of the body.[11] Displaying her seductive power before Leo, she nonetheless refuses to consummate their union until Leo has become as spiritual as she; when she is eventually persuaded to shorten the waiting period, Leo drops dead as soon as Ayesha embraces him, "slain by the fire of her love" (337).

Haggard's sequel reenacts with particular vividness the plot of men threatened by female sexuality and power in *She*. Indeed, we can see Ayesha's racial and sexual hybridity—her mingling of blackness and whiteness, sexual abstinence and sexual temptation—as an apt symbol for the generic hybridity of Haggard's imperial Gothic. Anticipating the literal killing off of British manhood in *Ayesha*, *She* is a strange miscegenation of the late-Victorian adventure tale, which as Patrick Brantlinger says is infused with "[u]pbeat racism and chauvinism," with the imperial Gothic narrative of degeneration, regression, and decline found in such *fin-de-siècle* texts as *Dracula* and *Heart of Darkness*. At once unbearably white and unbearably Other, Ayesha is thus the amalgam of racial and sexual anxieties that refuse easy containment.

Notes

1. My references to *She* are to the Oxford edition edited by Daniel Karlin.
2. See Auerbach (36–37), Gilbert and Gubar (3–35), and Stott. Among other critics who have discussed Ayesha as a New Woman figure are Murphy, Rodgers, and Showalter in *Sexual Anarchy* (83–89).
3. See Katz; Brantlinger ch. 8 (esp. 234, 244–46); McClintock (1–4; 232–57); Rodgers; Murphy.
4. I am indebted to Andrew Stauffer for bringing this example to my attention. Many thanks also to other participants in the Victoria Listserv—especially Tom Prasch, Ilona Salomaa, Stephen Holcombe, and Richard Fulton—who were very helpful in responding to my query about the racial classification of Arabs during the Victorian period.
5. As Sinha says in her discussion of masculinity and hunting in *She*, this lock of hair functions as a hunting trophy, and "trophies were themselves sexual emblems representing the war of males for sexual conquest" (6).
6. Ellen White, the subject of Numbers's study, is a fascinating example of a figure whose discourses on health were in many ways conservative (she wrote a book condemning masturbation), yet who was also a strong-minded woman who, while not a feminist, promoted dress reform, urging women to wear bloomers.

7. Colin Spencer discusses the association of vegetarianism with nineteenth century reform movements in *The Heretic's Feast* (274–94). For his discussion of Shelley, see 244–51. For more on Romantic-era vegetarianism, see Adams (124).
  8. I am indebted to James Gregory for sharing with me his extensive research on nineteenth century vegetarianism. As Gregory notes in "Vegetarians in the 'Kingdom of Roast Beef,'" the journal *The Vegetarian*, which he calls "the organ of the late-Victorian" vegetarian movement (3), devoted a year to discussing vegetarianism in *She* (19 n65).
  9. James Gregory's *The Vegetarian Movement in Victorian Britain* contains a thorough and useful discussion of gender issues in the Victorian vegetarian movement; see esp. ch. 5.2.
  10. For more on suffragettes and appetite control, see Schlossberg.
  11. I differ here from critics who see Ayesha in *The Return of She* as a domesticated figure; see, for example, Etherington (xxxvii) and Murphy, who claims that "The potent She of the 1887 version becomes, in *Ayesha*, a chastened and submissive handmaiden" (768). While in both *She* and in *Ayesha* Ayesha claims that her love for Leo has purified her of her lust for power, that her embrace kills Leo demonstrates that this power is far from dead. Rodgers perceptively discusses Ayesha's ambition and its emasculating effects (42–44).

Works Cited

Adams, Carol J. *The Sexual Politics of Meat: A Feminist-Vegetarian Critical Theory*. 1990. New York: Continuum, 2000.
Auerbach, Nina. *Woman and the Demon: The Life of a Victorian Myth*. Cambridge: Harvard University Press, 1982.
Bland, Lucy. *Banishing the Beast: Sexuality and the Early Feminists*. New York: New Press, 1995.
Brantlinger, Patrick. *Rule of Darkness: British Literature and Imperialism, 1830–1914*. Ithaca: Cornell University Press, 1988.
Brumberg, Joan Jacobs. *Fasting Girls: The Emergence of Anorexia Nervosa as a Modern Disease*. Cambridge: Harvard University Press, 1988.
Breuer, Josef, and Sigmund Freud. *Studies on Hysteria*, trans. and ed. James Strachey. Vol. 2. of *The Standard Edition of the Psychological Works of Sigmund Freud*. London: Hogarth Press, 1953–1974.
Etherington, Norman. Introduction to *The Annotated She*, xv–xliii. Bloomington: Indiana University Press, 1991.
Gilbert, Sandra, and Susan Gubar. *No Man's Land: The Place of the Woman Writer in the Twentieth Century*. Vol. 2 of *Sexchanges*. New Haven: Yale University Press, 1989.
Gilman, Sander L. "The Hottentot and the Prostitute." In *Difference and Pathology: Stereotypes of Sexuality, Race, and Madness*, 76–108. Ithaca: Cornell University Press, 1985.
Gregory, James. *The Vegetarian Movement in Victorian Britain*. Unpublished Ms, 2005.
_____. "Vegetarians in the 'Kingdom of Roast Beef': Representing the Vegetarian in Victorian Literature." In *Consuming Culture: The Eating Pleasures and Problems of Western Modernity*, ed. Tamara S. Wagner and Narin Hassan. Lexington Press, forthcoming.
Haggard, H. Rider. *The Annotated She*, ed. Norman Etherington. Bloomington: Indiana University Press, 1991.
_____. *Ayesha: The Return of She*. 1905. Mattituck, New York: Amereon Press, 1981.
_____. *She*, ed. Daniel Karlin. Oxford: Oxford University Press, 1991.
Katz, Wendy. *Rider Haggard and the Fiction of Empire*. Cambridge: Cambridge University Press, 1987.

"King Solomon's Mines." *The Spectator* (7 Nov. 1885), qtd. in Appendix A, H. Rider Haggard. *King Solomon's Mines*, ed. Gerald Mousman. Peterborough, Ontario: Broadview Press, 2002.
Knox, Robert. *The Races of Men: A Fragment*. 1850. Miami: Mnemosyne Publishing, 1969.
McClintock, Anne. *Imperial Leather: Race, Gender and Sexuality in the Colonial Context*. New York: Routledge, 1995.
Murphy, Patricia. "The Gendering of History in *She*." *SEL* 39.4 (Autumn 1999): 747–72.
Numbers, Ronald L. *Prophetess of Health: A Study of Ellen G. White*. New York: Harper and Row, 1976.
Pal-Lapinski, Piya. *The Exotic Woman in Nineteenth-Century British Fiction and Culture: A Reconsideration*. Durham: University of New Hampshire Press, 2005.
Rodgers, Terence. "Restless Desire: Rider Haggard, Orientalism and the New Woman." *Women: A Cultural Review* 10.1 (1999): 35–46.
Schlossberg, Linda. "Consuming Images: Women, Hunger, and the Vote." In *Scenes of the Apple: Food and the Female Body in Nineteenth- and Twentieth-Century Women's Writing*, ed. Tamar Heller and Patricia Moran, 87–106. Albany: State University of New York Press, 2003.
Showalter, Elaine. *Sexual Anarchy: Gender and Culture at the Fin de Siècle*. New York: Penguin, 1990.
Sinha, Madhudaya. "Hunting and Masculinity in Rider Haggard's *She*." Unpublished essay. University of Cincinnati, 2005.
Spencer, Colin. *The Heretic's Feast: A History of Vegetarianism*. 1993. Hanover: University Press of New England, 1995.
Stoker, Bram. *Dracula*, ed. Nina Auerbach and David J. Skal. New York: Norton, 1997.
Stott, Rebecca. *The Fabrication of the Late-Victorian "Femme Fatale": The Kiss of Death*. Hampshire: Macmillan, 1992.
Veldman, Meredith. "Dutiful Daughter Versus All-Boy: Jesus, Gender, and the Secularization of Victorian Society." *Nineteenth Century Studies* 11 (1997): 1–24.

4

Frankenstein's Other:
The Monstrous Feminine in Maryse Condé's Célanire cou-coupé

DAWN FULTON

Maryse Condé is one of the few writers from the francophone Caribbean to have established a sustained dialogue with the anglophone literary and critical canon. In this respect she is best known for her revision, or what she has more recently called her cannibalization, of Emily Brontë's *Wuthering Heights* in her 1995 novel *La Migration des cœurs*, but Condé's intertextual work has extended in less explicit form to a number of other texts in her *œuvre* as well, elaborating a uniquely bilingual and transnational literary heritage.[1] Condé's 2000 novel *Célanire cou-coupé* is one of the most recent installations in this intertextual exchange, suggesting a link both allusively and thematically to Mary Shelley's *Frankenstein*. Like Dr. Frankenstein's creature, the eponymous Célanire exists in defiance of natural laws, undergoes the rejection of her maker and embarks on a violent and frightening quest for vengeance. But Condé's "cannibalized" vision transposes the monstrous creature to Guadeloupe, France, the Ivory Coast, and Peru in the early part of the twentieth century, thus offering an extensive reflection on the conditions of transgression and monstrosity in these myriad cultural backdrops. Condé's implicit juxtaposition of Shelley's narrative with her own, moreover, allows us at the same time to revisit a number of the transgressions haunting the 1818 British classic. By positing Célanire's gender as one of the foremost conduits of her transgressive power, Condé suggests that ultimately Célanire and Frankenstein's monster may provoke strikingly similar nightmares surrounding femininity, procreation, and miscegenation. Through its formal engagement of the fantastic genre, the novel points in particular to the monster's ineffability as its fundamental trait, thus tracing the unreadable female body as a crucial specter in both nineteenth century England and the twentieth century Atlantic world.

The first few moments of Célanire's life establish her affiliation with the monstrous on both moral and physical levels: as a newborn she is found in the street in Guadeloupe, the victim of an attempted human sacrifice ordered by a desperate politician hoping to save his career. This "inhuman" crime is followed by the "unnatural" operation that saves her, as Dr. Jean Pinceau spends seven hours reconstructing the body of this tiny infant, who, upon her arrival on his operating table, had lost all of her blood and was "clinically dead" (106). Having recently read with fascinated interest Shelley's *Frankenstein*, Dr. Pinceau sets himself to his task with heady enthusiasm: "Je devais raccorder les artères, les veines, les nerfs, les tendons tranchés.... J'ai transfusé celui de deux poulets.... Tout le temps, je sentais qu'enfin j'étais l'émule de mon héros Victor Frankenstein" (117). ("I had to reconnect the severed arteries, veins, nerves, and tendons.... I transfused the blood from two chickens ... The whole time I felt that here I was at last emulating my hero Victor Frankenstein" [107]). Like Victor Frankenstein, Pinceau is intoxicated by his own power at this moment of creation, and like the Swiss doctor he too is suddenly horrified by the sight of the creature he has brought to life. Although he adopts Célanire and gives her his name, he remains unable to feel any affection for her, and is instead repulsed by her existence and especially by the scar around her neck, a constant reminder of his unnatural act.

The introduction of Célanire as an adult in the opening pages of the novel replicates this element of difference that marks her. Although her monstrous scar is concealed beneath an ever-present scarf, she nonetheless simultaneously troubles multiple social, religious, and racial boundaries. The initial description of her is given through the eyes of Father Huchard as she arrives with other missionaries in the Ivory Coast in 1901, having completed her religious education in Paris. For Huchard, this woman is clearly out of the ordinary: "Elle ne parlait guère ... sa couleur la mettait à part, cette peau noire qui l'habillait comme un vêtement de grand deuil. Elle n'était pas franchement négresse. Plutôt métisse d'on ne savait combien de races" (14). ("She hardly spoke ... her color set her apart, that dark skin that clothed her like a garment of deep mourning. Her features were not strictly black—rather, a hybrid of goodness knows how many races" [1]). Célanire's situation at the novel's opening is emblematic of her position at the crossroads of a number of cultural, geographical, religious, and racial allegiances: she is a Guadeloupean woman in Africa, a Christian missionary who has not taken her vows, a person of mixed race in European clothing and with a European education. Her physical "monstrosity" thus manifests ontologically as a sociocultural indeterminacy.

In a significant departure from the Frankenstein model, however, the creature in Condé's text is strikingly beautiful. Rather than inspiring universal horror and being categorically rejected from human society, as is the case for Shelley's monster, Célanire incites fascination as well as fear, holding a seductive power over men and women alike. Her beauty does little to normalize her, however; instead her mysterious sexuality is aligned with sorcery, as characters wonder if she has bewitched those who appear to have lost themselves under her influence. Condé thus suggests here a striking connection between Célanire's monstrosity and female sexuality; Célanire becomes a kind of Medusa figure, dangerous to those who dare to look at her, especially if their gaze is returned. While her admirers compare her eyes to stars, diamonds, and other precious stones, they are also frightened by their light: "leur éclat était insoutenable" (142). ("it was difficult to sustain the look in those gleaming eyes of hers" [131]). Dr. Pinceau, furthermore, compares Célanire's scar to female genitals, describing it as "obscène, violacée comme un sexe infibulé" (119). ("obscene ... purplish as an infibulated labium" [109]). The doctor's horror at his creation thus evokes a Freudian castration anxiety, an anxiety reinforced later in Célanire's story by the mysterious deaths that accompany her on her journey, as two of the men who die are castrated.[2] Célanire would seem to represent the very embodiment of female sexual power, seen as dangerous and unnatural by others, and, in this instance, doubled by the presence of a monstrous scar.

In fact Célanire's power is all the more threatening in that she maintains control over the very sign of her monstrosity: unlike Frankenstein's creature, Célanire can conceal her scar at will, thus defying the interpretive efforts of her public. In this sense Célanire subverts even the social role attributed by her monstrosity, since, as Chris Baldick has underlined in regard to *Frankenstein*, the moral function of the monster is primarily to render visible the results of aberration or unreason.[3] Instead of acting as a legible indicator of contemporary forms of ostracism, Célanire suspends the other in a constant state of uncertainty as to her symbolic function. In a sense her covered neck provokes even more anxiety for those who encounter her than would the scar itself: they are troubled not by the sight of something unnatural, but rather by the uneasy sense that something unfamiliar or threatening *could* be concealed beneath her scarf. The considerable force of this interpretive insecurity highlights Célanire's creative control as the most disruptive aspect of her presence: Célanire behaves as an unpredictable agent of moral disclosure, capable of exposing and transforming society's ills without warning.

Foremost among the ghosts she chooses to exorcise in West Africa is the sociopolitical condition of women. Célanire's initial efforts on the mission grow out of a conscious effort to repair the unacknowledged gender imbalance that she sees as an unfortunate lapse in an otherwise exemplary African society: "il n'y avait qu'une ombre à cette belle civilisation: le traitement des femmes" (34) ("there was only one dark side to the beauty of its civilization: the treatment of women" [24]). Upon her arrival in the Ivory Coast, then, Célanire (thanks to the sudden and, according to some, all too convenient death of the former director) takes over the Foyer des métis and transforms it into a haven for women, where girls can take classes alongside their male peers, and where young women can find protection from abusive husbands or from the practice of female excision. She also determines that the Foyer will provide a more nurturing home for orphans, insisting on their education and careful attention to their health. As the land surrounding the Foyer is cultivated, Célanire almost literally transforms the place into a garden paradise for her harbored women and children, a world apart from their previous lives of abuse, subservience, or neglect.

By separating married women from their families and offering them an education equal to that of men, Célanire fundamentally disrupts the religious and cultural order to which they belong, provoking widespread anxiety and mistrust. Meanwhile the physical work she does on the land is also viewed with suspicion: "car les terres entourant le Foyer n'étaient pas sans maître. Elles appartenaient aux Ebriés" (28). ("For the land around it [the Home] did in fact belong to someone. It belonged to the Ebriés" [18]). No act of hers can be neutral, since the land, the space she occupies is not a blank page: in every domain she enters there is a pre-existing order she disturbs. Here in Adjame-Santey she pointedly disregards the indigenous codes of ownership and tradition, replacing them with her own "monstrous" vision of society. Added to this complexity is of course the fact that she is transforming these social orders in the name of the French state and as a member of a Christian mission. Despite her proclaimed devotion to African culture, then, she is nonetheless performing these cultural and religious transgressions as an outsider.

Célanire's presence in Adjame-Santey and later in Guadeloupe represents a threat not only because she promotes the liberation and education of women, but also because she blatantly violates sexual taboos. The two projects are in fact closely linked, since it soon becomes apparent that at the Foyer in Adjame-Santey Célanire has also founded a brothel, with the specific goal of encouraging interracial love. In her mind, the solution to colonialism is to be found in the intimate relationship between the African woman and the European man: "Le Foyer des métis serait ... l'endroit privilégié où naîtrait, croîtrait, se multiplierait l'amour entre les races" (51). ("The Home for Half-Castes would be ...

a privileged place where love between the races would fructify, grow, and multiply" [41]). Through her Foyer Célanire thus institutionalizes sexual practices that until her arrival had remained unacknowledged, silenced by social convention. Beyond the disruption caused by the visibility of these transgressions and the intentionality of her project, Célanire also leaves her mark on the economic system in Adjame-Santey. The African women receive gifts from their French partners that, in combination with the education they complete, allow them to substantially shift their social status. Célanire's project fundamentally transforms the economic system of exchange in the region, giving rise not only to a changed relationship between the races, but also to a new social class.

The heroine's own sexuality of course participates in this particular transgression, as she has an affair with and eventually marries the French colonial officer Thomas de Brabant in a direct violation of his own personal interdiction of physical intimacy with African women. According to several reports from those working at the Foyer, she is also sexually involved with two women: Mme Desrussie, the widow of the mysteriously deceased director of the Foyer, and Tanella, an African woman accused of murdering the king's uncle in a refusal of his sexual advances. Célanire provokes further disturbance by allowing this intimacy to be publicly legible: one of the instructors at the Foyer recounts that Célanire and Tanella "s'enfermaient dans la même chamber.... Même en public, c'étaient des 'ma cocotte' et des 'ma chérie doudou' qui n'arrêtaient pas et des caresses sans équivoque" (84) ("locked themselves in the same room.... Even in public it was a never-ending serenade of 'my pet' and 'my little darling' and unequivocal caresses" [74]). Again, Célanire's transgressive acts are doubly so in that she chooses to make them visible as such, maintaining control over the social perception of her actions. Later, in Guadeloupe, she once again uses institutionalization as a means of reinforcing the visibility of supposedly unnatural behavior. Through her relationship with a lesbian separatist and founder of a women's association, she designates a space for this association which will allow women to live in isolation from men. The surrounding Guadeloupean society reacts, not surprisingly, with a mixture of shock and fear. As in Africa, Célanire's initiative, specifically because of its transgressive nature, transforms the landscape and causes a fundamental shift in the systems of economic exchange in the region.

Condé's creature, then, is monstrous not only because of her unknown origins, her unnatural re-creation, and her hideous scar, but also because she represents transgression in her acts—in the space she occupies, the partners she chooses, the politics she enacts, the institutions she builds. In each of the religious, cultural, and spiritual spheres she encounters, she exposes the limits of socially sanctioned behavior by violating those limits. Just as Victor Frankenstein's creature can be seen as the manifestation of a range of contemporary social anxieties, from Enlightenment science to maternity to revolutionary upheaval in France, Célanire exposes the fears and concerns particular to the various worlds she enters.[4] Her sociopolitical project of revising gender roles and racial divisions at the Foyer des métis and her own enactment of that project through her relationship with Thomas de Brabant in particular suggest a proscriptive link between female sexuality and miscegenation—or more specifically between procreation and racial indeterminacy—in the colonial context. Indeed, Condé's formal insistence on epistemological instability in the novel serves to showcase the anxieties provoked by Célanire's transgressive sexuality as fears grounded principally in the threat of the racial unknown.

Public perception is central to Célanire's experience. As we have seen, her transgressions are twofold, in that she disrupts the limits of social convention and then forces society to confront her disruptive acts by making them visible. To return to the image of her scar, however, Condé's monster reminds us that the *concealment* of transgression can be equally disruptive: just as she covers the mark of her physical deviance with her clothing, Célanire is all the more threatening socially because those around her are not entirely sure who she is or what her true motivations are. Versions and explanations conflict; first-hand accounts of her behavior meld into rumor and exaggeration; interpretation vacillates with shifts in audience. By maintaining this aura of mystery, Célanire keeps her public suspended in a constant state of interpretive uncertainty, and it is perhaps in this sense that she is most "monstrous," since she refuses even the hermeneutic proscriptions of a society constantly thwarted in its attempts to fix her identity.

In this context, the genre which Condé chooses to tell Célanire's story merits closer consideration. The novel is designated a *"roman fantastique,"* signaling a narrative form well suited to echo Shelley's classic. But beyond the thematic link to the monster's creation, the genre mirrors the conception of this heroine in crucial ways: even in its most general definition, the fantastic narrative elicits the collision of various worlds, of the real and the unreal, the known and the unknown, the natural and the supernatural. It is thus first and foremost a transgressive genre, in that it depends upon the departure from the familiar, the escape from the normative. Linked to the fantasy, it suggests the breaking of social codes and boundaries.[5] Roger Caillois pinpoints the departure from the familiar as the fantastic narrative's defining characteristic, and notes that the introduction of the unknown is characterized principally by its destruction of coherence: "In the fantastic, the supernatural appears as a rupture of universal coherence. The marvelous becomes a forbidden and threatening aggression that shatters the stability of a world whose laws had until that moment been considered rigorous and immutable. It is the impossible, intruding unexpectedly on a world from which the impossible is by definition banished."[6] The fantastic is thus a threatening narrative that crumbles the boundaries between the possible and the impossible, destabilizing codes and laws that had previously seemed immutable.

Inherent in this collision of worlds is also the encounter with the Other—the alien, the demon, the monster, the sorcerer, the mythical creature. The newly formed narrative world of the fantastic thus inscribes multiple modes of understanding and communication; the fabric of the fantastic is necessarily a patchwork one, combining various and conflicting perceptions of reality and suggesting a context in which such perceptions might coexist. In this sense, the fantastic can itself be seen as a "monstrous" narrative: much like Frankenstein's creature, it is an entity constructed from the suturing of materials from disparate sources.[7] Condé's novel too follows this model, not only because of the element of the supernatural but also due to its diverse cultural lexicons and multiple spheres of reference. The conflicting worlds inhabited by Célanire produce fragments of information that shift constantly and refuse to cohere around any single vision of reality. The narrative is thus "monstrous" in that it does not represent a coherent whole through the lens of any particular interpretive context.

There is, however, an important substantial (in the literal sense) difference between Shelley's creature and Condé's: for Célanire as a physical being is not a patchwork of disparate human body parts but a *single* human body severed in two and then reattached. In fact, the splitting of her body is (just barely) incomplete, as when she is discovered in the street her head hangs by a thread. Presumably it is this fragile remaining connection between body and head that allows Jean Pinceau to perform his miraculous operation. This difference is not forceful enough to "naturalize" the event in any way: the revival of Célanire's bloodless body (not to mention the replacement of her human blood with that of a chicken) ensures the potential incursion of the unnatural. But it is important to note this critical morphological difference between the classic creature and Condé's heroine: the result of Jean Pinceau's labor is, while monstrous and incoherent, the (re)assemblage of parts from a single human body.

If we return to the question of form, then, the discursive function of Célanire's reassembled body is instructive. For, as we have seen, the circumstances of Célanire's re-creation mean that she can, if she chooses, *appear* to be a scientifically coherent physical form; she can appear to belong to the natural world, with only the mysterious scarf as a disturbing suggestion of other possibilities. Her monstrosity thus does not have to be immediately apparent, but will emerge depending on how she is seen by others. Similarly, the fantastic as a genre functions crucially on interpretation: the categories navigated by the fantastic—of realism and fantasy, of possible and impossible, of known and unknown—are categories established by the reader. Depending on such factors as cultural or historical background, religious belief, gender, age, sexuality, and individual experience, a given reader will be equipped with his or her particular conception of the "natural" or the "real," and will recognize the fantastic as a disruption of that specific set of codes.[8] In *Célanire coucoupé*, by invoking such systems of understanding as animism, Christianity, Islamic faith, and Western science, Condé allows for a culturally diverse lexicon in order to produce a potentially limitless number of "monstrous" narratives, both of Célanire herself and of events in the novel. The text thus insists on a multicultural reading, an interpretive participation in its monstrosity.

What is striking about Condé's novel is that these various possible interpretations of events coexist simultaneously. Multiple accounts of a single series of events are offered side by side, conferring no priority of the rational over the irrational, the secular over the sacred, the known over the unknown. In particular, the numerous deaths that coincide disconcertingly with Célanire's presence produce heightened interpretive tension in the novel, as each one of them has a number of possible explanations, none of which is confirmed within the narrative. The body of Thomas de Brabant's French wife Charlotte, for example, is discovered deep in the forest, destroyed almost beyond recognition: "On aurait dit que des fauves, mangeurs de chair humaine et buveurs de sang frais, avaient eu affaire à elle" (62). ("It was as if wild beasts, eaters of human flesh and drinkers of fresh blood, had done her in" [52]). As evidenced by this citation, the passage describing the discovery of Charlotte's body emphasizes the limits of the possible that, through the lens of the natural, the rational, the scientific, appear to have been severely tested. The hypothesis of an attack by wild animals as the means of death is undermined by the lack of concrete evidence; meanwhile it seems implausible that the less than sturdy Charlotte could have walked alone across the kilometers of dangerous terrain between the forest and her home. General opinion in the community proposes that Célanire is guilty of this murder, yet while the Europeans attempt to find a scientific explanation for how the crime was carried out, the African population sees Charlotte's death as further proof that Célanire is a "cheval," a carrier of evil spirits seeking vengeance on the living and certain to strike again. The novel offers no resolution to this conflict and, as the deaths associated with Célanire multiply, preserves the status of Célanire's culpability as a suggestion, but never as definitive. The conflicting readings of these events thus maintain an unsettling coexistence in the narrative, each representing the impossibility of the others but forced to occupy the same discursive space.

Given this interpretive instability, Condé's novel corresponds to the more strict definition of the fantastic genre elaborated by Tzvetan Todorov in his *The Fantastic: A Structural Approach to a Literary Genre*. Here the fantastic is not simply a genre that allows for departures from the real or the familiar, but one that is characterized above all by the simultaneity of two conflicting worlds, and by the resulting uncertainty on the part of the reader: "The fantastic is that hesitation experienced by a person who knows only the laws of nature, confronting an apparently supernatural event" (25).[9] Once the reader chooses between the natural and the supernatural, the narrative is no longer a fantastic one. The two (or, in the case of Condé's novel, multiple) possible interpretations must carry equal discursive weight throughout the narrative, must conflict with one another without canceling each other out. The effectiveness of the fantastic narrative as elaborated by Todorov thus rests in the power of suggestion, rather than in the power of conviction: "'*I nearly reached the point of believing*': that is the formula which sums up the spirit of the fantastic. Either total faith or total incredulity would lead us beyond the fantastic: it is hesitation which sustains its life" (31). The reader of the fantastic can and should wonder, but must never be certain.

Much as the physical composition of Frankenstein's creature imitates the patchwork construction of Shelley's novel, Célanire's body provides a striking evocation of the fantastic narrative in this strict definition. Even without the piece of cloth to obscure her scar, the "natural" reading of Célanire's body is disturbingly coincident with the "unnatural" one: she is at once whole and divided, at once a living creature and a physical impossibility, at once known and unknown. Unlike Frankenstein's project, Dr. Pinceau's work represents an effort to recover a preexisting form: Célanire's body thus refers back to the real, even as its scar points to its distance from the natural world. Like the fantastic narrative, then, this heroine's form is a simultaneous suggestion of two conflicting worlds, and her scar is the sign of that disturbance.[10] The anxiety produced by the sight of Célanire, even or perhaps especially when her scar is covered, marks a sudden awareness of the unknown. Célanire thus represents at the same time a body existing wholly in the familiar world and the suggestion, necessarily inconclusive, of an unfamiliar one.

As we have seen, the transgressive nature of Célanire's existence rests to a significant degree on the uncertainty she produces in the other. In fact, this uncertainty and the simultaneity that inheres in the fantastic are closely linked. As Andras Sandor observes in his analysis of the genre, the anxiety provoked by the fantastic disturbance reveals above all the tenuous quality of the epistemological divisions that are ruptured. The confrontation of the unfamiliar instantly puts the bounds of the familiar into question, since the perception of that unknown object or event sheds doubt upon its position "outside" perception: "Fantastic stories establish a beyond against which the actual world can be noticed, and they project a mental field in which incomprehensible and/or only subliminally noticed aspects of the actual world can be suggested to experience" (350). The simultaneity of conflicting worlds, in other words, points to an added paradox: that to confront the unknown is in some sense to allow for its knowability. The result is a sphere of interpretation whose boundaries have shifted. The encounter with the supernatural points out the arbitrariness of the natural, and the perception of the inhuman that of the human.

Condé's novel in fact evokes such troubled distinctions at various points in the narrative, particularly with reference to the popular knowledge of native communities in the Ivory Coast and in Peru. A reaction to the first mysterious death in Adjame-Santey, for example, proclaims that "aucune mort n'est naturelle" (18) ("there is no such thing as a natural death" [7]), thus putting the very category of the natural into question. Indeed, the notion of a natural death implies that it is an event that can be understood and known, while in fact death may be one of the most obvious examples of the ubiquitous unknown. Meanwhile in Peru a violent death yields the following comment: "Dans nos pays où l'imagination est souveraine, la curiosité populaire ne se satisfait pas de mystères. Chaque chose doit avoir une explication, de préférence surnaturelle" (224). ("In our countries, where imagination reigns supreme, popular curiosity is not satisfied with a mystery. Everything has to have an explanation, preferably supernatural" [215]. Here the idea of the supernatural as a way to elucidate a mysterious event redefines the concept of the explanation as a demystifying, rational process: instead of being reasoned away, the supernatural *is* the explanation for the unknown. Like Célanire's scar, these passages evoke a division between two worlds even as they suture them together again, insisting on the arbitrary quality of such distinctions.

In the closing pages of the novel, Célanire seems to have completed a significant chapter in her journey: if she has indeed been pursuing her enemies, the last of their injustices has perhaps been avenged. Greatly transformed after recovering from a nearly fatal illness, and seemingly drained of her previous thirst for revenge, she claims that she needs a new purpose. Once in Guadeloupe, this newly formed ambition is made clear, as Célanire appears unexpectedly in her husband's bedroom, dressed in silk and lace and telling him she wants a child: "C'est tout ce que je peux être à présent: une bonne mère" (242). ("All I can do now is be a good mother" [232]).

Célanire's new reason for living, then, is procreation. With this dramatic conclusion, Condé would seem in a single gesture to recuperate a number of the monsters haunting Shelley's classic narrative: Célanire's claim is an assertion of female creativity, of birth, and of motherhood—a motherhood specifically characterized as "good," and thus an implied revision of the orphan's fate so frequently evoked in *Frankenstein*. But in the cross-cultural contexts of Condé's novel, it seems especially telling that Célanire also revives another monster destroyed in Shelley's narrative: the creature's bride. For Victor Frankenstein's refusal to allow his female creature to live arises out of a phobia of procreation; the thought of "a race of devils ... propagated upon the earth" (144) gives him pause and prevents him from granting the creature's demand. The repression of this new species represented by the destruction of the female is thus categorically refused by Célanire's final words: Condé's creature *will* reproduce herself, she will create a new race of monsters.

In the context of Condé's novel, of course, the "race" of monsters spawned by Célanire would be monstrous in part because of their *race*: the product of her union with Thomas de Brabant would be interracial, or worse, racially indeterminate, thus realizing a primary colonial phobia. Again, Célanire's affirmation recuperates *Frankenstein*'s censored material, since the geographical setting of the doctor's anxiety points to a colonial preoccupation hovering also in the shadows of Shelley's novel: in Frankenstein's imagination, it is in the New World that the creature and his bride would have released their race of devils upon an unsuspecting earth.[11] In *Célanire cou-coupé*, the colonial nightmare made real is miscegenation: Célanire's creation will violate the boundaries of race, power, and culture upon which the colonial system depends. Furthermore, as Condé's use of the fantastic genre reminds us, this child will represent the unknown, an invisible link to her monstrous mother and her mother's own undetermined origins. Read through the framework of the fantastic, the child's mixed race connotes not an assemblage of multiple parts, but rather a simultaneously whole and discontinuous being, a coexistence rather than an accumulation of different races. In this sense the disturbance of social codes provoked by Célanire's and Thomas's offspring also troubles the very categories of race: by expressing the simultaneity of racial difference, Célanire's imagined progeny implies that the "parts" of which she or he will be composed are themselves arbitrary categories.

In the final pages of her fantastic narrative, Condé thus culminates a chain of anxieties from female sexuality to reproduction to racial hybridity and indeterminacy. Célanire's child, like her mother, will exist in defiance of both natural and social codes, but will also expose the fundamental anxiety of race as an unknown. Given the novel's literary inheritance of Shelley's monster, Condé implicitly associates this epistemological instability with the reproductive powers of Frankenstein's bride, revealing that the fear of procreation connoted by the feminine stems not only from the vision of an uncontrollable population of monsters but more tellingly from the potential replication of a racial unknown. That a radically illegible being could not only control but also reproduce her monstrosity indefinitely, adding exponential layers of interpretive uncertainty, would seem to pose the greatest threat to social structures in both postrevolutionary England and the colonial Atlantic. Condé's *Célanire cou-coupé* thus reveals that, much like the author's anglophone and francophone literary genealogies, the Gothic hauntings of female sexuality and racial indeterminacy are inextricably linked.

Notes

1. Condé's award-winning 1986 novel *Moi, Tituba sorcière ... noire de Salem*, for example, not only reinvents the Salem witch trials of 1732 from the perspective of its only recorded slave witness but also envisions a friendship between Tituba and Hawthorne's Hester Prynne. The more recent *La Belle Créole* (2001), set in late twentieth century Guadeloupe, suggests somewhat less directly an affiliation with Lawrence's *Lady Chatterley's Lover*. Emily Apter reads this transnational dialogue in Condé's works as the "exchange [of] a French literary genealogy for a British one" that, especially in the case of *La Migration des cœurs*, suggests the formation of a "Caribbean Gothic" (438).

2. On the links between the creature's gaze in *Frankenstein* and the Freudian model of the Medusa figure, see Salotto (194–96).

3. Baldick proposes this reading of the Frankenstein myth through Foucault's etymological definition of the monster as a being or object to be *shown* (*monstrare*) in order to *warn* (*monere*) humanity of the potential consequences of vice or unreasoned behavior (10 ff).

4. See for example Ellen Moers's reading of *Frankenstein* as a "birth myth" (92), Fred Botting's analysis of the inscription of the French Revolution in Shelley's text, or Chris Baldick's reading of the "mad scientist" anxiety (141–42).

5. On the function of the fantasy in *Frankenstein*, see Rosemary Jackson's essay in *Aspects of Fantasy*.

6. "[D]ans le fantastique, le surnaturel apparaît comme une rupture de la cohérence universelle. Le prodige y devient une agression interdite, menaçante, qui brise la stabilité d'un monde dont les lois étaient jusqu'alors tenues pour rigoureuses et immuables. Il est l'impossible, survenant à l'improviste dans un monde d'où l'impossible est banni par définition" (Caillois 9).

7. The conception of Shelley's novel as a monstrous narrative, first suggested by the author herself in her introduction to the 1831 edition of the novel with a reference to her "hideous progeny" (25), has been taken up by a number of critics. Fred Botting, for example, has described the novel as "an 'assemblage' of fragments, a disunified text that subverts the possibility and implications of textual and semantic coherence" (27), while Eleanor Salotto proposes that Shelley's text falls into the mon-

strous inasmuch as it is an autobiographical text, the self-representation of a multiple subject. See also Baldick (30–33).

8. On this aspect of the fantastic, see Morse's introduction to *The Fantastic in World Literature and the Arts* (1–3).

9. Todorov's definition of the genre has not, of course, escaped criticism (see for example Brooke-Rose, Lem, and Sandor), but his emphasis on the *simultaneity* of conflicting interpretations captures an essential component of Condé's narrative.

10. In his work on myths and the fantastic, Andras Sandor uses the image of the scar to evoke the confusing simultaneity of the genre: "The fantastic suggests a scar that cannot be smoothed out, a scar that cannot heal" (349).

11. As Helena Woodard has proposed, this reproduction of the Other is the ultimate colonial fear, "a colonial power's worst nightmare: Caliban's threat to Miranda to people the world with 'little Calibans'" (26).

Works Cited

Apter, Emily. "Condé's *Créolité* in Literary History." *The Romanic Review* 94.3–4 (2003): 437–50.
Baldick, Chris. *In Frankenstein's Shadow: Myth, Monstrosity, and Nineteenth-Century Writing.* Oxford: Clarendon Press, 1987.
Berman, Jeffrey. *Narcissism and the Novel.* New York: New York University Press, 1990.
Botting, Fred. "Reflections of Excess: *Frankenstein*, the French Revolution and Monstrosity." In *Reflections of Revolution: Images of Romanticism,* ed. Alison Yarrington and Kelvin Everest, 26–38. London: Routledge, 1993.
Brooke-Rose, Christine. *A Rhetoric of the Unreal: Studies in Narrative and Structure, Especially of the Fantastic.* Cambridge: Cambridge University Press, 1981.
Caillois, Roger. *Anthologie du fantastique.* Vol. 1. Paris: Gallimard, 1966.
Condé, Maryse. *Célanire cou-coupé.* Paris: Laffont, 2000.
_____. *La Migration des coeurs.* Paris: Laffont, 1995.
_____. *Moi, Tituba sorcière ... noire de Salem.* Paris: Mercure de France, 1986.
_____. *Who Slashed Célanire's Throat?* Trans. Richard Philcox. New York: Atria, 2004.
Jackson, Rosemary. "Narcissism and Beyond: A Psychoanalytic Reading of *Frankenstein* and Fantasies of the Double." In *Aspects of Fantasy,* ed. William Coyle, 43–53. New York: Greenwood, 1986.
Lem, Stanislaw. *Microworlds: Writings on Science Fiction and Fantasy*, ed. Franz Rottensteiner. New York: Harcourt, 1984.
Moers, Ellen. *Literary Women.* New York: Doubleday, 1976.
Morse, Donald E., ed. *The Fantastic in World Literature and the Arts.* New York: Greenwood, 1987.
Reichardt, Jasia. "Artificial Life and the Myth of Frankenstein." In *Frankenstein, Creation and Monstrosity,* ed. Stephen Bann, 136–57. London: Reaktion, 1994.
Salotto, Eleanor. "*Frankenstein* and Dis(re)membered Identity." *The Journal of Narrative Technique* 24.3 (1994): 190–211.
Sandor, Andras. "Myths and the Fantastic." *New Literary History* 22.2 (1991): 339–58.
Shelley, Mary. *Frankenstein*, ed. Johanna M. Smith. New York: Bedford/St. Martin's, 2000.
Todorov, Tzvetan. *The Fantastic: A Structural Approach to a Literary Genre.* Trans. Richard Howard. London: Case Western Reserve University, 1973.
Woodard, Helena. "The Two Marys (Prince and Shelley) on the Textual Meeting Ground of Race, Gender, and Genre." In *Recovered Writers/Recovered Texts: Race, Class, and Gender in Black Women's Literature,* ed. Dolan Hubbard, 15–30. Knoxville: University of Tennessee Press, 1997.

Part II
THE SATANIC MALE

5
"There Was a Man": Dangerous Husbands and Fathers in The Winter's Tale, A Sicilian Romance *and* Linden Hills

RUTH BIENSTOCK ANOLIK

In the second act of Shakespeare's *The Winter's Tale* (1610), before the commencement of the betrayal and murder that furnishes the central plot, we witness a poignant moment between the young prince Mamillius and his mother, the queen Hermione. In this close Oedipal scene of mother and son, Hermione playfully asks her son for a story: "Pray you sit by us, / And tell's a tale" (2.1.29–30). Although Hermione asks for a tale "As merry as you will" (2.1.31), Mamillius replies: "A sad tale's best for winter. I have one / Of sprites and goblins" (2.1.33–34). And so, the audience and Hermione settle in for a story that will deliver the promised horror of the supernatural. Hermione challenges her son: "Come on, and do your best to fright me with your sprites" (2.1.36–7). But Mamillius confounds the expectations of his audience in beginning his winter's tale: "There was a man" (2.1.38).

And yet, as the audience, Mamillius and Hermione soon discover, the story that begins with a man is as horrifying as the story of sprites and goblins. For before Mamillius's story concludes, his father Leontes intrudes in classic Freudian manner into the close moment between mother and son. As "They talk privately" (stage direction), Leontes seizes the boy from the unbelieving mother. Soon after, Mamilius is dead, his heart broken by the imprisonment of his mother. The baby girl that Hermione bears in prison is abandoned to die in Bohemia, after Leontes rethinks his initial plan to have her "instantly consumed with fire" (2.3.169). And the audience and Leontes are pained to learn that Hermione too has died, as reported by Paulina. As Shakespeare tells us in this story of paternal intervention, it is the human male, not supernatural sprites and goblins, who is to be feared as the source of horror and death.

In making this statement, Shakespeare enacts one of the "critiques of patriarchy" (30) that A.E.B. Coldiron observes in the play.[1] Shakespeare responds to the traditional association of the woman "outside patriarchal structure, unmarried, widowed, or sexually active" (K.G. Rosenfield 1) with the dangerously supernatural witch.[2] Traditionally, witchcraft was associated with the male fear of uncontained and unmonitored female sexuality and its consequence: maternal power. The witch was frequently accused of having sexual intercourse with the Devil, an extreme case of undisciplined female sexual activity. Moreover, the process of childbirth entailed mystery and secrecy, thereby curtailing the extension of male surveillance over the lives of women. As Deborah Willis asserts: "Witches were women ... because witches were mothers" (99). The patriarchal anxiety evoked by the mysterious female power of creation was further amplified by the mystery of paternity. Thus the mother was a female who had greater power and knowledge than the male: she could create life as he could not, and she could easily subvert the unwitting patriarchy through infidelity. In exercising this uncontrollable power, the mother was abetted by her assistant, the midwife, who was also privy to the mysteries of life and of paternity and thus often associated with witchcraft in the patriarchal imagination. Richard Wilson suggests yet another aspect to the threatening power of the birthing assistants, the power over death as well: midwives were also "mistresses of infanticide and abortion" (Wilson 130).[3]

Shakespeare's play vividly illustrates all the contemporary patriarchal anxieties.[4] Janet Adelman notes that *The Winter's Tale* portrays a patriarchy that feels threatened by the childbearing female; the play articulates "the anguish of a masculinity that conceives of itself as betrayed at its point of origin, a masculinity that can read in the full maternal body only the signs of its own loss" (149). As Rosenfield notes, "Leontes's formulation of Hermione as witch/unnatural mother both acknowledges the power of her presence and the threat of his paternal line, and simultaneously reinforces his patriarchal authority by containing her as the accused witch is contained" (Rosenfield 4).[5] Leontes's quick slide into jealous instability, the speed with which he loses his rational balance, also reveals the destabilizing power of maternity over the patriarch. The ambiguous powers of the midwife are revealed in the person of Paulina. Although Paulina does not act literally as Hermione's midwife—she learns from Emilia that the baby has been born to the imprisoned queen— Paulina acts metaphorically in this role, a fact Leontes recognizes in disparagingly referring to her as a "midwife" (2.3.198). Like a good midwife,

Paulina works to stabilize the paternity of the baby, insisting to Leontes that "It is yours" (2.3.123). She also acts as midwife in helping the baby to live; in interceding on behalf of Perdita, Paulina saves her from her dangerous father. Even more significantly, Paulina also demonstrates the quasi-godlike power of life and death in her dealings with Hermione. It is by the power of Paulina's word that Hermione is consigned to the dead. Pauline announces to the court that "the Queen, / The sweet'st, dear'st creature's dead" (3.2.219–220) and for the sixteen years that follow, Hermione is given up for dead. In fact, Paulina emphasizes her linguistic power: "I say she's dead. I'll swear't" (3.2.224). Paulina also demonstrates her linguistic power to restore life in bringing Hermione back from the dead. As Leontes gazes at the supposed statue of his dead wife, Paulina speaks a series of commands[6]: "Music, awake her! Strike.... Descend. Be stone no more. Approach. / Strike all that look upon with marvel" (5.3.124–126). The extension of Paulina's power to the adult Hermione reveals the kind of leakage that amplifies the sense of the power of the midwife and thus explains the great fear that this largely benevolent figure generated in the patriarchal imagination.[7]

Yet in *The Winter's Tale* Shakespeare warns against the association between the woman and the witch, moving to reverse the cultural connection between bearing life and bringing death by revealing the shaky foundations of this thinking. As Rosenfield notes, the play "reveals these associations as accusations designed to contain the threat of the transgressing woman" and "identifies these linkages as cultural constructions.... Witchcraft is exposed as the rhetoric of threatened masculinity.... The play suggests that the conflation of sexuality and maternity with witchcraft is a projection of male anxiety about birth, paternal proof and the male construction of self" (2). Thus when Polixenes suggests that wives lead men to the transcendental evil of sex, Hermione rebukes him and warns him against claiming that "Your queen and I are devils" (1.2.104). And Shakespeare's play sustains this rebuke. Paulina's seemingly supernatural resurrection of Hermione is realistically explained and is completely benign. As Rosenfield says, "The witch no longer bears evil and chaos but presides at Hermione's rebirth.... The last scene thus enacts a containment of patriarchal fear and loathing as well as a gradual exorcism of the specter of witchcraft" (6). Thus any supernatural threat by the female is diminished and we are left with a fear and loathing of the true source of danger: the patriarch, the uncontained male tyrant whose role as the prime source of danger in this play is clear. It is he and not witches, goblins or sprites who is responsible for the horror that unfolds. And it is the life-giving women who reverse his death-dealing commands.

In his preface to the second edition of *The Castle of Otranto*, Horace Walpole, the putative inventor of the English Gothic, recognizes Shakespeare as an influence for this mode. In writing of his use of servants to delay action and to amplify suspense, Walpole notes, "The great master of nature, Shakespeare, was the model I copied" (10). And certainly, the Gothic owes much more to Shakespeare than mere comic relief. A cursory reading of Shakespeare's plays reveals the origins of many familiar Gothic staples: usurpation, appropriation and restoration, played out on the domestic and national levels; supernatural intervention; young love thwarted by domestic and political tyranny. Virginia Woolf insightfully writes, "What Horace Walpole began half in fun was continued seriously and with considerable power by Mrs. Radcliffe" (215).[8] Indeed, Ann Radcliffe, like Walpole, was a great admirer of Shakespeare. In "On the Supernatural in Poetry" (1826), she writes of "the perfection of Shakespeare" (167), crediting his use of the supernatural with an expansion of the audience's emotional response to his characters. Interestingly, the plays that Radcliffe praises in her piece are *Hamlet* and *Macbeth*, in which Shakespeare deploys supernatural devices that are undeniably unrealistic, while Radcliffe's strategy is to deny the existence of the seeming-supernatural. In fact, the quasi-supernatural, which is realistically explicable, that Shakespeare deploys in *The Winter's Tale* is much more aligned with Radcliffe's approach.

Indeed, although no previous critic seems to have remarked on this textual relationship, a strong line connects *The Winter's Tale* to Radcliffe's *A Sicilian Romance* (1790). Both are set in a safely distanced time and place, present similar plots and characters and highlight the theme of the malevolent male relative replacing the supernatural as a source of danger and horror.[9] The setting of Radcliffe's novel recalls Shakespeare's play, also set in Sicily.[10] The period of the novel—"towards the close of the sixteenth century"—might also be a bow to Shakespeare. Even before the opening line of the novel, the epigram reveals a clue as to its source. Although the epigram is from *Hamlet*, indicating to Alison Milbank, the editor of the Oxford edition of *Romance*, that "Radcliffe's plot is a non-supernatural version of *Hamlet* (Radcliffe 200 ff), the epigram provides a link to *The Winter's Tale*: "I could a tale unfold." This epigram recalls not only the title of Shakespeare's play but the phrase "old tale" that is repeated in act 5 (2.30,65; 3.146) as a way to account for the miraculous return of both Perdita and Hermione from the dead. In fact, the tale that Radcliffe tells is replete with allusions to *The Winter's Tale*. The villainous husband and father of Radcliffe's piece is the Marquis Mazzini, like Leontes an autocrat who cruelly exerts his power over his family. As in Shakespeare's play, the long-suffering wife of the tyrant is restored to life after seeming to be dead for many years, "about fifteen" (175), very close to the sixteen-year interval bridged by Time, the chorus in Shakespeare's play (4.1).

But Radcliffe revises the play in some important ways. In her text, the wife, unlike Hermione, is completely powerless; she does not withdraw willingly but is shut away by her husband, who knows that she is, in fact, still alive. Radcliffe thus heightens the malevolence of the husband who, unlike Leontes, is unrepentant for the duration of his wife's incarceration and who, in fact, dies by being poisoned by his second (bigamous) wife. While Radcliffe's novel, like Shakespeare's play, also ends on a note of restoration, in her case the mother and children (two daughters and a son) are restored to each other. Whereas in the play the male child is eliminated and the male tyrant is rehabilitated, in the novel the male tyrant is eliminated while the mother and children endure. Yet Radcliffe's novel, like Shakespeare's play (which ends with the implication that Perdita, the only surviving child, will succeed her father[11]), ends with an instatement of the female line.

Radcliffe then finds in Shakespeare's text, with its reversal of the association of supernatural danger and the witchlike woman, a sympathetic model for her novel. Certainly Shakespeare's location of the horror associated with the supernatural onto the human male strikes a chord with Radcliffe, famous for her use of the "explained supernatural." In this version of the supernatural, present in all her novels, Radcliffe implies a supernatural presence that is rationally explained by the closure of the novel, thereby suggesting supernatural terror without disabling the realism of her text.[12] In fact, in deploying the explained supernatural in *A Sicilian Romance* (and this argument might certainly be extended to her other novels), Radcliffe emphasizes the message in Shakespeare's play: in the real, material world in which women live, the human male is a far greater threat than any supernatural presence.

Radcliffe deploys typical Gothic repetition to emphasize the dangerous nature of the male relative throughout book. The prospective husband of Julia, the protagonist, has a history of being a dangerous husband: "He delighted in simple undisguised tyranny. He had been twice married, and the unfortunate women subjected to his power, had fallen victims to the slow but corroding hand of sorrow" (57). Radcliffe emphasizes the connections between marriage and death in writing of Julia's planned marriage to this tyrant: "she was to be ... sacrificed to the ambition of her father, and the absurd love of the Duke" (69). Another form of male danger emanates from the metaphorical "father," the Abote who heads the abbey to which Julia flees for sanctuary. Too late Julia discovers that she has placed "herself in the power of a man, stern and unfeeling in his nature, and from whom, if he thought it fit to betray her, she had no means of escaping" (128). Whereas Julia's father pressures her to marry, the Abote pressures her to "renounce the world, and dedicate your days to God ... assume the veil" (141). Finally Julia falls into the hands of men more explicitly evil, the only men in the book whose oppression of women is not sanctioned by law: a group of banditti who threaten to rape her.[13]

But the central image of male danger in this novel is the husband and father of the Mazzini family, the Marquis Mazzini. The marquis is "voluptuous and imperious ... arrogant and impetuous" (3). His "heart was dead to paternal tenderness.... Many persons believed that his unkindness and neglect put a period to her [his first wife's] life" (3). At the end of the novel, the three children discover that their father is actually their mother's jailer and potential murderer. Julia stumbles into a small room where she discovers "the pale and emaciated figure of a women, seated, with half-closed eyes" (174), her mother, immured for fifteen years in "the southern building of the castle of Mazzini" (175). This discovery unveils "the vices of her [Julia's] father" (175)—the mother calls him "my cruel tyrant" (177), and explains the full extent of his power, and thus his danger: "The marquis, you know, has not only power to imprison, but also the right of life and death in his own domains" (180).

The description of the marquis's unbridled power, which allows him to destroy his wife's life, connects this seemingly fanciful story of a husband run amok to the contemporary situation of Radcliffe's readers. A principle of English common law, written into the Commentaries on the English Constitution by Blackstone in 1758, states that when a women married, she became a *feme covert* and ceased to exist as a separate legal entity. A married woman thus underwent a civil death and forfeited all rights to possess property, custody of her own children and, indeed, to herself.[14] In the words of a popular saying "ascribed to the great eighteenth-century jurist Sir William Blackstone.... 'In law husband and wife are one person, and the husband is that person'" (Holcombe 18). Joan Perkin's rendering of this principle is somewhat less whimsical; quite correctly, she notes that under coverture, the wife became "a feme covert, a hidden person.... In Orwellian language, she became an 'Unperson.'" (2).

In metaphorically killing his wife—declaring her dead, burying her in effigy and immuring her in his dungeons—the marquis is thus re-enacting the process of coverture, which resulted in the civil death of the married woman. Radcliffe's representation of the marchioness, imprisoned, effaced and even at risk of being killed by her husband, literalizes and thereby demystifies this legal abstraction, reflecting the legal reality that the husband and the father who promote marriage, whose economic plots and possession of the woman are supported by marriage, are the primary causes of the civil death of the woman. The marchioness's loss of access to her children—she is dead to them—literalizes the absolute paternal rights within the system of coverture.[15] She tells of a bitter moment of her imprisonment: her husband, the marquis, informs her "I might see [her children] from a window near which they would pass.... I saw my children—and was [not] permitted to clasp them to my heart (178).[16]

The enforced absence of the mother in *A Sicilian Romance* also highlights the cruelty of the system of primogeniture, another legal system that served to destabilize the situation of women in Radcliffe's time. Primogeniture is the "common law doctrine" (Erickson 8) that limits the rights of the woman to possession,[17] determining that all of the father's property is bequeathed to the firstborn son: "The common law only allowed [women] to inherit land if they had no brothers, under a system of primogeniture" (3). This system, intended to preserve large estates, and to keep capital within the family, effectively erased the female presence from the line of property transmission.[18] Indeed, the wickedness of the marquis is identified by his commitment to the structures of primogeniture. In addition to imprisoning his wife, thereby illustrating the erasure of the mother from the patrilineal line within the system of primogeniture, the marquis rejects his daughters, demonstrating their inutility within patriarchal systems. Casting off Julia and her sister Emilia, the father elevates their brother: "His son ... was the sole object of his pride" (10).

And yet, although the male relative is a clear source of danger throughout the book, endangering his wife and neglecting his daughters, whose fates reflects the insecure situation of women in Radcliffe's time, the misguided young protagonists ignore the dangers posed by their own father. They focus instead on the imagined dangers of a supposed supernatural presence, located in the uninhabited southern part of the Mazzini castle. This manifestation appears early in the book in "the appearance of a light through the broken window-shutters of an apartment belonging to a division of the castle which had for many years been shut up ... A report was soon raised, and believed that the southern side of the castle was haunted" (8–10). When their evil stepmother moves Julia and Emilia, her sister, into "gloomy" rooms that "formed a part of the southern building," Julia decides that she is at risk because of a supernatural threat: "The late mysterious circumstances ... now arose to her imagination, and conjured up a terror which reason could not subdue" (27). In fact, her fears appear justified. Julia starts hearing strange sounds: "a low hollow sound which arose from beneath the apartment" (35); "strange and alarming sounds" (45). Seeking to help his sisters, Ferdinand also hears "a sullen groan" (46) and then a "hollow" (47) groan near their rooms. Radcliffe emphasizes that Julia and Emilia fear the supernatural more than they fear their father's wrath. "When he [Ferdinand] related the circumstances of his late adventure, the terror of Emilia and Julia was heightened to a degree that overcame every prudent consideration. Their apprehension of the marquis's displeasure was lost in a stronger feeling, and they resolved no longer to remain in apartments which offered only terrific images to their fancy" (47).

Certainly the siblings are wrong to exaggerate the dangers of the supernatural and to ignore the dangers emanating from their own father. In fact, the seemingly supernatural manifestations that Julia and Ferdinand witness—the lights and repeated groans from the southern part of the castle—are not supernatural phenomenon; they emanate from their imprisoned mother, and thus represent natural rather than supernatural danger. Radcliffe quite explicitly identifies the magnitude of the siblings' error and quite pointedly warns her young readers not to be distracted by ghost stories. In fact, the marquis deploys a ghost story to distract his children from the dangerous truth. In an attempt to keep Ferdinand away from the southern buildings where his mother is hidden, the marquis invents a story about an ancestor who kidnapped and killed a member of a rival family. As a result, says the marquis, "A rumor had prevailed long before the death of my father that the southern buildings of the castle were haunted.... One night.... I had such strong and dreadful proofs of the general assertion that even at this moment I cannot recollect them without horror" (53). The narrator confirms the motivation for this story at the conclusion of the novel:

> The story which the marquis formerly related to his son concerning the southern buildings, it was now evident was fabricated for the purpose of concealing the imprisonment of the marchioness.... the circumstance related was calculated, by impressing terror, to prevent further enquiry in to the recesses of these buildings. It served, also, to explain by supernatural evidence, the cause of those sounds and of that appearance which had been there observed but which were, in reality, occasioned only by the marquis [195].

The careful young reader of Radcliffe's novel, then, will learn not to be distracted by ghost stories but to focus on the real source of danger: fathers and husbands, the men trying to steal their property and curtail their freedom. This was, indeed, a timely warning for Radcliffe's young contemporary readers, who were immersed in a rising flood of Gothic fiction. The late eighteenth century saw the consolidation of the systems of coverture and of primogeniture in response to the emergence of the Industrial Revolution. Donna Dickenson asserts, "Coverture was the culmination and consequence of a long decline in women's civil rights, including their rights in property" (81).[19] Dickensen also indicates that the strengthening of primogeniture was also a relatively recent event in

Radcliffe's time: "In the period up to and including the seventeenth century, with the centralization and consolidation of states into absolutist monarchies, inheritance through the female line was barred" (82).[20]

Radcliffe thus unveils to her readers the dangers that lurked in the seemingly mundane legal system. In writing of Blackstone's formulation of coverture, Dickenson states: "Blackstone presents this doctrine of coverture not as irrational, or anomalous ... but as the revealed truth of reason, in conformity with natural law" (83). Radcliffe's revelation of the dangerous husband and father demystifies and denaturalizes the legal metaphors, revealing the horror that lurks beneath the neutral language of Blackstone's explication. In fact, Radcliffe reverses the construction of the metaphor of civil death to describe the situation of married women. In literalizing the situation of women, taking the metaphor of death and making it a reality, Radcliffe shows that the legal fictions are not fictions at all: in fact, real horrors lie within the seeming abstractions of the law. Thus in *A Sicilian Romance,* Radcliffe removes the seemingly dangerous veil of the supernatural and reveals that the supernatural is dangerous only in being a distraction from more serious threats. Radcliffe warns her readers of the true threat to women: the husband and father excessively empowered under the systems of coverture and primogeniture.

The line that connects *A Sicilian Romance* to *The Winter's Tale* continues across the centuries and across the Atlantic Ocean to Gloria Naylor's American Gothic novel, *Linden Hills* (1985). It is not particularly original to note that Gloria Naylor structures her novel *Linden Hills* within a network of other texts: Saunders quite accurately locates Naylor's tendency toward allusion in *Linden Hills* and in her other novels with Henry Louis Gates's notion of "'signification,' that is the utilization of others' characters and themes" (1–2), a strategy long used by African-American writers, who borrow from others to create a tradition. Yet, although much critical attention has been devoted to Naylor's use of allusion,[21] no critic, it seems, has noticed the strong connecting thread between *A Sicilian Romance* and *Linden Hills*.[22] Similarly, although Shakespeare is recognized as a strong influence in other novels by Naylor, most notably *Mama Day*,[23] the references in *Linden Hills* to *The Winter's Tale* are unnoted in the critical literature.

Although subtle, the web of allusions to *The Winter's Tale* is indisputable. One of Naylor's unlikely heroes, significantly named Willie, is an aspiring poet who has hopes of being a "black Shakespeare" (283). In *Linden Hills*, Naylor tells her own "winter's tale," explicitly setting her story in the time period of December 19th through December 24th. As in Shakespeare's play, the jealous and tyrannical father imprisons his wife because he irrationally suspects that she has been unfaithful and that her child is the product of adultery, conveying to her "insane messages about adultery [and] the complexion of the child" (280). As in the play, the son who is the focal point of paternal and patriarchal anxiety dies as the result of his father's insane and irrational jealousy, thereby paradoxically ending the paternal line so prized by the father.

Naylor thus revisits the anxiety of paternity that many critics identify in Shakespeare and that is visible in *The Winter's Tale*.[24] Like Leontes, Luther is preoccupied with, and perhaps driven mad by, the imperatives of bequeathing his dynasty to a legitimate male heir. The problem for Luther, who is dark-skinned like the line of men who preceded him, is that his light-skinned wife has produced a light-skinned son; like his predecessor Leontes, Luther leaps to an accusation of infidelity based on flimsy and inaccurate evidence, falsely believing that "there was no way that this child could be his son" (19). Perhaps Naylor is also alluding to the African-American history of slavery in which questions of paternity were riddled with anxiety and a light-skinned child born to a slave wife might indeed signify a forced infidelity. Part of Luther's danger as a husband is that he reverts to these archaic models in his dealings with his late twentieth century wife.

Naylor's allusions to *A Sicilian Romance* are equally rich and productive. Naylor clearly works to contextualize her contemporary realistic novel in the Gothic mode. One of the villainous husbands constructs "an artificial lake (really a moat) ... totally around his house and grounds" (6). A character reports that Luther always talks as if he is "straight out of a gothic novel" (86). Luther's house is "like walking into a movie set for *Wuthering Heights*" (290). Most significantly, Naylor like her precursors shows that in twentieth century America, as in England during the Renaissance and early modern era, the real source of Gothic horror is the husband and father. Like the Marquis Mazzini, and Leontes before him, Luther imprisons the wife who does not conform to his patriarchal plans; he reopens "the old morgue in his basement" (19) and locks in his supposedly unfaithful wife. In fact, the imprisonment of this wife, like the imprisonment of her extra-textual precursors, simply highlights her already-dependant situation: "By now she understood that he controlled her food and water and lights. Whatever she had been allowed—upstairs or down—was hers not by right, but as a gift" (68–69). Like the imprisoned mother in *A Sicilian Romance*, Willa emits howls that fill her auditors with a dread of the supernatural. When the first characters hear "the long, thin howl" it make "the hair stand up on their arms" (42). As in *A Sicilian Romance*, this sound is repeated: "a long thin wail" (60), winding its way through the text, emanating from the woman who is locked in her basement dungeon. Following the course set by her predecessors, Naylor shows her readers that the locus of true horror is not the haunted castle, but the suburban house in which lurks the dangerously powerful husband.[25]

Naylor creates a dynastic line of malevolent husbands, all named Luther Nedeed, who have long been a source of danger to their wives. These men deploy forms of legal oppression—coverture, primogeniture, and the particularly American system of slavery—to efface and erase the women they marry. The Nedeed version of primogeniture is evident in the heredity of the male line; each son is physically and psychologically identical to his father, inheriting no traits from his mother. As one of the wives realizes about her son: "it is not just that he is Luther's son, he is Luther" (123). As in the case of primogeniture in which property is passed from father to son, bypassing the invisible mother, so is the genetic property of these fathers passed directly to their sons. The biological invisibility of the mothers is paralleled by the social and psychological invisibility that evokes the systems of coverture and primogeniture. The line begins with the great-great-grandfather of the contemporary villain. This Nedeed sold his own "octoroon wife and six children for the money that he used to come North" (2). His descendants are equally dangerous to their wives, who had all "been brought to Tupelo Drive to fade against the whitewashed boards of the Nedeed home after conceiving and giving over a son to the stamp and will of the father" (18), a clear nod to the dangers of primogeniture. The diary of another Nedeed wife continues Naylor's indictment of the political systems that contain wives: "Luther told me today that I have no rights to my son.... I thought my sale to him was only a formality" (116). This wife, no less than her successors, discovers that her relation to her husband is that of a "slave" (116). Each wife takes on the cloak of invisibility that envelops every wife through primogeniture and coverture. One Nedeed wife starves herself to death, emblematizing the invisibility she already experiences in her family. Another records her disappearance from her family in a series of family photographs in which she becomes progressively less visible: "the only thing growing in these pictures was her absence" (209). The current Luther Nedeed has learned well from the patriarchy: "His father was right: breaking in a wife is like breaking in a new pair of slippers" (67). His wife is almost invisible to him: "Luther's eyes rest on the shadow floating through the carpeted rooms.... He heard the lilt in the voice when it spoke" (19). Using the prerogatives of coverture, this husband steals his wife's identify; covering her identify with his, he calls his wife Mrs. Nedeed and only at the end of the book, as she is dying does she assert her identity, revealing her name to the reader (as point-of-view character): "Her name was Willa Prescott Nedeed" (277).[26]

Naylor echoes her precursor, Shakespeare, in explicitly refuting the connection between the female and the evil supernatural. When one of

Naylor's male characters says: "it's cold as a witch's tit,"[27] a female character rebukes him: "Why do you men always apply something bad to a woman? Why can't it be cold as the devil's balls?" (32). Naylor develops this possibility, adding the aura of the supernatural to her representation of the malevolent male relative. This depiction of the quasi-supernatural radically and surprisingly reverses the earlier works. Both *The Winter's Tale* and *A Sicilian Romance* emphasize that it is the realistic powers of the male—the legal and economic powers—that render him so dangerous to the woman. Rather than displacing the supernatural and highlighting human, male danger, Naylor locates the male as the site of supernatural as well as natural danger. In her representation of the male, civil, legal and realistic danger is supplemented by supernatural danger; the dangerous and metaphorically demonic husband is literally demonic, even Satanic. His name Luther evokes the name Lucifer, and Nedeed may be read in reverse for "de," meaning "to undo," Eden.[28] The first Luther Nedeed plans "for exactly seven days" (2) before setting up his infernal enterprise, reversing God's seven-day, life-creating enterprise. Like Satan, he rebels against established power, dreaming of "a true black power" that would become "a real weapon against the white god." (11). Many critics, including K.A. Sandiford, note the connection between Dante's Inferno, at the core of which lies Satan, and the numbered Crescent Drives of Linden Hills, where the Nedeeds live in the center of the lowest crescent in house number 999, reflecting an inversion of the number associated with the Devil. The modern Luther Nedeed, like Lucifer, decides who gets to live in his always available domain: "Luther often wondered why none of the applicants ever questioned the fact that there was always space in Linden Hills" (18), and like Lucifer, his boots leave "triangular prints" (212). The implacable perpetuation of the male line in the Nedeed family also links the Needed family to supernatural power; the original Luther is immortal, although in a quasi-supernatural, realistically explicable way. Since each male in the dynastic line is identical, "It seemed that when old Luther died in 1879, he hadn't died at all, especially when they spoke to his son and especially when they glanced at those puffed eyelids and around those bottomless eyes" (4). Certainly there is an ambiguity in the supernatural representation of Luther Nedeed; nothing about him cannot be explained in realistic terms. But the accumulation of details does suggest a man whose demonism extends beyond the mundane planes of economics and law. One final ghostly association of the Nedeeds is a telling allusion to *The Winter's Tale*. The Nedeeds live next to a graveyard, engaging in the family undertaking business. Naylor thus pointedly recalls the opening sentence from Mamillius's story that begins "There was a man," and continues, "Dwelt by a churchyard" (2.1.40).

Naylor's revision of *The Winter's Tale* and *A Sicilian Romance* raises an important question: why evoke the Old English systems of coverture and primogeniture and the old texts that address them in late twentieth century America? The answer to this question may be found in the political history of the United States. As Winston E. Langley, Vivian C. Fox, and Amy Louise Erickson note, coverture had a significant impact upon early American law.[29] And although modifications were made in the law in the nineteenth century to improve the situation of women,[30] the process was not as complete as the history of law indicates. Linda Kerber asserts that the vestiges of coverture endured well into the twentieth century. Indeed, not until 1992, six years after the publication of Naylor's novel, "did the Supreme Court specifically announce that it would no longer recognize the power of husbands over the bodies of their wives. That is the moment when coverture as a living legal principle died" (307). And so, Naylor's novel, published in 1986, reveals a very real threat to her contemporary readers. In the tradition of her precursors, Naylor deploys the conventional dangerous male of the Gothic to highlight a real horror abiding within the legal system. In doing so, she alerts her perhaps-complacent readers to the dangers that are still lurking beneath the surface of a seemingly advanced society in which women seem to be protected by the law.

Yet, why conflate male danger with the supernatural two hundred years after the Enlightenment? Why reverse the movement of her precursors and risk distracting her readers with references to the supernatural? These questions are further amplified when we recognize that despite the whiff of the supernatural, Naylor is even more committed to the political realism of her text than are her predecessors, as revealed in the closure of the three texts. In Shakespeare's and Radcliffe's texts, the dangerous male is ultimately transformed into the endangered male; despite the unbounded power associated with these threatening men, each is ultimately reduced in some important way. Leontes repents immediately after Mamillius dies and spends sixteen years at Hermione's mercy, the deserving victim of the narrative that Hermione constructs as she chooses to withdraw and pretends that she is dead.[31] The impotence of Leontes's malignancy is further amplified by the denouement of the play: all the losses he has inflicted are magically restored. Hermione and Perdita return from the dead, and the truly dead Antigonus and Mamillius are replaced by their doubles: Camullus and Florizel.[32] Radcliffe's marquis is also unmanned by his author and text; he is eventually poisoned by his evil and treacherous second wife, who also dies. The family he threatens, wife and children, all survive and flourish. The paternal line of which the marquis is so proud withers: Ferdinand accepts "a command in the Neapolitan army," focusing on "promoting the happiness of his [maternal] family"(199) rather than marrying and perpetuating the Mazzini line. Nor is Radcliffe's disordering of the system of primogeniture limited to the Mazzini family (or this text—most of Radcliffe's novels end with female inheritance). Radcliffe creates a web of narratives in which the recurring theme is the disruption of the patriarchal Law of the Father, the law of primogeniture, frequently through the agency of a good brother.[33] Perhaps, even more than the ghostly tricks that are, after all, eventually explained, it is the reversal of patriarchal damage that marks *A Sicilian Romance*, like *The Winter's Tale*, as a romantic fantasy. The political realism of Naylor's text is evident in the closure of *Linden Hills*, in which Naylor deviates from the pattern of her precursors. Rather than end her text with a satisfying fantasy of restoration and female reinstatement, Naylor shows, quite plausibly, that the malignancy of the husband and father results in the destruction of his wife and child as well as himself. Why then, in this remorseless politically realistic text, add the aspect of the supernatural to the picture of male danger?

The answer to this question lies in Teresa Goddu's concept of "haunting back." Goddu develops this concept in her discussion of the way that the American Gothic "tells of the historical horrors that ... must be repressed" (10) for the project of national identity. These horrors include, of course, the horror of slavery. In her discussion of Harriet Jacobs's deployment of the Gothic to convey the horrors of slavery, Goddu asserts that a marginalized writer like Jacobs will take the strategy of "haunting back." That is, the marginalized writer, in Jacobs's case, the slave, the racial Other who is spectralized by the dominant society, will invert the model, asserting her subjectivity and her humanity and recasting the dominant and truly frightening oppressor as the inhumanly supernatural specter. Certainly Jacobs's model of inverted spectralization has sexual as well as racial relevance: her protagonist is spectralized because she is a woman as well as an African-American slave; her long imprisonment in the attic garret of her grandmother places her solidly in the tradition of marginalized women, including Gothic heroines. In relocating the supernatural from the barely visible ghostly wife, who haunts the margins of her husband's house, onto the dangerous husband, Naylor amplifies the gendered aspect of "haunting back." It is certainly appropriate that Naylor, an African-American woman writer, would deploy a strategy used to interrogate racial oppression in order to interrogate gender oppression. Thus Naylor's use of "haunting back" is not a diversion from the representation of real political problems but a strategy to invert the myths that perpetuate the oppression.

In writing of the Gothic, and anticipating the evil that the human heart would reveal in the twentieth century, Virginia Woolf says: "In our day ... it is at the ghosts within us that we shudder" (215). That is true, and much twentieth century literature written in the Gothic mode does reveal the Self as the locus of modern horror. Yet, as Gloria Naylor emphasizes, from the female perspective, the specter of the male Other who seeks to spectralize women is also frightening indeed.

Notes

1. In fact, as Coldiron suggests, not only is Leontes indicted by the play. The scene in which Polixenes interrogates Perdita shows that "Polixenes, like Leontes, suspects the woman" (52).
2. As Rosenfield notes, "*The Winter's Tale* [was] written during the height of public interest in witchcraft" (2). In fact, "Every primary female character is eventually accused of this specifically female crime" (1).
3. Richard Wilson also reminds us of the Renaissance conflict between male physicians and female midwives for control over childbirth, a conflict that the midwives ultimately lost. Richard Burt and John Michael Archer point out that the Renaissance was a time in which social power over women was being consolidated, and point to connections between "the enclosure and consolidation of land ... and the redefinition and enclosure of sexuality and the body within the symbolic order which accompanied this process" (1), and connections between "bodily enclosure and the enclosure of property" (2). They add: "The theater of ... Shakespeare played a key role in the representation of enclosure and containment" (7).
4. The play also reflects the political implications of the anxieties of the uncontained woman on the national level. As Wilson notes, "Anne Boleyn was condemned on testimony that she had been delivered of a deformed fetus, which was taken as proof of her sexual relations with five men.... In *The Winter's Tale* ... Hermione's ordeal recapitulates that of Elizabeth's mother" (134–135).
5. Rosenfield adds, "the public displays of Hernione's infidelity, invoke the format of the witch hunt" (4). When Leontes considers burning his baby girl, the supposed product of his wife's infidelity, he recalls this association.
6. Although the characters of this play are pagans and worship the classical gods, Paulina's power of creation reflects the linguistic powers of the patriarchal god of Western culture. Pauline reinforces the divine nature of her powers earlier when, in announcing Hermione's death, she tells Leontes that if he *were* able to revive Hermione (as she does in this concluding scene), she, Paulina, would "serve you as I would the gods" (3.2.227–228).
7. In *Woman and the Demon*, Nina Auerbach develops an explanation of how the idea of the woman as benevolent life-giver is transformed into the idea or woman as death-bringer.
8. Marilyn Butler develops this insight to argue that the very seeming frivolity of the Gothic is what makes it so useful for women writers: the detachment from realism and the real world frees Radcliffe to explore the very real issues of female sexuality and the female unconscious that contemporary women writers could not address in a realistic way.
9. Another possibility for Radcliffe's affinity for *The Winter's Tale*: the repugnance for witchcraft charges that she expressed in "On the Supernatural in Poetry." She calls witchcraft "that obsolete superstition which destroyed so many wretched, yet guiltless persons" (165).
10. James Ellison indicates another link between the two texts in "*The Winter's Tale* and Religious Politics." The essay argues that the play "deals with ... [the] strategic question facing English Protestantism in the early seventeenth-century: whether to offer armed support to the embattled European Protestants" (195). Not only does the play align itself with the Protestant stance; it also demonizes the Catholic presence; Ellison argues that Shakespeare sets the court of Leontes in Sicily because "Sicily was known for its succession of tyrants" (176). In Ellison's reading, then, the play aligns itself with the religious politics of Ann Radcliffe's novel (and indeed all of her

other novels and much of the English Gothic): the Italian Catholic represents irrational malevolence.

11. Recalling the succession of Elizabeth I.

12. Various critics provide explanations for Radcliffe's recurring use of the "explained supernatural." Virginia Woolf, somewhat skeptical about unrestrained Gothic excess, ironically attributes Radcliffe's explanations to her "conscience" (215). E.J. Clery suggests that the strategy allows Radcliffe to accede to the imperatives of gender: "a woman wishing to publish fiction in a supernatural vein needed to be prepared to negotiate" (106).

13. Hippolitus, her lover in hiding, observes them disputing the objectified body of Julia: "neither of the ruffians would give up his claim to the unfortunate object of their altercation" (163). Finally "the ruffians agreed to give up the lady in question to him who had fought for her and leav[e] him to his prize" (164).

14. In Blackstone's formulation:

> By marriage, the husband and wife are one person in law: that is, the very being or legal existence of the woman is suspended during the marriage, or at least is incorporated and consolidated into that of the husband: under whose wing, protection, and *cover* she performs everything; and is therefore called in our law-french, a *feme-covert*, *foemina viro co-operta*; and is said to be *covert-baron*, or under the protection and influence of her husband, her *baron*, or lord; and her condition during her marriage is called her *coverture* [1: 442].

15. Under coverture, not only does the husband have full control over the wife, as discussed above, additionally, "the father had the absolute right to custody of the children; the mother had no rights at all" (Holcombe 33). Joan Perkin adds, "The legal custody of children belonged to the father. During the lifetime of a sane father, the mother had no rights over her children ... and the father could take them from her and dispose of them as he thought fit" (14–15). Joan Perkin cites instances of fathers appropriating their children that are as horrifying to read as any Gothic novel.

16. The passage is curiously echoed in the slave narrative *Incidents in the Life of a Slave Girl* by Harriet Jacobs, an instance of Jacobs appropriating the strategies of popular literature to lend power to her autobiographical narrative.

17. As Amy Erickson points out, this also effectively limited a woman's ability to accumulate wealth since "land was the basis of wealth in an agricultural society" (18).

18. Concerns regarding inheritance of property, particularly inheritance by women, are evident in *A Sicilian Romance* as in all of Radcliffe's novels. The possession and appropriation of physical space in the form of real estate is an early preoccupation of this novel; before Julia is completely ejected from the castle there is much interfamilial maneuvering for space. Early in the narrative, Julia stakes out her own territory in "a small closet" adjacent to her room, within her father's castle. Within this room (a room that anticipates Woolf's "room of her own"), Julia safeguards "her favorite authors" and "her musical instruments" (5). This closet is later the site of the declaration of love by Hippolitus, who demonstrates his worthiness by apologizing for invading Julia's space: "forgive this intrusion, so unintentional" (51). The malignancy of Julia's presumed stepmother becomes apparent when the marchioness appropriates her stepdaughters' space: she claims "the chambers of Emilia and Julia" and leaves to "Julia only her favorite closet" (27).

19. Dickensen adds that during the Middle Ages "women's economic activity and autonomy were substantial.... In the long run, the transfer of production from home to factory made the economic contribution of women appear less significant.... Women were restricted from public participation and civil rights.... The English property codes ... gave the husband all control over his wife's property and earnings. ... as *The Lawes Resolutions of Women Rights, or the Lawes Provision for Women* (1632) enunciated in the seventeenth-century doctrine: 'That which the husband hath is his own ... that which the wife hath is the husband's.' The situation of married women was worse in England and America during Locke's time ... than on the Continent ...

because of the way the common law developed.... A married woman was effectively dead at law" (81–83).

20. Clery adds, "the legal provisions for the maintenance of landed inheritance were actually strengthened in the eighteenth century, notably by introduction of the device of 'strict settlement'" (76).

21. John Moore provides a useful summary of the contexts of *Linden Hills*: "Critics have closely examined some of these intertexts, especially Dante's *Inferno* (Ward), Plato's *Allegory of the Cave* (Houmans), Virgil's *Aeneid* (Ward, Saunders), and the Gothic novel (Sandiford)" (1410). Moore himself adds the Bible, the fairy tale, the epic and the Romance to this list. Yet although Sandiford does locate the Gothic novel as an influence of *Linden Hills*, he only briefly names Beckford's *Vathek* and mostly speaks in general terms of "the gothic vision" (137) in Naylor's novel.

22. It is also useful and important to note the debt of Naylor's novel to Lewis's *The Monk*. Like Lewis's nun, Agnes, Naylor's protagonist is immured in a subterranean space with the body of her dead child.

23. Naylor names the fictional setting of *Mama Day* Willow Springs, invoking the initials of William Shakespeare's name. Naylor quite clearly alludes to *Hamlet*, *King Lear* and *The Tempest* in the novel.

24. Wilson quotes Louis Montrose: the Shakespearean drama often "frets over 'the physical link between a particular man and child.' ... Aggravating this anxiety ... is that 'what we call the facts of life have been established as *facts* only recently.... Although maternity was apparent, paternity was a cultural construct for which ocular proof was unattainable" (127–8). Coldiron adds that this anxiety was heightened by the material implications of maternal infidelity: in early modern times the "pregnant body was a magnet for masculine fears, particularly fears of cuckoldry based in inheritance law. Legitimate children of a legal marriage inherited property.... [I]n a patrilineal economy and before DNA testing, concerns about paternity, cuckoldry, and inheritance turn the pregnant wife's body into a magnetic, swelling question mark" (Coldiron 33–34).

25. The joking conjecture of two characters, who notice the absence of the wife and hear her cries, emphasizes the horror embedded in contemporary marriage. They laughingly say, "Maybe old Nedeed's down there embalming someone who wasn't quite ready" (42), and "Maybe he's got her roped to his bed for safekeeping" (153). That this seemingly far-fetched conjecture is close to the truth highlights the reality that Gothic horror is alive and well in the American domestic setting.

26. In fact, as Kimberly A. Costino notes in "Weapons Against Women: Compulsory Heterosexuality and Capitalism in *Linden Hills*," part of Luther's villainy is that he imposes the model of heterosexual marriage not only upon his own wife but upon all the inhabitants of Linden Hills, usually with tragic results for those who accede to his demands. Thus a female tenant who is being evicted because she cannot live in Linden Hills without a husband accuses Luther of "telling me that I don't exist. That *I* don't live in this house" (245). Then she kills herself, enacting another conventional method of female self-erasure.

27. Deborah Willis notes that "The revelation of the witch's teat was usually among the last pieces of evidence to be entered against the accused woman.... [T]he witches' teat is an *extra* one" (113), expressing the fear of super-natural female maternal power.

28. Another way of reading this surname is as an anagram of "needed." All the Luther Nedeeds focus upon their needs, their appetites, rather than considering the subjectivity of their wives and the members of their community.

29. "The peculiar English system of coverture was taken to extremes in the American colonies, particularly the northern colonies" (Erickson 233). Winston E. Langley and Vivian C. Fox note the continuing influence of English common law on the American legal system: "English settlers brought with them to the American colonies the common law system.... [T]he *Commentaries* of William Blackstone ... became the ... primary reference on women's position throughout the nineteenth century" (6–7).

30. By the 1830s and 1840s (decades before parallel changes in England) the situ-

ation for American women was improving: "the legal fiction of marital unity began to undergo modification through the enactment of married women's property acts, which allowed married women to keep their property in their own name" (Langley and Fox 80–1). The nineteenth century change in the status of women included "greater control over their inheritances from their fathers and husbands ... new rights to manage what was now stipulated as their property (Brown 108).

31. As Cristina Alfar recognizes, "Hermione rejects Leontes when, in his tyranny he disregards the oracle's pronouncement of his wife's innocence.... [S]he departs from the play's action, independent of any patriarchal judgment; and it is she who returns, deliberately, when her daughter is found living" (163). Leontes's reversal is amplified by the death of Antigonus, also a husband—to Paulina—who is eaten by a bear as he is fulfilling Leontes's sentence upon his own daughter: abandoning her in Bohemia.

32. Camullus marries Antigonus's wife, Paulina, and Leontes recognizes Florizel as standing in the stead of his son. Seeing Florizel and his restored Perdita together, Leontes says: "I lost a couple that 'twixt heaven and earth / Might thus have stood begetting wonder, as / You, gracious couple, do" (5.1.160).

33. Julia learns from Hippolutus's sister, Cornelia, that he "desired to resign [to Cornelia] a part of this estate which had already descended to him in right of his mother" (120), representing thus a double disruption of the patrilineal line. Another instance of maternal transmission of property is located in Louisa's biography: she had been the only heir of her father after her brother and mother were killed in an eruption of Mount Etna. Yet another instance of female inheritance of property occurs when Madame de Menon's husband's property is restored to her. The estate was originally usurped because her husband "died without a will, and his brothers refused to give up his estate, unless I could produce a witness of my marriage" (33). The return of her friend Louisa to the world affords Madame de Menon such proof and her property is restored—a subversive, if fantastic, instance of male appropriation of property being countered by the power of the female word.

Works Cited

Adelman, Janet. "Masculine Authority and the Maternal Body in *The Winter's Tale.*" In *Shakespeare's Romances,* 145–170. New Casebook Series, ed. Alison Thorne. New York: Palgrave Macmillan, 2003.

Alfar, Cristina León. *Fantasies of Female Evil: The Dynamics of Gender and Power in Shakespearean Tragedy.* Newark: University of Delaware Press, 2003.

Auerbach, Nina. *Woman and the Demon: The Life of a Victorian Myth.* Cambridge: Harvard University Press, 1984.

Blackstone, William. *Commentaries on the Laws of England.* Vol. 1. Philadelphia: Rees Welsh, 1897.

Brown, Laura. *Ends of Empire: Women and Ideology in Early Eighteenth-Century English Literature.* Ithaca: Cornell University Press, 1993.

Burt, Richard and John Michael Archer, eds. *Enclosure Acts: Sexuality, Property and Culture in Early Modern England.* Ithaca: Cornell University Press, 1994.

Butler, Marilyn. "The Woman at the Window: Ann Radcliffe in the Novels of Mary Wollstonecraft and Jane Austen." In *Gender and Literary Voice,* ed. Janet Todd, 128–148. New York: Holmes and Meier, 1980.

Clery, E.J. *The Rise of Supernatural Fiction.* Cambridge: Cambridge University Press, 1995.

Coldiron, A.E.B. "'Tis Rigor and Not Law': Trials of Women as Trials of Patriarchy in *The Winter's Tale.*" In *Renaissance Papers,* ed. Christopher Cobb and M. Thomas Hester, 29–68. Raleigh, NC: The Southeastern Renaissance Conference, 2004.

Costino, Kimberly A. "'Weapons Against Women': Compulsory Heterosexuality and Capitalism in *Linden Hills.*" In *Gloria Naylor's Early Novels,* 39–54. Gainesville: University Press of Florida, 1999.

Dickenson, Donna. *Property, Women and Politics: Subjects or Objects?* New Brunswick: Rutgers University Press, 1997.
Ellison, James. "*The Winter's Tale* and the Religious Politics of Europe." In *Shakespeare's Romances,* 171–204. New Casebook Series, ed. Alison Thorne. New York: Palgrave Macmillan, 2003.
Erickson, Amy Louise. *Women and Property in Early Modern England.* New York: Routledge, 1993.
Gates, Henry Louis, Jr. *The Signifying Monkey: A Theory of Afro-American Literary Criticism.* New York: Oxford University Press, 1988.
Goddu, Teresa A. *Gothic America: Narrative, History, and Nation.* New York: Columbia University Press, 1997.
Holcombe, Lee. *Wives and Property: Reform of the Married Women's Property Law in Nineteenth-Century England.* Toronto: University of Toronto Press, 1983.
Kerber, Linda K. *No Constitutional Right to Be Ladies: Women and the Obligations of Citizenship.* New York: Hill and Wang, 1998.
Langley, Winston E. and Vivian C. Fox, eds. *Women's Rights in the United States: A Documentary History.* Westport, CT: Praeger, 1994.
Moore, John Noell. "Myth, Fairy Tale, Epic, and Romance: Narrative as RE-vision in *Linden Hills. Callaloo* 23.4 (2000): 1410–1429.
Naylor, Gloria. *Linden Hills.* New York: Penguin, 1986.
Perkin, Joan. *Women and Marriage in Nineteenth-Century England.* Chicago: Lyceum, 1989.
Radcliffe, Ann. "On the Supernatural in Poetry." In *Gothic Documents: A Sourcebook, 1700–1820,* ed. E.J. Clery and Robert Miles, 163–172. Manchester: Manchester University Press, 2000.
_____. *A Sicilian Romance.* Oxford: Oxford University Press, 1993.
Rosenfield, Kirstie Gulick. "Nursing Nothing: Witchcraft and Female Sexuality in *The Winter's Tale.*" *Mosaic* 35.1 (March 2002): 95–103. http://proquest.umi.com, 1–10.
Sandiford, K.A. "Gothic and Intertextual Constructions in *Linden Hills.*" *Arizona Quarterly* 47.3 (Autumn 1991): 117–139.
Saunders, James Robert. "The Ornamentation of Old Ideas: Gloria Naylor's First Three Novels." *The Hollins Critic* 27.2 (April 1990): 1–11.
Shakespeare, William. *The Winter's Tale.* Folger Shakespeare Library, ed. Barbara A. Mowat and Paul Werstine. New York: Washington Square Press, 2005.
Walpole, Horace. *The Castle of Otranto.* New York: Oxford University Press, 1982.
Willis, Deborah. "Shakespeare and the English Witch-Hunts: Enclosing the Maternal Body." In *Enclosure Acts,* ed. Richard Burt and John Michael Archer, 96–120. Ithaca: Cornell University Press, 1994.
Wilson, Richard. "Observations on English Bodies: Licensing Maternity in Shakespeare's Later Plays." In *Enclosure Acts,* ed. Richard Burt and John Michael Archer, 121–150. Ithaca: Cornell University Press, 1994.
Woolf, Virginia. "Gothic Romance." In *The Critical Response to Ann Radcliffe,* ed. Deborah D. Rogers, 214–251. Westport, CT: Greenwood Press, 1994.

6

Sexual or Supernatural: Threats in Radcliffe's The Italian

ELIZABETH HARLAN

Gothic novels of the eighteenth and nineteenth centuries typically contain a plethora of supernatural events and characters. Supernatural monsters are common, from the vampires in Le Fanu's *Carmilla* and Bram Stoker's *Dracula* to Mary Shelley's man-made horror in *Frankenstein* to Robert Louis Stevenson's treacherous Mr. Hyde. The Devil and his assistants are among the villains in Matthew Gregory Lewis's *The Monk*, which also contains the ancient Wandering Jew and the specter of the Bleeding Nun. However, this is not the case in the works of Ann Radcliffe, who is "not, strictly speaking ... a supernatural writer at all" (Cavaliero 26).[1] Rather, "Radcliffe explained the supernatural as the product of natural causes" (Miles "Ann Radcliffe" 41). Though *The Italian* (1797), Radcliffe's final work, is a Gothic novel and hints of the mystical and uncanny abound, there is actually nothing supernatural at all in the novel. Mysterious apparitions appear and disappear, deliver foreboding messages, leave trails of blood, and do all that they can to incite superstition, but these instances are entirely explained away as, for example, when the reader learns that the hero, Vincentio di Vivaldi, is not visited by a ghost in his cell in the Inquisition, but by the completely human monk Nicola di Zampari using secret passages. Likewise, an injured Zampari is the cause of the frightening blood trail, and it is he, not a ghost or something superhuman, who locks Vivaldi and his servant Paulo in a ruined chamber. In Radcliffe's novel, then, the supposed supernatural is merely the result of human motives and behavior.

In delineating her villain, Schedoni, as a Catholic priest, Radcliffe elaborates on her dismissal of the supernatural; she presents the mystifying and quasi-supernatural powers of the Catholic Church only to negate their potency. For the primarily English Protestant readers of the novel, Radcliffe's intended audience, Schedoni represents the Other in a variety ways that would not be recognizable to Schedoni's victims within the novel. His dark Italian foreignness (he is set up by the framed narrative as *the* Italian referenced in the title) and his position as a representative of the Catholic Church (Schmitt 861) link him to much that is mysteriously dangerous in the mind of the late eighteenth century English reader. Yet, although Schedoni, the Catholic Italian, is supported by fearsome institutions like the convent of San Stefano and the Inquisition, the Church is always thwarted in its evil plots. Ellena is able to escape the convent and her punishment for refusing to become a nun. Although Vivaldi is constantly threatened with torture as he is imprisoned by the Inquisition, and indeed even hears the sound of others being tormented, these threats are never carried out. The inquisitors listen to his accusations concerning Schedoni, investigate them, then the guilty are punished and Vivaldi is freed. Radcliffe thus explains away the dangers of the Catholic Church much as she explains away supernatural danger.

As Radcliffe diminishes the power of all the mysterious and supernatural sources of fear and anxiety in her novel, the only remaining cause for terror is the threat of sexual assault posed by the sexual predator, as mysterious and inhuman in motivation and behavior as the supernatural specters of other Gothic novels. The ominous presence of the treacherous and sexually threatening monk Schedoni, whose evocation of dread is most prominent when his aims are sexualized, is the true source of danger. Schedoni's strange sexuality identifies him as an Other, a character whose subjectivity is inexplicable both to the readers of the novel and to the other characters. This monk is filled with "passion": "There was something in his physiognomy extremely singular, and that can not easily be defined. It bore the traces of many passions" (35). We soon learn that Schedoni's passions are not all of the theological sort as he is frequently depicted leering at or caressing the women in the novel.[2]

On the surface, Schedoni's motives might seem to be either ambition or pride, associated with the hierarchy of the Catholic Church. He works tirelessly to advance himself by helping the Marchesa to prevent the marriage of her son, Vincentio di Vivaldi, to Ellena, whom the Marchesa believes is both socially and financially beneath her family. Such a wealthy and influential benefactress as the Marchesa could help Schedoni equalize his position amongst his peers: he has watched many of his fellow monks rise above him within the Church, though his own demonstrations of piety are unequaled. However, soon after the duo's machinations begin, Schedoni's motivation is revealed: he must conceal his secret sexual past as a sexual predator, which he believes that Vivaldi knows and will reveal.

Ansaldo, the confessor, ultimately and agonizingly reveals to the officials of the Inquisition what Schedoni told him:

> "I have been through life ... the slave of my passions, and they have led me into horrible excesses. I had once a brother! ... That brother had a wife! ... She was beautiful—I loved her; she was virtuous, and I despaired.... It overcame or communicated its own force to every other passion of my soul, and I sought to release myself from its tortures by any means. My brother died! ... Father, I was his murderer!" [339].

In fact, because of his quasi-incestuous sexual desire for his older brother's wife, Schedoni has resorted to murder and subsequently informed the confessor that after the widow refused his offer of marriage, she was forced to accept it in order to "retrieve her honor" (340), strongly implying that Schedoni raped her. His horrifying sexual treachery continued when, wrongly suspecting that his wife was adulterous, Schedoni stabbed her, believing her dead, which ultimately led to his decision to become a monk to conceal his identity.

Thus even when Schedoni threatens a character with death, the motivation has an underlying sexual cause. For instance, jealous of his brother, Olivia's husband, Schedoni had him killed. Later, afraid of Ellena's betrothed, Vivaldi, and the secrets he believes that Vivaldi could reveal, Schedoni has him imprisoned by the Inquisition. Although the threat he provides to men is not overtly sexual, it is still motivated by sexuality. Conversely, when Schedoni attempts to murder Ellena, to placate the murderous rage of the Marchesa, his assault takes the form of an encoded rape. He approaches the sleeping Ellena with his phallic knife poised. After he sneaks into her room, ready to stab a sleeping Ellena, "he again drew near, and prepared to strike. Her dress perplexed him; it would interrupt the blow, and he stooped to examine whether he could turn her robe aside, without waking her.... vengeance nerved his arm, and drawing aside the lawn from her bosom, he once more raised it to strike" (234). At this time, Ellena is asleep and clad in a fine linen gown. It is difficult to imagine what could be perplexing about her dress and how it could possibly interfere with a dagger, particularly one dipped in a deadly poison, as Schedoni's is. Though Schedoni is indeed considerably anxious at his moment, it seems as if his anxiety is surpassed by his desire to disrobe Ellena, an obviously unnecessary ploy before stabbing her. Ultimately, a miniature portrait Ellena is wearing causes him to incorrectly surmise that she is his daughter and this halts his attempt at murder.[3] However, while Schedoni is still under this delusion, he holds her tightly "to his bosom" (237) as she, still confused and afraid, struggles "to permit his caresses without trembling" (238). Thus the layer of potential incest is added to the threat of rape, amplifying the sexual nature of Ellena's danger.

In the world of Radcliffe's novel, even the threat posed by the older powerful woman to the young woman is couched in sexual terms: the Marchesa di Vivaldi is also presented as a source of sexual danger to Ellena. Although she is a woman, Radcliffe portrays her as desiring male power; Schedoni, her confessor and advisor, villainously manipulates the Marchesa's desire. This plays out in many conversations that "are masterpieces of mutual guilt and hypocrisy" (Aers et. al. 109). For example, as he attempts to cajole her into authorizing the assassination of Ellena, Schedoni plays upon the Marchesa's desire to be more masculine, as he declares: "Though the law of justice demands the death of this girl, yet because the law of the land forbears to enforce it, you, my daughter, even you! though possessed of a man's spirit, and his clear perceptions, would think that virtue bade her live, when it was only fear" (168). The Marchesa's masculine spirit is hampered because, as she claims, "some woman's weakness still lingers at my heart" (169). They ultimately "verbally dance around the marchesa's desire not only to have Ellena ... killed but to have Schedoni do the deed himself" (Hoeveler 113).[4]

Moreover, the threat the marchesa poses to Ellena is sexual. Unable to successfully maintain her masculine, patriarchal role by forbidding her son's marriage, the marchesa attempts to assert her control of Ellena by controlling her sexual activity. In this, the masculinized marchesa is aided by yet another woman, the abbess. Ellena, held captive in a convent, is given a choice. As explained to Ellena by the abbess, the "generous" marchesa "allows you to enter into our society; or, if you have not strength of mind sufficient to enable you to renounce a sinful world, she permits you to return into it, and gives you a suitable partner to support you through its cares and toils,—a partner much more suitable to your circumstances" (Radcliffe 83). Not able to sexually invade her as a man would, and not able to succeed in a father's typical role and control her own child, the marchesa resorts to trying to determine Ellena's sexual future.

The ability to discern the nature of danger is one important way in which Radcliffe distinguishes between her hero and her heroine, and promotes the superiority of her heroine. Vivaldi consistently misidentifies danger as having supernatural origins; while Ellena quite correctly realizes that the source of danger is the sexually exploitative male. For example, even when he is in the midst of the very real threat of being imprisoned by the Inquisition, Vivaldi, who often believes he is in the presence of ghosts or other otherworldly emissaries, misattributes the appearance of a monk in his cell to a supernatural cause. In fact, Schedoni promotes and capitalizes upon the misguided belief in the supernatural, exhibited by Vivaldi, to pursue his sexually exploitative aims. He has likely learned this skill from his fellow monks, who are accustomed "to excite the superstitious wonder of the devotees" (138), a strategy similar to that used by Ann Radcliffe herself. This strategy characterizes his behavior towards Vivaldi, against whom Schedoni consistently uses superstition in his plot to destroy the young man in order to protect his sexual history. As Schedoni admits to Vivaldi when confessing that he was behind Nicola's ominous warnings, "I trusted more to the impression of awe, which the conduct and seeming foreknowledge of that stranger were adapted to inspire in a mind like your's [sic]; and I thus endeavoured to avail myself of your prevailing weakness.... A susceptibility which renders you especially liable to superstition" (397). Schedoni thus has encouraged Nicola's mysterious behavior in order to distract Vivaldi from the planned abduction of Ellena. Superstition is thus a veil behind which Schedoni is able to hide his true sexual threat from those unable to discern reality.

Ellena, however, is able to penetrate the veil of danger that surrounds her, much as she ultimately penetrates the mystery of the veil over the wax *memento mori*. Ellena's great fear of Schedoni, as well as the threatening aura inherent in the monk, is evident upon their first encounter. They meet while walking on the beach, as Ellena is contemplating an escape from her captor, Spalatro. Initially, when she sees Schedoni from afar and only notes his monk's attire, she has hopes that he may be able to protect her. However, moving closer, "she perceived his large eyes looking from under the shade of his cowl, and the upper part of his peculiar countenance" (220). Schedoni's inhumanly sinister nature and dangerous passions are recognized as soon as Ellena sees his face and feels the power of his penetrating phallic eyes. Ellena's immediate and acute ability to identify her danger is demonstrated in her initial collapse when she sees Schedoni. It is to Ellena's credit that she recognizes the correct source of danger, the sexual predator. Although for all of Radcliffe's characters terror depends upon "the imaginative power of the half-seen and half-explained" (Aers et. al. 110), the characters distinguish themselves in the way they interpret this terror. Unlike the misguided Vivaldi, Ellena never exhibits any fear of supernatural threats. As in the case of Radcliffe's other heroines, Ellena's challenge is the challenge of interpretation, sensing suspicious phenomena that she needs to interpret: "Radcliffe's heroines hear breathing, see something move, discern a shape indistinctly" (DeLamotte 43). For Ellena, mysterious phenomena always signify a human threat. Where Vivaldi imagines specters, Ellena knows there is a man.

The perceptive recognition of this message elevates Radcliffe's heroine. Ellena di Rosalba encounters a myriad of human obstacles and physical dangers, which she recognizes are not in any way supernatural. Radcliffe and Ellena realize that an assault upon a woman's virtue and an attempt to control her sexuality (and thereby her property) are far more frightening than anything otherworldly; thus for Radcliffe's women, the "most fundamental anxiety [... is] fear of physical violation" (DeLamotte 29). As the situation of Ellena's mother demonstrates, rape is not a romantic episode, nor is it simply an attack that affects a woman's physical and emotional well being. Her social standing was undermined as well: Olivia was forced to marry her rapist in order to "retrieve her honor" (340). Thus Radcliffe emphasizes Schedoni's threat to both mother[5] and daughter. The threat of sexual assault that he poses is far more dangerous than a supernatural manifestation.

This is precisely because of the existence of something more terrifying than ghosts in Radcliffe's time: the threat of sexual violation. In her early and influential work, *Against Our Will: Men, Women and Rape* (1975), Susan Brownmiller reminds us that the Gothic tendency to romanticize rape glossed over a brutal reality: "Gothic literature has made heiress stealing a subject of great romance, replete with midnight assignations, loyal maidservants and a great thundering of horse's hooves, but in actuality it was predicated on the desire for land, not love" (16). That is, if a rapist could convince the victim to retrieve her honor by marrying him, he would come into possession of all her property, under English common law. The perceptive Gothic heroine (like Ellena), and reader, was the one who recognized that rape had nothing to do with love and that it represented a threat to the personal integrity as well as the property of the victim. Interestingly contemporary slang hinted at this reality: Anna Clark writes that in the eighteenth century, "'commodity' [was] the slang word for female genitalia" (32).

Anthony Simpson presents a compelling case for the foregrounding of rape in the minds of readers and writers of the Gothic in the late eighteenth century. Indeed, the threat or execution of rape is a common motif in eighteenth century novels, seen also in Samuel Richardson's *Pamela* and *Clarissa*, Henry Fielding's *Joseph Andrews*, and Lewis's *The Monk*, to name just a few. Simpson writes of the "sensational" (3) trial of Francis Charteris in February 1730. The trial of Charteris was, according to Simpson, "the media event of the decade, and one of the most famous criminal cases of the century" (2). Simpson mentions several instances in which the character of Charteris emerges in literature and art, identifying him as the model for the rake in Hogarth's "The Harlot's Progress" (1732). As Hogarth's prints were "immensely popular" (2), they extended the influence of the figure of Charteris. Simpson indicates that both Pope and Swift referred to him as an "exemplar of venality and excess among the privileged" (2).

Anna Clark's history of rape in the eighteenth century further explains the prevalence of this theme in literature. According to Clark, in the eighteenth century rape was justified through "the Enlightenment elevation of nature" which supported "the libertine philosophy of taking pleasure at every turn" (34). In fact, Clark contends that "scandalous rape trials provided titillating reading for literate wealthy men" (35). In these texts, Clark asserts, Charteris and his fellows were depicted as "'heroic rapists'" (35). And yet, as Clark demonstrates, there were no counter arguments in the public discourse, warning young women of the dangers and miseries of rape: "there is little or no evidence for such warnings in court records [or] newspapers," nothing to counter "the libertine pamphlet literature [that] presented rape as titillating to men" (43). Moreover, "rape was not publicized as a warning to women because so many men seemed to regard rape as a trivial issue" (44). Hence the utility of Radcliffe's novels and the other novels warning young readers of the dangers of rape, reminding those readers that rape and romance are not one and the same even though the handsome rapist might exhibit some superficial allure. Charteris, the "heroic rapist," may thus be seen as the archetype for the attractive and aristocratic rapist who haunts the Radcliffean text, including Schedoni and the even more famous Montoni of *The Mysteries of Udolpho*. But as Radcliffe, shows, these potential rapists are no heroes. The message that emerges in her texts is that the sexual violation on the part of a handsome aristocratic is a source of danger, not romance, to a young woman. She reminds her readers to remain undistracted by supernatural effects and to stay focused on the dangers of the natural world.

Yet paradoxically, Schedoni, the sexual Other, is not monolithically evil. As he gazes at an unconscious Ellena and attempts to revive her, he struggles with a battle between his passions, one of which *might* be compassion: "The conflict between his design and his conscience was strong, or, perhaps, it was only between his passions" (223). His desire for vengeance wages war with his sexual attraction to Ellena and both wage war with his better nature. He finds it difficult to behold "the innocent, the wretched Ellena, without yielding to the momentary weakness, as he termed it, of compassion" (223). While Schedoni can blithely separate the young lovers, have his brother murdered, stab his wife in a jealous rage, arrange to have Vivaldi imprisoned in the Inquisition and Ellena held captive in a convent, when he is actually forced to face his victim in the form of a beautiful and "fascinating young woman" (228), he actually exhibits a conscience. Thus, while Radcliffe presents Schedoni, the sexual Other, as dangerous and threatening, she also portrays some surprising sympathy in him. When Ellena is at her most defenseless, he is unable to harm her. Additionally, when believing her to be his daughter, he is anxious to help her win Vivaldi (though, of course, his own ambition is involved in this attempt) and to maintain his fatherly image by preventing her from learning of any of his past misdeeds. Because

Schedoni is, in the end, a man, no matter how monstrous, he cannot be entirely bad. In this it is possible to see the hopeful nature of Radcliffe's explained supernatural. As long as the source of evil is human there is always some hope of redemption.

Notes

1. Radcliffe is widely acknowledged as a pre-eminent author, not only of her particular genre, but also of the late eighteenth century. She was "the dominant novelist of the decade, certainly as far as commercial success is concerned—and for many readers critically too" (Miles, "1790s" 45). Furthermore, she is one of the earliest, as well as one of the most prolific, writers in the genre. While other Gothic pioneers like Horace Walpole and Matthew Gregory Lewis produced only a single novel each, Radcliffe wrote throughout the decade and produced several extraordinarily popular works: "To a very real extent 1790s Gothic writing happened in her shadow" (Miles, "1790s" 45).

2. Overall, according to an early reviewer, "his boldness and barbarity are equal to any purpose which villainy and ambition could project" (qtd. in Rogers 51).

3. In fact, she is the daughter of Schedoni's presumed dead wife, Olivia, and his murdered brother; the daughter of Schedoni and Olivia has died.

4. Even her behavior with her son demonstrates her more masculine, paternal relationship with him. She simply does not act like a mother, but rather like a father. "Throughout history and across cultures it is generally the father who sells the daughter in exchange for economic and political power among men. The Marchesa's assumption that she has the right to control her son's sexual behavior subverts this arrangement" (Greenfield 62). The marchesa is upending patriarchal society, taking her husband's role, and attempting to be the parent who makes marital decisions for the child. She is thus not only taking on the role of the father, but also placing Vincentio di Vivaldi in that of the daughter. These scenes, written in 1797 and occurring in 1758, emphasize the eighteenth century tendency to attribute the qualities of strength, courage, and rationality to men, while attributing emotions like compassion to women. Yet as Mary Wollstonecraft asserts in *A Vindication of the Rights of Woman* (1792), eighteenth century women were not taught to use their minds, and thus relied solely on their emotions; the differences thus were not inherent but based on educational practices. Interestingly, Radcliffe accentuates the masculine nature of the marchesa and rarely shows her in the traditional roles of wife and mother. Her very few encounters with her son quickly dissolve into dictatorial tirades over his choice of a bride. No encounter with her husband is directly shown in the novel. The one that is discussed by a few characters near the close of the novel does not occur until she requests to see him in a moment of deathbed repentance. Until her final moments are approaching, the marchesa seems far more comfortable in the masculine role of avenger than with that of the feminine nurturer.

5. This is a typical situation in Gothic novels, one likely originated by Radcliffe. "Almost always a victim of patriarchal violence and sexuality, the mother is usually missing or dead; she is a horrific symbol of the fate that may await the daughter when she becomes sexual" (Greenfield 58). Before Ellena has any sexual feelings, she is safe from the likes of Schedoni. However, Olivia is a perfect example of what Ellena has to fear when she enters the world of love and sexuality: Schedoni. Once Ellena falls in love with Vivaldi, she becomes an appropriate victim for a sexual predator like Schedoni. Mother and daughter share the same potential fate of a loved one being torn away and the threat of violation.

Works Cited

Aers, David, Jonathan Cook, and David Punter. *Romanticism and Ideology: Studies in English Writing 1765–1830*. London: Routledge and Kegan Paul, 1981.
Birkhead, Edith. "'The Novel of Suspense': Mrs. Radcliffe." In *The Critical Response to Ann Radcliffe*, ed. Deborah C. Rogers, 206–214. Westport, CT: Greenwood Press, 1994.
Brissenden, R.F. *Virtue in Distress: Studies in the Novel of Sentiment from Richardson to Sade*. London: Macmillan, 1974.
Brownmiller, Susan. *Against Our Will: Men, Women and Rape*. New York: Bantam, 1976.
Cavaliero, Glen. *The Supernatural and English Fiction*. Oxford: Oxford University Press, 1995.
Clark, Anna. *Women's Silence; Men's Violence: Sexual Assault in England 1770–1845*. New York: Pandora, 1987.
DeLamotte, Eugenia C. *Perils of the Night: A Feminist Study of the Nineteenth-Century Gothic*. Oxford: Oxford University Press, 1990.
Greenfield, Susan. "Veiled Desire: Mother-Daughter Love and Sexual Imagery in Ann Radcliffe's *The Italian*." In *The Critical Response to Ann Radcliffe*, ed. Deborah C. Rogers, 57–70. Westport, CT: Greenwood Press, 1994.
Hoeveler, Diane Long. *Gothic Feminism: The Professionalization of Gender from Charlotte Smith to the Brontës*. University Park: Pennsylvania State University Press, 1997.
Miles, Robert. "Ann Radcliffe and Matthew Lewis." *A Companion to the Gothic*, ed. David Punter. Oxford: Blackwell, 2000. 41–57.
_____. "The 1790s: The Effulgence of Gothic." In *The Cambridge Companion to Gothic Fiction*, ed. Jerrold E. Hogle, 41–62. Cambridge: Cambridge University Press, 2002.
Punter, David. *The Literature of Terror: A History of Gothic Fiction from 1765 to the Present Day*. Vol. 2 of *The Modern Gothic*. New York: Addison Wesley Longman, 1996.
Radcliffe, Ann. *The Italian*. Oxford: Oxford University Press, 1998.
Schmitt, Cannon. "Techniques of Terror, Technologies of Nationality: Ann Radcliffe's *The Italian*." *ELH* 64.1 (1994): 853–876.
Simpson, Antony E. "Popular Perceptions of Rape as a Capital Crime in Eighteenth-Century England: The Press and the Trial of Francis Charteris in the Old Bailey, February 1730." *Law and History Review* 22 (Spring 2004): 27–70. www.historycooperative.org, 1–31.
Rogers, Deborah C. *The Critical Response to Ann Radcliffe*. Westport, CT: Greenwood Press, 1994.

7
Investigating the Third Story: "Bluebeard" and "Cinderella" in Jane Eyre

VICTORIA ANDERSON

> *I, by dint of groping, found the outlet from the attic, and proceeded to descend the narrow garret staircase. I lingered in the long passage to which this led, separating the front and back rooms of the third story—narrow, low and dim, with only one little window at the far end, and looking, with its two rows of small black doors all shut, like a corridor in some Bluebeard's castle.*
>
> —Charlotte Brontë, *Jane Eyre*

"Among its other distinctions," writes John Sutherland, "*Jane Eyre* can claim to be the first adult, non-burlesque treatment of the Bluebeard theme in English Literature" (314). Quite so. Wives incarcerated in secret rooms in the bowels of rambling mansions are precisely the stuff of "Bluebeard," of which breed of men Edward Fairfax Rochester proves himself a fine specimen. In fact, there can be no denying the close correlation between "Bluebeard" and the general trajectory of the Gothic novel, from *The Mysteries of Udolpho* to *The Turn of the Screw* and beyond.

The eighteenth century marked a decisive shift from oral to print culture, whereupon print was suddenly distributed to a mass audience— not just as novels, but in chapbooks, as well. Chapbooks contained "real-life" stories not dissimilar from our contemporary tabloids and scandal sheets, but also English (Scottish, Irish) ballads, fairy tales (often derived from literary versions which chiefly originated in aristocratic France) and, by the latter half of the century, much-abridged popular novels. Thus the enormous distinction which our contemporary culture makes between novels and fairy tales (which we identify as simple children's tales on a par with nonsense rhymes) was not present in eighteenth century Britain, when oral tradition was still in existence, diminishing, certainly, with the onward march of print, but alive nonetheless. Furthermore, despite our twenty-first century conception of fairy tales as being profoundly unfeminist, it was only when fairy tales began to be widely disseminated in print that the heroines became uniformly vapid. Tales that preceded and, in remote communities, eluded print domination (which tales were, fortunately, to some degree preserved by nineteenth century folklorists), more often than not present a female protagonist as actively combating obstacles and assailants, rather than waiting passively to be saved by a man. Since the passive femininity with which we often associate fairy tales is typically confined to its printed manifestations, when British women began to write novels in the eighteenth century, the only model for female heroics upon which they could reasonably draw was that of fairy tale and oral culture.[1]

The tale that we know as "Bluebeard" was written by Charles Perrault and included in his 1695 collection of Mother Goose Tales: *Histoires ou Contes de Temps Passé*. The story runs thus: a young woman is courted by an ugly man with a blue beard; his wealth induces her to accept his proposal. One day he forbids her to enter one particular chamber; as soon as he has left the house she tries the door and finds, to her horror, a bloody chamber full of the corpses of women. On Bluebeard's return he is enraged by her transgression and prepares to kill her; she asks for a moment or two to say her prayers, and in the time gained her brothers fortuitously turn up and save her.

Versions of similar tales long pre-existed Perrault's, circulating orally.[2] Although the tales vary, there is almost always a "forbidden chamber" sequence; if there is no specific chamber in which dead bodies are sequestered, the girl spies on the murderer from a concealed spot and establishes his criminal intent. In fact, all the conjoined props that would come to be identified as Gothic (the mansion, the secret chamber, the murderous patriarch, our goodly heroine) pre-existed the Gothic in tales of the "Bluebeard" type. Through all the variations of the basic story, the defining feature is a murderous husband or fiancé who keeps the corpses of his previous victims sequestered in his large house.

So for example, the Grimms collected a tale called "Fitcher's Bird," which details a wizard who abducts one of three sisters, and takes her to be his bride. He forbids her access to one room only; however, she disobeys this injunction, discovers the bloody chamber and drops the key in the blood. The key will not come clean, so her transgression is visible; she is dispatched and her blood and limbs wind up in the chamber also. Then the next sister is abducted and meets the same fate; the third sister is also abducted, but when she investigates the chamber she has the presence of mind to put the key away first; thus her transgression passes unnoticed. The balance of power now shifted, she then magically revivifies her sisters and burns the whole house down, wizard and all. (We should take note of this house-burning, which prefigures the burnings in *Jane Eyre*, *Rebecca* and *Wide Sargasso Sea*.) "The Robber Bridegroom," a related story, is also collected by the Grimms. In the Grimm version, a young woman is betrothed by her father to a suitor whom she finds unaccountably sinister. Her fiancé invites her to come to his house on a particular day, and she accepts the invitation warily. When she gets there she is warned to turn back by a caged bird: "Turn back, turn back, young maiden dear, / 'Tis a murderer's house you enter here" (Grimm and Grimm 201). Inside she moves about the house but finds no one until she comes to the cellar. There she finds an old woman who tells her she is betrothed to a murderer who will kill and eat her. She then hides the girl behind a hogshead, and as soon as she has done so the groom and "his godless crew" return, dragging a girl with them; they drug, strip and dismember her, before eating her. A ring belonging to the dead girl flies up and lands in the hidden girl's lap; the old woman distracts the robbers from looking for it, thus saving her. When the robbers are asleep, both girl and old woman escape; the girl runs home and tells her father what she has seen. Subsequently the groom comes to a great dinner at the girl's house. She relates what she saw at his house as if she has dreamt it, before revealing the ring, still attached to the dead girl's finger, as proof of the deed; the bridegroom and his crew are then executed.

It should be noted that continental European tales such as "Fitcher's Bird" and the Italian tale "How the Devil Came to Marry Three Sisters" figure a supernatural instead of a human male villain. This villain also abducts his victims in a manner of bride capture rather than courting their attentions legitimately. On the other hand, the Grimms' "The Robber Bridegroom" is grounded in realism, featuring a girl whose betrothal is led by her father, against her own better judgment. The parallels between this type of plotting and the Gothic—*The Mysteries of Udolpho*, for example—are evident, for in both the heroine is posited as representing male property, the object of exchange and violent dispatch. In fact, Radcliffe's *oeuvre* typically tracks the root of supernatural fears to a living man rather than a specter. Austen too engages in this process in *Northanger Abbey*, where the fear is tragicomically severed from a supernatural origin, or even an exoticized Italianate context, and re-established within a mundane, non-spectral, English environment.

In the examples mentioned thus far, the villain is *not* the heroine's lover, even if he contrives to have her as his bride. Rather he is a predatory male for whom the heroine holds no sympathy, only fear and loathing. However, what we see in novels in the Gothic mode, certainly during the nineteenth century—possibly inaugurated by Wollstonecraft's *Maria, or The Wrongs of Woman*—is the scenario in which the villain is not only human and non-supernatural, he is actually the woman's husband or lover. Here we should backstep to look at the folkloric antecedents for this development. Among the oldest varieties of this folkloric schema is the old English tale "Mr. Fox"; this fascinating tale is unusual since the heroine's murderous lover is hers by choice rather than betrothal or abduction. However, she discovers his secret before the marriage and ultimately has the villain slain. In that sense it differs from all European versions of any of these grouped-together "sister" tales, since in other versions of the tale the suitor is either outright repellent but rich ("Bluebeard"), indecipherably sinister ("The Robber Bridegroom"), or an abductor ("Fitcher's Bird"). Only in "Mr. Fox" is the female protagonist in love with her charmingly murderous suitor.[3] What we see in novelistic representations of these character relationships is that prior to *Jane Eyre*, the male villain/protagonist tends to be one of either the "Mr. Fox" or "Fitcher's Bird" variety: either a seemingly attractive suitor whose reptilian underbelly is exposed, or a clearly rapacious abductor. In *Jane Eyre*, however, Bluebeard's secret is exposed, excused and altogether palliated when Jane marries Rochester. Yet, we do not forget (even if Jane does) that a woman who has been incarcerated for years in a secret room now lies dead.

The idea that it is the human husband, rather than a rapacious and inhuman villain, who is at fault reveals a connection to Middle Eastern folk tales; in fact, both "Bluebeard" and *Jane Eyre* share distinctly Asian aspects. Brontë was herself responsible for those to be discerned in *Jane Eyre*, but Perrault was quite innocent of the posthumous "ameliorations" made to his story. For example, in Sir Arthur Quiller-Couch's 1912 retelling of Perrault's "Bluebeard," the story is set somewhere near Baghdad, and Bluebeard gorges his new wife, Fatima, on "eastern" delicacies (Perrault and Quiller-Couch 33). Winfried Menninghaus observes that there existed a "(pseudo) orientalizing vogue for *Märchen* [German folk tales] in the eighteenth century." Following Perrault (who, as we know, did not add eastern flavor to his rendition), the tales of the celebrated fairy-tale writer Madame d'Aulnoye (whose tales, such as "The Blue Bird," were also extremely popular in England) "and the first translation of the *Tales of 1001 Nights* by Antoine Galland [in 1704]," it became the case that "the fairytale-like" was identified "with the Oriental and vice versa" (Menninghaus 72–3). In other words, since the vogue for fairy tales coincided temporally with the eighteenth century fad for Orientalia, the two became conflated.

During the eighteenth century England relied on France for cultural guidance; literary fashions were watched from across the Channel and followed obsessively (Conant 238). Perrault's collected *Contes* were not translated into English until 1729, owing, Martha Pike Conant suggests, to the French specificity of the tales that did not immediately lend itself to the English imagination. Thus the English translations of *The Thousand and One Nights* preceded the arrival in England of Perrault, allowing the *Contes* to settle down into an arabesque nest that, to the English, seemed ready-made. Both came from fashionable France to an insular England (Conant 234), where the *Mother Goose Tales* were suddenly exotic by association. But it was not only *The Arabian Nights* that stirred the French and English imaginations—a flurry of oriental and, as Conant terms it, "pseudo-oriental" literary outpourings flooded the scene; in England, she tells us, the "pseudo" tales were derived from French arabesques (Conant vii).

Though fairy tales and Arabian tales may well have been conflated during the eighteenth century, by the mid-nineteenth century only "Bluebeard" retained its oriental associations. It is unclear at what point "Bluebeard" became particularly associated with oriental themes, but by the nineteenth century all British illustrations accompanying versions of the tale showed orientalized characters[4] and in many cases the text was altered to include such oriental ameliorations as setting the tale in Baghdad. Hand-colored engravings from an 1804 edition of *Tabart's Popular Stories for the Nursery* show contemporary European settings for all the tales but Bluebeard's; he wears an ornate turban as he prepares to decapitate his wife. Such depictions continued as the norm throughout the nineteenth century and into the twentieth, finely wrought by the likes of Aubrey Beardsley, Arthur Rackham, W. Heath Robinson and Edmund Dulac.[5] Menninghaus observes that the conjunction between oriental themes and fairy tales "made it possible later for the disquietingly violent aspects of fairy tales—such as the serial murder of women—to be blamed on its oriental pedigree" (Menninghaus 73), thus displaying the strategy of cultural and geographic distancing common in the Gothic. But in fact it was Bluebeard alone who continued to carry that particular train of associations long after the eighteenth century Arabian vogue had peaked and waned. Since "the East" had in any case become, to some considerable extent, a metonym for "fabulous wealth or excessive tyranny" (Conant 234), as well as a world that, as Edward Said demonstrates, "exuded dangerous sex" and "perverse morality" (*Orientalism* 166–7), it ought not to surprise us that the so-called "oriental" world came to carry a particular association with "Bluebeard," in which all these elements are present in quantity.

Suggestions of orientalism are overt within Brontë's text. As Joyce Zonana notes, *Jane Eyre*'s "diffusely orientalist background has long been recognized" (Zonana 595).[6] Zonana lists the numerous instances of orientalism in the novel, from the framing of *Rasselas* (Brontë 87) to Jane's objections to *suttee,* but pays particular attention to the "harem as a metaphor for aspects of Western life" (Zonana 598), since in the novel Rochester is frequently cast as a despotic (and polygamous) sultan and Jane his slave. Zonana argues that the orientalism within *Jane Eyre* is primarily "a rhetorical strategy (and a form of thought) by which a speaker or writer neutralizes the threat inherent in feminist demands and makes them palatable to an audience that wishes to affirm its occidental superiority" (Zonana 594). While this may be true (and an example of Gothic distancing), in fact the orientalism within *Jane Eyre* is also a clearly identifiable link to the orientalism of "Bluebeard." The Bluebeard associations and the harem metaphor both indicate marital despotism that may, moreover, be differentiated from the antifeminist violence presented in the tales themselves. In fact, even in Perrault's "Bluebeard" the wife is complicit to some degree with her husband's illegal acts. Shifting the action to an oriental setting revisits and amplifies the implication that such marital despotism is *not* in opposition to the law and, indeed, is sanctioned by the law of the land, if not actually promoted and enforced by that law. Therefore, although in one sense one could accuse Brontë of transparent Eurocentricism in her use of oriental metaphors, at the same time she is indicting an Englishman, Rochester, in terms usually reserved for Arabian despots. Brontë thus suggests that this despotism is *not* something that only exists abroad, thereby reversing conventional Gothic distancing in her novel. Indeed, the fact that the concealed wife is actually from the slave colonies of the Caribbean is a frightful, truly shocking reminder (albeit one not fully explored by the novel, which leaves that task to Jean Rhys) that overseas is not necessarily all that far away, and that Elsewhere, with all its attendant horrors, can still be Here.

"Bluebeard" is certainly not the only folk tale that resonates in *Jane Eyre*. Over the years a number of critics have identified Brontë's novel as following a "Cinderella" patterning (Burkhart; Moglen; Clarke; Sullivan). In his introduction to Marian Roalfe Cox's exhaustive volume on the tale-type, Andrew Lang describes "the fundamental idea of Cinderella" as "a person in a mean or obscure position, by means of supernatural assistance" who "makes a good marriage" (vii). By a "good marriage" we are, of course, given to understand a marriage that raises the protagonist from poverty. This does not completely apply to Jane, as she is independently rich before she finally marries Rochester. However, the narrative certainly adheres to some sort of "Cinderella" plot up until the first marriage sequence, when Jane is still poor as she stands at the altar, and Mason exposes Rochester as a would-be bigamist. It is worth noting here that the marriage sequence strongly echoes what Cox designates the "false bride" motif that is evident in many "Cinderella"-type stories, including the Grimms' "Aschenpüttel."[7]

In Brontë's novel, Jane is propelled into flight after Rochester tries to induce her to become his mistress. In fact, Jane's ascent from "poor, obscure, plain and little" (281) beginnings is not linear; she ascends twice. Her first ascent takes her up to the failed wedding, where it is she herself (or then again, Rochester) who assumes the "false bride" position usually assigned to one of the horrid stepsisters. Following this she descends back into meanness, once again "the poor orphan child" (54); again she rises and ultimately weds Rochester without incident. This extended fairy tale format follows more closely the structure outlined by Propp in his study of the more elaborate Russian fairy tale, but in terms of its second phase alone is structured almost to the letter in terms of a "Catskin-Cinderella."

"Catskin" is the British variant of a tale also made famous by Perrault, and called "Peau D'Ane." There are many echoes of the "Catskin" story in *Jane Eyre*. In the fairy tales, the endangered princess seeks counsel from a fairy godmother–type character. Ironically, Rochester plays this role when he assumes the disguise of a gypsy fortune-teller. In *Jane Eyre* it is ultimately the moon that fulfils the magical maternal function (Rich 102), advising Jane to flee, like the fairy tale princess who escapes unseen. The Lang version ("Donkeyskin") says that the princess slips away "without being seen by anyone" (Lang 7); in the Grimm version, "Allerleirauh," the title character runs away from the castle at dead of night, taking only a few magical belongings. Alone in the world, our heroine "walked on a long, long way, trying to find someone who would take her in, and let her work for them; but though the cottagers, whose houses she passed, gave her food from charity, the ass's skin was so dirty they would not allow her to enter their houses" (Lang 7). In the corresponding section in *Jane Eyre*, Jane leaves what little money she has in the carriage, begs door-to-door for employment, then charity, though she is repelled by most on account of her impoverished appearance. Hannah, the Rivers' housekeeper, agrees to give her a piece of bread but then turns her out: '"You are not what you ought to be, or you wouldn't make such a noise. Move off"'(361). In the folk tales the refugee finally secures menial work, as does Jane, who is quick to announce that she "felt degraded" by her work in the schoolroom (385).

The "Catskin" stories, "practically worldwide in distribution" (Briggs 424), are according to Cox part of the "Cinderella" family. But there is one important motif that distinguishes them: the "unnatural father,"[8] the father who wishes to marry his daughter. Many "Catskin" tales in the British tradition have had this particular element edited out of them, but it is present in Perrault's "Peau D'Ane," the Irish tale "The Princess in the Catskins," and the Grimm tale "Allerleirauh." This motif too resurfaces in *Jane Eyre*. Paula Sullivan draws attention to Rochester's paternal function, pointing out the several occasions within the text when the "twenty-year difference in their ages is called into question"; she also points out that "Rochester's blindness and subsequent partial recovery of vision correspond to Mr Patrick Brontë's near-blindness and partial recovery due to a cataract operation." Nevertheless, Sullivan continues, "Rochester figures primarily as a lover rather than a surrogate parent" (Sullivan 67). This notwithstanding, Rochester's paternalist role as Jane's master is further underscored by Mrs. Fairfax's observation that '"He might almost be your father."' Jane refutes this statement with an uncharacteristic pique that reveals her discomfort: "'No, indeed, Mrs Fairfax!' I exclaimed, nettled; 'he is nothing like my father! No-one, who saw us together, would suppose it for an instant. Mr Rochester looks as young, and is as young, as some men at five-and-twenty'" (293). Yet when at the local pub she later hears her own story recited back to her, she discovers that it is not only Mrs. Fairfax who sees her relationship with Mr. Rochester in this light: "'She was a little, small thing, they say, almost like a child.... Mr Rochester was about forty, and this governess not twenty.... Well, he would marry her" (452). Rochester himself observes that he "should entertain none but fatherly feelings" (460) for Jane; moreover, as Sullivan observes, Jane sits on Rochester's knee in a daughterly fashion (67).

Thus in casting Rochester in a paternal relationship with Jane, Brontë reminds us that he is the "unnatural father" of the fairy tales, hoping to marry his daughter, just as she suggests that he is Bluebeard, the "unnatural husband." In referencing the fairy tales, Brontë encodes her message regarding the dangers posed by Mr. Rochester to Jane and to her reader: he is not merely the dangerously powerful Victorian husband, legally authorized to lock up his insane wife; he is the preternaturally dangerous husband and father of the folk tale. Thus while it may seem puzzling to note the conjunction of seemingly opposite tale-types—one that directs itself towards the blissful union of marriage; the other predicated upon the murderous reality of marriage—in fact, in the "Catskin-Cinderella," as in "Bluebeard," it is a man who is the source of terror. In layering the two tales, Brontë reminds her readers that husbands and fathers are both preternaturally dangerous.

This encoded, but nevertheless clear, message amplifies a troubling aspect of *Jane Eyre*, the masochism of the protagonist who refuses to heed the encoded warning and who accepts the terms of her problematic marriage, eventually returning to the man who has attempted bigamy and who has—directly or indirectly—killed his wife, having incarcerated her in a garret. The explanation for Jane's wilful disregard of the textual warnings, too, may be found in the fairy tale sources of her story. Significantly, in Perrault's "La Barbe-Bleue," the wife's ambivalent complicity with the terms of her marriage hinges on scopic terms; it is a matter of *seeing or not seeing* that determines her choices. For instance, her paramour's blue beard makes him frightful to women; however, after he showers her with expensive gifts and shows her his expansive mansion (most of it, at least) she decides that his beard is not so blue after all. When she looks inside the secret chamber, she does not see straight away: "at first she saw nothing, since the windows were closed; after some moments she began to see that the floor was covered in clotted blood, and that in this blood were reflected the corpses of several women hung from the walls" (Perrault 63). And as we know, even at that point *she does not attempt to escape*, but rather tries to pretend she has *seen nothing*. The denouement returns to the question of sight. While waiting for the arrival of her brother, the protagonist asks Sister Anne up on the tower if she sees them coming: "Anne, ma soeur Anne, ne vois-tu rien venir?" ("Anne, Sister Anne, do you see nothing coming?") This famous phrase is repeated three times, while Anne replies: "Je ne vois rien que."[9] Sister Anne sees *nothing*; even when she sees *something*, it is cast as *nothing*, since it is not the approach of the two phallic brothers: "Je ne vois rien que le soleil qui poudroie et l'herbe qui verdoie." ("I see nothing but the dappled sunlight and the rippling grass.")

The sightlessness with which Perrault's "Bluebeard" is infused seems to travel to *Jane Eyre*. Jane is wilfully blind in ignoring Rochester's flaws. The physical blindness with which Rochester is ultimately blighted is the price he pays for rendering Jane figuratively blind. And yet, as the folk tale suggests, Jane herself is to blame for her blindness. Thus, if Mr. Rochester's blindness appears to put Jane and him on an equal footing, in fact it merely enables Jane to accept her own sightlessness without acknowledging it. Meanwhile, a house is burned and a woman is dead, as if she never existed; and the future promises nothing better for Jane, who refuses to learn from the all-too-visible examples of all her predecessors.

Notes

1. It is important that we recognize the extremely close connections between the fairy tale and the early novel. Indeed, the inception of the European novel occurred in the salons of seventeenth century France, where novels and fairy tales were written and created in tandem, as noted by DeJean and Seifert.
2. The Aarne-Thompson folklore classification system differentiates schematically between three essentially similar tale-types: type 312, wherein the endangered woman's brothers rescue her from the murderous man; 311, where she is typically the last of three sisters to be abducted by a wizard or devil, and saves herself and her sisters through trickery (the Grimms' "Fitcher's Bird" is of this type); and type 955, known as "Robber Bridegroom" tales, wherein a suitor is foiled in his murderous/cannibalistic aims by the girl who discovers his plot and exposes him, often using riddles to expose the murderer in a public space.
3. This scenario is exploited to perfection by Beatrix Potter, whose Jemima Pud-

dleduck became positively enamoured of "the foxy gentleman" who showed her to his wood-shed: "quite full of feathers—it was almost suffocating; but it was comfortable and very soft." Indeed, "Jemima thought him mighty civil and handsome" (Potter 164).

4. French illustrations, it should be noted, do not seem to follow this trend to a significant degree; woodcut illustrations from the eighteenth century show contemporary settings.

5. The association between Bluebeard and "the oriental" existed too in Germany, since, as Menninghaus notes, in 1797 Ludwig Tieck published his *The Seven Wives of Bluebeard,* which featured the "bibliographic mystification" of presenting the publication details as "'Istanbul by Heraklius Murusi, Court Bookseller of High Gate; in the Year of Hedschrach 1212'" (Menninghaus 71).

6. One explanation of this is the larger context provided by Edward Said: "everywhere in nineteenth and early twentieth century British and French culture we find allusions to the facts of empire, but perhaps nowhere with more regularity and frequency than in the British novel" (Culture and Imperialism 73).

7. In tales of this type, the prince, having only the mystery woman's shoe by which to recognize her, goes about the land having all the women try the shoe for size. Cinderella's stepmother has one of the stepsisters mutilate her foot by slicing off toe or heel so that it may fit the shoe; the prince is fooled and a wedding arranged with the false bride. However, the false bride is exposed as she walks up the aisle, usually by a bird who draws attention to the bleeding foot with a rhyming song.

8. The opening pattern of all these tales runs thus: The queen on her deathbed bids the king promise that he will marry no one who is not as wise and beautiful as she. After the queen's death, the heartbroken king has the land scoured for just such a woman and finds not a one who can in any way compare with his dead wife. Finally his eye lights upon his daughter and he sees that only she is as beautiful and wise as her mother; he wants to marry her. The daughter, understandably, is appalled by the suggestion, but the king will not be put off.

9. "Anne, ma soeur Anne" rhymes with "rien"—indeed, this may be the only reason why Anne comes into it at all, since she has figured in the tale neither by name nor reference prior to her sudden appearance on the tower.

Works Cited

Aarne, Antti. *The Types of the Folktale: A Classification and Bibliography.* Trans. Stith Thompson. 2nd ed. Helsinki: Suomalainen Tiedeakatemia, Academia Scientiarum Fennica, 1961.
Briggs, Katharine M. *A Dictionary of British Folk Tales in the English Language.* Vol. 1. London: Routledge and Kegan Paul, 1970.
Brontë, Charlotte. *Jane Eyre,* ed. Q.D. Leavis. Harmondsworth: Penguin, 1988.
Burkhart, Charles. *Charlotte Bronte: A Psychosexual Study of Her Novels.* London: Gollancz, 1973.
Clarke, Micael M. "Brontë's *Jane Eyre* and the Grimms' 'Cinderella.'" *Studies in English Literature 1500–1900* 40.4 (2000): 695–710.
Conant, Martha Pike. *The Oriental Tale in England in the Eighteenth Century.* London: Frank Cass, 1966.
Cox, Marian Roalfe. *Cinderella: Three Hundred and Forty-Five Variants of Cinderella, Catskin, and Cap O'Rushes.* London: David Nutt, 1893.
DeJean, Joan. *Tender Geographies: Women and the Origins of the Novel in France.* New York: Columbia University Press, 1991.
Grimm, Jacob, and Wilhelm Grimm. *The Complete Fairy Tales.* Ware: Wordsworth, 1997.
Lang, Andrew. *The Grey Fairy Book.* New York: Dover, 1967.
Menninghaus, Winfried. *In Praise of Nonsense: Kant and Bluebeard.* Stanford, Calif.: Stanford University Press, 1999.

Moglen, Helene. *Charlotte Brontë: The Self Conceived*. New York: Norton, 1978.
Perrault, Charles. *Contes*, ed. Marc Soriano. Paris: Flammarion, 1991.
Perrault, Charles, and Sir Arthur Quiller-Couch. *Perrault's Fairy Tales*. London: Folio, 2001.
Potter, Beatrix. "Jemima Puddleduck." In *The Complete Tales*, 161–72. London: Frederick Warne, 2002.
Rich, Adrienne. *On Lies, Secrets and Silence: Selected Prose, 1966–1978*. New York: Norton, 1995.
Said, Edward. *Culture and Imperialism*. London: Chatto and Windus, 1993.
____. *Orientalism*. London: Routledge, 1978.
Seifert, Lewis Carl. *Fairy Tales, Sexuality, and Gender in France, 1690–1715*. Cambridge: Cambridge University Press, 1996.
Sullivan, Paula. "Fairy Tale Elements in Jane Eyre." *Journal of Popular Culture* 12.1 (1978): 61–74.
Sutherland, John. *The Literary Detective: 100 Puzzles in Classic Fiction*. New York: Oxford University Press, 2000.
Zonana, Joyce. "The Sultan and the Slave: Feminist Orientalism and the Structure of Jane Eyre." *Signs* 18.3 (1993): 592–617.

8

Monstrous Men: Violence and Masculinity in Robert Browning's The Ring and the Book

MICHAEL ACKERMAN

> Yet here is the monster! Why, he's a mere man—
> (Browning. *The Ring and the Book* 4:1603)

Of Monsters and Men

Although well known for his dramatic investigations into abnormal psychology and murder in macabre settings, Robert Browning is not usually considered a Gothic author.[1] This may be due, in part, to temporal and generic issues. As Fred Botting notes, "less identifiable as a separate genre in the nineteenth century, Gothic fiction seemed to go underground" (11). The Gothic is often viewed as waning in the mid-Victorian period and resurging towards the *fin de siècle*. This view is filtered through scholarly emphasis on the novel as the pre-eminent manifestation of the Gothic. If, however, we accept that the Gothic is a poetic tradition, as Anne Williams claims, we will find the Gothic surfacing from the literary and cultural "underground" in much of the dramatic verse that marks the mid-Victorian period. Robert Browning's poetic investigations into the abnormal psyche created a coterie of terrifying male figures, and his experiments in the Gothic almost always emphasize men as generators of fear, men who are violent (often towards women), and men who struggle to interpret the cultural codes for regulating and maintaining masculine identity. As his troupe of Gothic villains respond violently to moments of personal and cultural crisis they reveal a nexus of Gothic tropes that interrogate the terrifying technology of masculine subjectivity. While the unnamed confessor in "Porphyria's Lover" and the infamous Duke in "My Last Duchess" are examples of such men, none are more monstrous than Count Guido

Franceschini from Browning's Gothic masterpiece *The Ring and the Book* (1868–9).[2]

The terrorizing activities of many of Browning's male characters are rooted in their own sense of terror at the thought of being emasculated men, seemingly unable to produce the fear necessary in the domestic realm to completely control the woman who is held captive there. Abjected from the patriarchal social structures that provide them with an illusory stable self, these characters murder the women in an attempt to reassert their place in the system of patriarchal authority that rejected them. This rejection, and the concomitant loss of identity, leads to the violent reassertion of authority in a bid to reappropriate their shattered sense of a proper masculine self. This perspective on Browning's villains aligns with Cyndy Hendershot's interpretation of the intersection between the Gothic and gender.[3] Hendershot notes that "the Gothic reveals ... the myth of masculinity as a whole and dominant, rather than concealing fissures that threaten to expose the male subject as a subject like the female one, one lacking and incapable of ever achieving wholeness and mastery" (3). The violent conclusion to such works, the complicit social structures that are depicted, and the manner in which male subjectivity is rooted in the death of the female Other shift the situation's horror from the characters within the text to the readers who have been invited to view them from the inside out.

Browning's magnum opus, *The Ring and the Book* (1868–69), was based on found documents regarding an actual seventeenth century domestic murder case in Italy.[4] Such cases of familial murder often generated a wide array of literary and dramatic representations, including broadsheets, pamphlets, handwritten notices, ballads and plays that, like Browning's poem, focus on actual events. The Gothic's debt to Jacobean and Elizabethan drama has long been established, but, more specifically, Browning's Gothic monodramas share elements with domestic tragedy. Like Browning's *The Ring and the Book*, in "domestic tragedies (also known as murder plays) ... the action is usually precipitated by a murder, the basis of which is an actual and recent crime recorded in a ballad, chapbook, chronicle or pamphlet" (Comensoli 4). The broadsheets, pamphlets, plays and ballads that accrued around domestic murder cases often deployed the term "monstrous," "unnatural," and "strange,"[5] not so much to condemn the savagery of the offenders but (especially in the case of fathers and husbands) in order to show that these monstrous men were aberrations, thereby eliding the complicity of the patriarchal power structures that helped create them. As Michel Foucault notes, "if these accounts were allowed to be printed and circulated, it was because they were expected to have the effect of an ideological control" (67, 68). While there are important generic differences, Browning's text, the Gothic, and the early domestic tragedies share a nexus of social and familial signifying practices and dramatize their violent unraveling. Thus, Browning's Gothicizing of the original narrative is not surprising given the discourse of "the monstrous" that was utilized in the public reporting of such incidents.

David Punter reminds us that "the term 'monster' is often used to describe anything horrifyingly unnatural," and that "etymologically speaking, the monster is something to be shown, something that serves to demonstrate (Latin: *monstrare*: to demonstrate) and to warn (Latin, *monere*: to warn)" (263). The public destruction of the monster is of utmost importance, as Foucault reminds us: "the public execution ... belongs, even in minor cases, to the ceremonies by which power is manifested" (47). Thus, even before the early Gothic novels create their monstrous aristocrats, early modern applications of the term "monstrous" to men were used to signal their "horrifying unnaturalness"—meaning that these men either lack the particular cultural signifiers of masculinity at play in that historic moment, or have embraced them to excess, and therefore serve as a demonstration of what manliness is *not*. Indeed, the crucial aspect of domestic tragedies that were based on men as the protagonists was to show "that a man who would murder his wife was no longer a representative of order and authority" (Dolan 103).

While early Gothic monsters function similarly (as emblems that threaten to wreak havoc on the social order and, even in their very bodies, signify chaos over order and authority), the term shifts in usage within the Gothic from individual monstrosities to monstrous social structures. As Punter explains, "rather than being the demonic other to mainstream society, the monster is explicitly identified as that society's logical and inevitable product: society, rather than the individual becomes the primary site of horror" (266). Thus, the Gothic displays a certain ambivalence towards the "monster"—depicting both horrific individuals whose destruction is welcomed and applauded, and "sympathetic" creatures whose very existence demonstrates the social forces that form a "technology of monsters."[6]

Browning's multiple narratives structure *The Ring and the Book* as, in Isobel Armstrong's phrase, "a double poem." As Armstrong explains, "the double poem is a deeply skeptical form. It draws attention to the epistemology which governs the construction of the self and its relationships and to the cultural conditions in which those relationships are made" (13). In this case, the double poem enunciates both meanings of "monstrous" and allows for individual guilt *and* the complicity of culture. Guido must face the consequences for terrorizing Pompilia and her family, even as the reader recognizes that Guido is subject to forces, both dark and violent, that are deeply enmeshed in the production of masculine monstrosity.

Fear and Loathing in the House of Franceschini

The poet/speaker in Book 1 of Browning's twelve-book masterpiece begins by telling readers, in summary, each of the ten versions of the Roman murder trial. Readers are given brief but lurid details of the horrific crime, and the series of events that led to it. The events are adapted from a legal discourse in which a society was attempting to come to terms with the limits of domestic violence in relation to the importance of domestic fidelity, "wherein it is disputed if, and when, / Husbands may kill adulterous wives, yet 'scape / The customary forfeit" (129–31). For Browning, the case reads, and writes, like a Gothic novel filled with the mode's most obvious characteristics: an aristocratic line that is in jeopardy, an innocent young woman immured in the palace of a monster, corrupt clergy, deceptive usurpations, a vicious and bloody triple murder, and a sense of terror that seems to permeate victim and perpetrator alike.

Book 1 not only establishes the Gothic plot, but also introduces the cast of monstrous characters. The "house" of Franceschini is depicted as a lust-driven "satyr-family" (1:570) that includes two "obscure goblin creatures" (1:549) who serve as Guido's brothers, and the count's mother who, with her "monkey-mien" (1:571), mocks Guido's new young wife, Pompilia, with wild gestures and grotesque faces. While her parents, "in the potency of fear, / Break somehow through the satyr-family," this dark cohort surrounds Pompilia, preparing to "wring the uttermost revenge / from body and soul" (1:579–80) of their young captive. This melodramatic tableau, in which "the victim stripped and prostrate" (1:582) is encircled by the feral family members in front of a fiery cauldron, echoes the depiction of macabre aristocratic families, and their feminine prey, in the Gothic novels of the late eighteenth century. In this scene, not only is the family structure Gothicized, but so is the "main-monster" (1:551) of this horrific clan, Guido, who must produce a male heir to perpetuate the family name, and legitimate his place in the patrilineal line.

Guido pursues this reproductive necessity with absolute ferocity. When Pompilia escapes and flees in fear for her life, Guido and his men pursue her. When they find her, the scene contrasts the "warmth and light" (1:614) that pours out of the villa, with what lies just outside its idyllic promise of domestic tranquility: "All was grave, silent, sinister,—when, ha? / Glimmeringly did a pack of were-wolves pad, / The snow, those flames were Guido's eyes in front" (1:610–12). The were-wolf, Guido, and his pack stand outside Pompilia's threshold with their "blood-bright eyes, / And black lips wrinkling o're the flash of teeth, /

And tongues that lolled" (1:616–19). Browning's use of the term "were-wolf" is specific in invoking a particular type of monstrous, unnatural savagery. It also speaks to the level of bloodlust in the men, and to the count's voracious consumption of Pompilia and her family. Rather than relating the group's wolfishness to Rome's mythic founders,[7] the speaker's image of the were-wolf insists upon the animal/human hybridity that marks the Franceschini household's "unnatural" relations.

The next two monologues, while reflecting the public's divided opinion regarding the case, begin by talking about the gruesome remains of Guido's crime. Half-Rome perversely delights in "trying to count the stabs" (2:23) of the mutilated bodies on display within the church, fascinated that Violante "took all her stabbings in the face" (2:27). A more discreet Other Half-Rome simply describes Pompilia's "flower-like body" ... stabbed through and through again" (3:5–6). The books then recount how "penury" (3:23) did "brutify and beastialize" (2:24) the nobleman's "immense hate" for "the solitary / Subject to satisfy that hate, his wife" (3:699–700). Discovering that Pompilia is, in fact, the purchased bastard child of a prostitute further enrages the count, not only because his noble family line has been polluted, but also because the revelation terminates all of the financial benefits he had expected to acquire from the marriage. Pompilia cannot immediately break free from Guido's "cage and torture-place" (1:502) or the increasingly monstrous actions of her husband, and finds no respite "From tooth and claw of something in the dark" (3:787). While the sadistic Half-Rome chalks up Guido's treatment of Pompilia to "the regular jealous-fit that's incident / To all old husbands that marry brisk young wives" (2:828–29), Other Half-Rome views Guido's cruelty as springing "like an uncaged beast" ... "on the weak shoulders of his wife" (3:966–67). Lacking in both monetary and conjugal rewards from the marriage to his thirteen-year-old bride, Guido begins a "slow sure siege laid to her body and soul" (3:1434) in which his "cruelty graduated dose by dose" (3:525).

As expected, when the domestic terror shifts from simple torture to murder, Half-Rome relishes the gory details of the family that has been "hacked to pieces" (2:1443). Aligning *cosmos* and *domus*, Half-Rome depicts the event as a type of apocalyptic cleansing that will renew the "world" through blood and fire:

> Vengeance, you know, burst like a mountain-wave
>   That holds a monster in it, over the house,
>   And wiped its filthy four walls free again
>   With a wash of hell-fire—father, mother, wife,
>   Killed them all, bathed his name clean in their blood [2:1433–37].

At least half of the public feels that Guido's only fault is that he took the "new path" (2:1525) by appealing to the law for justice, which left him "stuck in a quagmire" (2:1526), until he scrambled back "Into the safe sure rutted road once more, / Revenged his own wrong like a gentleman" (2:1527–28). The link between violence as means of domestic control and masculinity is made explicit as this personified segment of the population rejects the new path, and advises the listener to "take the old way trod when men were men!" (2:1524). Half-Rome views this violent "road" to manhood as somewhat excessive, yet socially necessary, "the better for you and me and all the world, / Husband and wives, especially in Rome" (2:1438–39).

Pompilia's own deathbed testimony in Book 7 confirms her husband's cruelty and her "miserable three drear years / In that dread palace" (7:947–8) at Arezzo. She remembers that her lot as a woman was "terrible and strange.... And [she] was found familiarized with fear" (7:118–22). She describes her "dreadful husband" as a "serpent towering and triumphant" (7:1589) and a fiend. But, like most Gothic narratives, the most horrific terror is that which cannot be spoken. Despite the fact that she was "firm, withstood, refused" (7:719) Guido and his brother's sexual advances, her confession to the priest is riddled with telling ellipses, which silently signify the rapes she undergoes at the hands of her husband. The trauma is hinted at when she pleads to the archbishop for the "right" to refuse Guido her body since they are in "estrangement, soul from soul" (7:723), and he replies with a sadistic smile that she is to "swallow the burning coal your husband proffers you!" (7:730). In the end, Pompilia states that "this blood of mine / Flies forth exultingly at any door" (7:1716), glad to have death deliver her from Guido's cruel hate.

Guido is introduced by the poet in Book 1, in the context of the "dark question" of domestic violence in a masculinist culture. Guido speaks for himself in Book 5, invoking ideologies of class and gender in puzzlement at being held criminally accountable for performing a husband's regrettably necessary duty when obedient "wifeliness" is lacking and therefore threatening to the "social fabric" (5:444). He freely admits he had vindictively hated, beaten, and threatened Pompilia. The count reminds the court of his "obligation" to "practice mastery [and] prove my mastership" (5:716–17) of his new wife, whose duty was to "submit herself, / Afford me pleasure, perhaps cure my bile" (5:718–19). The count invokes the traditional alignment of theological authority and social practice to justify his treatment of Pompilia, asking, "Am I to teach my Lords what marriage means, / What God ordains thereby and man fulfills ...?" (5:720–21). That the count's "mastery" is an attempt to maintain control through sexual violence and the production of extreme fear marks him as a monstrous figure well worthy of the Gothic name. Seeing that the role of husband is one of the central ways in which masculine identity is formed and maintained, his control over her must be complete. The count claims that he has "taught [his] wife her duty, made her see / What it behooved her see and say and do, / Feel in her heart and with her tongue declare, / ... And who finds fault here?" (5:856–58, 860). The count desires absolute rule over his wife. It is not enough for the count to control her speech, her actions, and her perception; he must also control what she "feels in her heart" (5:858). His failure to shape her interior attitudes leads to her eventual death. This echoes another of Browning's aristocrats who resorted to violence because he could not alter his wife's heart, which was "too easily impressed" ("My Last Duchess" 23) by things other than his "nine-hundred-years-old name" (33).

The count's shaken confidence in his cultural identity produces a maddening rage that is fueled by the fact that his failures were made public. Not only did he fail in his obligation to control his wife, but this failure and shame was "published before my lords, / put into print, made circulate far and wide" (5:765–66). In fact, the count defends murdering his wife by claiming that his only fault was that he had been too kind. He suggests that when he first suspected his wife of flirting he should have "Calmly and quietly cut off, clean thro' bone, / but one joint of one finger of [his] wife" (5:93–54), with the threat of cutting off a bit more each time she was at the window. His line of argument is that he should be allowed the brutal murders of his wife and her family because he restrained himself so long when they clearly deserved worse treatment. Guido is correct, of course, that neither church nor state would have charged him if he had privately dealt in such a violent manner with Pompilia. His defense becomes, however, an inadvertent confession revealing his emasculated state within his own house. The fact that he was not violent enough at home, that he was unable to produce the a level of fear necessary to control his wife, proves this lack of "mastery." In this sense, the patriarchal powers of the state and church, designed to establish and maintain masculine domestic authority, potentially emasculate the men subject to their authority. This is particularly true of Guido, who must consistently rely on help from the archbishop and the governor to try and control Pompilia.

Guido's desperate attempt to restore a masculine identity that, like his palace, lies in ruins, manifests itself in his attempt to possess Pompilia's soul, control her body, and forcibly impregnate her with a legitimating heir through a series of rapes, demanding that she "give [him] the fleshly gesture [he] can reach / And rend and leave fit for hell to burn!" (7:783–84). As Judith Halberstam points out, often within the Gothic "rape ... is not the sexual enactment of violence ... it is violence enacted with bodily or fleshly weapons. *Sex is a metaphor for violence* not the other way around" (156). For Pompilia, the rapes are terrifying harbingers of Guido's desperate bid for absolute authority, which culminated in the "twenty-two dagger wounds" (7:38) that he savagely inflicts on her after brutally killing her father, and stabbing her mother's face beyond recognition. Within this series of events, the rapes are not a simple reversal of the sex/violence metaphor. This is not a replacement of "penis for knife" instead of the more common substitution of "knife for penis." It is a moebius band of "penis is knife is phallus is power is me" in continual, ontologically productive, circulation. This circulation is temporarily halted by Pompilia's own "unlawful appropriation of phallic authority" (Boose 204)—the use of her tongue. When facing imminent death at the hands of her husband, after an escape attempt, Pompilia's outburst reveals the gendered and dehumanized horror she is determined to resist: "Never again degraded to be yours / The ignoble noble, the unmanly man, / The beast below the beast in brutishness!" (3:1295–99).

As Lynda E. Boose points out, "a discourse that locates the tongue as the body's 'unruly member' situates female speech as a symbolic relocation of the male organ, an unlawful appropriation of phallic authority in which the symbolics of male castration are ominously complicit" (204). Pompilia's words here are like daggers piercing Guido in his "tremulous part" (5:30)—and her cut to Guido's social rank, and more importantly, his masculine identity, leaves him "unmanned," unable to act, and helplessly calling "on the law to adjudicate" (3:1320). That feminine speech has emasculated Guido in this scene is important. The early modern period dedicated an "obsessive energy" to "exerting control over the unruly woman—the woman who was exercising either her sexuality or her tongue under her own control rather than under the rule of a man. ... [I]llogical as it may seem—being a scold and being a so-called whore— were frequently conflated" (195). Thus after years of being subject to Guido's degrading treatment, Pompilia refutes his mastery over her by reversing the signification of phallic power. Again, Boose notes that "genital differentiation tended to be subsumed within a problematically gendered orality ... her open mouth the signifier for invited entrance elsewhere. Hence the dictum that associates "silent" with "chaste" (196). Guido's continually uninvited entrance into Pompilia is reversed through her oral rejection of his manhood. Her tongue finds words that are able to penetrate Guido to the core, and render him impotent to act. Guido's revenge for this emasculation is brutal and compensatory murder. However, the fact that Pompilia survives for four days, pouring forth speech, unsilenced by Guido's attack, intimates that he has, once again, failed to master his wife. This incident is reported by the Other-Half Rome, indicating that the public is acutely aware of the ways in which masculinity's stability is imbricated not only with social rank, but also with acts of violence.

Guido's Guilt and the Mystery Revealed

"Yet here is the monster! Why, he's a mere man—/ Born, bred and brought up in the usual way" (4:1603–04). So says Tertium Quid, prefiguring the foundation for Guido's confusion after he has been condemned to death. In his final moments, Guido is perplexed, searching in baffled rage for the basis of his crime. Richard D. McGhee depicts the count as "the champion of the law and the order of society; duty and law become ends in themselves and their enforcement assumes highest priority" (84). In Guido's mind, he is fighting to preserve social order, to return to a time when "the wholesome household rule" may be "in force again" (11:2041). This old "wholesome rule" is the ancient privilege of *paterfamilias*: absolute authority over all family members, even adjudicating over their life and death. Over and over Guido tells his jailers, that "all this trouble has come upon me / Through my persistent treading in the paths / where I was trained to go" (5:123–25). Guido reminds them that these codes of masculinity were reinforced by class structures: "Were we not put into a beaten path, / Bid pace in the world, we nobles born and bred?" (11:91–92). In Guido's mind, "whoever owned wife, sister, daughter—nay / Mistress" (11:40) approved his vicious actions, and— more importantly—"These manly men / Approved!" (11:43–44). Guido appeals to his place within a validating homosocial tradition and pleads "obedience" to the patriarchal structures that govern Rome, asking, "Who taught the dog that trick you hang him for?" (11:950).

Throughout the monologues, it becomes increasingly clear that the major patriarchal social structures of his time, the state and the church, are complicit in enacting violence on Pompilia in both ideological and physical ways. Ideologically, the legal system maintains that women are chattel, and religious doctrines inculcate both husband and wife that a woman's duty is to "cleave" to her husband in unwavering obedience. In addition to the numerous times Guido quotes scripture to justify his cruelty, he mentions the play he saw at the "Vallombrossa Convent, made / Expressly to teach what marriage was!" (11:908–909).

But in Browning's poem, these institutions also have a more active role. Guido is shocked that his crime is so horrific to a court who "brands a woman black between the breasts / For sinning by connection with a Jew" (5:1243–44). Several characters remark in surprise that Pompilia was not publicly whipped when she was caught with the priest. Certainly either of these two institutions, church or state, could have prevented the crime from happening. Even the public knew of her need for protection, and that "She cried / To those whom the law appoints recourse for such, / The secular Guardian—that's the Governor, / And the Archbishop—that's the spiritual guide, / And prayed them take the claws from out her flesh" (3:967–71). The Other Half-Rome tells us that "Three times she rushed, maddened by misery" (3:1003), to the archbishop, who was a "friend / of her husband" (3:1004–1005), and he "Thrice bade the foolish woman stop her tongue" (3:1009). Not only did he fail to provide her with protection, he "Coached her and carried her to the Count again," (3:1011), stating that "His old friend should be master in his house, / Rule his wife and correct her faults at need!" (3:1012, 1013).

Guido's perplexity also stems from the conflict he feels between the law as an embodiment of patriarchal authority and the social enforcement of patriarchal tradition. The law has condemned Guido (officially) for the murder of his wife and her parents. Yet it also condemns him for not killing her when she was first discovered with the priest, Caponsacchi. He hears in his head the court's objection that "[he] shrank from Gallant readiness and risk. / Were coward" (5:1090–91), and attempts to appease them by agreeing: he pleads guilty to "having been afraid" and aligns himself with "eunuchs, women, children" (5:1099) who are all "shieldless quite / against attack" (5:1100). In his invoking of the law for his own protection, his choice of associations speaks to the earlier question—what kind of man is under the law? In Guido's eyes: one that is emasculated and effeminized. Yet Guido's final and bloody assertion of his manhood is precisely what makes him an unnatural monster. Ultimately, Dolan notes, "Such exaggerated, grotesque characterizations evade the relationship between wife-murder and the dominant ideology of male supremacy ... murderous husbands are monstrous exceptions, not husbands whose 'legitimate' correction of their wives gets out of hand" (106).

Donna Heiland points out that "masculinity as a masquerade may be articulated through Gothic texts, which frequently reveal the fragility of traditional manhood. ... the Gothic continually reveals the gulf between the actual male subject and the myth of masculinity" (4). Guido's manliness is on trial, and it is measured against an impossible and horrifying ideal. The collapse of his decaying house, his inability to be a master in his own home, his public display of domestic weakness draw attention to the gap between the masculine ideal and the male subject. Paradoxically, he is also punished for his revelation in such a public fashion of the violence that constitutes the foundation for male authority within both the state and church settings.

The reproduction of this patriarchal control is dependant upon two key roles: husband and father. This is not only the system through which patriarchal power is transmitted, but one which is meant to transform those who participate in it, reproducing masculinity even as their idealized structures are entered into. Failure in either realm is subject to anything from private ridicule, public torture, or even, as in Guido's case, death. John Tosh reminds us that "Early Modern society was merciless in pillorying men who appeared to have surrendered their mastery in [the area of regulating his wife's sexual behavior] and an immense amount of litigation stemmed from the need to defend the sexual reputation of husbands (and wives also) from the imputations of cuckoldry" (3). The reason for such vigilant policing of masculinity, as legitimated by spousal and paternal roles, rests on the fact that failure in either realm was a threat, both to social "order" and to the ontological foundation of masculine subjectivity.

Thus there is a continual sense of terror that operates at two levels; there is the fear of violent hegemonic control, which threatens the body, and the terror of facing an ontological void if such structuring mechanisms are abandoned, or simply fail to shore up the fragile masculine self. Guido displays both types of terror. This does not keep him from benefiting fully from the power structure that is condemning him (hence his outrage, and bewilderment when he finds himself cast out), but it does foreground the reality that in the late seventeenth century, even for men, there were few ways out of such a structure. Browning links this complex of horror to the homosocial affiliation between Guido, Church, and State, indicating a complicit relationship in the patriarchal structures that perpetuate the violent subjection of women.

In the end, Guido is not punished for his treatment of Pompilia so much as he is for exposing the violence that forms the foundation for the law (theological and social) in such a public fashion. Thus, in official culture, masculinity itself seems predicated on a violence that must terrorize and eradicate the very feminine Other on which it depends for its patrilineal succession and self-identification. Perhaps this is what Donna Heiland means when she claims that "patriarchy is not only the subject of gothic novels, but is itself a gothic structure" (11). However, in Heiland's study of Gothic and gender, she claims that "gothic novels are all about patriarchies, about how they function, what threatens them, what keeps them going" and that "patriarchy inevitably celebrates a male creative power that demands the suppression—and sometimes the outright sacrifice—of women" (11). While this is true, what becomes equally clear is that the Gothic reveals what the consequences are for the men who, for one reason or another, have made that structure their home, one that becomes particularly *unheimlech* as they realize that patriarchy's phantasmatic dominance can also demand the suppression—and outright sacrifice—of men with equal vengeance. That is the punishment for "Count Guido, who reveals our mystery" (11:2010).

Notes

1. The earliest example is perhaps James Thompson, who refers to the Gothic "richness of detail" in *The Ring and the Book* (1882). While other reviews of *The Ring and the Book* had commented on the various grotesqueries of Browning's style, it was not until Henry James's address to the Royal Society of Literature on the occasion of Browning's centenary (1912) that the word "Gothic" was reassociated with the work. In a particularly Wordsworthian echo, James associates the "monstrous magnificence" of the poem with a labyrinthine Gothic structure. More recent scholarship, particularly that of Adam Roberts (2004), has reevaluated Browning's entire body of work as a type of "necromancing poetics" (110) that returns "again and again to figures that straddle life and death" (112), but Roberts, for all his Gothicized language, deliberately avoids using the term in reference to Browning's works.
2. I have used the original 1868–69 edition of the poem, published by Penguin and edited by Richard Altick. The Oxford edition was consulted and is invaluable for its textual commentary; however, the Oxford edition has added material based on Browning's latter revisions, and I am interested in the poem as it appeared in its original form.
3. For similar interpretations see Williams, Smith, Brinks, and Heiland, and Botting's article "Aftergothic: Consumption, Machines, and Black Holes."
4. Browning's poem is based on two sources. The first is what Browning referred to as the "old yellow book"—a collection of seventeenth century pamphlets, manuscripts and legal documents concerning the case that had been bound together, which he providentially discovered while in Italy, a process he describes in Book 1 of *The Ring and the Book*. The second (often referred to as the "Secondary Source") was an Italian manuscript titled "The Execution by Beheading of the Wife-Killer Guido Franceschini" (1698). Five other pamphlets describing the case have since been found, and while Browning would not have had access to (or knowledge of) these documents, they speak to the public fascination with the case. Here again we might see traces of early Gothic "formulas" in which the plot would be set in Catholic Europe, often Italy—or in the trope of the "found document." Walpole is infamous for his notoriously forged "translation" of a found document. In this case the documents, and the case, actually exist, but Browning still "Gothicizes" the scenes as means of "repristinating" the horror of the original crime.
5. Examples of pamphlet titles include *Strange and Lamentable News from Dullidg-Wells* (1678), *The Unnatural Father* (1621) and *Two Most Unnatural and Bloodie Murthers* (1605). Likewise two popular ballads were titled "The Bloody-Minded Husband" (1690) and "The Inhuman Butcher" (1697).
6. While Judith Halberstam uses this term in her 1995 text *Skin Show: Gothic Horror and the Technology of Monsters*, I am employing the term in a somewhat different manner. While she is interested in separating the "stories of mad monks, haunted castles, and wicked foreigners" (3) that permeated the later eighteenth century from the "nineteenth-century Gothic tales of monsters and vampires" (3), I am offering a link between them—a cultural moment in which the division between man and monster was particularly permeable. Moreover, while her technological trope is invested in "a particularly modern emphasis upon the horror of particular kinds of bodies" (3), I am identifying ideological mechanisms that function to produce particular types of terror both *in* and *through* masculinity as a social construct.
7. In the midst of the debate surrounding "the precedent for putting wives to death, / Or letting wives live, sinful as they seem" (1:219–20), one of the voices shouts to "Quote the code / Of Romulus and Rome!" (1:222–23). Romulus and Remus were the savage twin brothers who "founded" Rome, and who were said to have been nursed by a she-wolf.

Works Cited

Armstrong, Isobel. *Victorian Poetry: Poetry, Poetics and Politics.* London: Routledge, 1993.
Browning, Robert. *The Ring and the Book,* ed. Richard D. Altick. New York: Penguin, 1981.
_____. *The Ring and the Book.* The Poetical Works of Robert Browning. Vols. 7–9, ed. Stefan Hawlin and T.A.J. Burnett. Oxford: Clarendon, 2004.
Boose, Lynda E. "Scolding Brides and Bridling Scolds: Taming the Woman's Unruly Member." *Shakespeare Quarterly* 42:2 (1991): 179–213.
Botting, Fred. "Aftergothic: Consumption, Machines, and Black Holes." *The Cambridge Companion to Gothic Fiction,* 277–300, ed. Jerrold E. Hogle. Cambridge: Cambridge University Press, 2002.
_____. *Gothic.* The New Critical Idiom, ed. John Drakakis. New York: Routledge, 1996.
Brinks, Ellen. *Gothic Masculinity: Effeminacy and the Supernatural in English and German Romanticism.* Lewisburg: Bucknell University Press, 2003.
Comensoli, Viviana. *"Household Business": Domestic Plays of Early Modern England.* Toronto: University of Toronto Press, 1996.
Dolan, Frances E. *Dangerous Familiars: Representations of Domestic Crime in England 1550–1700.* Ithaca: Cornell University Press, 1994.
Foucault, Michel. *Discipline and Punish: The Birth of the Prison,* trans. Alan Sheridan. New York: Vintage, 1995.
Halberstam, Judith. *Skin Shows: Gothic Horror and the Technology of Monsters.* Durham: Duke University Press, 1995.
Heiland, Donna. *Gothic and Gender: An Introduction.* Malden: Blackwell, 2004.
Hendershot, Cyndy. *The Animal Within: Masculinity and the Gothic.* Ann Arbor: University of Michigan Press, 1998.
McGhee, Richard D. *Marriage, Duty and Desire in Victorian Poetry and Drama.* Lawrence: Regents Press of Kansas, 1980.
Punter, David, and Glennis Byron. *The Gothic.* Malden: Blackwell, 2004.
Roberts, Adam. "Browning, the Dramatic Monologue and the Resuscitation of the Dead." In *The Victorian Supernatural,* ed. Brown et al., 109–127. Cambridge: Cambridge University Press, 2004.
Smith, Andrew. *Victorian Demons: Medicine, Masculinity and the Gothic at the Fin-de-Siecle.* Manchester: Manchester University Press, 2004.
Tosh, John. *A Man's Place: Masculinity and the Middle-Class Home in Victorian England.* New Haven: Yale University Press, 1999.
Williams, Anne. *Art of Darkness: A Poetics of Gothic.* Chicago: University of Chicago Press, 1984.

9

"I Am God": The Domineering Patriarch in Shirley Jackson's Gothic Fiction

BERNICE M. MURPHY

Shirley Jackson's Gothic fiction is often associated with the supernatural, largely because of the commercial and critical success of her 1959 novel *The Haunting of Hill House*. However, the dangers which confront her troubled female characters arise more often from the men in their lives than from any otherworldly force. After all, the reasons for teenager Natalie Waite's catastrophic mental breakdown in *Hangsaman* (1951) have much to do with the stifling influence of her father and with a vaguely-alluded-to incident at a party when she is sexually assaulted by one of his friends. Similarly, in *The Bird's Nest* (1954), the incompetence and arrogance of Elizabeth Richmond's male psychiatrist, the ironically named "Dr. Wright," significantly complicates her recovery from multiple personality disorder. In addition, Jackson suggests that abuse may be a factor in a Jackson heroine's mental dislocation: as a child, Elizabeth may well have fallen victim to the sexual predation of her mother's boyfriend. The largely unpleasant group chosen to wait out the end of the world in *The Sundial* (1956) do so at the alleged behest of the long-dead Mr. Halloran, whose typically over-bearing demands are communicated to them by his downtrodden daughter. Even the haunted Hill House evidences malign patriarchal influence, built to the exact specifications of the tyrannical Hugh Crain, whose lingering malevolent influence may well be more dangerous that that of any ghosts. It is perhaps not altogether surprising then that Jackson's final completed novel, *We Have Always Lived in the Castle*, features a psychotic heroine who blithely resorts to mass murder and arson in order to elude the control of greedy and tyrannical male relatives.

The frequency with which the male becomes a source of danger in Jackson's work is obvious, although upon first glance men may not seem to play a particularly prominent role in her fiction. After all, four of Jackson's six completed novels (*Hangsaman, The Bird's Nest, The Haunting of Hill House* and *We Have Always Lived in the Castle*) have as their principal characters troubled young women, and while the other two novels, *The Road Through the Wall* and *The Sundial,* both feature a much larger cast of characters, women still carry the main burden of narrative interest. To date, relatively little had been written of the role that male characters play in Jackson's fiction.[1] This may in part be due to the fact that there are virtually no conventional romantic or sexual relationships in Jackson's novels. Even though her heroines are all young, single women in an era where marriage was considered a woman's highest calling, such orthodox (and, as often suggested by Jackson, suffocating) entanglements rarely occur. There *is* a tentative understanding between librarian Essex and teenager Gloria Desmond in *The Sundial,* but they are minor characters and the relationship is actually of little importance. Tellingly, Jackson's young men, like Luke Sanderson in *The Haunting of Hill House* or Cousin Charles in *We Have Always Lived in the Castle,* are typically foolish, vain dilettantes who pose only a fleeting temptation to her troubled heroines. The most significant male in Jackson's fiction is actually the recurring figure of the domineering, "God-Like" father figure. These men are godlike in that they deliberately align themselves—often wryly but always with a serious eventual impact—with the malign figure of a despotic, supernatural, and patriarchal god. In two instances—*Sundial* and *Hill House*—the men even seem to have taken on some sort of supernatural power themselves. It is entirely possible that the psychological and emotional damage these domineering, blundering patriarchs consistently inflict upon Jackson's troubled young women explains in no small part their characteristic abhorrence of conventional romantic attachments.

The first Jackson novel in which the despotic patriarch plays a significant role is her overlooked second novel, *Hangsaman.* This is the first (but not the last) Jackson novel in which a heroine's descent into madness blurs the thin lie between reality and fantasy and imbues the narrative with a pervasive atmosphere of Gothic unease. From the outset, it is clear that Natalie Waite is an unusual young woman. She has a rich, disturbing inner life and is accompanied everywhere by voices, such as that of a police detective who interrogates her about imaginary murders (significantly, the victim is usually her father). In her own quiet way, Natalie is as cowed and confined as any heroine of the classic Gothic, and her gradual disengagement from sanity is undoubtedly in part an unconscious attempt to evade the control of her pretentious, boorish father.

Apart from the very important relationship between Natalie and

Tony, her imaginary college friend, the most meaningful exchanges in the novel are those that take place between Natalie and her father. He is by far the most important presence in Natalie's life, the subject of her first conscious memory (193), and the authority figure whose opinions matter most. Their relationship is in many ways the key to a proper understanding of the novel. Arnold Waite, "husband, parent, man of his word," is first described as "looking with some disbelief" upon his wife and children (3). His importance in the novel is underscored by the fact that it is he, not Natalie, who is the focus of the novel's opening pages, laughingly declaring, "I am God," at the breakfast table in order to irritate his wife. However ironically the comment is meant, the fact is that he really is in many respects a godlike figure to his daughter, and sees himself as such, the first of several godlike patriarchs in Jackson's novels. He even has access to his daughter's innermost thoughts thanks to his daily review of her journal—the journal that will soon chronicle her mental collapse.

Mr. Waite's influence on Natalie is much more powerful than that of her mother; in fact, her mother's ineffectualness drives Natalie even closer to her father. When her mother rather desperately tries to communicate genuine feeling, as when she tells Natalie that "'A mother gets very lonesome without her daughter,'" she expresses herself with "an air of girlish whimsy which irritated both Natalie and Mr. Waite as no flat statement of hatred could have" (25). Natalie can only respond, "'You'll find something else to do.'" Notably, Mrs. Waite's whimsy is said to irritate Natalie and her father in the same manner. Natalie has internalised her father's scornful assessment of her mother. Yet her mother, and not her father, is the model of adulthood she is supposed to follow: according to the cultural propaganda of the time, girls like Natalie were supposed to become housewives, not intellectuals. This contradiction perhaps goes some way towards explaining Natalie's resentment towards domesticity and the rapid disintegration of her personality: she has absorbed two radically conflicting models of adult behavior, neither of which is particularly positive.

Because her father is so important to her, at college Natalie is quick to find a father substitute in the form of literature teacher Arthur Langdon, an ambitious, philandering academic, to whom she feels an instant if unsurprising connection: "He was subtly familiar to her, as though his words were meaningful on more than one level, as though there was an established communication between them in the course of five minutes" (105). Arnold Waite is predictably jealous of his rival: first he writes, "'be extremely cautious with Arthur Langdon,'" and then he revealingly declares:

"Do not under any circumstance allow Arthur Langdon to convert you to any philosophical viewpoint until you have first consulted me. As the person who knows you most dearly, and who loves you always best, I am equally the one most capable of telling you these things" [152].

These letters are Mr. Waite's way of maintaining control over his daughter even from afar. They vary in tone: some teasing and gently mocking in which she is his "princess" trapped in a tower and he is her "knight in shining armor"; some sterner missives which, like the one quoted above, use almost biblical language—"'let me, then, warn you direfully against false friends'" (150). Although Mr. Waite acknowledges that he has written to his daughter in the style of "'an old-testament God,'" he continues his letter in that vein nevertheless. He reminds his daughter "'that even your despair is part of my plan,'" thereby casting her acute unhappiness and growing psychological distress in malignantly divine terms. There is a strangely revealing moment too when he adds the following: "'Remember, too, that without you I could not exist: there can be no father without a daughter. You thus have a double responsibility, for my existence and for your own.'" Here Mr. Waite aligns himself with post-Enlightenment notions of the divine: God is a human construction, requiring human belief to exist. Mr. Waite concludes that letter with a dire (and accurate) warning: "'If you abandon me, you lose yourself.'" This is exactly what happens to Natalie, who rapidly spirals into severe mental illness, thus confirming the quasi-divine extent of Mr. Waite's malevolent power.

A dangerously controlling father figure also appears in Jackson's follow-up to *Hangsaman*, *The Bird's Nest*. Although, at first glance, *The Bird's Nest*, like *Hangsaman*, is a psychological novel (and the novel indeed has much in common with the popular psychiatric case-study subgenre of the 1950s), Jackson's clever reworking of classic Gothic tropes and willingness to immerse the reader in her protagonist's distorted worldview again mean that it also belongs to the Gothic tradition. Elizabeth Richmond is initially a less interesting protagonist than the more obviously disturbed Natalie. Her life, Jackson tells us, is one of dutiful routine and lifeless stoicism: "She had no friends, no parents, no associates and no plans beyond that of enduring the necessary interval before her departure with as little pain as possible" (8). However, it soon becomes clear that something is badly amiss. She suffers from constant, crippling headaches; she arrives at her boring desk job to find a nasty, puzzling letter that is only one in a series of such missives. Much to the displeasure of Aunt Morgen, her guardian and only living relative, she has been sneaking out of the house late at night yet claims not to remember a thing. At a social gathering she blacks out and causes several embarrassing scenes. At this point, it is decided that Elizabeth should receive professional help. She is referred to the affable, pompous Dr. Wright, who, having placed his patient under hypnosis, soon discovers the real reason for her odd behavior: multiple personality disorder.

We learn that Elizabeth's real father, Ernest, died when she was two years old, leaving her the large fortune that she will inherit upon turning twenty-five. Dr. Wright soon adopts a bluffly paternal role, cosily characterising her coterie of personalities as "'my little group of girls'" (141). Like Arnold Waite, and indeed, like many of the male figures in Jackson's novels, as Darryl Hattenhauer has noted, the ironically named Dr. Wright has academic pretensions, yet lacks the ability to comprehend much beyond his own jaundiced opinion (Hattenhauer 120). Like Waite, he also jokingly refers to himself as "God" since it is up to him, or so he believes, to decide which of Elizabeth's personalities survives. At one point he smugly compares himself to "'a great idol who has just seen a whole calf roasted at his altar'" (145). Once more, then, the most controlling person in the life of the disturbed Jackson heroine is an arrogant father figure with decidedly godlike pretensions, albeit one whose whose powers are more psychological than supernatural.

In naming the characters of this novel, Jackson alludes to the tradition of the alignment of the quasi-scientific and quasi-supernatural in the Gothic, in particular Mary Shelley's novel *Frankenstein*. Dr. Wright's first name, Victor, is just one of the many points of comparison between him and Victor Frankenstein, one of the most famously inadequate fictional fathers ever created. The name of Jackson's heroine, Elizabeth, recalls the name of Victor Frankenstein's doomed fiancée, the indirect victim of his disastrously unregulated scientific pursuits. In Jackson's novel too, a young woman suffers the consequences of male arrogance and misapplied science wielded by a man who appropriated to himself divine powers. Like his namesake, Wright meddles with forces he will not, or cannot, fully understand, forces that blur the line between magic and science. Like Frankenstein, he too is terrified of the unruly subject of his experiments. While his patient is under initial hypnosis, a charming, attractive alter ego, Beth, replaces the rather boring, colorless, Elizabeth: Dr. Wright quickly becomes very fond of this paragon of traditional femininity and harbors hopes of making her the dominant force in Elizabeth's troubled psyche. Soon after, another, rather less wholesome persona surfaces, "A Devil's mask" (50) that both repulses and disorients the doctor, recalling Frankenstein's response to the monster that he creates. Wright consistently describes Betsy, or "R3," in monstrous terms: she has "'The dreadful grinning face of a fiend'" and is a "'possessing demon,'" (54). Wright soon abandons all scientific detachment, justifying his deeply alarmed reaction to Betsy by claiming, "'even a man of science cannot always be impartial, and sensible, and invulnerable'" (132). Adding to his discomfiture is the fact that the undesirable Betsy can actually pretend to be both Beth and Elizabeth. This weakness is soon taken advantage of when Betsy absconds to New York, like Frankenstein's monster escaping the control of the scientist-father.

As Elizabeth and her various personas become even more rebellious, Jackson explicitly identifies the connections to Shelley's novel. Wright directly compares himself to his namesake, seemingly unaware of the disastrous consequences of *his* scientific pursuits:

> I saw myself, if the analogy be not too extreme, much like a Frankenstein with all the materials for a monster ready at hand, and when I slept, it was with dreams of myself patching and tying together, trying most hideously to chip away the evil from Betsy and leave what little that was good, while the other three stood by mockingly, waiting their turns [135].

As his influence further wanes, and Elizabeth's greediest, most immature personality, Bess, begins to take control for longer and longer periods of time, Wright can only berate himself in excessively melodramatic terms which clearly resemble those employed by Shelley's rogue scientist, as when he laments, "'I have made a monster and turned it loose upon the world'" (177). He may not have created Elizabeth's alter egos, but Wright's ignorance of modern psychiatric theory and insistence upon seeing her case as a struggle between good and evil, rather than as symptoms of a deeply rooted trauma, certainly do her little good. It is appropriate therefore that the climactic crisis and apparent resolution of his patient's condition happens when he is absent, as Elizabeth finally comes to terms with the blameless part she played in her dissolute mother's death and, as in *Hangsaman*, her various personalities seem to merge into a unified new persona.

Even then Dr. Wright and Aunt Morgen appear determined to maintain their influence. In the closing pages, Wright pompously declares, "'our responsibility is, clearly, to people this vacant landscape—fill this empty vessel ... and, with our own deep emotional reserves, enable the child to rebuild'" (234). They even jokingly suggest renaming their charge "Morgen Victoria." The fact that the new Elizabeth has cut her long hair short without their permission and laughs loudly at their suggestion presents the possibility, however, that their new charge, like Frankenstein's monster, will continue to elude the control of her creator.

We now move from discussing paternal figures who *believe* themselves to be godlike to a patriarch who seems godlike—to his descendants at least—speaking to them from beyond the grave: the founding Mr. Halloran in Jackson's fourth novel *The Sundial* (1956). This text constructs a knowing homage to the eighteenth century novel, presenting a wry reconfiguration of the traditional Gothic castle and of the conventional Gothic patriarch. Not surprisingly, the plot concerns the re-emergence of patriarchal control, in the form of the original (and dead) Mr. Halloran, a rich man who "could think of nothing better to do with his money than set up his own world" and apparently continues to boss his family about long after his death. The house he constructs, intended for his wife who died shortly after coming to live there,[2] has been built to his specifications of exact mathematical perfection.

Though long dead at the time that the novel's action takes place, the founding Halloran nevertheless manages to make himself alarmingly present, at least according to his daughter, Fanny Halloran, mouthpiece for his alleged warnings of impending doom. In the novel's opening pages, Aunt Fanny is a faint, doddering presence, ignored by everyone. Her profound attachment to the house and its grounds has no impact upon her domineering sister-in-law Orianna, who announces her intention to purge the house of all its unnecessary inhabitants and to send Fanny to live in a disused tower—in the tradition of many Gothic heroines. Significantly, Fanny's first "revelation" occurs the morning after this bombshell has been dropped. Shortly thereafter, Fanny finds herself at the titular sundial, which is "set badly off center," and experiences her first "revelation."[3] Fanny attributes the voice she suddenly hears in her head to her beloved father, creator of her beloved home. It is unsurprising therefore that there is only one truly safe place in the coming cataclysm: "'Tell them in the house, tell them, in the house, tell them that there is danger. Tell them in the house that in the house it is safe. The father will watch the house, but there is danger. Tell them'" (28). The source of this "danger," we are soon told, is an apocalypse that will come "'from the sky and from the ground and from the sea'"; there will be "'black fire and red water and the earth turning and screaming.'" Unsurprisingly, when Fanny staggers back inside with the news, everyone is unimpressed. It takes a "miraculous" sign to lend credibility to her remarkable claim: "a small, brightly banded snake was watching them from the fireplace, seeming frozen with attention, and then, turning at once into liquid movement, slipped from the fireplace across the heavy carpet ... angled behind a bookcase and disappeared" (22).

Despite the tenuous nature of the manifestation in question, the fact that it seems to confirm Fanny's outlandish revelation is enough to convert the others to her new creed. It also helps that it suits almost everyone (except Orianna) to believe in her story. After all, Essex (the librarian), Mary Jane (Lionel Halloran's widow), Miss Ogilvie (Fancy's governess) and Fanny herself have all just been told to leave the house. The prophecy conveniently gives them all an excuse to stay on indefinitely. For Fanny the prophecies also mean new standing within the house. For the first time in her life, she is the center of attention. Her spiritual dispensation means that she can behave in any manner she likes, and attribute it to her visions.

In fact, it is likely that in this case, the seemingly powerful father has been appropriated by his daughter for her own uses and that Jackson is suggesting a subversion of the powers of the patriarch. The incorporeal Mr. Halloran seems the apotheosis of Jackson's godlike patriarchs: where we once had Arnold Waite facetiously declaring, "'I am God,'" in *The Sundial* we have a long-dead father who is presented as God. Having created his own world, it seems as if Halloran is corresponding from the afterlife in order to ensure that his "chosen people," his bickering descendants, remain there forever. Yet since the more believable explanation is that Fanny is hallucinating, or even making up the whole story, either to ensure that she is not evicted, or, most suggestively, out of a genuine attempt to articulate what she believes her father's feelings would be, the father is revealed to be powerless, and actually nonexistenct.

The power of the father is further subverted as Fanny's privileged position as new-world prophet is overtaken by that of Orianna, self-proclaimed "Queen" of their future state. Orianna compiles a list of rules to be adhered to in the new world; among these is damning stipulation that "'It is expected that all members of the party will keep in mind their position as inheritors of the world, and conduct themselves accordingly'.... 'Father, what have you done to me?'" wails Fanny as she reads Orianna's rules, realizing that her revelations have been hijacked by her ambitious, possibly murderous, sister-in-law, as Lenemaja Friedman suggests. This power too is destabilized as the rebellious, devious Fancy, youthful heir to the Halloran mansion, voices opposition towards Orianna's divinely sanctioned bossiness: "'I'm sick and tired of hearing God bully everyone'" (153).[4] The novel ends on the eve of destruction, with the discovery of Orianna's body at the foot of the stairs. Given the resentment her domineering ways had inspired there are plenty of suspects, the most likely of which is Fancy, who has long coveted her grandmother's gold crown. Thus Jackson concludes this novel with the last of a series of rebellions, showing the instability of the power constructed by the patriarchy.

In *The Haunting of Hill House*, Jackson continues the pattern of young women victimized by malevolent male patriarchy, although on the surface the novel appeals more supernatural than psychological. While several critics have rightly noted the importance of mothers in *The Haunting of Hill House*, the role of fathers has yet to be scrutinized to the same extent.[5] However, it is important to recognize the malignant presence of the builder of Hill House, Hugh Crain, a man who has much in common with the founding Halloran in *The Sundial*; for both men their self-designed houses are a powerful means of control.

We are pointedly told that Hugh Crain "made his house to suit his mind" (105), a far from complimentary statement, given that "every angle is slightly wrong" and the building is "a masterpiece of architectural misdirection," with the potential to cause madness in those foolish enough to stay there for any length of time. We get a further disturbing insight into the mind of Hugh Crain from a book written for the edification of his eldest daughter, titled: "Memories for Sophia Anne Lester Crain." The book consists of excerpts appropriated from other works and handwritten epistles from the man himself. Unsurprisingly, his first precept is the suitably biblical "'Honor thy Father and Mother'" (168), and the rest of the work is composed of gruesome etchings and his helpful thoughts on topics such as the everlasting agony meted out to those who go to hell for disobeying the Law of the Father. The *pièce de résistance* comes in the closing pages, which Crain has, of course, written in his own blood:

> Live virtuously, be meek, have faith in thy Redeemer, and in me, thy father, and I swear to thee that we will be joined together hereafter in unending bliss. Accept these precepts from thy devoted father, who in humbleness of spirit has made this book.... Thy ever loving father, in this world and the next, author of thy being and guardian of thy virtue; in meekest love, Hugh Crain [169].

Note that, yet again, we have a bullying patriarch who urges his daughter to have "faith" in him and to obey his precepts as she would those laid down by God. Like Arnold Waite, Dr. Wright and the founding Halloran, Hugh Crain used suggestively old-testament-style language while laying down his fatherly commandments. Like his predecessors, he also has an elevated view of his own status.

Although he does not *explicitly* proclaim himself to be godlike, Crain urges Sophia to have "faith" in him and in "thy Redeemer" in the same sentence, and concludes by declaring himself "'author of thy being and guardian of thy virtue.'" Like Halloran, Crain sees his status as a creator manifested in two varieties of creation: his children and his house. Both men built their houses to reflect the eccentricities and aspirations of their respective minds, and both men, like Dr. Wright and the autocratic Arnold Waite, seek to exert the same degree of objectifying control over their potentially troublesome daughters. The fact that such conduct consistently has disastrous consequences for the daughter (or daughter substitute) is irrelevant to the project of the patriarch who is malignantly unaware of the subjectivity of the daughter.

It is hardly surprising to learn that, in keeping with Gothic tradition, Crain's wives died young, and in tragic circumstances. The daughters to whom he bequeathed his malign property found no happiness there either: they spent their adult lives quarreling over the house until the older sister, who lived there, died under predictably questionable circumstances. This is a place in which terrible things happen to vulnerable women. Jackson's Hill House reveals then that the Gothic house, often associated with the maternal, is perhaps as actively misogynistic as it is monstrously maternal.

Eleanor, the protagonist of the novel, recognizes the danger of the house during the introductory tour; the new guests come across a marble statue to which both Eleanor and Theo, a fellow research subject, react with instinctive abhorrence, half facetious, half genuine. It is the perceptive Theo who hazards the best guess as to what the statue represents:

> It's a family portrait, you sillies. Composite. *Any*one would know it at once; that figure in the centre, that tall, undraped—good heavens!—masculine one, that's old Hugh, patting himself on the back because he built Hill House, and his two attendant nymphs are his daughters [103].

Dr. Montague, the researcher who has himself adopted a paternalistic tone towards his young companions,[6] not surprisingly sees the statue as "'a symbol of the protection of the house, surely.'" Yet Eleanor perceptively and correctly views the statue as a potential threat: "'I'd hate to think it might fall on us'" (103). As she unconsciously recognises at the time, the claustrophobic, oppressive family dynamic depicted in Crain's statue—the powerful male flanked by submissive daughters—is one that has the power to do her great harm: in a sense, the statue—or rather, what it represents—*does* fall on her. When Eleanor has ultimately been destabilized by the paternal malignancy that surrounds her, she roams the house at night, curtsies before the statue, and asks, "'Hugh Crain ... will you come and dance with me?'" before climbing up the library tower and almost falling to her death. Eleanor's inability to resist the desire for a place of her own, which an inherently patriarchal cultural consensus has ingrained within her, ensures that for her, as for Hugh Crain's unfortunate wives, this homecoming will be fatal.

Even before Eleanor arrives at Hill House, though, she is under the influence of another patriarch, her father. We are told that her psychokinetic abilities, the likely cause of much of the novel's supernatural occurrences, were triggered by the death of her father. We are told that "She could not remember a winter before her father's death on a cold winter's day" (15) and that the shower of stones which eventually brought her to the attention of paranormal investigator Dr. Montague happened soon after (7). The trauma caused by her own father's early death made Eleanor all the more susceptible to the deadly charms of Hugh Crain's monstrous house.

The dangers of the house appear to be supernatural—and Jackson deploys all the supernatural Gothic tropes in her depiction of this haunted house. The famous, magnificently atmospheric opening paragraph of the novel leaves the reader in no doubt as to three things about Hill House:

that it is somehow alive, that it is "not sane" and that something malevolent resides there. Dr. Montague, who has been "looking for an honestly haunted house all of his life" believes, with good reason, that he has found it here (4). "'Some houses are born bad,'" he tells the others as they huddle round the fireplace on their first night there. On her second night there, Eleanor is awoken by a loud rapping on the walls which reminds her of her invalid mother: she and Theo huddle together on the bed while something tries to find its way inside their room. Dr. Montague finds a cold spot that cannot be scientifically measured. At night, there is the sound of hysterical laughter, and a message found written on the wall in red letters says "HELP ELEANOR COME HOME" (146).

Ultimately, however, it is left up to the reader to decide to what extent the supernatural activity in the house is a manifestation of Eleanor's own troubled psyche; it does seem likely that she is indirectly responsible for at least some of what occurs. After all, as we are frequently reminded during the course of the novel, this is an "evil" house—Dr. Montague calls it "deranged," "sick" and "disturbed" (70). Indeed, Hill House specializes in targeting those most susceptible to its malign influence. Dr. Montague hopes that by bringing Eleanor and Theo, who both seem to possess some psychic ability, to the house, he can intensify the forces already at work there. Although Eleanor vehemently denies any such talent, there is no doubt that from early on, she feels a strange kind of affinity to this "masterpiece of architectural misdirection" and that the escalating intensity of the disturbances (which mimic those of an angry poltergeist, a phenomenon often associated with disturbed young women) parallels her own increasing psychological distress. And so, even in Jackson's most overtly supernatural ghost story, there is room to believe that the supernatural is only a code for the dangers of the patriarch and the damage inflicted by the patriarchy.

It seems all the more fitting therefore that Jackson's final completed novel, *We Have Always Lived in the Castle*, should feature a heroine who successfully rejects (and ultimately even *exorcises*) the precepts of a tyrannical father figure—twice—albeit in a manner that suggests that she is even more mentally disturbed than her predecessors. At the tender age of twelve, Mary Catherine (Merricat) Blackwood spiked the family sugar bowl with arsenic in retaliation for having been sent to bed early by her overbearing father. The sole survivors of this precocious act of mass murder are her beloved elder sister Constance (who disliked sugar) and her uncle Julian, whose mind has been permanently befuddled by his ordeal.

What facts we learn about John Blackwood, head of the family, suggest that he was greedy and materialistic, took great pride in his fine house and in his many possessions, and had a strong miserly streak. Public relations are clearly not the Blackwood forte, and John, like his daughters later on, had few friends in the local village. His relationship with the rebellious Merricat, who as a second daughter is inessential to the patriarchy, seems to have been a difficult one: as Constance notes, "'Merricat was always in disgrace'" (432). Indeed, it is the kindly, sane-enough-seeming Constance's reaction to the murders which suggests to the reader more than anything else that he and the rest of the clan may well have gotten their just desserts. She apparently "told the police those people deserved to die" (432) and took the blame on Merricat's behalf, although a jury later acquitted her.

Jackson repeats the pattern of the exorcism of the male in the episode of Cousin Charles. The six-year idyll that follows the death of the tyrannical patriarch is suddenly disrupted when the last able-bodied male in the Blackwood line, scheming Cousin Charles, turns up on the doorstep. Merricat immediately recoils from Charles for two reasons: First, he reminds Constance of the world she has been cut off from for so long, and of the chance for a normal life she has forfeited by remaining in exile with her mad sister. Secondly, and even more threateningly, Charles not only "looks like Father" (151) but also possesses a similarly domineering personality. "Charles is a ghost," Merricat plaintively declares soon after his arrival, as he strides around the house covetously cataloguing its contents, and it is true, for while Charles may not be a revenant in the *supernatural* sense, he *is* a powerful reminder of the patriarch she had previously gone to such violent extremes to overthrow.

As the novel, all of which is relayed to us via Merricat's obviously subjective first-person narration, progresses, Charles's intrusion becomes an ever-greater threat to her carefully constructed fantasy world. He insists that Constance consider leaving the house, sets himself up as potential husband, allies himself with the hostile locals and, ominously, sleeps in John Blackwood's room (which suggests that he is trying to become some sort of combination lover/father figure to the naïve and submissive Constance).[7] He also suggests that something be done about the unruly and obviously disturbed Merricat—the implication is that she be placed in a home of some kind—and, for a moment, it looks as if Constance is beginning to come round to his point of view. Once her magical charms and incantations have failed, the only option Merricat can see is to resort to the kind of violent behavior she exhibited six years previously: she knocks her cousin's smouldering pipe (itself a suggestive symbol of masculinity) into a wastepaper basket and semi-accidentally burns the house down. Violence, it would seem, is the only sure way to counter such a powerful threat.

The arrival of a mob of resentful locals who do nothing to put the fire out—and actually loot and smash what is left of the smouldering house—vindicates Merricat's paranoid world view. In the aftermath, she and Constance at last retreat to a completely female and weirdly domestic world of their own amid the ruins. Charles, having been denied Constance, the house, and the wealth he feels to be rightfully his, is last glimpsed trudging around the grounds with a newspaper reporter, unsuccessfully trying to get the women to show themselves. Whereas Charles was once the "ghost" picking up where Merricat's domineering father had left off, ultimately then he and the tyrannical patriarchal control he represents have forever been exorcised from the house. Indeed, it is the Blackwood women themselves who, embracing their new-found status as modern-day witches and settling into a bizarrely domesticated existence amid the ruins of their home, contentedly haunt the place now, albeit in a manner that is more metaphorical than supernatural.

Despite Jackson's reputation as a supernatural novelist then (a notion belied by the fact that only one of her six novels and a handful of her stories have such a slant) we can see that the *real* horror in her Gothic fictions all too often arises from real-world threats, and in particular from the always complex, often threatening, and sorely overlooked relationship between fathers and daughters in her work. Given that Jackson herself must have been all too aware of the immense pressure placed upon young women during the post–World War II era to conform to a highly conservative, often stifling set of cultural and social expectations, it is perhaps unsurprising that her fiction should so consistently enact narratives in which troubled young women struggle to escape the control of domineering father figures. By reconfiguring the tropes and settings of the classical Gothic in order to reflect the anxieties of her own era, Jackson dramatizes the flexibility of the Gothic that evolves to respond to historical anxieties.

Notes

1. The troubled nature of father-daughter relations in Jackson's novels is in many respects as significant a factor in the construction of her unique brand of the psychological Gothic as the often discussed mother-daughter dynamic.

2. A similar fate befalls Hugh Crain's wife in *The Haunting of Hill House* (1959). Like Hill House too, the Halloran mansion is constructed according to unusual architectural requirements; both houses recall Horace Walpole's Strawberry Hill.

3. It is interesting to note that the source of Fanny's revelation—her father—and the message given have much in common with the real life case study recounted by Leon Festinger *et al.* in the sociological study *When Prophecy Fails*. The book follows the development of a group which believed that their founder, a Mrs. Marian Keech, had received messages from outer space, mediated through the spirit of her dead father. Soon, Mrs. Keech received notice that a devastating global flood, caused by the reemergence of the lost continents Atlantis and Mu, was going to destroy the world and wipe out all but a few chosen survivors. Festinger's sociologists made contact with the group when their revelations were made public, and observed the consequent failure of the end to arrive as scheduled. It is possible that the UFO worshipping "True Believers" that Jackson satirizes in *Sundial* may be based upon

this group. My thanks to Judie Newman for this observation; see also Richard Pascal's comments on the same case in "New World Miniatures: Shirley Jackson's The Sundial and Post-war American Society."

4. Significantly, in *We Have Always Lived in the Castle* (1962) the only girls who actively resist patriarchal control are violent sociopaths.

5. The psychic disturbances which mark Eleanor's ill-fated stay in Hill House can therefore be said to have as much to do with the trauma caused by the loss of her much-loved father as with the more recent death of her mother.

6. Dr. Montague is, of course, yet another male scientist indicted by Jackson for scientifically and paternalistically objectifying a young woman.

7. Those interested in delving more into inter-familial dynamics in the novel should read Karen J. Hall's interesting article "Sisters in Collusion: Safety and Revolt in Shirley Jackson's *We Have Always Lived in the Castle*," which quite persuasively posits that Merricat's disturbed mental state and violent actions are the result of sexual abuse by her father.

Works Cited

Festinger, Leon, et al. *When Prophecy Fails*. Minneapolis: Minnesota University Press, 1955.

Friedman, Lenemaja, *Shirley Jackson*, Boston: Twayne, 1975.

Hall, Karen J. "Sisters in Collusion: Safety and Revolt in Shirley Jackson's *We Have Always Lived in the Castle*." In *The Significance of Sibling Relationships in Literature*. Bowling Green, Ohio: Bowling Green University Press, 1993.

Hattenhauer, Darryl. *Shirley Jackson's American Gothic*. Albany: State University of New York Press, 2003.

Jackson, Shirley. *The Bird's Nest*. London: n.p., 1956.

_____. *Hangsaman,* London: Victor Gollancz, 1951.

_____. *The Haunting of Hill House*. 1959. New York: Penguin, 1987.

_____. *The Sundial*. 1958. New York: Ace Books, n.d.

_____. *We Have Always Lived in the Castle*. 1962. *The Masterpieces of Shirley Jackson*. London: Robinson, 1996.

Pascal, Richard. "New World Miniatures: Shirley Jackson's *The Sundial* and Post-war American Society." In *Shirley Jackson: Essays on the Literary Legacy*, ed. Bernice M. Murphy, 81–103. North Carolina: McFarland, 2005.

Part III
HOMOSEXUAL HORROR

10

Other Love: Le Fanu's Carmilla *as Lesbian Gothic*

ADRIENNE ANTRIM MAJOR

> *The lesbian is never with us, it seems, but always somewhere else: in the shadows, in the margins, hidden from history, out of sight, a wanderer in the dark, a lost soul, a tragic mistake, a pale denizen of the night. She is far away and she is dire.*
> —Terry Castle, The Apparitional Lesbian

> *Was there here a disguise and a romance? I had read in old story books of such things. What if a boyish lover had found his way into the house, and sought to prosecute his suit in masquerade, with the assistance of a clever old adventuress?*
> —Sheridan Le Fanu, Carmilla

In *Carmilla* (1872) Sheridan Le Fanu encodes both the language of feminine intellectual discourse and transgressive feminine sexuality in the trope of lesbianism. At once subversive and transgressive, his lesbians revel both in their illicit sexuality and in their manipulations of the possibilities of Gothic narrative. The anxiety of the text is experienced solely by the men who are left out of the lesbian love equation and out of the female Gothic. The patriarchal protections set in place to shield women from their own sexuality, and thus men from the anxiety of feminine power, are demonstrated throughout the text to be useless in the face of the lesbian manipulation of its mores. In *Carmilla,* Le Fanu presents us with a text that is, throughout its length, neither didactic nor contained. Instead it poses a paradigm of feminine power and lesbian love that might well create terror in the hearts of his contemporaries: the specter of their women seduced away from them into a world of illicit sexuality and uncontrollable perversion.

The term "lesbian Gothic" is here problematic. As generated by such theorists as Terry Castle and Paulina Palmer, it has been used to describe a contemporary subset of Ellen Moers's Female Gothic which "centres on female sexual representation—its cultural and political ramifications"

(Palmer 3).[1] In the work of these theorists, "lesbian Gothic" has signified the work of women who are lesbian, and who use the Gothic as a way to explore and celebrate "transgressive" sexuality, while at the same time honoring the victimization and sacrifice (what Terry Castle terms "ghosting" in *The Apparitional Gothic*) suffered by lesbians. Le Fanu, however, anxiously recasts the Female Gothic mode[2] in *Carmilla*, attempting to ensure protection for the patriarchy from lesbian—and indeed, female— horror. However, due to the nature of the Gothic genre, be it male or female, slippages[3] remain in Le Fanu's narrative which serve to allow the lesbian, yet un-ghosted, to continue in circulation. These slippages include a sneaking sympathy throughout the narrative for the sexually vital yet languid Carmilla on the part of the narrator, and a significantly Gothic failure of resolution—Carmilla is destroyed, but will her victims become vampires? And what of the other mysterious figures surrounding and abetting Carmilla? Both the endeavor to create a patriarchally "safe" narrative by suppressing the lesbian vampire,[4] the sign of transgressive female power, and the conflicting Gothic uncertainty about whether or not the "pure" narrator herself has become a vampire mark this work as a seminal foray into the lesbian Gothic.

Related to us through the first-hand narrative of a woman of unknown patronymic,[5] whose very name is suppressed for thirty-eight pages,[6] the story of Carmilla emerges as a forbidden tale of the horror of feminine evil, represented by lesbian lust, which exposes, in its sexual extravagance, a terror of any woman, even the consumptive and collapsing, but above all the dead. The eponymous Carmilla, indeed, has been dead for several generations before the story begins.[7] As the "Chinese-box"[8] of a narrative reveals its secretive inner chambers, we learn that Laura, the primary narrator, has descended through her (dead) mother's side from the mysterious and evil family of the Karnsteins. In the beginning of the nouvelle, Laura is disappointed to hear that the prospective visit of Bertha Rheinfeldt, a young lady similarly situated to herself in birth and beauty, must be denied due to that young lady's sudden and mysterious death. Instead a chance visit from a beautiful stranger, also Laura's contemporary, leads to the revelation and potential destruction of the revenant strain haunting the family of the Karnsteins. This mysterious stranger is the eponymous Carmilla, and her ravishing of Laura provides one of the lesbian contexts to this convoluted tale of blood ties and blood lust. Interwoven into this primary seduction tale are two more: Carmilla's own, and Bertha's. Unlimned and shadowy behind these three tales, there lurks a fourth tale concerning the mysterious mother figure who appears in each of Carmilla's amorous seductions as the chaperone and pander for Carmilla. As the tale unfolds, we learn that Bertha has been romanced and destroyed by Carmilla, that Carmilla herself is actually Laura's maternal ancestress, and that the sexual relationship between Laura and Carmilla must result in Laura's death and metamorphosis into a vampire herself. The tale ostensibly ends with Carmilla's ritual destruction by a largely unnamed bevy of men who flock to the village of Karnstein in order to rid the world of Carmilla's "atrocious lusts" (327).

However, Le Fanu's heroes—scientist, philosopher, soldier—fail: Laura still belongs in part to the bloodline of the Karnsteins and to Carmilla. Laura and Bertha are carefully chaperoned, protected girls in households headed by powerful men: Laura's father an Englishman, and Bertha's guardian a general. These men are well-read, rational, pious models of Victorian middle-class virtues. So too their daughters, carefully brought up, educated, innocent and shielded from masculine importunities. Such evil as unfolds throughout the tale unfolds through and because of the women, despite all of the protections of domesticity. It becomes clear that feminine sexuality and insidious female bloodlines are at fault; against feminine sexuality, men are powerless. That is the nature of degenerative feminine evil, Le Fanu concludes. It cannot be completely banished by the rational, scientific process of staking and decapitating the vampire's corpse. Somehow, Carmilla still exercises a fascination over Laura, "the consumptive sublime,"[9] never quite recovering her health or her nerves after the "terror of recent events" (336). Since Le Fanu reveals at the beginning of the text that Laura is dead by the time we read her narrative, the ambiguous thoughts she has of Carmilla during her decline and death indicate that she herself has metamorphosed into a vampire. The lesbian has overcome masculine precautions to emerge all-powerful, self-regenerating. What kind of woman is Laura after all, the reader is to ask, if, after all has been explained, she still feels fondness for her lover/murderer?

Authorial ambivalence marks the tale throughout its length: Le Fanu achieves a pervasive duality by presenting the traditional comforts of distance and alienation, and then effacing them by enfolding them within a domesticated narrative that teases the ordinary out of the Other. Through this endeavor, the lesbian Other lurks invidiously within the domesticated angel despite all that can be done to preserve its purity. Considerable critical argument has gone into the positioning of Laura as an "everywoman" (Senf 28). The elision of her name, her patronymic anonymity, her ur-conventional response to the experiences that she undergoes, mark her as such. Thus by positioning her within the primary lesbian relationship of the nouvelle, Le Fanu exposes the possibility of corruption for any woman by the discovery of her own sexual response. The mere fact of lesbian possibility, deemed so threatening that even in 1921 it was not mentioned in law for fear that the utterance of the possibility would lead to its promulgation and practice (Castle 12), haunts

Le Fanu's aesthetic through Laura's acceptance of and pleasure in Carmilla's c/overt caresses.

Le Fanu creates the schema that will mark the lesbian relationship within his description of the setting of the tale. Markers of traditional Gothic alienation, such as distance and isolation, appear comfortingly in the first pages of the narrative. It takes place amidst ubiquitous sylvan desolation and isolated *Schlösser*; Laura's nearest neighbors are, she is careful to tell us, "nearly twenty miles away to the right" (275), not counting, of course, the ruined village only "three miles to the westward" (275) and the nearest inhabited village "seven of your English miles to the left" (275). The narrative is set carefully on nights in which the full moon emits "odylic[10] and magnetic influences" (281). This is what we expect of a Gothic novel—a lonely and isolated spot comfortably removed from the ordinary. Le Fanu, however, remorselessly removes any of the comfortable Otherness of the scene by presenting terms that evoke Jane Austen's practical and prosaic detailing of a suitor's income. The *Schloss* is managed on "eight or nine hundred a year" and the location "is marvelously cheap" (275). The moon's "odylic" influences are related by Laura's two governesses, Madame Perrodon—"fat, middle-aged, and romantic" (276)—and Mademoiselle De Lafontaine—"assumed to be psychological, metaphysical, and something of a mystic" (276). Laura describes their discussion as a "tinkle" in her "listless ears" (278). Even the mysterious arrival of Carmilla—a moonlight carriage accident, a distraught mother, mysterious menservants, a nameless black woman sneering through the carriage window—wreathes itself in appropriate shrouds of respectability. The mother seeks the chivalrous protection that Laura's father is pleased to offer, the girl is clearly upper-class and gently bred. Assured of proper chaperonage (*two* governesses), Carmilla is allowed to remain at the *Schloss* for a period of three months' time. Thus Le Fanu deftly inscribes and then effaces all of the signifiers of Gothic distancing safety: the mysteriousness of the locale and the landscape, the power of the moon and the circumstances of the vampire's invitation to the household are all laid before us with ruthless domestic detail.

Le Fanu further works at the level of the narrative structure itself to demonstrate the possibility of loss of male narrative control. Falling into the traditional rubric of Gothic narration,[11] he produces his text from the fictional distance of a series of chimerical[12] removes with which he attempts to protect both himself and the reader from the lesbian contamination of the narrative itself. These removes attempt to surround and contain the text by imposing a rational, "scientific" framework through which both author and reader are "protected" by distance and death from an otherwise suspicious and disturbing evocation. Le Fanu himself abjures authorial agency by inventing two men, both physicians, to act as intermediaries and transmit the narrative, itself told in first person by a woman. The first of these men purports to be an editor, a nameless creation who bears full responsibility for transcribing the text for publication to interest the "lay" reader. The second is Dr. Martin Hesselius, who has collected the tale and used it as a footnote in his formal, scientific writing, presented to us in the introduction elusively as an "Essay [sic] on the strange subject which the MS. illuminates" (274). Having thus assured his readers that the tale upon which we are about to embark has been carefully read and commented on, dissected, analyzed and made safe, Le Fanu then proceeds to destabilize or to remove all of this elaborate protection: "I have determined, therefore," the "editor" informs us, "to abstain from presenting any *précis* of the learned Doctor's reasoning, or extract from his statement on a subject which he describes as 'involving, not improbably, some of the profoundest arcana of our dual existence, and its intermediates'"(274). In this single gesture of inscription and erasure, Le Fanu is able to present a wildly unstable text: voices are called upon only through a feminine agency, and the touch of the story itself, with its fevered eroticism and explicit pleasures, escapes from the suppression of masculine analysis, however anxiously reassured we may be at the existence of such suppression.

Having created a pattern of the domesticated Other, Le Fanu embarks on a tale of sexuality between women living under the "protection" of the patriarchy. Laura, in her compromised position as narrator, relates three tales of vampire seduction that are distinctly lesbian: the players are all women engaged in intensely physical relations with one another. Each of the narratives is intermingled, so that no one narrative is distinct from the others. Personality and individuality becomes indistinct and indeterminate, chronology is suspended, and even identities become fixed within the other. Laura remarks, "The first occurrence in my existence, which produced a terrible impression upon my mind, which, in fact, never has been effaced, was one of the very earliest incidents of my life which I can recollect" (276). Note the emphasis on the formative in this moment: this is the *first* occurrence in her *existence;* similarly, it is one of her *earliest ... recollections.* Laura is not safe, not protected by youth or femininity but rather exposed immediately upon remembrance to the sexuality that runs within (m)other love: "I saw ... a young lady who was kneeling, with her hands under the coverlet. She caressed me with her hands, and lay down beside me on the bed, and drew me towards her, smiling; I felt immediately delightfully soothed, and fell asleep again" (277). The infant Laura experiences both the comfort of the mother's caress and the beauty of the lover. The pain she undergoes—"I was awakened by a sensation as if two needles ran into my breast very deep at the same moment" (277)—marks her precipitation into consciousness, both from the sleep into which her mother/lover has caressed her, and into the self-knowledge of a distinctly remembering being. However, upon her first meeting with Carmilla, Laura's own conscious identity, as it has been establish by the vampiritic incident, is called into question. Carmilla exclaims: "I saw *you*—most assuredly you— as I see you now; a beautiful young lady, with golden hair and large blue eyes, and lips—your lips—you, as you are here" (288). Laura's identity or at least the incident at which she marks the onset of her consciousness is usurped by Carmilla, and we are given, at the same time, our first physical description of the narrator: the reader's own vision becomes elided within the conscription of consciousness as all lose identity within the amorphous lesbian whole. Traditionally, of course, the elision of identity comes with marriage: the woman loses her name, her property, her legal identity within the identity and consciousness of the man. Here, men are dangerously missing from the politics of female identity, and women identify themselves as the Other.

The confusion of gender and identity marks the growing anxiety with which Le Fanu manipulates his lesbian text. As the attraction between Laura and Carmilla becomes more explicit, it is more frantically coded as evil/Other and, even more threateningly, unavoidable. Women, Le Fanu warns, are naturally attracted to one another because of their identification with the mother, and their lack of understanding of themselves within a differential. Looking at the Other, they see themselves. Laura's response to Carmilla, having identified her mysterious guest as the stranger who appeared by her bed at the beginning of her existence, is one of attraction and yearning. Again and again she confesses that she longs to know more about Carmilla, and yearns for the day when Carmilla will keep no secrets from her. And it is not merely knowledge that Laura would take from Carmilla. Her own attraction to Carmilla's beauty upsets and excites her:

> Now the truth is, I felt rather unaccountably towards the beautiful stranger. I did feel, as she said, "drawn towards her," but there was also something of repulsion. In this ambiguous feeling, however, the sense of attraction immensely prevailed. She interested and won me; she was so beautiful and so indescribably engaging [289].

Despite this confession of ambiguity, the prevailing feeling here is one of attraction; Laura desires Carmilla because of her beauty, but also because of a quality which Laura cannot express. Lacanian analysis would seem to be prefigured here, with the obvious caveat that completion, the conjoining of the self within the mirrored whole, which in Lacan is unobtainable, in Le Fanu is supernatural and ultimately evil. The Lacanian infant undergoes a mirror stage as a rite of passage or an initiation to the fragmented self. Le Fanu's overturning of the fragmented self with the lesbian whole evokes his deep suspicion of the projected yearning of the self for the whole, particularly when the whole refers to women. That which Laura and by extension Le Fanu then cannot express is the monstrous completion of the singular sex, here configured as lesbian love.

Le Fanu carefully and overtly sexualizes the "friendship" between Laura and her guest: Carmilla's behavior toward Laura is one of intense physicality: she gazes "passionately" at Laura (289); places her "pretty arms" about her neck (291); rests her cheek next to Laura's; whispers softly in her ear. We are thus left to understand that the "engaging quality" so irresistible, so completely unnamable must be sexual. Laura herself is not reluctant to return these physical marks of friendship. While together in Carmilla's bedroom, she loosens her friend's hair, fondling and playing with it, remarking on its color and weight with passionate intensity (290). When she seeks information from Carmilla—a transgressive act which she has promised her father she would not do—she does so by mounting a direct "attack," using "caresses" to accomplish her purpose (291).[13]

Both women recognize their affection for one another as love: Laura explains, "Young people like, and even love, on impulse" (289), when describing her initial—and continuing—response to Carmilla. Carmilla exclaims to Laura in a moment of blinding honesty that she is required to destroy Laura's life because she loves her so much:

> Dearest, your little heart is wounded; think me not cruel because I obey the irresistible law of my strength and weakness; if your dear heart is wounded, my wild heart bleeds with yours. In the rapture of my enormous humiliation I live in your warm life, and you shall die—die, sweetly die—into mine. I cannot help it; as I draw near to you, you, in your turn, will draw near to others, and learn the rapture of that cruelty, which yet is love [291].

The language that Carmilla uses here is perversely accurate: because of Carmilla, Laura will have orgasmic experiences (here configured as "the little death" of Shakespearian punning—"sweetly die"), and in order to maintain Carmilla's "life," she will die, but in that death be released from the trammels of social/cultural constraints, and roam with the essentially masculine license to choose her own love objects, as Carmilla has chosen her.

Neither does Laura reject Carmilla's proffered love, even though she does protest that it makes her feel uncomfortable. Since Le Fanu is using the unstable position of a purportedly naïve narrator who nevertheless knows the ending of the story even as she tells it, this discomfort is suspect: it could easily have been written in as an editorial gloss rather than a clear reflection of Laura's response to Carmilla. Indeed, when Carmilla makes her most direct announcement of love to Laura, Laura's reaction is to comment on the loveliness of the moon, as if to inscribe the beauty of the night with the wonder of her lover's declaration. When Laura begins this interchange with an attack of her own, declaring that such a romantic and beautiful figure as Carmilla must already have a lover, Carmilla's response is to confirm the women's love for one another: "'I have been in love with no one, and never shall,' she whispered, 'unless it should be you.'" Laura frames this avowal: "How beautiful she looked in the moonlight!" (300).

Laura's exclamation seals the love of the women, and marks the beginning of their sexual union. Here Le Fanu is careful to provide a duality of reading experiences. Laura's actual memories of Carmilla's nighttime seductions are carefully occluded, in the narrative that is allowable. Yet Laura's catalogue of her physical reactions—"trembling"; "strange, tumultuous excitement that was pleasurable" (292); "lassitude" and "languor" after a night visitation, and intimations of "unaccountable fascination with earlier symptoms" (307)—point to sexual arousal, excitement and satisfaction. As the nouvelle progresses, the "safety" of sickness and clinical diagnosis are cunningly overlaid on a more sexually explicit narration, until that point when Laura finally recounts the first (renewed) visit of the vampire and orgasmic consummation:

> Sometimes there came a sensation as if a hand was drawn softly along my cheek and neck. Sometimes it was as if warm lips kissed me, and longer and more lovingly as they reached my throat, but there the caress fixed itself. My heart beat faster, my breathing rose and fell rapidly and full drawn; a sobbing, that rose into a sense of strangulation, supervened, and turned into a dreadful convulsion, in which my senses left me, and I became unconscious [307].

Clearly the union here is physical, sexual and pleasurable. Laura describes multiple experiences in this single catalogue (three weeks of such intense nightly visitation) and notes that the only symptoms she displays, besides the languor, is a tendency to be rather more pale than usual. Her narrative voice records "horrible sufferings" (308) but what she actually describes has been narrated in far more complicitous language. Despite the adjectival iteration of "dreadful," the primary color of her remarks is found in such adverbs as "softly" and "lovingly." Indeed, her inclination, during the weeks that elapse, is to deny any "suffering" at all, and to refuse to recognize her newly found sexuality as an illness: "My father asked me often whether I was ill; but ... I persisted in assuring him that I was quite well.... In a sense this was true" (308).

In fact, during the entirety of the narrative, her response to the "horrors" that entrap her is always first to worry for Carmilla's safety and security. Even after learning that Carmilla is actually one and the same as the Mircalla whom the general claimed had murdered his ward, Laura's feelings of gratitude upon returning home turn to "dismay" (335) upon learning that her beloved Carmilla, whom she has not seen since one fleeting glance revealed her in the tomb of the Karnsteins, has not returned there before her. Of the termination of her relationship with Carmilla, she remarks only that her disappearance marks "the discontinuance of my nightly sufferings" (309). After this, her narrative turns businesslike, drawing its information from "a copy of the report of the Imperial Commission, with the signatures of all who were present ... attached in verification of the statement" (336). In recording her own emotional response to the loss of her lover, she betrays only the ambivalence which marks the text. However, it is telling that both Laura's narrative and physical selves discontinue with the destruction of Carmilla. The story "ends" and Laura drifts off into invalidism and early death.

The eroticism of the text and continual sexualization of the relations between Carmilla and her lovers strenuously resist any alternative reading that denies or removes the lesbian context.[14] Even when Laura attempts, as in the epigraph of this essay, to offer a heterosexual gloss to Carmilla's clearly homosexual advances, she immediately writes the fiction off as unworkable (293). Laura must struggle with Carmilla as a woman, with desires for a woman, and all of the odd and exhilarating feelings these yield for her. Laura's homosexual feelings and heterosexual interpretations reveal an exquisite dialectic of repulsion and desire that refuses resolution within the text. As the narratives progress and the narrators change under the rubric of the ur-text from Laura to Carmilla to the general, this dialectic becomes, instead, more acutely pronounced. Laura tries to gloss her narrative heterosexually—indeed, she never allows herself to think or to tell her tale as a conscious lover. Carmilla's narrative, on the other hand, marks a segue from a heterosexual to a homoerotic world by first acknowledging and then firmly leaving behind the heterosexual.

Pressed by Laura's insatiable curiosity to confess something about her past—"'Do you think ... that you will ever confide fully in me?'" (302)—Carmilla first offers to tell everything, couching her language in elliptically erotic terms: "'The time is very near when you shall know everything.... You must come with me, loving me, to death; or else hate me, and still come with me, and *hating* me through death and after'" (302). The confluence here of hatred and love, the ambivalence with which Carmilla regards her own existence and the future of her lover impress upon the reader the toll which must be paid in order for these women to complete their Hyde-like translation into vampires. Carmilla's masochistic elision confuses Laura, forcing Carmilla to couch her narrative in more heterosexual terms in order to lead Laura into the contemplation of her lesbian theme. Thus Carmilla begins her narrative with a ball, but the event does not receive the prominence it would in a paradigmatically patriarchal text. Instead the ball—that heterosexual sublime of meeting and breeding—becomes suppressed and subverted by Carmilla's subsequent homosexual seduction:

> I remember everything about it—with an effort. I see it all, as divers see what is going on above them, through a medium, dense, rippling, but transparent. There occurred that night what has confused the picture, and made its colours faint. I was all but assassinated in my bed, wounded *here*," she touched her breast, "and never was the same since [303].

The tale that Laura expects and keeps insisting on throughout Carmilla's narratives, the patriarchal tale of a girl who finds completion at a dance, becomes all but irrevocably lost when Carmilla asserts that she can only remember the scene with effort, and that even then it is unreal to her. She turns away from the romantic world of the ball to the sexual and taboo world of the bed. Carmilla's real tale is the joining of woman to woman, rather than of woman to man. The occurrences of the night "confused the picture" that the insistently patriarchal narrator would like to establish. Carmilla's imagery conjures up not the penetration of a male lover, but the eroticism of "assassination" by a female; we can finish Carmilla's tale by invoking Laura's own nursery experience: the scene which has "made the colours [of the ball] faint" undoubtedly includes the lovely female figure under the sheets, the mysteriously caressing hands erotically stroking Carmilla's body "under the coverlet," and the sensation of the twin needles puncturing her breast (*"here"*).

Carmilla's half-untold narrative betrays a deeper textual fear: the "pleasure" of the orgasm is reached not by masculine penetration (configured in vampire lore as the stake to the heart) but feminine "assassination" (308). Given the lingering Renaissance link between death and orgasm, Le Fanu strongly implies orgasm without penetration. The anxiety of the text focuses on the vexed question of women's sexual pleasure; the text worries that women find pleasure without the presence of a man. This pleasure is what must be vigorously excluded from Le Fanu's text as demonic, vampiritic, corrupt, deathly. That it nevertheless tantalizingly remains in focus is one of the slippages that move the text beyond Le Fanu's control and into the realm of the lesbian Gothic.

Le Fanu attempts to order his narrative within the confines of the "normal" by eliding the vampire's voice within the auspices of other narrations: Laura's naïve descriptions and finally (although still through Laura, of course) the general's bracing masculinity. It is in the general's narrative that we see the effects of a patriarchal interpretation upon this lesbian text. Although recognizing that his is a tale of the "preternatural" (317), the general nevertheless removes his narrative from the breathless adjectives and torrid experience of Laura's personal prose and presents his own rubric of patriarchal care and suppression to the vampiritic excesses of Carmilla's machinations. The most telling level of alienation comes with the now-familiar bedroom scene. When told by Laura and Carmilla, a beautiful stranger inhabits the bed and ushers in the strange seduction. When told by the general, the beautiful stranger becomes "'a large black object, very ill-defined'" which, in its feeding "'swelled ... into a great, palpitating mass'" (331). Revealed to the masculine gaze, then, the lesbian Other is monstrous, and must be destroyed as such. The masculine monster narrative thus ends with the triumphant destruction of the monster. Laura's gaze is sequestered from this turn of events as she is hastily removed from the scene of destruction, and is left to rely on "a copy of the report of the Imperial Commission" (336) for the final details of Carmilla's story.

Yet, despite the general's tale, the report of the Imperial Commission, the framing editors, and other representatives of male reason, the text remains relentlessly feminine. In an age which sought to disembody women's sexuality through its fascination with women who were consumptive, sleeping, collapsing or dead,[15] Le Fanu suggests that contemporary reliance upon illness and death to cloister women from the evils of their transgressive sexuality is unreliable and dangerous. Consumptive and even dead women can re/turn to wrest control and power over purer wives and daughters. These "pure" vessels, submitting to the sublime of unfettered and unspoken sexuality, demonstrate in their very susceptibility the dangers inherent within a femininity which abjures the sexuality offered by men. Female vampires can seduce chaperoned and protected young women under the eyes of their doting fathers and potential (male) suitors. The culturally accepted habits of Victorian feminine friendship, the walks under the moonlight, twining arms while exchanging sighs and sweet kisses, become unabashedly sexualized within Le Fanu's poetic, while at the same time he exposes the apparatus of patriarchal protection—chaperonage and constant female companionship before marriage, and the erasure of the female family name and legal status after marriage—as helpless in the face of female sexuality and blood connections.

Indeed, Le Fanu ultimately acknowledges female resistance to male reason. Carmilla, early on in the tale, refers to a book by "M. Buffon," undoubtededly a corruption of "buffoon," in explaining a metaphor to Laura about vampirism and girlhood: "'Girls are caterpillars while they live in the world, to be finally butterflies when the summer comes; but in the meantime there are grubs and larvae, don't you see—each with their peculiar propensities, necessities and structure. So says Monsieur Buffon, in his big book, in the next room'" (297). Carmilla manages at once to insult masculine scientific knowledge while using its patterns to delineate the process she is asking Laura to undergo. Laura manages the same subversive tactic when, in the chapter comfortingly entitled "Conclusion," Laura describes the texts collected by Baron Vordenburg, an impoverished vampire expert. He has collected both ancient treatises and the latest scientific discourse, all of which seek to contain and control the irrational powers of the supernatural.[16] Lest we be concerned that these works perhaps do not exist, Le Fanu includes a brief list in several languages: "'Magia Posthuma,' 'Phlegon de Mirabilibus,' 'Augustinus de curâ pro Mortuis,' 'Philosophicæ et Christianæ Cogitationes de Vampiris,' by John Christofer Harendberg; and a thousand others, among which I remember only a few of those which he lent to my father" (336–337). Laura, however, takes it upon herself to contradict these experts: "I may mention, in passing, that the deadly pallor attributed to that sort of *revenants*, is a mere melodramatic fiction. They present, in the grave, and when they show themselves in human society, the appearance of healthy life" (337). Having coolly dismissed the vampire experts carefully listed to reassure us that the vampire question has been examined, diagnosed and laid to rest, Laura proceeds calmly with her own narrative, and continues to open the possibility of feminine ambivalence and inconclusion in the face of patriarchy's imperatives of explanation.

Le Fanu's responds to this subversion of his "Conclusion" with an indictment of the perfidy of the women in a tale untrammeled by masculine containment and commentary. Both writer and reader are immediately coded as feminine, and their intimacy, given the nature of the text, laden with sexual overtones. The nameless editor comments that the writer is an "intelligent lady" who, although now dead, has nevertheless managed to convey the narrative with reasonable accuracy to an anonymous lady friend of hers living in an unspecified city. Le Fanu thus taps into the contemporary fear of women writing for women readers,[17] and uses as his transgressive symbol of this fear the lesbianism that underlies the text. Both lesbianism and female writing are discourses in which women attain satisfaction without the necessity of male intervention. In creating a text ostensibly written by a woman for a woman, Le Fanu elides his own and the reader's sexuality within a lesbian encoding, creating at once a position of safety (the author and the presumed reader are men, and therefore untainted) and a wildly unstable signifier (the author purports to be a woman writing a private discourse to another woman, and therefore lesbian). The Gothic mode of course has long been considered a "female mode," in which women write for women.[18] Le Fanu understands and uses this trope in order to emphasize both the danger and the power inherent in women's writing and in women's sexuality. The lesbian text with its labyrinthine exposition and its emphasis on the monstrosity of women's sexuality stands as an object lesson in horror for the masculine writer/reader. The posited feminine reader, on the other hand, is incessantly and unperturbedly curious about the text, and urges its interlocutor to add detail upon detail in order to satisfy a perhaps insatiable appetite:

> Nothing but your earnest desire so repeatedly expressed, could have induced me to sit down to a task that has unstrung my nerves for months to come, and re-induced a shadow of the unspeakable horror which years after my deliverance continued to make my days and nights dreadful, and solitude insupportably terrific [336].

Only the profound desire of another woman forces Laura to take up the pen and to write of her awakened and destructive sexuality.

Laura's motivation becomes significant when we remember that Tammis Ellis Thomas interprets curiosity itself as a code for sexuality (51). Thus Carmilla's "ever-wakeful reserve" (290) about herself, her mother and her history sets up a dialectic between Carmilla's unspeakable secret and Laura's unspeakable curiosity. In this dialectic Laura's curiosity impels her to engage in a serious of violating investigations in attempts to penetrate the forbidden realm of Carmilla's secret identity. Laura assumes the role of the aggressor, which in turn places Carmilla in the position of warding off Laura's attacks. Even more to the point, in the course of these attacks, Laura's sexual desire for Carmilla's person is metonymically transposed into a desire for truth. Laura claims to be unsettled by the fact that she does not know the name of Carmilla's family, armorial bearings, or country of origin, but it is clear that Laura's curiosity is an inherently sexual rather than genealogical project: "I watched opportunity, and rather insinuated than urged my inquiries. Once or twice, indeed, I did attack her more directly. But no matter what my tactics, utter failure was invariably the result. Reproaches and caresses were all lost upon her" (291). In the conclusion of Carmilla, we see this curiosity/sexuality/desire palimpsest made explicit in Laura's act of gratifying her friend's curiosity in a way that Carmilla refused.

We can thus sense the acute loneliness of the lesbian alone ("insupportably terrific") and the irremediable nature of her malady. In this text, once a woman loves a woman, once a woman embarks upon inditing a text for another woman, there can be no return to the world of masculine signifiers. There is no husband in this scene, no patronymic, no promise of traditional cultural closure. This is, then, the final working of Le Fanu's lesbian/lexicon image, in which the reader recognizes that the lesbian text is, of necessity, a coded text. The lesbianism itself becomes the key for interpretation, the lexicon that decodes the rest of the text. Le Fanu thus allows the reader to see that despite the necessities of cultural closure, despite the traditional masculine language of conclusion, there can be neither in the desire or the text of a woman. Indeed, the last lines of Le Fanu's nouvelle demonstrate at once the lingering horror, the ruthless domesticity and the impossibility of narrative closure that pertain to *Carmilla*:

> It was long before the terror of recent events subsided; and to this hour the image of Carmilla returns to memory with ambiguous alternations—sometimes the playful, languid, beautiful girl; sometimes the writhing fiend I saw in the ruined church; and often from a reverie I have started, fancying I heard the light step of Carmilla at the drawing room door [339].

In a brilliant gesture that is at once presence and absence or erasure and inscription, Le Fanu presents both the ideal and the ghoul, allowing his narrator to reflect upon the impossibility of disentangling the image, or of removing it from her domestic space. Carmilla, beauty and fiend, lurks always a footstep away from the drawing room door, and although by this time she is staked through the heart, decapitated and burned, she lies threateningly close, haunting the mind of the narrator.

Thus Le Fanu encodes as lesbianism the dangers of feminine intellectual discourse that eliminates the male through the exchange between female writers and readers and the development of a narrative using the patterns of a feminine literary tradition, the Gothic. Le Fanu ultimately fails, just as his masculine heroes fail in the text, to contain his narrative because of the power he has invested in the lesbian Other. Unable to understand the feminine, unable to protect her, unable to keep her from her own sexuality, and ultimately unable to draw her voice into the reasonable conclusion desired by the patriarchy, Le Fanu's text frees the lesbian Laura to a half-life of living death and unlooses the bonds of narrative closure to the possibilities of continuation. Ultimately, then, Le Fanu is both anxious respondent to the Female Gothic and unconscious promulgator of its projects.

Notes

1. For Ellen Moers's concept of Female Gothic, see *Literary Women* (xii).
2. Michael Smith argues for such a cross gendered reading as Bram Stoker's strategy both in *Dracula* and in *The Jewel of Seven Stars*. I here invoke his language because such a project speaks to the way that Le Fanu can be read as radically ambivalent about his own authorship of Female Gothic.
3. James R. Kincaid is very amusing about this need to keep Gothic endings incomplete, parodic or ironic—at least on the part of the reader: "Consider the gothic: it's got always to reach toward what cannot be spoken; if all can be spoken, then there is no gothic.... [T]he gothic has to alert us to the presence of agencies we cannot explain ... because they lie outside the realm of ... language.... That's why the endings of gothic novels, the explanations, are always read by good readers as parodic. They expose the inadequacy of explanations" (3).
4. Interestingly, it is not because she is lesbian that Carmilla is destroyed, but because she is a vampire. Thomas notes: "the sexual orientation of Carmilla ... is not causally related to her metamorphosis into a vampire. In other words, Le Fanu does not present Carmilla's vampirism as a form of homophobic punishment for her homosexuality" (53).

5. One of the strategies Le Fanu uses to protect the patriarchy is to suppress Laura's family's patronymic throughout. Thus we entertain a narrative spoken by a women whose only living relative is her father, but whose mother's maiden name is the only patronymic given, and that name protected over and over again with the compulsive labeling of "extinct" (272, 298, 319, 329).
6. Until it is uttered by the father, when comparing his daughter's want of looks with Carmilla's blooming health (312).
7. Her portrait is dated 1698 (299).
8. Milbank uses the Chinese box figure to suggest a metaphorical connection between the pattern of the text itself and the "failure" of its author to "penetrate and deal with the origin of the evil let loose in the [story]."
9. Dijkstra's term.
10. Adjectival form of "od": a hypothetical force formerly held to pervade all nature and to manifest itself in magnetism, mesmerism, chemical action; an arbitrary name coined by Baron Karl von Reichenbach (1788–1869); according to Dijkstra, a pervasive "scientific" theory during Le Fanu's lifetime.
11. See Eve Sedgwick's overview of Gothic narrative conventions (8).
12. I mean this word in both its senses: monstrous (in that it calls upon its root: "Chimera") and wildly, absurdly fantastical.
13. I am indebted to Thomas for this reading. See her fascinating analysis of Laura's response to Carmilla's sexual invitation (51).
14. See, for example, the off-hand remark in Veeder (197), Senf's dismissive mention of critical obsession in "Woman and Power" (30) and of course Terry Castle's list of the lesbian in Gothic fiction, *The Apparitional Lesbian* (7).
15. See Dijkstra (69 and *passim*).
16. Dijkstra argues that only masculine scientific influence, a sort of "Scientific Sublime" can legitimize and dismiss the taint of feminine evil: "And when the hero, the true male, the intellectual male—he is usually a scientist or a philosopher—comes back to release her.... He must exorcise the inherently regressive, degenerative susceptibilities of woman with a broad sweep of his superior, light-born male intellect" (340). We see this anxiety both in this list of male experts and in the proto-scientific team brought in at the end to rescue Laura as a protective patriarchal endeavor.
17. See Haggerty (6–7).
18. Haggerty suggests that the Female Gothic in particular is a site of feminine empowerment: "Gothic writing, 'Female Gothic' as it has traditionally been called, carries romance techniques into magical and threatening other-worlds that allow female characters a surprising degree of initiative and a range of victimization that could be in certain ways described as an attractive alternative to passive femininity" (13).

Works Cited

Castle, Terry. *The Apparitional Lesbian: Female Homosexuality and Modern Culture*. New York: Columbia University Press, 1993.

Dijkstra, Bram. *Idols of Perversity*. Oxford: Oxford University Press, 1989.

Haggerty, George. *Unnatural Affections: Women and Fiction in the Later Eighteenth Century*. Bloomington, Indiana: Indiana University Press, 1998.

Kincaid, James. "Designing Gourmet Children, or, Kids for Dinner." In *Victorian Gothic: Literary and Cultural Manifestations in the Nineteenth Century*, ed. Ruth Robbins and Julian Wofreys, 1–11. Hampshire: Palgrave House, 2000.

Le Fanu, Joseph Sheridan. *Carmilla*. In *Best Ghost Stories of J.S. Le Fanu*, ed. E.F. Bleiler, 274–339. New York: Dover, 1964.

Milbank, Alison. "Doubting Castle: The Gothic Mode of Questioning." In *The Critical Spirit and the Will to Believe*, ed. David Jasper and T.R. Wright, 104–119. New York: St. Martin's, 1989.

Moers, Ellen. *Literary Women*. Garden City, NY: Doubleday, 1976.
Palmer, Paulina. *Lesbian Gothic: Transgressive Fictions*. London: Cassell-Continuum, 1999.
Sedgwick, Eve Kosofsky. *The Coherence of Gothic Conventions*. London: Methuen, 1981.
Senf, Carol "Woman and Power in *Carmilla*." *Gothic* 2 (1987): 25–33.
Smith, Michael. "Love, Freud and the Female Gothic: Bram Stoker's *The Jewel of Seven Stars*." *Gothic Studies* 6 (May 2004), http//www.manchesteruniversitypress.co.uk/information_areas/journals/gothic/sample%20issue.htm.
Thomas, Tammis Ellis. "Masquerade Liberties and Female Power in Le Fanu's *Carmilla*." In *The Haunted Mind: The Supernatural in Victorian Literature*, ed. Elton E. Smith and Robert Haas, 39–65. Lanham, Maryland: Scarecrow Press, 1999.
Veeder, William. "'Carmilla': The Arts of Repression." *Texas Studies in Literature and Language* 22 (1980): 197–223.

11

Preying on the Pervert: The Uses of Homosexual Panic in Bram Stoker's Dracula

DAMION CLARK

In *Fictions of Loss in the Victorian Fin de Siècle*, Stephen Arata writes, "High Victorian fictions banish problems by throwing them outward, toward the colonies. In this way they rid themselves of figures who disrupt or trouble the domestic order" (107). Yet this strategy begins to fail when the colonies come home. For the great influx of foreign strangers into Victorian England disrupts any possibility of banishing problems to some "distant" colony. Therefore, Victorian fictions must alter the direction of their discourse, and fix the locus of the problem onto the space where it lives, at home. However, since the foreign stranger has "come home" to England, the potential exists for the culture and its artistic representatives to continue placing the blame for the nation's problems on the shoulders of those who come from the outside.[1]

The power of culture, including that exerted by the novel, over the constructed identity of a nation and its people relies on a set of established anxieties and phobias to maintain its influence. In *Culture and Imperialism*, Edward Said notes that these anxieties and phobias depend upon the creation of identity-defining binaries that ensure their perpetuation: "culture comes to be associated, often aggressively, with the nation or the state; this differentiates 'us' from 'them,' almost always with some degree of xenophobia" (xiii). Additionally, Said writes, "Neither imperialism nor colonialism is a simple act of accumulation and acquisition. Both are supported and perhaps even impelled by impressive ideological formulations that include notions that certain territories and people require and beseech domination" (9). Yet the people who, according to the ideology of imperialism, "require and beseech domination" are not always the subjugated others against which the dominant culture defines itself; sometimes the members of the dominant culture also require domination and definition, to be reminded of the anxieties and the phobias that form their own culture. For if the dominant culture is to remain dominant, then the members of that culture who transgress against its norms must, through a discursive domination, be "re-educated" in the normative ideology, and brought back into the collective fold.

An example of this process is to be found in Bram Stoker's novel *Dracula,* in which Stoker deploys a complex of anxieties and phobias to manipulate the cultural discourse of Victorian Britain. In fact, Stoker revitalizes the faded Gothic genre to prey on the homophobic and xenophobic attitudes of his late-Victorian readers, reinforcing the horror of the Other who meets their outward gaze in an attempt to recreate "domestic order" and reify "normativity."[2] Breaking with the conventions of the Female Gothic typified by Ann Radcliffe and Charlotte Brontë, Stoker argues that fear and the supernatural cannot be explained away with reason; he aligns himself with the male Gothic of Matthew Lewis in showing that the dark and dangerous Other must be violently eradicated.

Yet there is an important distinction to note here: in *Dracula*, Stoker ultimately plays down xenophobia and plays up homophobia to locate himself—a heterosexual Irishman—within the norm. Thus, rather than seeking to relieve the cultural anxieties surrounding the introduction of the foreign stranger onto British soil, Stoker preys on the pervasive fear of the foreigner as a sexual degenerate who will rot the core values of Britain from the inside. Stoker further amplifies his argument by including in the novel two foreign male characters, Van Helsing and Quinsy, who as members of the "Circle of Light" are noble, heroic characters who seek to preserve normative, that is heterosexual, British values. Aligning himself with these foreigners, who are nevertheless normative heterosexual characters, Stoker informs his readers that it is the sexually perverted outsider they should fear, not the heterosexual outsider who shares their values. Moreover, Stoker justifies this course of action as necessary by evoking relevant current events, using them to intensify his readers' fear.

The anxieties of mid-nineteenth century England and those of the *fin-de-siècle*, while differing in intensity, share some commonalities that fall under the banner of degeneracy, specifically the "degeneracy" that Max Nordau blamed in 1892 for the corruption of Western culture.[3] This brand of degeneracy represents the destruction of all that is good and virtuous in the culture: gender roles, class structures, and religious practices. Yet, unlike Nordau, Stoker focuses on degeneracy in a very specific way. Whereas Nordau views degeneracy as a wide-reaching umbrella, Stoker is much more concerned with a degeneracy that is explicitly sexual. This type of degeneracy, as Arata notes, "afflicted the individual, but its supposed causes ... and effects ... reached deep into the collective life of the people. At every point the biological model of the degenerate provided ways to theorize social decay" (3). The overpowering fear of the effects of the "degenerate" upon the "healthy" creates a hostile environment for the "degenerate," and a desire to either cure or destroy it. The degeneracy that Stoker considers in *Dracula* includes all of the expressions above as well as introducing a significant addition: sexual deviancy. It is this form of degeneracy that will provide the focus of anxiety in Stoker's novel, deflecting some of the horror associated with other forms of cultural degeneracy. In this, Stoker's novel both reflects and attempts to mold the prevailing anxieties and prejudices of its period.

In fact, Stoker utilizes the "scandal plot" as a convention to reeducate his readers. William A. Cohen's definition of the "scandal plot" works to explain its dominance in late Victorian fiction: "it provides a way of working out the novel's double duty: the duty of telling stories composed centrally of incidents from private life and, simultaneously, of using these stories to teach widely applicable public lessons" (19). Indeed, the "incident from private life" that Stoker uses to "teach widely applicable public lessons" in *Dracula* is the Wilde scandal. The lesson is that Wilde's sexuality, not his nationality, is what makes him a "horrifying" figure.

Published in 1897, two years after the trials and imprisonment of Oscar Wilde, an event that brought the sex scandals[4] of the late nineteenth century to a feverish climax, *Dracula* reacts to a set of cultural anxieties and phobias that, rather than being speculative, seem rooted, for Stoker, in hard evidence. Wilde, as a homosexual Irishman, posed a double threat to the British norm: sexual and cultural. Furthermore, as with previous British notions that equated the Irish with an inferior species, race and class, the equation between the Irish and sexual deviancy seemed, after Wilde, inevitable. In his novel, Stoker, a heterosexual Irishman, works to separate Wilde's sexual perversion from his nationality. In reacting to the Wilde trials, Stoker creates an Other that his readers will recognize as threatening to heterosexual normativity, and by modeling Dracula after Wilde, Stoker demonstrates to his readers that what they need to fear is sexual Otherness, not cultural Otherness. As Philip Holden and Richard J. Ruppel cogently argue in *Imperial Desire*, "The need for, and yet constant disavowal of an Other, is constitutive not only of the colonial subject but also the heterosexual male subject in the second part of the nineteenth century" (xii). With Stoker, the emphasis on the sexual difference of the Other works to de-emphasize the cultural difference, thus rendering the heterosexual Irishman like Stoker acceptable within the British norm. Stoker thus frames his argument: "I am one of you; he is a sexual pervert." The simultaneous evocation and disavowal of the sexual Other works in *Dracula* to facilitate a reaffirmation of the core heterosexual values that Stoker wants to reestablish as the cultural norm.

Specifically, Stoker works to reassert the fixed gender and sexual conventions that he hopes will stabilize the norm that will include him by employing what Sedgwick terms "homosexual panic." In *Epistemology of the Closet*, Sedgwick explains the ways in which homosexual panic operates in the nineteenth century: "Because the paths of male entitlement, especially in the nineteenth century, require certain intense male bonds that were not readily distinguishable from the most reprobated bonds, an endemic and ineradicable state of what I am calling male homosexual panic became the normal condition of male heterosexual entitlement" (185). Although the homosexual panic that Sedgwick describes has a specifically xenophobic tinge to it, Stoker works to de-emphasize the xenophobia so that sexual degeneracy remains as the central focus and cause of horror. Although Dracula is a foreigner, his seductions radically disrupt gender identity and sexual normalcy, not cultural identify. Stoker thus utilizes homosexual panic in two distinct ways in the novel. First, and foremost, Stoker relies on the heterosexual British society's fear that homosexuals prey on impressionable youth, recruiting them as Wilde "recruited" the "rent boys," thereby threatening the norm. Secondly, Stoker feeds the heterosexual male fear that, because of their bonds with other men, they might be perceived as homosexual.

Many critics have explored the connection between Wilde and the character of Dracula based on sexuality, notably Talia Schaffer, who writes that "*Dracula* reproduces Wilde in all his apparent monstrosity and evil, in order to work through this painful popular image of the homosexual" (471). She continues her examination of Dracula as Wilde by noting that "[h]e represents not so much Oscar Wilde as the complex fears, desires, secrecies, repressions, and punishments that Wilde's name evoked in 1895. Dracula is Wilde-as-threat" (472). Byrne R.S. Fone also notes the "nearly hysterical outcry of the press and public for the blood of Wilde" (148). However, he too places this reaction solely on the shoulders of Wilde's sexual transgression. Yet Schaffer and Fone confine the connections between these two iconographic figures, Wilde and Dracula, to the realm of sexuality. They thus fail to take into consideration a far more pressing similarity that explains British culture's extremely violent reaction to Wilde's transgression: both Wilde and Dracula are foreigners who threaten to transform the culture. British culture in 1895 felt betrayed by Wilde. They had adopted this Irish-born stranger as their own. His literary work and his carefully crafted persona transformed the artistic identity of the nation. They had welcomed the stranger in, cele-

11. Preying on the Pervert (Damion Clark) 171

brated him as a champion of their national arts, only to be betrayed by his sexual transgression. Thus, his conviction for acts of "gross indecency" reveals not only a homophobic response by the populace, but a homophobic response coupled with xenophobic rage.

Stoker thus has a vested interest in sexually demonizing Wilde. As a heterosexual Irishman himself, Stoker has much to gain in de-emphasizing the cultural dangers of the Irish and in joining the dominant culture in its condemnation of sexual transgression. For if the dominant British culture continued to view the Irish stranger solely as a sexually and morally transgressive beast, then the Irish-born Stoker would find himself in the same category as Wilde. However, if Stoker joined in with the British in their condemnation of Wilde, he could show them that Wilde did not represent all Irishmen, and that a normal, healthy, and moral Irishman like himself could coexist with the English, on English soil. Thus, by joining with the dominant culture's condemnation of homosexuality, Stoker's novel contends that only the stranger's sexual transformations of the British homeland are horrifying and dangerous. Stoker thus attempts to transform cultural anxieties and to tell his readers when they should be afraid and what they should fear, using an encoded Wildean figure as an example to justify and perpetuate the particular anxieties that suit his purposes.[5]

By identifying the norm as heterosexual and discounting cultural degeneracy as a source of anxiety, Stoker feeds on "homosexual panic" to develop the homosexual identity of his villain. Stoker also taps into cultural fears of the Other who transgresses the boundaries that create and contain the norm. As Christopher Craft argues, Dracula's bite inverts the gender and the sexuality of his victims. He notes that this act of penetration

> entails both the dissolution of the boundaries of the self and the thorough subversion of conventional Victorian gender codes, which constrained the mobility of sexual desire and varieties of genital behavior according to the more active male the right and responsibility of vigorous appetite, while requiring the more passive female to "suffer and be still" [444–5].

Thus the norms that Dracula contravenes are sexual and not cultural. After the penetrating bite of Dracula, the women become like men in their expressions of sexual desire and the men become like women. At first glance, the novel's focus on Dracula's transforming effect on the women's sexuality does not appear to rely on "homosexual panic." Yet with deeper analysis, the sexual awakening of Lucy and Mina feeds directly into the cultural fear of homosexuality. The key to this analysis is that the sexuality that Dracula awakens in these women is not a female sexuality, but a male sexuality. This becomes problematic, not only in the sense that these women transgress their prescribed gender identities, but because the men in the novel have been and continue to be sexually attracted to Lucy and Mina, thus revealing a homosexual desire on the part of Arthur, Dr. Seward, Quincy Morris, and Jonathan, the "Crew of Light," the paragons of the ideal Western man.[6]

Yet Dracula's transformation of English sexuality does not begin with Lucy or Mina; Dracula begins to transform British sexuality before he ever arrives on its shores. This is evidenced through his sexual and gendered transformation of Renfield and Jonathan Harker. Both Jonathan and Renfield embody the ideal of British maleness before they encounter Dracula. Renfield was such an established member of the culture that, as he tells Lord Godalming, he "had the pleasure of seconding your father at the Windham" (215), a gentleman's club. Yet, after he mysteriously encounters Dracula, he is a sexually changed man. The Renfield who desires Dracula can no longer be considered respectable. Indeed, he is institutionalized for madness that manifests itself through his deviant desire to become servant, slave, mate, and bride of Dracula. After Dracula arrives in England, Renfield escapes from his cell and runs, naked, to Carfax Abbey and cries out to Dracula, "I am here to do your bidding, Master. I am your slave, and you will reward me, for I shall be faithful, I have worshiped you long and afar off. Now I await your commands, and you will not pass me by, will you dear Master, in your distribution of good things" (98). This intensely homoerotic scene portrays a former respectable British man, naked and begging a foreigner to "reward" him with his distribution of "good things." Although Dracula never physically penetrates a man in the novel, the case of Renfield indicates that he does not have to. Dracula is able to release the desire in Renfield through the promise of a "reward." The mere suggestion of penetration transforms Renfield into a sexual deviant who must be institutionalized in an attempt to "cure" his sexual hybridity.

In the case of Jonathan Harker, however, Dracula does indirectly achieve penetration through his "brides," his agents of penetration. Elaine Showalter writes in *Sexual Anarchy*, "In Transylvania, where sexuality is fluid, Dracula desires men as well as women, and men like Harker can also become breathlessly passive victims" (179). This penetration of Jonathan by the "brides" of Dracula embodies a homosexual act encoded by the male gendering of the vampire's teeth. The phallic teeth of the vampire perform the male role in the sexual act of penetration in the novel. Thus, when the brides penetrate Jonathan, his gender identity and sexuality alter, if only temporarily. Craft notes that the "virile Jonathan Harker enjoys a 'feminine' passivity and awaits a delicious penetration from a woman" (445). Harker writes in his journal, "the skin of my throat began to tingle as one's flesh does when a hand that is to tickle it approaches nearer—nearer ... I closed my eyes in a languorous ecstasy and waited—waited with beating heart" (42–3).

The difference between Jonathan's desire for the brides and Renfield's desire for Dracula himself determines the prescribed outcome for each. Renfield feels no sense of shame in his desire for Dracula's penetration, no wish to be "cured." For this Stoker punishes him: Renfield's desire, in the form of Dracula, violently murders him.[7] The sexually unrepentant Lucy, too, must be dispensed with: the men murder Lucy by penetrating her with a "stake" and decapitating her, thus restoring her to the correct place within the heterosexual paradigm and erasing her manifestations of the predatory male sexuality that continues to sexually excite them. Jonathan, on the other hand, having received the altering bite, does experience shame that initially drives him into a catatonic state from which he awakens with a renewed commitment to his heterosexuality and a vengeful desire to eradicate the foreign stranger's sexually mutating presence from England. Because Jonathan seeks a cure from the nuns who nurse him back to health after his escape from Dracula's castle, and because his shame drives him to marry Mina in a reaffirmation of his heterosexual maleness, Stoker allows him to live.

Of course Dracula, the emblem of sexual danger and difference, must be destroyed. The real men in the novel—and Mina, after she has been brought back into her proper place by the men—rabidly and violently strike out to find Dracula and remove him from their land by killing him. Stoker agrees that this action must take place. Dracula's transformation of the fixed gender and sexual norms of English culture must not be allowed to continue. Led by Van Helsing—who is significantly like Stoker, a foreigner committed to the sexual norms—Jonathan and the other men murder Dracula, the sexually degenerate foreigner. It is important to note here that the "Crew of Light" chases Dracula back to his own land to kill him instead of slaying him in England. The perversion—Dracula/Wilde/homosexuality—must be crushed in the filth/dirt/soil that he/it grows in. The deviant foreigner must be killed in his own land to provide a warning to other potential strangers who may seek to bring their perversion to England. As Matt Cook notes in *London and the Culture of Homosexuality*, "The defeat of the vampire marks not only the end of the lone sexual pervert but also the salvation of the family, future generations and the nation" (119). The movement of the action between countries emphasizes the political and national necessity of the eradication of the sexual Other; this action thus represents national and cultural salvation as well as sexual and personal salvation of the individual characters.

Yet, Stoker's prescription for the erasure of the homosexual may not be as easy as it seems. For as Nina Auerbach explains in "*Dracula*:

A Vampire of Our Own": "For Dracula and his acolyte Renfield, blood is the life, but the men who combine against him find life by drinking in each other's 'stalwart manhood'" (206). While these men do not actually "drink" each other's blood, they combine to fight Dracula, kill/fix Lucy, and save/cure Mina with a homosocial closeness that borders on the homoerotic. This suggests that Dracula's effect on the culture cannot be completely erased by his death. The men who come together do so in a homoerotic way. This is the aspect of "homosexual panic" to which Stoker can find no resolution. The homosocial bond that holds patriarchy together requires this closeness between men, as Sedgwick explains. It is the internal fear that holds the power machinery in place. Yet the line between homosocial closeness and homoerotic contact is a fine one. Stoker tries, but cannot fully bring himself to make this distinction sharp enough. Craft notes, "The result in *Dracula* is a child whose conception is curiously immaculate, yet disturbingly lurid: the child of his father's violations.... He is the unacknowledged son of the Crew of Light's displaced homoerotic union" (459). And so, the figure of Dracula further complicates the problem he has been created to solve. While Stoker evokes homosexual panic to stabilize the normative British heterosexual code with which he can align himself, the behavior that Dracula evokes in his British protagonists looks curiously homoerotic. Once again, Stoker, the staunchly heterosexual Irishman, stands in the margins.

Notes

1. Indeed, the novel seems to be the perfect cultural vehicle to express the anxieties of Victorian England at the same time that it relieves the British citizen of any responsibility for the creation and maintenance of these anxieties. For as a dominant form of cultural representation and creation in the Victorian age, the novel is able to address, diagnose, and prescribe a cure for the ills of the nation. D.A. Miller comments on the extreme power of the Victorian novel when he writes that "perhaps no openly fictional form has ever sought to 'make a difference' in the world more than the Victorian novel, whose cultural hegemony and diffusion well qualified it to become the primary spiritual exercise of an entire age" (x). Thus, in its effort to "make a difference," the Victorian novel has a definite agenda: to direct and control the cultural direction and the collective identity of the nation.

2. Most fascinating is that the homosexual subculture and its artists had been embracing the oriental aesthetic for a century. Indeed, the entire British culture had been doing the same thing. Appropriating foreign cultures and their aesthetics served to help define the British imperialist identity. Additionally, the Gothic genre was also a favorite of homosexual authors like Beckford, who is writing much earlier than Stoker, as Sedgwick notes in *Between Men* (92). It is interesting therefore that Stoker employs this homosexual and orientalist genre in a homophobic way that uses fear of a foreign aesthetic to urge the nation to reject the foreigner because of his deviant sexuality and his transformation of the British heterosexual norm.

3. Nordau makes this claim in *Degeneration*, originally published in 1892. This work blames artists and philosophers—specifically naming Wilde—for the destruction of virtue in the West.

4. For more on the sex scandals of the nineteenth century, see Cohen's *Sex Scandal: The Private Parts of Victorian Fiction*.

5. My reading of the source of danger in the figure of Dracula informs my reading of a critical debate between two critics of *Dracula*. In *Strange Country*, Seamus Deane argues for a reading of Dracula as the absentee Irish landlord. Dean contends that the soil Dracula brings with him from his native country represents the landlord's possession *in absentia* of Irish land. However, Talia Schaffer argues that the "soil" refers to transcripts from the Wilde trial that comment on Wilde's "filthy" bed. Since Stoker has crafted a sexually deviant "monster" as the Other who must be destroyed, I tend towards Schaffer's argument.

6. Nor is homosexuality the only sexual danger associated with Dracula. Dracula's sexual perversion and gender inversion is thus also a code for the dangers of miscegenation. So here too the fear is not of cultural invasion but of sexual/biological invasion and transformation. For Dracula achieves his sexual transformation of the nation through the medium of blood. By focusing on the mixing of blood as a racially and sexually mutating agent, Stoker mixes the culture's fear of the homosexual with the fear of race mixing. This particular phobia ran rampant across England beginning in 1892 with Francis Galton's "scientific" study on race, culture, and intelligence, *Hereditary Genius*. In this "scientific" text, Galton relays to his readers a "parable" of how the most highly developed society the world has ever known, ancient Greece, crumbled:

> We know, and may guess something more, of the reason why this marvelously-gifted race declined. Social morality grew exceedingly lax; marriage became unfashionable, and was avoided.... In a small sea-bordered country, where emigration and immigration are constantly going on, and where manners are as dissolute as were those of Greece in the period of which I speak, the purity of a race would necessarily fail [342–3].

It is no mere coincidence that Galton refers to Greece in this passage as a "small sea-bordered country, where emigration and immigration are constantly going on." The English readers would have immediately thought of their own land in this context. It is also no coincidence that Stoker employs this race anxiety in his sexual cautionary tale. For the combination of a hybrid race with hybrid gender and hybrid sexuality creates a powerful hybrid phobia that will justify Britain's reassertion of Anglo patriarchy and cultural superiority.

7. According to the plot of the novel, Dracula murders Renfield after Renfield "warns" Mina about Dracula. Yet the novel never explicitly states that this is the reason for the murder. One must ask the question here, why does Renfield warn Mina? Is it because he truly cares for her safety? Considering that Renfield has declared his devotion to Dracula while standing naked under his window, it is likely that warns her because Renfield wants to be the beloved of Dracula in her place.

Works Cited

Arata, Stephen. *Fictions of Loss in the Victorian Fin de Siècle*. Cambridge: Cambridge University Press, 1996.

Auerbach, Nina. "*Dracula*: A Vampire of Our Own." In *Bloom's Modern Critical Interpretations: Bram Stoker's Dracula*, ed. Harold Bloom, 191–228. Philadelphia: Chelsea House, 2003.

Cohen, William A. *Sex Scandal: The Private Parts of Victorian Fiction*. Durham: Duke University Press, 1996.

Cook, Matt. *London and the Culture of Homosexuality, 1885–1914*. Cambridge: Cambridge University Press, 2003.

Craft, Christopher. "'Kiss Me with Those Red Lips': Gender and Inversion in Bram Stoker's *Dracula*." In *Dracula*, by Bram Stoker, ed. Nina Auerbach and David J. Skal, 444–59. New York: Norton, 1997.

Deane, Seamus. *Strange Country: Modernity and Nationhood in Irish Writing Since 1790.* New York: Oxford University Press, 1997.
Fone, Byrne R.S. *A Road to Stonewall: Male Homosexuality and Homophobia in English and American Literature, 1750–1969.* New York: Twayne, 1995.
Galton, Francis. *Hereditary Genius.* 1892. New York: St. Martin, 1978.
Holden, Philip and Richard J. Ruppel, eds. Introduction to *Imperial Desire: Dissident Sexualities and Colonial Literature,* ix–xxvi. Minneapolis: University of Minnesota Press, 2003.
Miller, D.A. *The Novel and the Police.* Berkeley: University of California Press, 1988.
Nordau, Max. *Degeneration.* 1892. Lincoln: University of Nebraska Press, 1993.
Said, Edward W. *Culture and Imperialism.* New York: Vintage, 1994.
Schaffer, Talia. "'A Wilde Desire Took Me': The Homoerotic History of *Dracula.*" In *Dracula,* by Bram Stoker, ed. Nina Auerbach and David J. Skal, 470–482. New York: Norton, 1997.
Sedgwick, Eve Kosofsky. *Between Men: English Literature and Male Homosocial Desire.* New York: Columbia University Press, 1985.
_____. *Epistemology of the Closet.* Berkeley: University of California Press, 1990.
Showalter, Elaine. *Sexual Anarchy: Gender and Culture at the Fin de Siècle.* London: Virago, 1992.
Stoker, Bram. *Dracula,* ed. Nina Auerbach and David J. Skal. New York: Norton, 1997.

12
Horror and Homosexuality in Christopher Isherwood's Mr. Norris Changes Trains

BRIAN WHALEY

On June 30, 1934, the head of the Nazi SA paramilitary, Ernst Röhm, was, along with sundry others, murdered in what came to be known as the "Night of the Long Knives." Röhm's homosexuality and the specter of a like-minded, subversive cadre at the heart of Hitler's organization—an allegation immediately in circulation[1]—served as one of the more visible signs of the war of fascism against non-normative bodies and its attempted imposition of compulsory heterosexuality. Three weeks before Röhm was killed, Christopher Isherwood (having slipped out of Weimar with his German boyfriend) sat down to write *Mr. Norris Changes Trains*, a novel grounded in his experience of Berlin from 1929 to 1933, during the period of Hitler's rise. At the heart of Isherwood's book, alongside the charming and amoral figure of Arthur Norris himself, is Kuno Pregnitz, a gay man described as a monster of the city's making—a figure who, transformed by allegedly unnatural appetites, is condemned to the nocturnal pursuit of what he craves. Sinister and fussily cultivated, worldly and with an aura of forbidding yet alluring mystery, Pregnitz is a 1930s version of the decadent aristocrat of Gothic fictional lore. Isherwood completed the novel in which Pregnitz features in the middle of August, while the sensation surrounding Röhm's murder was still fresh.

In Isherwood's terms, Pregnitz is one of "those individuals whom respectable society shuns in horror."[2] And indeed Gothic horror, with its flickering polarities of revulsion and allure, is key: it is both the material out of which Pregnitz's marginalized sexuality is constructed and the discursive field in which the novel's ethical claims are played out. As Judith Halberstam reminds us, the Gothic is shifting, boundary-defying terrain: the "fear and monstrosity" which are its products "are historically specific forms rather than psychological universals" (24). One senses the intricacy of Isherwood's rendering of gay male sexuality in terms of "horror" and "respectable society" in a context where "respectable society" is comprised of Hitler's subjects. As horror tropes intersect with sexist and racist discourse in extreme forms, Isherwood's text interrogates the topography of horror itself—specifically, the power of fear-producing male sexual difference and its alleged opposite, normality. Like the Gothic as representational field, Isherwood's novel is unstable textual terrain, for depictions of sexual difference in 1930s Germany threaten to end up subsumed in the phobic imagination of newly ascendant Nazism. In *Norris*, Isherwood thus plays a delicate game, creating would-be monsters whose monstrosity—like that of Nazi Germany's categories of despised Other—is phantasm without essence, a mass of interrelated and projected anxieties, continually in motion.

Baron Kuno von Pregnitz—very rich, gay, and strange—is, in one sense, a caricature of the nineteenth century Gothic monster. He is, in Halberstam's terms, a "meaning machine" whose representation points insistently at sexuality, as opposed to other possible markers like race, as the locus of his monstrosity (21). Even his surname, with its suggestion of "pregnant," announces sexual horror and transgression, hinting at what lies below an ambiguously gendered surface. Moreover, the sexually insistent name locates Pregnitz as an embodiment of the "sexual pathology" that so captivated Nazi thought.

On New Year's Eve, when he and the text's narrator, William Bradshaw, first meet, one of Pregnitz's first actions is to maneuver Bradshaw into traveling alone with him across Berlin to an unknown, heavily Gothicized destination: "We were driving along a street bounded by a high dark wall," Bradshaw recalls, when "I suddenly caught sight of an ornamental cross. 'Good God,' I said. 'Are you taking me to the cemetery?'" (25). They are not, in fact, going to a cemetery—the cross, like the Baron's sleek, dark taxi, having served as a none-too-subtle nod in the direction of Gothic fiction—but to a raucously boozy party where Bradshaw will be inducted into "decadent," *demi-monde* Berlin. Thus "decadence," one of the central terms of Nazi discourse, is made to intersect with a Gothic pastiche in Isherwood's gay baron.

Isherwood's preferred term for Pregnitz is "fishy": he is a figure between elements; his representation wriggles—fishlike—refusing finally to settle into simple pastiche. In this, he embodies the horrific multidimensionality—the boundary-defying indeterminacy—that Halberstam identifies as central to embodied monstrosity (110). What makes Pregnitz "fishy" is, in addition to his scheming (for he tries to pressure Bradshaw into intimacy and later attempts to sell government secrets), the effects of the eyeglass he wears, which "look[s] as though it had been screwed into his pink well-shaved face by means of some horrible surgical operation" (23). This monocle, which gives the baron a glassy and distorted and strangely *assembled* air, is clearly intended as a synecdoche for a more general depravity. He is, it is implied, an urban excrescence: a monstrous amalgam thrown up from Germany's rotten core. The fact that he takes "artificial sunlight treatment" marks him as still more unnatural for abjuring the healthful light of day (29); this is underscored when Bradshaw, having declined an invitation to spend the night with Pregnitz, asks whether he should instruct the driver to take the baron home: "'No, thank you,' Kuno spoke rather sadly, but with an attempt at a smile. 'I'm afraid not. Not just yet'" (109). The implication is clear: craving flesh, Pregnitz endlessly trawls the streets of the darkened city. The "ghostly gleam" (109) in his eye is another means, like the ornamental cross in the graveyard, of rendering his "decadence" macabre and vaguely supernatural, in accordance with Gothic fictional conventions. The suggestion of a specifically vampiric, night-stalking monstrosity is insistent in the image of Pregnitz, a nocturnal creature driven by a particular hunger, just as his aristocratic social status invokes Dracula, the best known of Gothic vampires. Indeed, when Bradshaw later returns to the building to which the baron had taken him on New Year's Eve, he realizes that its narrow courtyard is "like a coffin standing on end. ... there was a deep twilight, like the light in a mountain gorge" (81). Isherwood thereby imbues the baron, by association, with two further standard horror characteristics: a macabre artifact (the gigantic coffin) and a generically appropriate setting (the darkening mountain gorge).

The representation of Pregnitz wielding his wealth and desire upon a semi-repulsed victim is, however, anything but unidirectional. Having outfitted Pregnitz with the characteristics of the sinister, Gothic aristocrat, Isherwood dilutes and undermines this representation by exposing the baron as a harmless fantasist—a pitifully compulsive reader of boys' adventure fiction whose conquests are largely imaginary. Indeed, despite his sinister coding, Pregnitz is solicitously concerned for Bradshaw's comfort. When, for instance, they reach their cross-town destination, "having arrived, it seemed, at the blackest corner of the night," the baron "obligingly [takes Bradshaw's] arm" (25). Elsewhere, Bradshaw finds himself again "tucked ... into the depths of [Pregnitz's] vast black limosine," silently cruising darkened streets with the baron's hand caressing his own under a fur rug (108).

At the same time as he establishes for him an aura of mystery and power, Isherwood mocks Pregnitz, containing whatever fear the baron evinces within the invisible quotation marks of camp comedy. As a result, one of Pregnitz's first questions to Bradshaw is patently, comically bizarre: "Have you read *Winnie the Pooh*, by A.A. Milne?" (24). Its 1926 publication, only four years prior to *Norris*'s narrative action, means this cannot be a fond memory from the nursery; rather, it renders Pregnitz slightly ridiculous: a man with a passion for children's stories. As this new strand of satirically comic discourse develops in relation to Pregnitz, it destabilizes competing images of the sinister-Gothic-predator, subverting associations as quickly as they take shape. Thus, having arrived at the baron's "lair," Bradshaw is not imperiled; rather, he has foisted upon him the contents of a "library of stories for boys" and the baron's "dark" secret: in fantasy, he imagines himself to be Jimmy, the hero of a book "cribbed largely from the *Swiss Family Robinson*" (116–17). There is another layer of destabilizing representation at work: as Isherwood explained in an interview, the baron is based in part upon "a stock figure in the Berlin homosexual bar world," the sham aristocrat (qtd. in Leyland interview 192). His laughter is therefore rendered in the novel as "a curiosity, an heirloom; something handed down from the dinner-tables of the last century ... [and] scarcely to be heard nowadays except on the legitimate stage" (*Norris* 107). Equated with play-acting, playing at boys' adventure, Pregnitz is declawed, as it were, reduced to a mere would-be Gothic villain. Whereas a classically monstrous entity like Dracula, for example, has "a smooth, resistless way" (Stoker 56), the "suave" baron is, we are given to understand, eminently resistible, his attentions risible. The perceived power of his exotic, erotic Otherness is self-consciously dispersed by a young narrator (and, indeed, author) who ridicules what he takes to be an essentially retrograde, closeted coyness.[3]

One could insist with some justice that this portrayal of Pregnitz exposes a basic insecurity about how to represent anything other than a tormented or laughable gay male. Like the novel's narrator (whom one contemporary reviewer tellingly dismissed as a "sexless nitwit"[4]), Isherwood perhaps lacked the rhetorical means, the imagination, or the courage to represent homosexuality positively and straightforwardly.[5] In this, he would hardly have been alone at a time when consensual sex between men remained a criminal offense in both Germany and Isherwood's native Britain. A more compelling explanation of the coexistence of mocking laughter and horrific fear, however, depends upon a reading of the full arc of Pregnitz's career in the novel. He is made to appear menacing *and* vulnerable, dauntingly powerful and yet curiously pitiable. Only apparently wealthy, Pregnitz is the victim of a blackmailer who, in possession of compromising love-letters, drains his resources and drives him, finally, to attempt to sell state secrets. In the latter attempt he is surveilled, flees the state agents who attempt to arrest him, shoots himself inside a public toilet, and dies shortly afterwards. Blackmail and a men's-room—the instrument and topography of horrors peculiar to pre-Stonewall gay men: the novel invokes them to shift the locus of horror from Pregnitz to the culture that produces him as monster. Indeed, Bradshaw's discovery of

12. Horror and Homosexuality (Brian Whaley) 181

Pregnitz's cruel death comes only as casual gossip from an uncaring reporter: "Good riddance to bad rubbish" (188) is her brutal, barely considered summary. The reporter's callousness figures as a tacit acceptance of the regime's actions, since "respectable society" needs to be protected against "monsters."

Such "protection," formulated as a defense of the family and body politic against corrupting agents, took increasingly hallucinatory forms as Hitler brought the German state into line. The notorious complement of the officially lauded Aryan family ideal was the eradication of, among others, the nation's non-reproductive subjects. Dagmar Herzog conveys this linked objective in the work of one Johannes Schulz, physician and author of a tremendously influential sexual advice manual of the period. On the one hand, Schulz produced information aimed at "enhancing heterosexuals' sex lives" while, on the other, he "choreographed torture":

> At the German Institute for Psychological Research and Psychotherapy ... Schultz and a commission of coworkers forced accused homosexuals to perform coitus with a female prostitute while the commission watched. Whoever performed heterosexually to their satisfaction under these conditions was set free; whoever did not ... was sent on to a concentration camp [Herzog 19].

The Weimar Republic was thus made to pay for its tolerant attitudes towards sexuality, disciplined by the Führer's horrified gaze. Accordingly, and as is well known, gay men were termed "alien to the species": carriers of their peculiar contagion, they were alleged to seduce and thereby corrupt right-thinking young men, spreading an "epidemic of homosexuality" (Micheler 96-7). This monstrous, vampiric, ability to produce men in their own image cast them as rivals to the pro-family apparatus of the state, thus targets of a vociferous crackdown. The demolition of Magnus Hirschfeld's Institute for Sexual Science—next door to which, not incidentally, Isherwood had taken a room upon arrival in Berlin in 1929—was, as the historian Richard J. Evans writes, "only one part, if the most spectacular, of a far more wide-ranging assault on what the Nazis portrayed as the Jewish movement to subvert the family" (376).[6] Ten thousand of the institute's books are believed to have been burned and the signal given for the dismantling of Europe's most progressive sexual liberation movement, with singularly dire consequences for gay men (Evans 376-77). Reformers had hoped to see Paragraph 175—the portion of the German civil code that criminalized homosexual activity—abolished; instead, by 1935, more and harsher penalties were added: penal servitude, psychiatric incarceration, castration, and, finally, murder in concentration camps notorious among them (Micheler 95). These ends, while gruesome, were not surprises sprung by the Nazis on an unsuspecting public; indeed, they feature in party literature from early on, as this official Nazi response to a question about its position on Paragraph 175 shows:

> It is not necessary that you and I live, but it is necessary that the German people live. And it can only live if it can fight, for life means fighting. And it can only fight if it maintains its masculinity. It can only maintain its masculinity if it exercises discipline, especially in matters of love. Free love and deviance are undisciplined. Therefore, we reject you, as we reject anything that hurts our nation [qtd. in Page 99].

Among the transformations effected by Hitler's takeover, *Norris* records a general paranoia that turns easily into violence against perceived Others: "The whole city lay under an epidemic of discreet, infectious fear" (181). The culmination of this fear is embodied in Kuno Pregnitz as he runs, fails to hide, and shoots himself in an attempt to keep his secret from becoming public. In an important sense, however, the baron *has* no secret: by naming him Kuno, Isherwood pointedly links him to the figure at the heart of one of Germany's most infamous homosexual scandals, Graf Kuno von Moltke—rather as if, in an English context, the baron's surname had been Wilde (Parker 247).

The documentation of mounting horror in late-Weimar Berlin is thus a major part of Isherwood's project in *Norris*. It represents an additional, parallel discourse to convey horror at—and fear of—social upheaval and collapse. As culture takes a Gothic turn, with a horrifying regime spinning supposedly horrific "monsters" from designated Others, Isherwood puts competing versions of Gothic horror in dialogue. Pregnitz, his deconstructed "monster," throws an ironic light upon the business of making monsters in a culture that depends for its power upon the creation and consumption of horrifying difference. Thus, "[h]ate explode[s] suddenly, without warning, out of nowhere," as Berlin descends into civil war; "The murder reporters and the jazz-writers had inflated the German language beyond recall" (86). Its corrupted language the symbol of underlying distortion, the surface of Berlin buckles and gives way to seething, interior hatreds.

The corresponding disintegration of Pregnitz is striking. During his first night spent drinking with the baron, Bradshaw remarks how, "[a]s intoxication proceeded, [Pregnitz's] face seemed slowly to disintegrate.... A rigid area of paralysis formed around the monocle. The monocle was holding his face together" (24). The strain of maintaining a discreet surface, of tamping down the secret, "monstrous" self within, is here rendered directly. The baron is clearly under immense optical pressure, his monocle figuring less as an instrument though which he sees than as a reminder that he is watched. The rough treatment to which he is increasingly subjected as the political climate changes and his secret is forced into the open is rendered obliquely, as simply "good fun." Thus, at his country villa in Mecklenburg, for instance, the "handsome young men with superbly developed brown bodies" who are his house guests "wrestled and boxed on the beach and did somersault dives from the springboard into the lake" in high-spirited homage to the Nazi fetish of "physical culture." Yet, "[w]ith good-humoured brutality the boys played practical jokes on him which smashed his spare monocles and might easily have broken his neck. He bore it all with his heroic frozen smile" (43). Eventually, the baron's smile disappears, along with the good-humored aspect of the boys' brutality. In another telling moment, Bradshaw catches a glimpse of Pregnitz at a party, "in the embrace of a powerful youth in a boxer's sweater, who was gradually forcing a mugful of beer down his throat. The Baron protested feebly; the beer was spilling all over him" (29).

The effect of such depictions is, thus, a systematic emptying out of Pregnitz's alleged monstrosity—an evacuation that simultaneously establishes another, public locus of horror, one that employs a distinct but parallel rhetorical style: namely, the discourse of social reportage. Both discursive styles—the one used to represent Pregnitz and that which depicts German society—are Gothic, centered upon unstable surfaces giving way to monstrous depths. They serve as analogues of one another yet produce quite different moral effects. Political rivals are killed in the streets; every day people are summoned by the police; street youths pay off old scores with razors and clubs: Isherwood's novel maps the, by now, familiar terrain of civic disorder that accompanies Hitler's takeover. Everywhere, people smile and seem pleased by the sight of uniformed Nazis—the regime's most visible manifestation of valorized masculinity—striding the streets: "They smiled approvingly at these youngsters in their big, swaggering boots.... And they thrilled with a furtive, sensual pleasure, like schoolboys, because the Jews, their business rivals, and the Marxists, a vaguely defined minority of people who didn't concern them, had been satisfactorily found guilty of the defeat and the inflation, and were going to catch it" (179). In this context, the baron appears as would-be monster, his increasingly terrified vulnerability contrasting sharply with the arrogant, masculine swagger of young Nazis. Where he seemed to be predatory he is shown to be afraid; what appeared mysterious about him becomes painfully prosaic. Pregnitz becomes, in a word, human; his alleged monstrosity dims as, increasingly, the surrounding culture figures as the text's true monster.

Despite the fact that *Norris* is drawn from intersecting lines of Gothic horror, Isherwood's writing is not generally associated with that rhetorical style or narrative structure. Indeed, the opposite is true: along a continuum separating Gothic fiction and "documentary" realism, Isherwood, along with George Orwell, is held to represent the latter among interwar British writers. Amid upheavals and displacements of 1930s Europe like those charted in *Norris*, he and Orwell are credited with developing an English style of lightly fictionalized social reportage that borrowed from the techniques of so-called direct cinema and exactly suited the political mood of the moment[7]: "I am a camera with its shutter open," the narrator of one of his Berlin books memorably asserts, "quite passive, recording, not thinking" (*Goodbye to Berlin* 1). And, despite the author's many subsequent protestations about the absurdity of the pose, this impression of Isherwood as recording instrument remains, largely and rather surprisingly, unchanged. Consequently, his Berlin fiction features regularly in historical accounts of the city, as though it could be more or less straightforwardly mined as historical record.[8] Such readings, however, tend to drain Gothic elements from the text, as though their presence vitiates a more worthy purpose. As evaluative practice, this is consistent with a well-entrenched approach to the literature of modernism—one initially promulgated by modernist writers themselves—that draws sharp lines of demarcation between genre fiction and serious literature.[9] In fact, as we have seen, Isherwood's *Mr. Norris Changes Trains* is a far more unstable, unsettling, and revealing text than is suggested by such circumscribed critical responses: a novel whose elements of reportage depend upon, rather than eschew, echoes and adaptations of popular literary forms, at the fulcrum of which lie conflicted, competing discourses of sexuality, history, and the Gothic.

As Samuel Hynes attests in his discussion of *Norris*, Isherwood "protested against this [insistently 'documentary'] view of the novel." Hynes asserts, however, that such protest is pointless, "for serious books are read for what people need from them, and at this time [the mid-1930s] what men needed ... was the truth about Europe" (181). Such ostensibly "low" and notoriously shifting forms as Gothic horror can have little purchase, given such a judgment. This is doubly strange and unfortunate, however, in light of *Norris*'s pronounced engagement with the Gothic and Isherwood's apprenticeship and abiding interest in the form. For Isherwood's Cambridge juvenilia, centered upon the surreally grotesque fictional village of Mortmere, is deeply indebted to Gothic fiction. Indeed, Isherwood draws for his depiction of *Norris*'s Pregnitz upon two characters he had invented for Mortmere: Reynard Moxon, a figure who looms into view in "an enormous limousine, painted all in a gleaming black" (Isherwood, *Mortmere* 81) in "The Garage in Drover's Hollow," and Kester, eleventh Lord Wranvers, from "The Horror in the Tower."

"The Garage in Drover's Hollow" and "The Horror in the Tower" are burlesques of horror and detection: massively inflated amalgams of Poe's tales of aristocratic madmen, Conan Doyle's Sherlock Holmes stories, and other popular fictional resonances. Reynard Moxon appears as a Pregnitz prototype in that he, like Pregnitz, is a rich and widely-traveled stranger who dresses all in black and displays "almost fiend-like nonchalance" (81) and an "oppressively languid" (84–85) manner of speech. He is exaggeratedly depraved: he regards without a murmur, for example, the "loathsomely mangled" (*Mortmere* 85) corpses of his victims; whereas Pregnitz merely conducts Bradshaw past a graveyard to a party where the bodies are those of "dead drunks" (*Norris* 31). For his part, Kester is more subtle than Moxon but no less wicked: a decadent, aristocratic coprophagist, he lures the hapless narrator to a Yorkshire estate ("lichenous," of course, and "gloomy beyond description") to indulge his peculiar vice (50–51). Fashioning his Berlin fiction, Isherwood obliquely references both of these figures. When Baron von Pregnitz is shown endlessly roaming the streets of Berlin by night, it is of Reynard Moxon, a figure of obscure evil "[who] never went out till after dark" (*Mortmere* 39), that one may well think. When Kester's secret is revealed and his body pumped with bullets, it is of Pregnitz's supposedly monstrous corpse that one is forcibly reminded.[10]

As Judith Halberstam writes, "Gothic ... is the breakdown of genre and the crisis occasioned by the inability to 'tell,' meaning both the inability to narrate and the inability to categorize" (23). Many of the Mortmere stories are aborted, magpie fragments—barely controlled and rather puerile jokes drawn from multiple genre sources that break off at peaks of nauseated horror where the narrator seemingly can go no further. Although he tried, Isherwood could find no way to link fantasy and reality, Mortmere and lived experience (Bucknell 14–15). Literally "alien to the species," his monsters failed to move. In *Norris*, by contrast, Isherwood discovered how Pregnitz—a figure coded as sexually monstrous—could cast into relief more vivid forms of horror, other intersections of fear and desire. In so doing, Isherwood depicts a history and culture far more frighteningly Gothic than any gay "monster."

Notes

1. As Stefan Micheler writes, Röhm's assassination, which Hitler justified in public statements as a preemptive measure against a homosexual fifth column, "is generally regarded as a turning point in the National Socialist regime's treatment of homosexuality" (105–06).
2. The quotation is from Isherwood's preface to *The Berlin Stories* (v), the name given to Isherwood's two Berlin novels, *Mr. Norris Changes Trains* (1935) and *Goodbye to Berlin* (1939), when they were issued together in 1945.
3. For useful discussion of the interpenetration of horror and laughter, see Avril Horner and Sue Zlosnik's *Gothic and the Comic Turn*.
4. The reference to a "sexless nitwit" was aimed at Norris's narrator—a figure widely identified with the author himself. Isherwood recalls the gibe and the prob-

lem of representing the narrator's sexuality in his autobiographical book *Christopher and His Kind* (186).

5. Edward Blake, the homosexual war hero from Isherwood's *The Memorial* (1932), though frankly and sympathetically portrayed, is hardly positive: he attempts suicide by shooting himself in the head, suffers, and departs ambiguously for Berlin at the end of the novel. For its part, the suggestion of Eric Vernon's sexuality in the same text remains precisely that: a hinted at possibility rather than a realized depiction.

6. For compelling analysis of the conflation of racism and homophobia under the Nazis, see Stefan Micheler's "Homophobic Propaganda and the Denunciation of Same-Sex-Desiring Men under National Socialism" (2005); for analysis of the convergence of racism and aversion to sexual difference more generally, see Judith Halberstam's *Skin Shows* (1995), chapter 1.

7. John Willett's *Art and Politics in the Weimar Period* provides a good, brief account of the kinds of ideas and techniques that Isherwood absorbed in Berlin and deployed in his writing. For the German political situation to which Isherwood's texts respond, see Richard J. Evans's superb *The Coming of the Third Reich*.

8. Such uses can be problematic. One danger is illustrated by Otto Friedrich's *Before the Deluge* (1972), which at times relies so heavily upon Isherwood's Berlin material for its rendering of Weimar Germany that it treats the historical and literary records as though they were identical. A different kind of caution needs to be exercised while reading accounts such as Anthony Reed's and David Fisher's *Berlin Rising: Biography of a City*, which, in addition to making a handful of minor errors of fact, draws upon Isherwood's writing only to render its author as the type of the dilettante Englishman, blithely pleasure-seeking while Hitler drove himself to power. While it is true that Isherwood enjoyed himself in Berlin, it is misleading to describe him merely "danc[ing] the night away as the Golden Twenties faded into the terrible Thirties" (Reed and Fisher 313), like some empty-headed swell or flapper. To do so is to reinforce the impression that "moral looseness" caused Hitler's regime—an enduring idea, persuasively contested by (among others) Linda Mizejewski in *Divine Decadence* (1992). See Siegfried Kracauer's classic formulation of the cultural decadence thesis in *From Caligari to Hitler* (1947).

9. Maria DiBattista's introduction to *High and Low Moderns: Literature and Culture, 1880–1939* offers an immensely useful overview and discussion of the reluctance of academic literary studies to recognize shifting and permeable boundaries between high, low, and middling modernist writers.

10. Isherwood's fascination with the possibilities of the Gothic, a genre hardly associated with his name, never left him. Given a free hand to write what he pleased in the 1970s, Isherwood produced *Frankenstein: The True Story*, a riveting adaptation of the Gothic classic that won best scenario at the International Festival of Fantastic and Science Fiction Films.

Works Cited

Bucknell, Katherine. Introduction to *The Mortmere Stories*, by Christopher Isherwood and Edward Upward. London: Enitharmon, 1994.

DiBattista, Maria and Lucy McDiarmid, eds. *High and Low Moderns: Literature and Culture, 1880–1939*. New York: Oxford University Press, 1996.

Evans, Richard J. *The Coming of the Third Reich*. New York: Penguin, 2004.

Halberstam, Judith. *Skin Shows: Gothic Horror and the Technology of Monsters*. Durham: Duke University Press, 1995.

Herzog, Dagmar. "Hubris and Hypocrisy, Incitement and Disavowal: Sexuality and German Fascism." In *Sexuality and German Fascism,* ed. Dagmar Herzog, 1–21. New York: Berghahn, 2005.

Horner, Avril, and Sue Zlosnik. *Gothic and the Comic Turn*. New York: Macmillan, 2005.

Hynes, Samuel. *The Auden Generation: Literature and Politics in England in the 1930s*. Princeton: Princeton University Press, 1976.
Isherwood, Christopher. *The Berlin Stories*. New York: New Directions, 1954.
____. *Christopher and His Kind, 1929–1939*. New York: Farrar, 1976.
____. Interview. In *Gay Sunshine Interviews,* ed. Winston Leyland, 190–99. San Francisco: Gay Sunshine, 1978.
____. *The Memorial: Portrait of a Family*. 1932. New York: Farrar, 1974.
Isherwood, Christopher, and Edward Upward. *The Mortmere Stories*. London: Enitharmon, 1994.
Kracauer, Siegfried. *From Caligari to Hitler: A Psychological History of the German Film*. Princeton, N.J.: Princeton University Press, 1947.
Micheler, Stefan. "Homophobic Propaganda and the Denunciation of Same-Sex-Desiring Men under National Socialism." In *Sexuality and German Fascism,* ed. Dagmar Herzog, 95–130. New York: Berghahn, 2005.
Mizejewski, Linda. *Divine Decadence: Fascism, Female Spectacle, and the Makings of Sally Bowles*. Princeton, N.J.: Princeton University Press, 1992.
Page, Norman. *Auden and Isherwood: The Berlin Years*. New York: St. Martin's, 1998.
Parker, Peter. *Isherwood: A Life Revealed*. New York: Random, 2004.
Reed, Anthony, and David Fisher. *Berlin Rising: Biography of a City*. New York: Norton, 1994.
Stoker, Bram. *Dracula*. 1897, ed. John Paul Riquelme. New York: St. Martin's, 2002.
Willett, John. *Art and Politics in the Weimar Period: The New Sobriety, 1917–1933*. New York: Pantheon, 1978.

13

Invasion of the Husband Snatchers: Masculine Crisis and the Lavender Menace in I Married a Monster from Outer Space

ANDREW SCAHILL

"It's the Day of the Gray Flannel Fag," reads the headline from a March 1958 article[1] in the men's lifestyle magazine *Sir!* : "Not All Homos Are Easy to Spot," it chides; "Many Have Muscles, Are He-Men in Everything—Except Sex." In the text of the article, the author asserts that fifteen to twenty percent of men are homosexual, though only four percent are "recognizable," and delivers a particular warning to heterosexual women: "Lady, take a good look at that date you're having cocktails with. Is he a real guy? Or is he a He-Man homo?" The warning continues: "They design dresses, decorate homes, sell antiques, make the rounds of Broadway producers' homes. But what throws unsuspecting women is that they can be found heading Wall Street firms, boxing in Madison Square Garden and playing baseball. There's no telling where a gray flannel he-man fag will turn up."[2]

The invocation of *The Man in Gray Flannel Suit*, a popular 1950s book and film about a conflicted man rejecting corporate greed in favor of everyman suburbia and familial bonds, is no coincidence. As Steven Cohan notes in *Masked Men*, "the white, heterosexual, corporate, WASP, suburban breadwinner [is] personified by the ubiquitous figure of The Man in the Gray Flannel Suit, the logo of the age which still represents it four decades later" (xi). The article in *Sir!*, therefore, speaks to more than simply a fear of a homosexual presence; this pointed reference makes it clear that the very archetype of normative 1950s male masculinity is in jeopardy. The article's list of spaces "invaded" by the invisible homosexual—the corporate office, the boxing ring, the baseball field—is also particularly telling. These spheres are, strictly speaking, homosocial spheres; a homosexual presence thus troubles the distinction between homosocial and homoerotic spheres. Indeed, given *Sir!* magazine's exclusive male readership, the article's admonition to heterosexual women is a thinly-veiled masking of heterosexual male culture's own paranoia about the tenuousness of the hetero-homosexual binary, and the uncertainty of defining masculinity in terms of gender performance. In the article's assessment, the one true way for men to determine "authentic" masculinity is in "sex"—potency, virility, and the ability to consummate in heterosexual couplings.

Like the article in *Sir!*, the 1958 film *I Married a Monster from Outer Space*, as Cyndy Hendershot argues, seems to be centered on the experience of female paranoia—a cautionary tale to young women about the alien Other who has slithered into her bed. But like the article in *Sir!* magazine, below the surface the film is less invested in its female lead's internal struggle and more invested in a form of large-scale, societal, masculine paranoia—quite literally, a paranoia *about* masculinity, and how to define it. In fact, *I Married a Monster from Outer Space* details this 1950s masculine paranoia as the intersection of two conflicting anxieties: concerns about postwar masculinity in decline—the fear of emasculation through marriage and suburban heteronormativity after the visibly masculine activities of World War II; and simultaneously, the fear of the "lavender menace" of a gay and lesbian subculture on the rise. The film responds to these anxieties by delineating homosocial and homoerotic spheres and policing the hetero-homosexual binary through recourse to those very same structures of normative reproductive heterosexuality.

Replicating (and Rejecting) the Replicant Formula: The Invasion Motif and the American Family

I Married a Monster from Outer Space opens with the staunchly single men of Anytown, U.S.A., at a bachelor party, bemoaning the loss of one of their own, Bill (Tom Tryon), to marriage. On the way home from the party, Bill is captured and replaced by a shape-shifting alien, whose mission is to breed with human women in an attempt to replenish its own declining population. Soon after the marriage, Bill's new wife, Marge (Gloria Talbott), grows weary of Bill's growing apathy and seeming indifference to their relationship; she learns the true secret of Bill's transformation when she pursues him to a midnight meeting with the mother ship at a local park. When Marge attempts to warn the community about the invasion, she discovers that the invasion has spread to police and government officials. Finally, a rescue party of other "real" men destroys the alien menace, including alien Bill. The movie ends with the reunification of Marge and real Bill, the human heterosexual couple.

The trope of "invasion" by the Other, marked by national, regional, or racial difference, is a recurring motif in American Gothic fiction. From the mischievous Carwin disrupting the rationalist ideal of the Mettigen estate in Charlie Brockden Brown's *Weiland* to the Misfit's moral relativism in Flannery O'Connor's "A Good Man Is Hard to Find," American Gothic literature is heavily populated with domestic threats from dubious figures. Indeed, as Dana Polan argues in *National Manhood: Capitalist Citizenship and the Imagined Fraternity of White Men*, America's very fraternal identity is tenuously structured upon the binary construction of racial and cultural difference and the persistent threat that Otherness poses to white, masculine identity (1–29). Teresa Goddu has additionally noted in *Gothic America: Narrative, History, and Nation* that Gothic horror often functions as a genre in which national anxieties can be mapped onto the domestic, so that threats of marital or familial invasion become national narratives as well.

It is commonplace to read the threat of domestic invasion in 1950s science fiction in terms of the Cold War paranoia concerning Communism. In "The Imagination of Disaster," Susan Sontag details the generic conventions of the "alien invasion" plot of the 1950s: a middle-class heterosexual couple discovers the "invader"; the couple seeks to warn the authorities, without effect; the invader's plot to conquer the planet or reproduce its race becomes clear; and finally, the invader is defeated and normalcy is restored. To a large extent, Sontag's analysis functions as a totalizing structure for the genre; therefore, the moments in which *I Married a Monster from Outer Space* deviates from Sontag's formula become all the more analytically useful. The major distinction to be made is that this film is one of a handful of science fiction films from the 1950s (including *Invasion of the Body Snatchers*, *It Came from Outer Space*, and *Invaders from Mars*) in which invasion takes the form of "doubles," or replicas of humans. As is the case with "possession" or doppelganger motifs in Gothic works such as Poe's "Ligeia" or Stevenson's *The Strange Case of Dr. Jekyll and Mr. Hyde*, this plot device ensures a particularly paranoid vision in which the perceived "threat" is virtually indistinguishable from the "victim." In the case of 1950s science fiction, the threat is generally read as Communism, and the victim is invariably white, middle-class, suburban society.

I Married a Monster from Outer Space, however, diverges from its predecessors in the surprising amount of empathy it demonstrates for its alien invaders, allowing for the possibility that the aliens can learn human emotions and subsequently integrate into society. The alien Bill becomes conflicted between his duty to proceed with the invasion and his ever-increasing "human" desires. Through the course of the film, he increasingly takes on the persona of his human counterpart and seeks to sublimate his alien Otherness. The question the film poses, then, is this: how does a film that expresses sympathy for the invader of marriage and that articulates criticism of marriage and heterosexual consummation ultimately become a film that champions heterosexual union and procreation as the sole arbiter of authentic masculinity? The few theorists who have addressed this film see it as either an extension of the anti-communist/anti-conformity messages of *Invasion of the Body Snatchers* or as a social commentary on the post-war fear of commitment and marriage. However, such readings do not address the film's overall anxiety about defining masculinity and homosocial environments. As Henry M. Benshoff describes it, *I Married a Monster from Outer Space* is a film in which "a newly married man ... finds it preferable to meet other strange men in a public park rather than stay at home with his wife" (130–1). Benshoff's decidedly tongue-in-cheek assessment of the film reveals the film's obsession with homosocial circles of men, and with delineating the hetero-homosexual boundary. Indeed, reading the film through the lens of queer theory opens up the possibility of seeing the film's incongruities with the typical invasion film narrative as evidence for the 1950s' conflicted relationship with "them/us" constructions of masculine culture as such distinctions based on sexuality became obfuscated. Though the film functions, in the traditional Gothic mode, to "unmask" the invisible Other and make its difference known, there is also a competing desire within the film's diegesis to integrate the sexual Other as well. Indeed, the film wrestles not only with the possibility of integrating the sexual Other, but also with the implications this act has for categories of sexual difference.[3] Unable (or unwilling) to both unmask difference and reveal that difference to be a fiction, the film ultimately must revert to the stock conventions of the alien invasion genre to destroy the alien invader who threatens the culture most by its very ability to integrate.

The Man in the Gray Flannel Space Suit: The Postwar Masculine Archetype in Crisis

In the 1950s, the suburban middle-class family unit, in addition to becoming the American ideal, became the vanguard for the post-war drive for industrial progress and a signifier of national welfare. Declaring in 1948 that "children and dogs are as necessary to the welfare of this country as is Wall Street and the railroads," President Harry Truman urged passage of a bill to provide "a decent home and suitable living environment for every American family" ("Housing Gets No. 1 Spot at Family Life Conference" 15). As men returned to the workforce and the white middle-class family found comfort in the uniformity of suburban living, the popular media of the time championed a new age of reified nuclear family constructions. Husbandhood and fatherhood, too, were being reassessed: to appropriate the title of a popular television show, father knew best, and what he came to know was that family, not work, was to be the true measure of a man—a lesson learned, not coincidentally, in *The Man in the Gray Flannel Suit*. As a 1954 *McCall's* article about parenting and suburbia states:

> Had Ed [a model father] been a father twenty-five years ago, he would have had little time to play and work along with his children. Husbands and fathers were respected then, but they weren't friends and companions to their families. Today, the chores as well as the companionship make Ed part of his family. He and Carol have centered their lives almost completely around their children and their home [qtd. in Johns 94].

Cohan notes that this reassessment of parental and matrimonial roles "ended up relocating masculinity in what had previously been considered a 'feminine' sphere, primarily by validating a man's domesticity (and consumption) over his work (and production) as the means through which he fulfilled societal expectations of what it took to be 'manly'" (xii).

Others were not so optimistic about these changes, however; many viewed the 1950s suburban husband and father as a feminized shell of his former self. For instance, *Look* magazine's article "The Decline of the American Male," published in February 1958, bemoaned the loss of American masculinity, stating, "scientists worry that in the years since the end of World War II, [the American male] has changed radically and dangerously; that he is no longer the masculine, strong-minded man who pioneered the continent and built America's greatness" (94). Embedded in such critiques was the anxiety that the new suburban "masculine domesticity" was no match for the wartime model of manhood; and, more ominously, that it would, in fact, have a negative impact upon the strength of the nation.

These two contradictory discourses, celebrating the post-war father's centrality in the family unit, and yet worrying that such a domesticizing drive would weaken the national interest, were in wide circulation during the period. As Cohan notes, "Cold war politics ... project[ed] contradictory ideals for American malehood, requiring a 'hard' masculinity as the standard when defending the nation's boundaries, yet insisting upon a 'soft' masculinity as the foundation of an orderly, responsible life" (xii). The binary contradictions of nationalism/domesticity, strength/vulnerability, and most succinctly in this case, masculinity/femininity, then set the groundwork for the anxiety upon which the Gothic/horror genres thrive.

The conflict between competing identities is played out in *I Married a Monster from Outer Space*. In the opening scene, as the group of men send their buddy off into the "constraints" of matrimony and suburbia, Bill's friend, Harry, details the sad state of affairs: "Every one us was married, is married, or is about to be married—give us all a drink." These drinks, it should be mentioned, are anything but celebratory: as will be evidenced later, liquor becomes a running conceit in this film for all that heterosexual, masculine bachelorhood symbolizes. Another friend continues the vitriolic tone towards marriage, chiming in, "[Bill's] such a nice guy ... it's a shame it [marriage] had to happen to him." The homosocial circle even trades strategies for escaping the bonds of marriage, and one friend details the most effective escape: "mass suicide." At this bar, for these men, marriage is a fate worse than death.

The synchronization of Bill's invasion and the eve of his wedding night is no mere coincidence: his marriage becomes, in every sense of the term, a "marriage of convenience." While the convergence of wedding and invasion (seemingly) ensures that the invader's victim will be actively procreating, it also provides an ingenious cover for the alien doppelganger. As the film makes clear, in the homosocial sphere, heterosexual emasculization through marriage looks deceptively similar to alien invasion. Nancy Steffen-Fluhr offers a convincing explanation for this commonality in her analysis of *Invasion of the Body Snatchers,* where she claims that the trope of "bodily invasion" often speaks to a fear of the male body becoming feminized: "loss of self, loss of individuality, surrender ... a dialectic between sleep and wakefulness, between deadly 'alien' passivity and passionate human activity" (141–4). It is the lack of passion, self-assertion, and emotion that mark the invaded victims as both "feminine" and "inhuman." However, in a portrayal quite divergent from the generic conventions of most bodily invasion films of the era, Bill's emotionless state and abrupt change of character are not seen as incongruous to his homosocial circle of friends—these changes are, the film tells us, synonymous with the changes that are to be *expected* when a man enters heterosexual marriage. In this, the feminization of the body through alien invasion and the feminization of the male body through marriage are virtually indistinguishable.

The Man in the Lavender Suit: Unmasking the Queer "Invisible Menace"

The conflicting constructions of "soft" domesticized masculinity and "hard" nationalistic masculinity in the 1950s are further complicated when the question of sexuality is added to the mix. *The Kinsey Report on Male Sexuality*, published to widespread sales in 1948, revealed that homosexual activity in men (the report on women was five years away) was far more prevalent than anyone at the time had suspected. According to the report, thirty-seven percent of adult men admitted to having at least one post-adolescent homosexual encounter. Kinsey's analysis of these statistics further contended that simple binary constructions of "heterosexual" and "homosexual" could not encompass the fluidity of sexual categorization, and suggested a seven-point sliding scale of sexual desire and identification. As Benshoff states, during the 1950s, "a newly inflected model of homosexuality gain[ed] prominence, one that recognized that all gay men weren't necessarily sissies and that all lesbians weren't necessarily butch ... [however,] the newly discovered 'invisibility' or 'passability' of homosexuals only led to more hysteria" (122). Thus the homosocial sphere, once an enclave from the fears of emasculization through marriage and family, became the site of paranoia as the possibility of the invisible homosexual presence led to fears of an imperceptible invasion.

So if in the 1950s public consciousness it was true that (in the words of *Sir!* magazine) "not all homos are easy to spot," and that "many have muscles, are he-men in everything—except sex," then the ultimate and only defining quality of the homosexual becomes the inability to engage in heterosexual sex. Masculinity becomes essentially a question of virility, potency, and the enunciation of exclusive sexual desire for women. This adds a new set of responsibilities, sexual performance, to the previous set of family responsibilities used to define maleness. Drawing upon the 1957 work of psychologist Helen Mayer Hacker, Cohan notes the "new burden of masculinity" that emerged in the 1950s, and the difficulty in defining normative masculinity in conflicting terms: both as a "social responsibility, with a man expected to perform his duty as the family breadwinner, and, simultaneously, as a question of sexual potency, with a man expected to perform in bed with vigor" (xv). As historian George Chauncey details, hetero-homosexual binarism became an essential component in defining this masculine construction, as "normal middle-class men increasingly believed that their virility depended on their exclusive sexual interest in women" (100). This recourse to exclusive, compulsory heterosexuality thus provided middle-class men with "a new, more positive way to demonstrate their manhood" (117). However, since this mode of differentiation was not socially visible, and could not be determined in homosocial spaces which excluded women (such as *Sir!* magazine's Wall Street firms, boxing rings, and baseball fields), these spaces became increasingly suspect.

The fear of the invisible homosexual man actually infiltrating the heterosexual institution of marriage was not far from the public consciousness, either. In addition to the revelations made by the *Kinsey Report*, a 1960 article by Eleanor Harris in the popular *Look* magazine detailed the invisible presence of "latent" homosexuals:

> A third troubled group consists of latent homosexuals. These fall into two classes—the "neuter" who practices no sexual activity of any kind, who is often found working in boys' schools and boys' organizations, and the Don Juan, who is so threatened by his fears of his unacknowledged homosexuality that he engages in affairs with women to prove his masculinity [29].

During this era, both the medical/psychiatric community and the popular media engaged in fierce debate about the origins and pathology of homosexuality. In the government, thousands of gays and lesbians were fired from their government jobs under suspicion of treason (Johnson 8), and homosexuality was deemed an "invisible menace" from the floor of Congress (Cong. Rec. 96.4) in much the same language used to hunt down the red menace. On the floor of the House of Representatives in 1950, Senator Miller of Nebraska employed the language of espionage to warn that the lavender menace was transmitting cryptic messages in plain view, stating "[t]hose people [homosexuals] like to be known to each other. They have signs used on streetcars and in public places to call attention to others of like mind" (Cong. Rec. 96.4).[4] As Chauncey asserts, "The fact that homosexuals no longer seemed so easy to identify made them seem even more dangerous, since it meant that even the next-door neighbor could be one. The specter of the invisible homosexual, like that of the invisible communist, haunted Cold War America" (100). Drafting their own Gothic narrative of spectral invasion for the nation, these government officials delivered an edict to unmask and eradicate the Communist and the homosexual, so often aligned in this era because of their invisibility.[5]

I Married a Monster from Outer Space thus performs the cultural work (that is so often done by Gothic/horror)[6] of revealing the invisible Other, showing the (imagined) horror that lies beneath the surface. The allegory of invisible alien (from space) invasion translates neatly into the equally fanciful tale of invisible alien homosexual invasion. As Cohan rightly observes, "[s]ince gender deviance was a conventional way of referring to homosexuality on screen without mentioning it ... fifties American films generally make the two comparable, so the representations of male gender trouble in movies of this period invariably raise problems of sexuality, too" (xvi). Indeed, the solidification of these representations as an understood "code" and the centralization of masculine crisis in homosocial circles in the film make such readings possible, certainly for queer spectators.

Moreover, the level of interpretation added by the casting of the film should not be overlooked. The male lead, Thomas Tryon, would come out of the closet in the 1970s, and certainly his sexuality adds an additional level of nuance to the film. As Gary Westfahl aptly puts it, "Tryon was bright enough to see the story's relevance to the terrible secret that many young men in the repressed 1950s were actually hiding—a sexual desire that dare not speak its name—and he gave an edgy, unnerving performance as the monster pretending to be, almost wanting to be, but ultimately unable to be a genuine husband to his lovely bride."

Already a feminized body through the trope of alien invasion, the alien Bill soon discovers that he is not alone; rather, he is one of many, a community of men that communicate through coded language and averted stares. In a particularly telling scene, one we might call alien Bill's "coming out" sequence, his old friend Sam (now a doppelganger himself), pays a visit. In this scene, Bill fetches Sam a gin cocktail, but neither he nor Sam take a drink (liquor, the earlier signifier of male heterosexual bachelorhood, is a liquid that the aliens apparently cannot drink). "Aren't you going to drink?" asks Sam. Bill responds, stating, "I guess I've lost my taste for it." The two exchange tentative glances in the pregnant pause that follows, each sizing one another up. Sam then offers the first "hint" of his alien/homosexual orientation, responding, "You know, I guess I've lost my taste for it, too." Another pause, but still Bill is unwilling to return the cryptic references. Sam persists, asking Bill, "Make many mistakes at first? Wearing this 'thing' [his human body]? The design—pretty lousy." And yet Bill still rejects the coded speech and insists on artifice, until Sam finally "outs" himself by physically revealing his inner "alien" self by removing the "mask" of humanness. Both men then smile, and draw close to one another as Bill lightly whispers, "Well ... congratulations." Though they do not signal each other in streetcars, this is certainly a moment of Sen. Miller from Nebraska's worst fear realized: an invisible cabal of queer Others in communication with one another, but hidden from public view.

The reading of alien invasion as homosexual invasion is strengthened by the structural similarities between homosocial and homoerotic circles of men. In another instance of parallel construction it soon becomes clear in the film that the homosocial circles of "alien" men look eerily similar to the homosocial circles of "human" men: both are exclusionary of women, both take place in the evening away from the home (or when in the home, as earlier, the females "excuse" themselves to leave the men to their work), both involve the "troubles" of heterosexual courtship, and both view sex and marriage as separate—as alien Bill says, on his home planet, men and women came together "for breeding purposes only." And finally, both homosocial circles even take place in a centralized location—the downtown bar.

In fact, it is through the trope of drinking that the film works to make the distinction of the invisible Other clear. Though the aliens have invaded the heterosexual male space of the bar (as they have invaded the heterosexual marriages), the alien doppelgangers cannot drink liquor, much to the disgust of Max, the bartender. Since the link between drinking liquor and heterosexual pre-feminized masculinity has already been strongly established by the opening bachelor party sequence, it becomes clear that the performance, or mask, of heterosexual masculinity, then, is not complete. Indeed, the inability to drink alcohol becomes one of the essential ways in which the delineation between (heterosexual) "human" men and (homosexual) "alien" men is made. The other mode of distinction, which brings about the ending of the film (and the aliens), is discovered when Marge visits her gynecologist, Dr. Wayne. Together, they realize that the alien husband has been unable to procreate due to a genetic incompatibility. To battle the invaders, they turn to the last bastion of true, authentic, heterosexual masculinity: the maternity ward waiting room. That is, they collect all of the town's expectant fathers: men who have verifiably been able to impregnate their wives and thus could not be part of the invading menace. In this film, as in the 1950s in general, the hetero-homosexual binary is policed through recourse to male virility and potency, and the true marker of a man (and in this case, a *hu*man) is his ability to procreate in the bonds of heterosexual consummation. In the end, the band of proven, virile heterosexuals (and their dogs) pounce upon the unsuspecting aliens at their mother ship, and literally rip them from limb to limb. Marge, who once was central to the tale, lags behind in the chase as the film's new central protagonists destroy the alien menace and restore the human victims. In the final battle, the binary distinction between the "real" men and the "alien" men is completely realized: invisible difference (no alcohol, no procreation) has given way to visible, bodily difference as the virile humans combat the aliens in their true reptilian form. In the end, the pogrom finally destroys the alien invaders and restores the heterosexual couple, Marge and (human) Bill; Anytown, U.S.A., returns to normalcy.

I Divorced a Monster from Outer Space: The Return to Normalcy Reconsidered

But we need to back up a moment: what seems to set *I Married a Monster from Outer Space* apart from the other bodily invasion films of the era is the surprising amount of empathy it demonstrates for the alien invaders.[7] Midway through the film, alien Bill begins to abandon his strictly procreative assessment of Marge, and begins to notice her aesthetic qualities, stating quite queerly, "You're very beautiful, aren't you?" By the end of the film, it is even suggested that alien Bill may even have begun to "love" Marge; or as he says, "I'm beginning to learn what love is." In a particularly sentimental scene, an alien is even seen gazing longingly into a shop window at a baby doll, suggesting a paternal affection heretofore unacknowledged.[8] Indeed, it seems that many of the alien invaders have developed, or learned, human emotions as a result of their prolonged stay on Earth. During a picnic scene in the latter half of the film, the suburban couples, invaded and uninvaded partners alike, chat playfully about their courtships, marriage, and cheery suburban lives. This suggests that the aliens have almost fully integrated themselves in the suburban society, as the "alien" men are virtually indistinguishable from the "human" men. Even alien Bill's final words to Marge before being eviscerated, "I never knew happiness, or love, or any emotion when we came to your Earth ... I'd just begun to learn," suggest the aliens could, conceivably, integrate themselves into the "human" world.

Yet, why does the film raise the possibility of a "reformed" alien population, only then to turn around and destroy it? We can best address this incongruity by saying that this film's politics cannot be contained within the formula of 1950s science fiction cinema. Although human Bill and Marge reunite at the film's close, their union does not carry with it the genre's conventional promise of a return to normalcy and security. Indeed, that portrait of matrimonial "normalcy" has already been established as loveless, sexless, and altogether rather bleak. The film's fear of the "decline of the American male" in marriage and suburbia is genuine; however, the alternative it offers—the safety of homosocial circles of men—is no less troubling. As the film demonstrates, these spheres are disturbingly similar to homoerotic circles. Therefore, a delineation is made through a recourse to the generic conventions of 1950s sci-fi, which requires that it exorcize the alien Other and reify heteronormativity. But the irony of this film's placement within 1950s science-fiction is that it ultimately reveals the genre's structural inadequacy in dealing with gender anxieties. This provides a point of entry to reinterrogate the genre as a whole,[9] and to recognize that a body of work so troubled by the Red Scare is also haunted by the fear of a more lavender hue.

Notes

1. As much as I would love to take credit for this discovery, this article is quoted from Harry Benshoff's *Monsters in the Closet* (131–2).
2. This article could also be read as a distinct "warning" for gay male readers to conform to heterocentric expectations. As Benshoff notes, the thriving "men's magazine" industry (*Esquire, Stag, Sir!, Saga, Showdown for Men*) defined American masculinity through "'true adventure stories' of intense homosocial bonding and the ever-increasing objectification of women as sex objects" (126). Intermingled with these tales were more explicitly homoerotic material, such as Charles Atlas physique pictorials—visual culture, which, as many theorists have noted, became a burgeoning gay male proto-pornography industry during the decade.
3. Drawing upon the work of Eugenia DeLamotte, Ruth Bienstock Anolik notes in her introduction to *The Gothic Other: Racial Constructions in the Literary Imagination* that "the essential fear of the Gothic is that there are actually no categories of Otherness" (10).
4. It is worth noting that Sen. Miller also explicitly cultivates racial anxiety in his vilification of homosexuality, stating "It is a known fact that homosexuality goes back to the Orientals, lone [sic] before the time of Confucius; that the Russians are strong believers in homosexuality, and that those same people are able to get into the State Department and get somebody in their embrace, and once they are in their embrace, fearing blackmail, will make them go to any extent" (Cong. Rec. 96.4).
5. This fear thus echoes the fear of the invisible Catholic and the invisible Jew that troubled earlier governments and societies.
6. For a similar perspective on the Gothic response to the invasion threat from the "invisible Other," see Ruth Bienstock Anolik's "The Infamous Svengali: George Du Maurier's Satanic Jew," in which Anolik discusses George Du Maurier's attempt to unmask and demonize the religious Other in his novel *Trilby*.
7. A possible exception to this would be *It Came from Outer Space*, although I would contend that the sympathy elicited in that film comes from the fact that alien "invaders" seek only to flee from Earth, rather than to conquer it.
8. Although it is not quite clear, the toy also appears to be an African-American baby doll, additionally suggesting a sense of shared "alienation," and a parallel between racial and sexual Otherness. Certainly other films from the era, such as John M. Stahl's and Douglas Sirk's versions of *Imitation of Life* (1934 and 1959, respectively), explored instances of African-Americans "passing" as white.
9. Considering, for instance, the genre's conventional "interruption" of heterosexual coupling when the alien invasion occurs, or the gender-based paranoia that populates so many of the films (perhaps most succinctly in Miles Bennell's climactic admission, "I never knew the meaning of fear until I kissed Becky," from *Invasion of the Body Snatchers*).

Works Cited

Anolik, Ruth Bienstock. "The Infamous Svengali: George Du Maurier's Satanic Jew." In *The Gothic Other: Racial and Social Constructions in the Literary Imagination,* ed. Ruth Bienstock Anolik and Douglas L. Howard, 163–193. Jefferson: McFarland, 2004.

_____. Introduction: "The Dark Unknown." In *The Gothic Other: Racial and Social Constructions in the Literary Imagination,* ed. Ruth Bienstock Anolik and Douglas L. Howard, 1–14. Jefferson: McFarland, 2004.

Benshoff, Harry M. *Monsters in the Closet: Homosexuality and the Horror Film.* Manchester: Manchester University Press, 1997.
Chauncey, George. *Gay New York: Gender, Urban Culture, and the Making of the Gay Male World, 1890–1940.* New York: Basic Books, 1994.
Cohan, Steven. *Masked Men: Masculinity and the Movies in the Fifties.* Indianapolis: Indiana University Press, 1997.
Connelley, James. "It's the Day of the Gray Flannel Fag." *Sir!* March 1958, 20–1, 40.
D'Emilio, John. *Sexual Politics, Sexual Communities: The Making of a Homosexual Minority in the United States, 1940–1970.* Chicago: University of Chicago Press, 1998.
81st Congress, 2nd Session. *Cong. Rec.* 96.4. 29 March–24 April 1950: 4527–4528. http://www.english.upenn.edu/~afilreis/50s/gays-in-govt.html.
Goddu, Teresa. *Gothic America: Narrative, History, and Nation.* New York: Columbia University Press, 1997.
Harris, Eleanor. "Men Without Women." *Look Magazine,* 22 November 1960, 124–30.
Hendershot, Cyndy. *Paranoia, the Bomb, and 1950s Science Fiction Films.* Bowling Green: Bowling Green State University Popular Press, 1999. 51–65.
"Housing Gets No. 1 Spot at Family Life Conference." *Journal of Housing,* May 1948, 15.
I Married a Monster from Outer Space. Dir. Gene Fowler, Jr. Perf. Tom Tryon, Gloria Talbott. Paramount, 1958.
Johns, Michael. *Moment of Grace: The American City in the 1950s.* Berkeley: University of California Press, 2003.
Johnson, David K. *Lavender Scare: The Cold War Persecution of Gays and Lesbians in the Federal Government.* Chicago: University of Chicago Press, 2004.
Moskin, J. Robert, George B. Leonard, Jr., and William Attwood. *The Decline of the American Male.* New York: Random House, 1958.
Polan, Dana. *National Manhood: Capitalist Citizenship and the Imagined Fraternity of White Men.* Durham: Duke University Press, 1998.
Sontag, Susan. "The Imagination of Disaster." *Liquid Metal: The Science Fiction Film Reader,* ed. Sean Redmond. London: Wallflower, 2004.
Steffen-Fluhr, Nancy. "Women and the Inner Game of Don Siegel's *Invasion of the Body Snatchers.*" *Science-Fiction Studies* 11:2 (1984): 139–153.
Westfahl, Gary. "Thomas Tryon (1926–1991): American Actor and Writer." *Gary Westfahl's Biographical Encyclopedia of Science Fiction Film.* 8 June 2004. http://www.sfsite.com/gary/try001.htm.

Part IV
VIVE LA DIFFÉRENCE: CELEBRATING THE SEXUAL OTHER

14
The Lesbian Vampire: Transgressive Sexuality[1]
PAULINA PALMER

The vampire is the queer in its lesbian mode.
—Sue-Ellen Case, "Tracking the Vampire" 9

The image of the vampire has been frequently in the public eye in recent years. In addition to inspiring numerous novels and stories, it has generated two major critical studies. Ken Gelder, in tracing the creature's shifting fortunes in literature and myth from the eighteenth century to the present day, explores the varied and at times bizarre assortment of interpretations that theorists and writers assign to it. Meanings that he discusses include the foreigner, such as the Jew or black, contact with whom imperialist nations fear will contaminate their blood; communist tyranny in Eastern Europe; queer relationships; and (unlikely though it sounds) the Lacanian concept of "the Real."[2] Nina Auerbach, adopting a more populist approach in *Our Vampires Ourselves*, focuses on the vampire's links with contemporary politics and culture; she examines, among other things, the significance it assumes in relation to the fears of communism and nuclear war that haunted the American imagination in the 1950s and 1960s. However, there is one topic which both writers, different though their perspectives are, prioritize. This is the vampire's homoerotic associations.[3]

The vampires that dominate the story lines of film and fiction, whether their sexual preferences are heterosexual or gay, are generally represented as male. However, female vampires have also achieved a degree of notoriety—frequently of a misogynistic kind. Nineteenth century artists and writers utilized the motif as a vehicle to delineate the woman who takes excessive pleasure in sex and to illustrate the destructive effect her inordinate sexual demands have upon men. Philip Burne-Jones portrays her gloating over the limp body of her unconscious lover, while Franz Flaum, in a powerful sculptural representation, depicts her in the act of stalking her prey.[4] Although centering his novel on the activities of Count Dracula, Stoker also introduces a clutch of female vampires. Lucy Westenra, who, on becoming Dracula's victim, is herself transformed into a member of the undead, reveals, prior to her metamorphosis, symptoms of the sexual promiscuity associated in nineteenth century *fin-de-siècle* culture with the figure of "the New Woman." This is signaled by her inability to choose between the three suitors who compete for her love and by her playfully voiced remark that she wishes that society would allow her to marry all three.[5]

Appearing less frequently in nineteenth century literature, though representing an even greater threat to marriage and the fabric of society, is the lesbian vampire. Bonnie Zimmerman traces her origins to the Countess Elizabeth Bathory, a sixteenth century aristocrat who allegedly engaged in the gruesome practice of bathing in the blood of local virgins to preserve her youth, and to the Countess Millarca Karnstein, the eponymous heroine of Sheridan Le Fanu's *Carmilla* (1872).[6]

In contrast to Le Fanu's relatively liberal accepting approach, other nineteenth century writers treat the lesbian vampire in a homophobic manner, associating her with evil and sexual depravity. Samuel Taylor Coleridge portrays her in his unfinished poem *Christabel* (1816) seducing her victim and winning her trust with a display of insidious charm, while Charles Baudelaire's *Les Fleurs du Mal* and Algernon Charles Swinburne's "Faustine" utilize vampiric imagery to typecast the lesbian as decadent and morally corrupt. Swinburne describes in vampiric terms the "shameless nameless" love in which the Roman empress Faustine, inspired by "the stray breaths of Sapphic song that blew through Mityline," supposedly indulged. As Clement Dane's *The Regiment of Women* (1917) and Francis Brett Young's *White Ladies* (1935) illustrate, the introduction of vampiric imagery to stigmatize the figure of the lesbian continued in the twentieth century. D.H. Lawrence's *The Rainbow* (1915) contains a particularly vicious example in the portrayal of Winifred Inger, the school teacher who becomes the lover of the heroine Ursula. Having transformed Winifred into a kind of predatory lamia by comparing her to "a prehistoric lizard," Lawrence emphasizes the vampirish nature of her lovemaking by describing it depleting Ursula's vitality and leaving her with a "heavy, clogged sense of deadness" (344).[7]

With the advent of the horror film, directors have tended to exploit the image of the lesbian vampire for sensationalistic, pornographic ends, taking advantage of the appeal of the motif to male fantasy. *The Vampire Lovers* (1970) and *Twins of Evil* (1971) illustrate this trend, associating lesbian love with violence and narcissism.[8] Nonetheless cinematic representations, despite their misogynistic resonances, frequently display an element of ambiguity. As Zimmerman's reading of *Daughters of Darkness* (1970) and Barbara Creed's discussion of *The Hunger* (Creed 59–72) illustrate, the lesbian vampire, though ostensibly portrayed as monstrous and unnatural, simultaneously emerges as a signifier of female power. She displays a potential for lesbian/feminist revision. Her shape-changing abilities can be read as denoting her refusal to become entrapped in the conventional domestic role, while her erotic relations with women represent a challenge to the institution of marriage and the control men seek to exert on female sexuality.

Transgressive sexuality is a key feature of the lesbian vampire's representation differentiating her from the other mythic images of womanhood that feature in lesbian Gothic. Whereas the witch is utilized by Barbara Hanrahan and Emma Tennant[9] to explore the disruptive effects of female eroticism, and the spectral visitor, as illustrated by the novels of Paula Martinac and Molleen Zanger, acts as a signifier of repressed desire, the vampire, on account of her connections with blood and oral sex, is explicitly sexual in significance, carrying associations of a perverse eroticism that violates accepted taboos.[10] The vampire's reputation for transgressive sexuality explains, of course, the popularity that the motif is currently enjoying in lesbian and queer culture. Although the reclamation of the lesbian vampire commenced in 1984 with the publication of Jody Scott's *I, Vampire*, only in the late 1980s and the 1990s has it captured the imagination of writers and readers, and texts centering on the motif have proliferated.[11] The lesbian vampire's rise to fame has coincided with the emphasis on the sexual dimension of lesbianism promoted by the sexual radicals and the queer movement. Three of the fictional texts discussed in this essay, Jewelle Gomez's *The Gilda Stories* (1991), Katherine V. Forrest's "O, Captain, My Captain" (1993) and Pat Califia's "The Vampire" (1988), reveal the influence of these movements and can be read, in certain cases, as manifestos for them. The three writers portray the lesbian vampire as a signifier of an alternative economy of sexual pleasure which is more emotionally intense and fulfilling than its heterosexual counterpart. The descriptions of lesbian sex that they create, in some cases successfully and in others less so, function as a fantasy space of transgressive eroticism which exists beyond the limits of mundane reality and the confines of patriarchy. These passages foreground the relationship between sexuality and the body, exploring its boundaries, flows, ruptures and exchanges.[12]

In challenging the homophobic associations of the lesbian vampire and transforming the motif into a signifier of lesbian sexual pleasure, the writers discussed in this essay appropriate ideas from both classic vampire narratives and feminist/queer readings and critiques. Instead of portraying her as the epitome of the monstrous Other, as is the case with texts reproducing a hetero-patriarchal viewpoint, they position her as the narrator or protagonist and allow her to address the reader directly. They also tease out the metaphorical connections between "lesbian" and "vampire." These, as illustrated below, are both numerous and complex.

A key point of affinity between the lesbian and the vampire, which writers frequently exploit, is their dual existence both as independent loners and members of a loosely knit network or group. Both figures experience a tension between the need for privacy and anonymity on the one hand and interaction with members of "their own kind" on the other. While concealing their lesbianism/vampirism from the prying eyes of the world, they seek to recognize and be recognized by a group of like-minded sisters. The association of the vampire with the period of twilight, since the sunset is supposed to liberate her from her coffin and permit her to venture abroad to stalk her prey, is pertinent in metaphoric terms to the closeted lesbian who, having concealed her sexual orientation during the day, emerges at night to seek romance in the half-lit world of clubs and bars. The popularity that lesbian vampire fiction is currently enjoying, in addition to reflecting the interest in the sexual dimension of lesbianism which characterizes present-day lesbian/queer culture, also mirrors the re-evaluation, frequently nostalgic in tone, of the lesbian social life of the 1950s with its emphasis on a furtively illicit lifestyle centering on the night-time scene.[13] The reason the lesbian and the vampire feel forced to conceal their identities and lead a double life is that they are targets of persecution. Terms of abuse such as "unnatural," "perverse" and "monstrous" are directed at both. As Sue-Ellen Case observes in her essay "Tracking the Vampire," where she discusses the potential the motif displays for lesbian and queer appropriation, "the identification with the insult, the taking on of the transgressive, and the consequent flight into invisibility" traditionally typifying lesbian existence "are inscribed in the figure of the vampire" (2).

The association of the vampire with sterility and death is also, sad to say, applicable from a homophobic point of view to the figure of the lesbian. Although many lesbians and gay men do in fact raise children, homosexuality tends to be linked in the mind of the general public with barrenness and sterility. Gillian Hanscombe and Jackie Forster in their study of lesbian motherhood comment on the fact that, on account of the confusion existing between female sexual pleasure and reproductive sex and the notion that lesbians are psychologically or physiologically "masculine," many people assume that they are incapable of bearing children. Alternatively, if by some quirk of fate they do bear them, they are deemed unfit to care for them.[14] The connection existing between homosexuality and death is illustrated by Jonathan Dollimore; he points out that the linking of the two in homophobic studies of AIDS is by no means new since reference to death is, in fact, common in discussions of same-sex desire throughout history.[15] Yet, despite the fact that, particularly in the present era of AIDS, male homosexuality and lesbianism, like vampirism, tend to be associated with sterility and death, they also paradoxically carry connotations of immortality. Though frequently experiencing intense pressure to submit to heterosexual norms, lesbians and gay men staunchly refuse to do so. Resisting harassment and persecution, they continue, like the vampire, to pursue an alternative lifestyle and survive.

The lesbian and the vampire also reveal links in terms of sex and sexual politics. Anna Livia foregrounds three significant points of affinity when in *Minimax* (1991), a novel discussed in this essay, she commands the reader with evident relish to "think of all those beautiful female heads rising superbly from between their lovers' thighs, mouths dripping with menstrual blood. Triple taboo: no oral sex, no sex during periods, no female to female sex" (112). And, while as Livia humorously emphasizes, the lesbian, like the vampire, breaks the "triple taboo" of sexual relations with women, oral sex and sex during menstruation, she also challenges the institution of marriage by forming primary attachments with women. Whereas the vampire unsettles our assumptions of clearly defined categories by traversing the borderline between the living and the dead, the lesbian destabilizes conventional gender roles by usurping the male prerogative of choosing a woman as love-object. In addition, both display perverse connotations with the maternal. The lesbian vampire, as Barbara Creed argues, is a particularly terrifying creature since, in causing woman's blood to flow while initiating her into eternal life, she reworks, with perverse displacements, the primal scene of birth. The lesbian, by taking a woman as her lover, indirectly embarks on a taboo return to the pleasures of the mother/daughter relationship (Creed 61).

The connections between the vampire and the lesbian furnish the frame for the novels and stories discussed in this essay. Writers treat them inventively, developing different aspects of vampire lore and utilizing them for a variety of intellectual and ideological ends. Scott and Livia, concentrating on the vampire's relation to the abject, humorously problematize the concepts of the monstrous and the abnormal which she conventionally embodies, exposing them as relative and arbitrary. They utilize the vampire's shape-changing abilities as a vehicle for addressing issues relating to the construction of role and identity. The excess which lesbian sexuality signifies in hetero-patriarchal culture is mirrored in the style the two writers employ. It finds expression in an unconventional mingling of genres, unexpected flights of humor and a witty utilization of parody and pastiche.

In the fiction of Forrest, Califia and Gomez the transgressive dimension of lesbianism and the excess that it signifies are expressed primarily by reference to sex and the body. The physical transformations the vampire enacts and the exchange of blood in which s/he engages inspire the three writers to create representations of the body in its grotesque form, foregrounding its orifices, protuberances, fluids and sexual rhythms. Experimental forms of sexual practice such as oral sex, S&M, and butch-femme role-play, also assume prominence. In a manner calculated to disturb the reader, Califia and Gomez juxtapose images of maternal nurture with depictions of lesbian/vampiric sexual encounters. The latter are emphatically violent, involving reference to blood and wounds.

As well as being reflected in the three writers' representations of the body and sex, a focus on the grotesque is also apparent in their treatment of the family. The vampire network or "family" they illustrate does not depend on the Law of the Father[16] but, on the contrary, reflects a genealogy based on the direct exchange of body fluids. It resembles queer relationships and groups in furnishing a transgressive alternative to the patriarchal familial formation and the values which it encodes.[17] In her essay theorizing the vampire as a signifier of queer politics, Case makes the point that the queer movement, like the vampire, seeks to deconstruct the binaries of normal/abnormal, nature/culture, fertility/infertility by untying the knot that traditionally links sex to procreation and by foregrounding other forms of creativity besides child-bearing. The novels and stories discussed in this essay, in exploring alternative familial formations and reproductive technologies and centering attention on examples of vampiric/gay creativity, furnish fictional illustrations of these ideas.

The texts which are the focus of this essay share a similarly transgressive perspective, while differing in style and ideological viewpoint. Lesbian Gothic as a genre evinces little interest in normalizing lesbian relations but highlights their socially disruptive aspect and foregrounds lesbian difference. As the grotesque nature of the vampire motif and its explicitly sexual character lead us to expect, a focus on lesbian "Otherness" and the problematizing of hetero-patriarchal norms and structures are particularly to the fore in the narratives which it inspires. Case's theorization of the vampire again endorses this point. She jubilantly affirms the fact that the queer movement is uninterested in normalizing or sanitizing homosexuality but, as she luridly puts it, "revels in the discourse of the loathsome, the outcast, the idiomatically proscribed position of same-sex desire" (3). A similarly celebratory emphasis on "difference" and "Otherness" is apparent in the texts discussed below.

Humor, Genre and Lesbian History

The period of the mid-1980s marked a decided upturn in the fortunes of the vampire. It witnessed its reclamation from monstrous Other to a creature which, if not exactly cuddly, is capable of enlisting the sympathy of the reader and audience. Three texts focusing on the vampire and, more significantly, assigning to her/him a subjectivity and a voice appeared around this time: Tony Scott's art film *The Hunger* (1983), focusing on the glamorous bisexual Miriam Blaylock (Catherine Deneuve) and her love affairs with mortal men; Anne Rice's *The Vampire Lestat* (1986), the second volume of her *Vampire Chronicles*, which explores the history and growth of a vampire network; and Jody Scott's *I, Vampire* (1986), which utilizes the vampire as a mouthpiece for the pleasures and problems of lesbian existence. The comic dimension of Scott's novel challenges the stereotypical image of lesbian feminists as a dreary, puritanical bunch who lack a sense of fun. Scott utilizes humor both to entertain the reader and as a strategy to address and popularize ideas relating to sexual politics.

The idea of treating the vampire in a comic light, which furnishes the germ of Scott's novel, has precedent in film. Roman Polanski's *The Fearless Vampire Killers* (1967) introduces a gay vampire and employs a brand of humor that is playfully camp in the scenes in which he appears. Stan Dragoti's *Love at First Bite* (1979), which portrays the vampire hero emigrating from Eastern Europe to New York when his castle is commandeered by the communist government, also exploits the vampire narrative's comic potential. Whereas film furnished Scott with a model for the humorous treatment of the vampire and the creature's homosexual associations, feminist science fiction provided her with a model for utilizing fantasy as a vehicle for sexual politics. *I, Vampire* is a work of lesbian feminist political fiction[18] in the tradition of Joanna Russ's *The Female Man* (1975). Scott emulates Russ in employing science fiction conventions and parodically manipulated stereotypes to investigate the construction of gender and to interrogate hetero-patriarchal norms and values. Like Russ, she also advertises the fictionality of her narrative and alerts attention to its ideological import by punctuating it with jokes, intertextual allusions and passages of authorial comment. In contrast to her predecessor, however, Scott chooses to rework not one popular genre but two. She inserts into a typical science fiction scenario of interplanetary travel the Gothic motif of the vampire, exploiting the explosion of wit in which the clash between the two genres results for ideological ends. By humorously interrogating the conventional notion of the vampire's monstrous nature, she problematizes not only the idea of lesbianism as monstrous and abnormal but also the concepts of monstrosity and abnormality *per se*, exposing them as inauthentic and arbitrary.

Scott structures her novel on a series of encounters between her vampire protagonist, Sterling O'Blivion, and Benaroya, a visitor from outer space, that exemplify the meeting of "the grotesque" and "the alien."

Benaroya and her fellow Rysemians are light-years ahead of the human race in intelligence. They number among their numerous talents the art of self-transformation, the enjoyment of immortality and the ability to manufacture their own physical forms and "realities." Benaroya has learned everything she knows about life on Earth from the novels and films she has studied on her native planet while preparing for her trip abroad. She is used to adopting different personae and, in order to win Sterling's trust, chooses to materialize before her in the guise of Virginia Woolf, signifier of female creativity and lesbian love. The aim of her visit to Earth is to prevent the human race from destroying the universe, a course on which, she angrily observes, it appears to be hellbent. As she informs the astonished Sterling, she has chosen her as mediator in the mission to save the earth because, as a vampire, she represents a link between the human and the immortal. Sterling, Benaroya flatteringly observes, in addition to being "the most advanced, and by far the oldest bat on the planet," is "very wise, and not only a damned good theoretical physicist but a square shooter!"[19] (51, 54). Though flattered by Benaroya's good opinion of her and quickly falling for her extraterrestrial charms, Sterling finds the encounter with her disconcerting and, in certain respects, humiliating. Up to now she has always regarded herself as the epitome of the weird and the perverse. She prides herself on the fact that in the sixteenth century she "vampirized a famous Shakespearean actor whose name was a household word" (31), grabbing the crucifix he was holding for self-protection and adding it to her collection of 947 similar items. Now, however, confronted by Benaroya in the unlikely guise of Virginia Woolf, she has to admit that there are creatures in the universe who are even more alien and weird than she herself. Her response to the image of the abject which, in her eyes, Benaroya represents, is typically ambiguous. While she finds the image of "a sea pig or fat dolphin, all flippers and bloated neck" (59), the form which Benaroya adopts on her native planet, utterly repulsive, she regards the Virginia Woolf persona she assumes during her visit to Earth as enthralling and delightful. Benaroya signifies, Sterling nervously admits, "the edge of something." Her description of Benaroya as combining both "the charm of the unhuman—and the *fear*" (59) agrees with Julia Kristeva's description of the contradictions of fascination and disquiet which the abject generally evokes.

Sterling's unexpected encounter with this highly intelligent visitor from outer space, as well as undermining her pride in her own "Otherness" and monstrosity, proves to be educational. She is astonished when, in response to her sarcastic quip "You're the superior alien who knows it all!" Benaroya promptly retorts, "There are no aliens" (61). The inauthenticity and arbitrariness of the concept "alien" is the novel's key theme. Its importance is illustrated by the way that, while Sterling projects the category "alien" on to Benaroya, Benaroya and her Rysemian colleagues, despite recognizing its inauthenticity, instinctively project it on to the human race. As they pointedly remark, parodically mimicking the expressions of bigotry and aggression which human beings habitually utter, "What I am is right, and if you're different, you're on an infantile level, so I have the right and duty to bully you until you act like *me"* (153).

In problematizing the concepts of the alien and the monstrous and exposing them as inauthentic, *I, Vampire* foregrounds the constructed aspect of culture and identity. Sterling acts as a mouthpiece for this by expressing irritation with the popular image of the vampire which people habitually project upon her. In a passage parodying lesbian/feminist complaints about the oppressive and degrading scripts which women are forced to enact, she mournfully laments the fact that she is "merely a mythological creature ... expected to act out a script written by others, one that ignores my true nature" (22). Relaxing in bed, flicking through the pages of the latest vampire novel, she denounces it for producing "boring writing, wooden characters, and no ideas" (22)—and, in consequence, failing to register the fact that, as she paradoxically states, "Vampires are as human as anyone, in fact, more so" (15). Disenchanted with the tacky culture of twentieth century America, she reminisces nostalgically about her youthful years in Renaissance Spain when, as she proudly puts it, "I was inventing, and I mean *personally creating*, that baroque dramatization known as the classic [vampire] style" (18). She is by no means pleased when Benaroya, instead of sympathising with her stories of the disrespect she meets in present-day New York, accuses her of wallowing in self-pity and manifesting symptoms of self-oppression—"Revelling," as she puts it, "in all the bad things that have been done to you" (62). Benaroya callously concludes, adding insult to injury by questioning her identity, "This vampire thing; what is a vampire? Who projected the image onto you?" (201).[20]

Scott's humorous treatment of the vampire motif as a strategy to problematize concepts of the alien and the monstrous and to discuss constructs of lesbian identity created a blueprint for later writers. Livia's *Minimax*, published in 1991, seven years after Scott's novel, develops many of its key features. The similarities between the two texts are in some cases so close as to suggest that Livia is deliberately reworking Scott's narrative with the aim of creating a postmodern version relevant to the lesbian culture of the 1990s. Both writers structure their novels on an encounter between the present-day protagonist and a lesbian icon from the past. Whereas in Scott's novel the figure with iconic status is Virgina Woolf, the persona which the extraterrestrial Benaroya adopts on her visit to Earth, in Livia's it is Renee Vivien and her ex-lover Natalie

Barney who unexpectedly materialize in 1990s Perth as members of the living dead. While Scott assigns the role of vampire to her protagonist Sterling, Livia ascribes it to Vivien and Barney.

The two novels also reveal stylistic and intellectual similarities. In addition to creating humorous versions of the vampire narrative, both utilize fantasy for antiessentialist ends. Whereas Scott, as we have seen, problematizes concepts of the alien and the monstrous, exposing them as ideological constructs, Livia investigates changing fashions in vampiric form and identity. The representation of Vivien and Barney in vampiric form enables her to resurrect the two women from the grave and bring them face to face with her present-day protagonist Minnie. The clash of attitudes and styles which the encounter generates is a source of lively humor throughout the text. It also gives Livia the opportunity to compare and contrast the "decadent" image of lesbianism which flourished in early twentieth century Paris with the constructs of lesbianism produced in the 1970s and early 1980s.

Minimax opens with a parodic description of the lesbian feminism of the 1980s, emphasizing the rigidity and narrowness which, after the heady radicalism of the 1970s, tended to descend upon the lesbian community. Livia playfully illustrates that the adoption of a lesbian identification, far from being a passport to behavior that is transgressive and individualistic, often brings with it a new set of rules—sexual, social and sartorial—which can be every bit as stifling as their heterosexual counterparts. Minnie, unemployed and living in London, is portrayed donning the lesbian feminist uniform of dark jeans and sweater, purchased from the local jumble sale, and sallying forth on a shopping spree to Marks and Spencer. Here she intends to purchase a new outfit to wear to a job interview which, by dint of much effort, she has succeeded in achieving. She is delighted when the arrival of two letters, both by the same post, relieves her from the dual responsibilities of deciding what to wear and finding herself a job. One is from her mother Beryl, who has recently emigrated to Australia, inviting her to pay a visit and offering to pay her air fare to Perth. The other is a mysterious missive with a New York postmark containing the succinctly worded summons, "Come. I must meet you" (15). It bears the signature of Natalie Barney. This understandably puzzles Minnie since, as an admirer of Barney's writing, she knows that she died in 1972. Minnie, however, has had enough of life in Thatcher's Britain and is in the mood for adventure. Enthusiastically taking advantage of both invitations, she contacts a travel agency and books a flight round the world, with stops in Perth and New York.

On meeting up with her relatives in Perth, Minnie is astonished to see the improvement that has occurred in their material circumstances. Whereas when last she heard from them they were homeless and on the breadline, now they are living in relative affluence. As she subsequently discovers, it her mother Beryl who is responsible for this unexpected upturn in the family fortunes. Beryl is also responsible for the transformation of Livia's narrative, which up to now has been feminist realist in style, to a version of comic Gothic, complete with the standard components of vampires, coffins and incidents of shape-changing. Beryl, we discover, has entered into a business agreement with Vivien, who, accompanied by crateloads of Parisian furniture and memorabilia, has set up home in Perth in vampiric guise. In return for agreeing to clean her decadent mansion with its black marble staircase and chandeliers and tend her conservatory of exotically funereal plants including "black orchids and Lethean lotuses" (71), Beryl can rely on Vivien's uncanny powers to ensure her family's health and financial security.

Livia's representation of Vivien and her ex-lover Barney as members of the living dead creates a comic pastiche of the decadent construct of lesbianism that Vivien herself cultivated in her lifetime,[21] humorously ridiculing the Gothic aspects of her image.[22] The decadent model of lesbianism that Vivien, with her anorexic looks and conservatory of funereal plants, epitomizes acts as a foil to the romantic Sapphic image exemplified by Barney. Conquered by the latter's seductive rhetoric, Minnie throws caution to the winds and, forgetting Barney's reputation for capriciousness and infidelity, accepts her invitation to become her lover. However, after a few weeks of happiness Barney, true to the belief in sexual freedom and experimentation which she championed during her life, tires of her new conquest and abandons her. She sails away on her yacht accompanied by Vivien to savor the Sapphic pleasures of California, leaving lesbian feminist Minnie standing forlornly on the quayside in the classic pose of jilted womanhood.

A feature of Livia's novel that differentiates it from Scott's is the focus it places on historical constructs of lesbianism. Unlike Scott who, writing in the early 1980s, makes only passing reference to the topic in her intertextual allusions to Virgina Woolf and Radclyffe Hall, Livia, influenced by the interest in lesbian history that emerged toward the end of the decade, gives it pride of place. *Minimax* can be read as a playfully inventive fiction of history which endorses the postmodern view that the investigation of the past involves the use of imagination as well as the documentation of facts. However, even regarded in postmodern terms, the methods of research that Livia assigns to her protagonist Minnie strike the reader as decidedly unorthodox and eccentric. Minnie gains information about two famous lesbian writers from the past not by reading the texts they produced or perusing their biographies but by conversing with them and embarking on a love affair with one of them. Ironically, rather than valuing the opportunity which the encounter offers for gain-ing an insight into an important episode of lesbian history, Minnie treats it very casually. She is more interested in flaunting what she regards as her own superior knowledge and in slotting Vivien and Barney into present-day cultural paradigms than in listening to their views and ideas. Livia cynically suggest that, when the present-day lesbian actually does have the chance to investigate lesbian history at first hand, her egocentricity and obsession with political correctness act as a barrier to communication and blinker her vision.[23] In addition to commenting on the current vogue for investigating and reconstructing the lesbian past, *Minimax* also critiques present-day images of lesbianism, exposing their contradictions and absurdities.

Sex and Erotic Fantasy

The sexual connotations of the vampire, which are instrumental in accounting for the popularity that the motif is currently enjoying, make it an appropriate vehicle for discussing other aspects of lesbian sex besides the topic of butch-femme role-play which Livia addresses in *Minimax*. Oral sex, S&M partnerships and different forms of erotic fantasy are all topics that achieve representation and analysis in the lesbian vampire narrative. The two stories by Forrest and Califia discussed in this section exemplify this focus. They are influenced by and contribute to the debates about sexuality which, surfacing in the 1980s, continue to provoke discussion and controversy among women who identify as lesbian or bisexual.[24] The sexual encounters on which the stories center are introduced not merely for purposes of characterization or to stimulate the reader erotically—though they are certainly erotic. They are ideological in emphasis, contributing to a deliberately worked out political agenda. Aligning themselves with the lesbian sexual radicals,[25] Forrest and Califia seek to affirm the importance of the sexual dimension of lesbianism and to expand the reader's appreciation of sexual pleasure. The image of sex they create differs from the lesbian feminist model by prioritizing experimentation and role-play. In foregrounding the interaction between dominant/submissive positions in butch-femme relationships or S&M encounters, it also represents lesbian partnerships as involving the negotiation of power. In contrast to the lesbian feminists who associated power and violence with heterosexual relations, the lesbian sexual radicals regarded them as intrinsic features of sex in general. They promoted butch-femme role-play and S&M scenarios as a vehicle for channelling and controlling these tendencies. In consonance with their belief in sexual experimentation, they also advocated an interest in erotic fantasy. These ideas, in addition to informing collections of essays and stories such as the groundbreaking volume *Desire: The Politics of Sexuality* (1984),[26] are also reflected in the lesbian magazines of the 1980s such as the American publication *On Our Backs* and the British *Quim*. *Serious Pleasure* (1989), a collection of erotic stories produced by Sheba Feminist Publishers, likewise aims to stimulate the reader's enjoyment of the erotic. It contains, it is interesting to note, "White Flowers," a story by Gomez, whose contribution to the lesbian reclamation of the vampire motif is discussed below. The vampire, with its associations of power struggle, transgressive eroticism and the image of sex as paradoxically pleasurable and dangerous, makes a suitable vehicle for the radical image of lesbian sexuality which Forrest, Califia and Gomez seek to convey. As we shall see, the three writers treat the motif from notably different angles—and with varying degrees of success.

Forrest's "O Captain, My Captain," interpreted in terms of the debates about lesbian sexual practice which dominated lesbian politics in the 1980s and early 1990s, creates a bridge between the approach promoted by the lesbian sexual radicals and the lesbian/feminist model. On the one hand, Forrest celebrates sexual pleasure, representing lesbian sex as involving the negotiation of power and introducing episodes that are explicitly erotic. On the other hand, however, by revising the conventional image of the vampire and repudiating the thirst for blood traditionally attributed to the creature, she rejects the focus on pain associated with S&M.

In addition to mediating between these contrary approaches to sex, Forrest also brings together two different styles of vampire narrative. She combines the focus on humor and the interplay of genres which Scott employs with the emphasis on the erotic reflected in the texts of Califia and Gomez. Like Scott, she utilizes the simple but effective device of inserting the Gothic motif of the vampire into a science fiction frame, thus subverting the masculinist associations of the latter. Captains of space ships are generally portrayed as male and heterosexual. They are certainly not depicted as lesbian vampires who engage in love affairs with female members of the crew and perform the uncanny trick of transforming themselves into bats—as is the case with Drake, the captain of *Scorpio IV*, the spacecraft that is the setting for Forrest's story.[27] In contrast to Scott, who concentrates on interrogating and problematizing the concepts of the alien and the monstrous, however, Forrest aims to affirm and celebrate lesbian sexuality. Her story hinges on a topic which, as we saw in the introductory section, creates a link between vampirism and lesbianism. This is oral sex and the breaking of the taboo relating to it in which both the vampire and the lesbian engage.

Captain Drake is accompanied on her voyage in space by her second-in-command, Lieutenant Harper, a re-creation of Stoker's Harker. Harper is positioned in the text as a naïve persona. Her initial inability to perceive the fact that Drake is a vampire, a discovery which the reader, alerted by the tell-tale signs of Eastern European origins, unnatural pallor and unusual sleeping habits, makes early on, is a source of humor that Forrest effectively exploits. Harper interprets Drake's reclusive habits and lack of interest in socializing as eccentricities stemming from long spells of duty away from home. When she unexpectedly sees Drake transform into a bat, Harper refuses to credit the evidence of her own eyes and thinks that she must be hallucinating. Even when, succumbing to Drake's androgynous beauty and flattered by her expressions of sexual interest, she finds her hostility giving way to feelings of attraction and, forgetting her lover Niklaus who patiently awaits her return on Earth, embarks on a love affair with her, she still fails to perceive the truth. Drake's lovemaking, though assertive, does not involve the infliction of pain. On the contrary, it is the height of sensual pleasure. It consists of her employing her supple fingers and tongue to caress Harper's body. As Harper pleasurably observes, commenting approvingly on her lover's sexual skills, "The velvet tongue stroked, and stroked and stroked her to an incandescence of orgasm" (200).[28]

When in the latter stages of the story Harper suddenly perceives Drake's vampire identity, she panics. Her fears center, of course, on the dreaded vampire bite which she assumes she must inadvertently have suffered. Humor escalates as, rushing into her cabin, she positions herself in front of the mirror and scrutinizes every inch of her skin for telltale fang marks. Her failure to find any puzzles her. How, she wonders, does Captain Drake acquire nourishment? The answer to this question, which Forrest, intent on keeping the reader in suspense, delays revealing, hinges on the topic of oral sex. Drake, we learn, is not the standard predatory vampire, familiar from film and fiction. She is a vampire with a conscience who seeks to pleasure her partners, not hurt them. In order to do so, she has succeeded in renouncing the vampire bite. As she explains to the astonished Harper, blood is unnecessary to her survival since she acquires nourishment just as good from imbibing female sexual juices. When Harper, angry at the act of deception which her lover has perpetrated on her, sarcastically enquires, "You mean you diet between lovers?" (223) and accuses her of exploiting her physically, Drake rejects the charge. She pointedly replies, "You body is not my food.... Your pleasure is" (225).

The modifications that Forrest introduces in the vampire narrative transmutes it from the conventional tale of horror to a playful celebration of the pleasures of lesbian sex. She transforms the lesbian vampire from a predatory monster who lives on human blood to the signifier of a feminine erotic economy. In describing Harper's initiation into vampirism as a result of her sexual encounter with Captain Drake, she also investigates the growth of the vampire network or "family." This, she illustrates, is not patrilineal in origin but, like the lesbian community which it symbolically represents, develops and expands by means of female contact and the sharing of erotic pleasure.

Forrest neatly concludes her story by bringing together the two themes of sexual pleasure and "family" around which it revolves. She portrays Lieutenant Harper, now safely returned to Earth, sitting in her study absentmindedly erasing the welcome home message that the ever-faithful Niklaus has inscribed on her computer screen. She is preparing to reply to another message which she has just received from a mysterious Colonel Westra. Colonel Westra introduces herself as a former shipmate of Captain Drake; very appropriately her name resembles Count Dracula's conquest Lucy Westenra. She invites Harper to meet her in order, as she euphemistically puts it, to "share a beverage" (226). The fact that Harper intends to accept her invitation indicates that she does not regard her love affair with Drake as a "one-off" but intends to pursue further vampiric/lesbian encounters. Forrest's story, it emerges, differs from the usual vampire narrative in that, as well as focusing on the production of vampires, it explores—more interestingly from the viewpoint of the lesbian readership to whom it is addressed—the production of *lesbians*. Harper's enthusiastic response to Captain Drake's lovemaking, and her readiness to embark on a lesbian lifestyle enable us to read it as a Gothic variation on that perennially popular fictional form, the "coming out" story.

In celebrating sexual pleasure and treating, albeit humorously, power relations between lovers, Forrest's version of the vampire narrative corresponds, in general terms, to the viewpoint of the lesbian sexual radicals. However, in revising the traditional image of the vampire, she goes out of her way to reject the emphasis on pain associated with S&M sex. Califia's version, on the contrary, as her reputation as a leading advocate of S&M who has published a study of the topic[29] leads us to expect, concentrates attention on it. Her story "The Vampire" takes the form of an S&M manifesto. Concepts relating to S&M such as the interplay of "power and trust" between the two partners, the consensual nature of the S&M relationship and the view of S&M sex promoted by its practitioners as exceptionally transgressive, are all interwoven in the narrative. So too are references to practices conventionally associated with it, such as role-play, whipping and cutting. The vampire motif makes, in many ways, an effective vehicle for S&M fantasy. Conventional features of the motif such as the power relationship between the vampire and her/his prey, the piercing of the skin in which the vampire bite results, the interplay between pleasure and pain which the victim experiences and the initiation of the victim into the vampire cult or "family" can, with a degree of imagination on the writer's part, find equivalents in S&M practice and theory.[30] Nonetheless, as we shall see, Califia's utilization of it, though inventive in many respects, reveals limitations and flaws.

An important aspect of lesbian S&M sex, according to its advocates, is the physical and emotional intensity that the experience offers. As Juicy Lucy observes in *Coming to Power,* a collection of essays and stories focusing on the practice, "In S&M sex each seeks to open as much as possible, to push past the limits, to turn each other on so intensely that there is no possibility but full satisfaction, not just physically but emotionally and psychically as well" (31). This is yet another feature of S&M sex that finds an equivalent in the vampire encounter. Commenting on Le Fanu's *Carmilla,* Williams argues that the eponymous protagonist's emotional commitment to the realm of the undead "does something other than simply assert the possibility to vampiric immortality," since it "suggests that women's fulfillment is to be had through a developmental route which is projected towards the liminal" (163). The sense of moving "towards the liminal," which S&M sex shares with the vampiric encounter, is central to Califia's story. To impress its significance upon the reader, she centers her narrative on two S&M scenarios of escalating intensity and power. The first takes place in the sex club, aptly named Purgatory, which furnishes the setting for the opening episode. It is here that the butch Kerry and the femme Iduna, the two characters around whom the story revolves, initially meet.

A tenet of S&M theory is the belief that, since power and violence are intrinsic features of sexual relations, they are best channeled into forms of play and theater, as this will have the effect of rerouting them away from uncontrolled outbreaks of cruelty and abuse. In keeping with this, an emphasis on stylized forms of role-play is strongly to the fore in Califia's description of the club. She builds into the scene the concept of "gender as performance," to use Butler's term. An air of theatricality is reflected not only in her description of role and costume but also in the reference she makes to voyeurism and spectacle. The club, as well as being the haunt of S&M practitioners, is frequented by a group of tourists who, intrigued by its notoriety, achieve a thrill from playing the spectator. Their presence introduces a note of self-reflexivity into the story since, like the reader, they furnish an audience for the activities taking place.

Califia intersperses references to S&M and butch-femme roles, covertly at first and later in a more explicit manner, with allusions to the role of vampire. Iduna, dressed in the femme costume of a low-cut black dress with a red stone shaped like a skull between her breasts, initially mistakes the butch Kerry for a young boy. Kerry wears leather, tellingly described as "the color of dried blood" (245). Kerry's taste for blood becomes even more apparent when, reacting to the taunts of a male client who claims that she is too physically feeble to dominate him, she invites him to position himself on the bondage frame, which forms the club's centerpiece, and proceeds to whip him until his back bleeds. This incident exemplifies the first S&M scenario. Iduna watches the event with interest. Her attention, however, is focused not on the pain the man is suffering but on a feature of Kerry's performance which furnishes a clue to her vampire identity: while inflicting the whipping, she concentrates her gaze not on her victim's face but on the stream of blood trickling from his back.

Having enacted this display of dominance, Kerry abruptly drops her whip and stalks out of the club. Iduna, eager to discover if her suspicions are correct and she is, in fact, a vampire, follows her. The sexual encounter between the two women which ensues commences on a note of antagonism. Kerry, aware that she has inadvertently revealed the secret of her identity, is on the defensive. Angered by Iduna's persistent questioning, she draws a knife and threatens to stab her. Iduna, however, manages to reassure her. Taking Kerry's hand, still clasping the knife, she guides it to her own cleavage, makes a cut in the skin, and offers Kerry her breast to suck. The act of vampiric intercourse to which this forms a prelude represents the second, climactic S&M episode. It differs from the first both in its intensity and in the fact that it involves two women. Advocates of S&M sex sometimes maintain that one of the ways which lesbian S&M differs from its heterosexual counterpart is that the pleasure it offers the participants, as well as being more intense, is reciprocal, frequently involving an element of role exchange (Juicy Lucy 32). Califia's description of the encounter between Iduna and Kerry makes precisely this point. Although in the initial stage Kerry is the aggressor, the roles which the two women play are subsequently reversed. The episode concludes, in fact, with Kerry relinquishing the dominant role and making herself vulnerable to Iduna who, in the concluding sentence of the story, is also unexpectedly revealed to be a vampire.

In describing the encounter between the two lesbian vampires—for so, with hindsight, we perceive them both to be—Califia foregrounds certain key features of S&M. These include the contradictions of pleasure/pain and liberation/discipline and, as mentioned above, a focus on role exchange. However, the most striking feature of her representation is the comparison of the S&M partnership, and the vampiric encounter which metaphorically represents it, to the relationship between mother and infant. Iduna describes Kerry's hand as "clasping the small of her back, holding her the way a mother holds an infant" and depicts herself as "being picked up, cradled" (259). She admits to finding the sensation pleasurable since, as she acknowledges, it enables her to enjoy access to "infantile pleasure" which "adults are not lucky enough to re-experience" (259). Her remarks recall the observation voiced by the theorist Tania Modleski. Modleski, perceiving the relevance of the terms "discipline," "trust" and "submission" utilized in S&M discourse to the mother/infant relationship, argues that the dominant partner in the S&M partnership represents "the symbolic mother," while the submissive partner enacts the role of "daughter." The dominant partner performs, according to Modleski, "an almost archetypal function, initiating symbolic order, but transferring and transforming a patriarchal system of gender inequalities into a realm of difference presided over by women" (156–7). This analysis is applicable to the sexual encounter between Kerry and Iduna. Califia's description of the encounter similarly transfers concepts of power relations and "difference" to a world where women reign supreme.

Califia's "The Vampire" successfully illustrates the tension that exists between pleasure and danger in sexual relations. It also furnishes the reader with an insight into the distinctive facts of lesbian S&M practice and the theoretical ideas underpinning it. The story nonetheless reveals problematic features. The most obvious hinges on its uniformity of mood. It is a truism of Gothic criticism that the most thrilling and disturbing examples of the genre create a tension between the familiar and the unfamiliar, the mundane and the surreal.[31] Califia appears to have this in mind when, in preparation for depicting the encounter between the two vampires, she shifts the location of the narrative from the indoor space of the club to the mysterious outdoor world of the city streets. However, this is insufficient to achieve the necessary contrast in mood. In fact, both her description of the S&M club and her representation of the vampire encounter strike the reader, despite the change of location and the escalating degrees of intensity in the S&M scenarios she describes, as similarly melodramatic. By the time we reach the concluding paragraph of the story we have become so accustomed to the highly charged emotional mode in which she writes that her final fantastic revelation—the fact that Iduna too is a vampire—fails to impress or interest us.

Another problem with Califia's story is her failure to critique or transform the stereotypical image of the lesbian vampire, which she appropriates from popular fiction and film, and the phallocentric image of woman that it encodes. In fact, she uncritically reproduces the very attributes that masculinist culture assigns to woman/lesbian. Kerry and Iduna, in addition to being related to darkness and the night, are portrayed as excessively sensual and are associated, in a displaced form, with the maternal. Kerry, in addition, as is illustrated by the attempt she makes to stab Iduna, is prone to fits of irrationality and violence. The two figures emerge, despite their superficial vestiges of radicalism and their ostensibly transgressive behavior, as very conventional members of the living dead.

Queer Encounters

The criticism of failing to transform the image of the lesbian vampire that Califia's treatment of the motif invites, certainly cannot be leveled at Gomez's *The Gilda Stories*. A distinctive feature of Gomez's version of the motif is the interplay that it establishes between tradition and innovation. In contrast to Scott and Livia, who employ strategies of humor to discuss issues relating to role and identity and to explore historical constructs of lesbianism, and Forrest and Califia, who focus on sex and erotic fantasy, Gomez creates a narrative which, in appealing to the reader's enjoyment of mystery and the uncanny, reproduces the traditional aspects of the genre exemplified by Stoker's *Dracula*. Gomez is also influenced by the updated version of the vampire narrative which transfers the creature to an urban location and portrays him frequenting bars and rock concerts, achieved by Rice in her *Vampire Chronicles*. Like Rice, she traces the growth of a vampire network and develops the concept of the vampire as a traveler in both time and geographical terrain. She further emulates Rice in portraying her vampire protagonist mixing with mortals in clubs and bars and, by joining a theater troupe and singing in nightclubs, participating in the entertainment scene.

However, Gomez's treatment of the vampire narrative, though undoubtedly indebted to Rice, reveals significant differences. Whereas Rice, while introducing a mixture of different races and ethnicities, focuses chiefly on characters who are white, Gomez prioritizes the experience of blacks and people of color. The characters whom she portrays include among their ranks, in addition to the African-American Gilda, a Creole and an American Indian. And, in contrast to Rice who, while exploring queer and homosexual lifestyles, reveals notably little interest in lesbianism, Gomez, though referring to bisexuality and male homosexuality, foregrounds lesbian experience and perspectives. It is the interaction she creates between the discourses of race, sexual orientation and gender which serves to distinguish her treatment of the vampire narrative from other versions and makes it imaginatively vital. It also gives it a politically subversive edge which the fiction of Rice lacks.

The Gilda Stories, as the title signals, takes the form of a series of loosely knit episodes, each of which forms a separate story. As Gilda discovers in the course of her travels, vampires represent a form of "living history" since they enshrine in their memories images of the distant past (177). As a result the novel displays links with the historical romance. In the unusually lengthy lifespan that vampires enjoy (in Gomez's version of the myth, vampires, though long-lived, are not necessarily immortal and can choose, if they wish, to terminate their life), Gilda experiences, in a variety of roles and guises, a number of different moments of American history. Having escaped from an American slave plantation at the age of fourteen, she is given refuge by the female owner of Woodards, a Louisiana brothel, and her partner Bird, who initiates her into the vampire cult. When the brothel owner, weary of longevity and disillusioned with hopes of political progress, moves away to seek solace in "the true death," Gilda appropriates her name and forms a partnership with Bird. In the 1890s she participates in the sophisticated *fin-de-siècle* world of Yerba Buena, drinking champagne and attending the opera as the guest of Sorel and Anthony, two homosexual vampires who run a fashionable nightclub. Other personae she adopts in the course of the novel include manager of a 1950s Boston beauty parlor, lighting technician to an alternative theater company in New York (1971) and performer in a chain of New Jersey nightclubs (1981). As this summary of her trajectory illustrates, the society she frequents tends to be alternative and bohemian. The novel offers an illuminating insight into the changing lifestyle of African-American women and the black community. While all the works of fiction treated in this chapter make inventive use of genre, Gomez's treatment is particularly imaginative. She interweaves the conventions of the travelogue and the historical romance with the family saga and the "coming out" narrative. The concluding episode, which represents Gilda and her companions struggling to escape the clutches of the vampire hunters and to survive the pollution which is speedily engulfing the planet, addresses, in futuristic style, two political issues that achieved prominence in the 1990s: the backlash against homosexuality and the recognition of the fragile state of the ecology. The pessimistic viewpoint that Gomez adopts towards these topics has the effect of moving the novel into the realm of dystopian fiction.

Another feature of *The Gilda Stories*, besides the interplay of different genres that contributes to the novel's success, is Gomez's radical remodeling of the image of the vampire. She replaces the bloodthirsty monster, familiar from popular fiction and film, with a portrayal that is sympathetic as well as psychologically complex. Vampire existence, instead of being represented as a sadistic round of violence, takes the form of a process of education and learning. Bird and Sorel, who act as Gilda's mentors, believe that vampires, rather than wantonly destroying life, have a duty to enhance it. Thus the acts of vampirism depicted in the novel take two different forms. There are "primary" acts involving a mutual exchange of blood which serve to initiate a new member into the vampire family. These take place relatively infrequently and are performed only after a period of careful consideration on the vampire's part. In addition, there are "secondary" acts which the vampire performs regularly, in order to survive. Having hypnotized the victim, the vampire takes a small amount of blood, heals the wound and, in return for this "gift," implants a dream or an idea. One of the first lessons that Gilda learns after her initiation into the vampire family is that "We draw life into ourselves, yet we give life as well. We give what's needed—energy, dreams, ideas. It's a fair exchange in a life full of cheaters" (45). The contribution Gilda herself makes to theater and literature exemplifies this creativity. The emphasis that Gomez places on gay creativity is self-reflexive, commenting by implication on her own narrative and on the relationship that it establishes with her reader. In exchange for winning the reader's attention and enticing her into the Gothic realm of fear and suspense, Gomez plants in the reader's mind a series of ideas and fantasies.

Auerbach complains, unfairly in my view, that Gomez's novel lacks tension, since, in her opinion, "Gilda exists entirely apart from antagonism" (185). This critique is unjust since Gilda is portrayed in terms of conflict, both external and internal. She and her companions are represented in several episodes combating those vampires who, rejecting the moral idealism of Sorel and Bird, take delight in bloodshed and behave with conventional cruelty. In addition, she also experiences conflict of an emotional kind. Feelings of loneliness or desire tempt her, on occasion, to renounce the principles of the vampire code and to initiate into the vampire family someone whom she knows rationally to be incapable of maintaining the high standards of secrecy and self-control on which, in Gomez's version of the myth, its survival depends.

Gilda's characterization, as well as revealing elements of conflict, is enriched by her ethnic identity and the experience of persecution this involves. Her memories of life on the slave plantation haunt her throughout her life, influencing her response to subsequent events, personal and political. The attempt which the white Eleanor makes to dominate her elicits from her the sarcastic retort "I'm no longer a servant. We been freed!" (99). Gomez exploits Gilda's vampiric longevity to allow her first-hand knowledge of certain formative moments in the history of the black community. The exceptionally wide perspective on events to which Gilda has access enables her to make connections between different episodes of ethnic oppression. For example, she relates the newspaper pictures of the murder of the blacks at Attica in the 1970s to the scenes of victimization that she witnessed as a child on the nineteenth century slave plantation. "The image," she poignantly remarks, "was always the same as her memories of the slave quarters: dark men with eyes full of submission and rage. Their bodies plumped with bullets were the same ashen color as those fallen besides the trees to which they had been tied as punishment" (169). In the course of her unusually long life, she encounters a range of relationships between blacks and whites, friendly as well a hostile, and comes to accept the shifts and contradictions which they display. Teasing out the meanings of the term "queer," Eve Sedgwick observes that "A lot of the most exciting recent work around 'queer' spins the term outward along dimensions that can't be subsumed under gender and sexuality at all." She draws attention to "the ways that race, ethnicity, postcolonial nationality crisscross with these and other identity-constituting, identity-fracturing discourses."[32] *The Gilda Stories*, in interrelating factors of race, genre and sexuality, re-creates this interplay in fictional form.

Another feature of Gomez's novel which carries queer resonances is its treatment of the "vampire family." This develops the idea of a vampiric/lesbian network, the formation of which, as other texts discussed in this chapter illustrate, depends not on the Law of the Father but on the direct transmission of blood and sexual pleasure. The vampire family, as Gomez describes it, further subverts hetero-patriarchal convention in that the relationships and roles which it comprises reveal, in terms of conventional familial roles, anomalies and contradictions. Roles that are generally regarded as incompatible combine and merge—as in Gilda's description of the way Bird acts as "mother, father, sister and lover" to her (177). The enfolding of one relationship into another is again exemplified by the way that Bird, in initiating Gilda into the vampire cult, transforms her into her daughter while simultaneously becoming her lover. It is also reflected in Gilda's comment that Anthony, who gently washes her back while she is having a bath, "seemed to be brother and sister to her at the same time" (71). A spectrum of transgressive sexualities, including homosexuality, lesbianism and bisexuality, are represented in the novel. While Gilda's primary attachment is to Bird, she also becomes involved with Julius, a young man whom she meets while working in the theater troupe in New York. Gomez's unorthodox treatment of sexual reproduction and familial relationships is notably queer in emphasis. It agrees with Case's representation of the vampire as a signifier of the queer movement's interest in deconstructing the binaries of nature/culture and fertility/infertility.

Gomez's approach to lesbian/gay political and ideological attitudes is as eclectic and unconventional as her perspective on race and sex. She reconciles and depicts as compatible contrary attitudes and lifestyles which have generated controversy among lesbians. Whereas her reference to a range of transgressive sexualities and her representation of lesbians and gay men living and working together is typically queer, the emphasis she places on the lesbian/feminist community and on acts of female support has more in common with the separatist position associated with the lesbian feminist movement. Examples of the latter abound in the novel. Bird and her partner give refuge to Gilda while she is escaping from the bounty hunters who seek to return her to the slave plantation, while Gilda herself, on reaching adulthood, goes out of her way to help the various women whom she encounters in different periods and social contexts. She treasures the "womanist atmosphere" of the beauty parlor she establishes in Boston; she describes it as "a woman's place, open and intimate, utilitarian like a kitchen but so easily transformed by heat and laughter" and delights in the fact that "Women came here to be massaged by other women, made beautiful by other women" (13).

As mentioned above, a key point of connection between the vampire and the woman who identifies as lesbian is the tension between the role of independent loner and member of a group or community. This tension underpins the design of Gomez's novel since Gilda's lifestyle alternates, like the hero of the traditional quest narrative, between periods of solitude and anonymity in which she travels alone and periods when she enjoys companionship by frequenting centers of vampire community. The brothel where she first encounters Bird, the club run by Sorel and Anthony, and the Boston beauty parlor which she herself creates exemplify centers of this kind. The security and warmth they represent is reflected in her comment, voiced in relation to the club: "To those like herself, it was home of sorts" (65).

The longing for "home," reflected in the emotional significance which Gilda attaches to these communal centers, carries resonances of woman's quest for maternal nurture. This, Gomez illustrates, informs Gilda's trajectory throughout the novel. Like Luce Irigaray[33] and Joanna Ryan, Gomez represents lesbian involvements as reproducing, with complex displacements, aspects of the infant attachment between mother and daughter. Her treatment of the topic, though superficially analogous to Califia's, displays a greater degree of emotional subtlety. At the center of the novel, and the relationships that Gilda forms with women in the course of her travels, is the figure of the absent mother—the mother from whom, when she escaped from the slave plantation in her teens, she was untimely wrenched. This moment of separation, as well as being, on a literal plane, a specific event in Gilda's life, also signifies in symbolic terms the experience of maternal loss that Lacanian psychoanalysis regards as intrinsic to the human condition; it forms the basis of both desire itself and the subject's entry into language and culture.[34] The interrelation between sexual and maternal impulses is exemplified in the descriptions of primary vampiric encounters which occur throughout the novel, in particular the episode in which Bird initiates Gilda into the vampire cult. Here Gomez folds together, in a manner which is typically queer, allusions to S&M sex with images of the child suckling the mother's breast, the act of birthing, and the mother's abject, bleeding body. She describes how Bird, having made an incision in the skin beneath her own breast,

> pressed Gilda's mouth to the red slash, letting the blood wash across Gilda's face. Soon Gilda drank eagerly, filling herself, and as she did her hand massaged Bird's breast, first touching the nipple gently with curiosity, then roughly.... To an outsider the sight may have been one of horror: their faces red and shining, their eyes unfocused and black, the sound of their bodies slick with wetness, tight with life. Yet it was a birth. The mother finally able to bring her child into the world, to look at her [140].

This passage is of interest in a number of ways. In addition to highlighting the ambiguous pleasure and violence of the primary vampire act and illustrating the processes involved in the production of vampires, it foregrounds, in symbolic terms, the way sexual relations between women indirectly reproduce features of mother-daughter relations, such as sensuous contact, emotional and physical interdependence, and patterns of dominance and submission. The act of breastfeeding, radically defamiliarized, is transformed here into the source of illicit *jouissance*. The pleasures of oral sex, the S&M partnership and the breaking of the interdiction again the return to the maternal body, all come together in a manner that is both powerful and disturbing. The passage also alerts us to the ambiguity that the image of blood acquires in the novel and the contradictions it inscribes. Blood is generally associated with death and violence. Simultaneously, however, through the connections with menstruation and childbirth, it has connotations of life and sexual vitality. As Kristeva comments, it represents "a fascinating semantic crossroads, the propitious place for abjection where *death* and *femininity*, *murder* and *procreation*, *cessation of life* and *vitality* all come together" (96).

However, while alerting the reader's attention to the connections between lesbian relationships and the mother-daughter bond, Gomez avoids sentimentally advocating a simple "return to the mother" by positioning her characters in some kind of utopian pre-oedipal realm. Episodes focusing on intimate female encounters of the kind cited above play, in fact, a minor role in the novel. They are juxtaposed with scenes of a very different kind in which Gilda, who is portrayed as essentially solitary, asserts her independence and travels alone. In juxtaposing these contrary images of her protagonist, Gomez combines a recognition of woman's nostalgic desire for the recovery of the maternal presence with a clear-sighted recognition of its illusory nature.

The vampire, as is evident from the popularity which the motif is currently enjoying in lesbian fiction and from the varied approaches writers adopt towards it, makes an effective vehicle for affirming lesbian difference and exploring the transgressive dimension of lesbianism. However, as the version of the motif Califia has produced illustrates, it is by no means easy to employ successfully. In treating it, writers run the risk of indulging in sensationalism and reproducing the very essentialist stereotypes of woman/lesbian which the writer of lesbian Gothic, in seeking to reclaim and recast the genre, aims to redress. A number of writers, however, succeed in steering clear of these pitfalls. Reclaiming the motif from its lurid and frequently lesbophobic past, they exploit the potential it displays for generating a discourse celebrating proscribed desire and exploring alternative reproductive technologies, transforming it into a vehicle for discussing issues of sexual and political interest.

The vampire motif, as the history of its narrative development illustrates, is notable for its versatility and the ability it displays to respond fluidly to shifts in culture and politics. Writers of lesbian fiction, as the texts discussed above illustrate, capitalize on these features, turning them to good account. Scott and Livia utilize the motif to humorously problematize concepts of the monstrous and the alien, to explore the construction of role and identity, and to re-create and comment on episodes from the lesbian past. With the emergence of the lesbian sexual radicals and the queer movement in the late 1980s and the 1990s, the motif's potential for celebrating lesbian sexuality and addressing issues relating to sexual practice has achieved fruition. While Forrest and Califia utilize it to explore and discuss oral sex and S&M roles, Gomez employs it to foreground the queer community's critique of the hetero-patriarchal family unit and its radical experimentation with alternative groups and familial formations. She also uses the motif as a vehicle to interrelate ideas relating to gender with reference to the politics of race and ethnicity. Another topic with erotic connotations on which Califia and Gomez focus is the interaction between the roles of mother and lover, and the enfolding of the one into the other which, as theorists point out, characterizes lesbian sexual encounters and partnerships.

As the reader will no doubt have perceived, a striking feature, from a literary point of view, of the novels and stories discussed above is the self-conscious and critical approach which the writers adopt to genre and convention. In transforming the vampire motif into a vehicle for representing the transgressive aspects of lesbian desire and identification, they challenge the prejudices that the vampire narrative conventionally encodes and, by drawing attention to the artifice and ideological limitations of the character-stereotypes it creates, expose its limitations and oppressive features. They highlight the lesbophobia it frequently inscribes and critique the chauvinistic and bigoted images of femininity and lesbianism it has produced. All in all, lesbian vampire fiction, like the mythical creature whose adventures it recounts, is lively and multifaceted, notable both for its shape-changing abilities and its powers of endurance. The popularity which it enjoys with writers and readers shows no sign of declining. It will be interesting to see the further ideological and stylistic modifications it undergoes in the future.

Notes

1. To Cambridge (U.K.) Lesbian Line.
2. Ken Gelder, *Reading the Vampire* (11–23, 48–52, 108–18).
3. Gelder and Auerbach concentrate attention on the character who, they agree, furnishes the model for the representation of the vampire as we are familiar with it today in fiction and film: Bram Stoker's Dracula. Whereas Gelder teases out the homoerotic nuances in the count's relationship with Jonathan Harker (74–6), Auerbach makes the interesting suggestion that his progenitor, rather than being John Polidori's Lord Ruthven or James Rymer's Varney, as critics generally assume, was the ill-fated figure of "Oscar Wilde in the dock" (85). Dracula's solitariness, the intense opprobrium which he arouses and the stance of silence he assumes in contrast to the loquaciousness of Van Helsing and his Crew of Light who hold forth volubly about their moral rectitude—all these features, she observes, correspond to the circumstances of Wilde during his trial.
4. See Bram Dijkstra, *Idols of Perversity: Fantasies of Feminine Evil in Fin-de-Siècle Culture* (350, 346).
5. Dijkstra discusses the connection between the vampire and "the New Woman" in *Idols* (345–51).
6. See Bonnie Zimmerman, "Daughters of Darkness: The Lesbian Vampire on Film." Le Fanu, although depicting Carmilla's transgressive behavior as being punished with death, portrays her with unexpected sensitivity. Her unconventional sexual attentions, though producing the usual symptoms of pallor and lethargy in her victims, elicit a response of pleasure from Laura, the young woman whom she loves. Carmilla, as Auerbach points out, is, in fact, "one of the few self-accepting homosexual vampires in Victorian literature" (41). Instead of resting content with homosocial bonding, as is the case with her male counterparts (Byron's Augustus Darvell in "Fragments of a Novel" and Polidori's Lord Ruthven, in "The Vampyre"), she has the courage to act on her desires and form a relationship that is overtly sexual.
7. Lillian Faderman discusses the use of vampiric imagery to stigmatize the figure of the lesbian in twentieth century fiction in *Surpassing the Love of Men: Romantic Friendship and Love between Women from the Renaissance to the Present* (341–5).
8. See Andrea Weiss, *Vampires and Violets: Lesbians in the Cinema* (92–6).
9. For a discussion of the representation of the witch in lesbian fiction see Paulina Palmer, *Lesbian Gothic: Transgressive Fictions* (29–58).
10. Christopher Frayling, quoting Ornella Volta, remarks, "First and foremost the Vampire is an erotic creation.... The vampire can violate all taboos and achieve what is most forbidden" (387–8).
11. Contemporary lesbian vampire fiction includes *Daughters of Darkness* and *Dark Angels*, both edited by Pam Keesey. Lesbian vampire stories also appear in *Embracing the Dark*, edited by Eric Garber, and Victoria A. Brownworth's collection *Night Bites: Vampire Stories by Women*.
12. Passages of this kind occur in Pat Califia's "The Vampire" (258–61), in Katherine V. Forrest's "O, Captain My Captain," and in Jewelle Gomez's *The Gilda Stories* (140).
13. See Case, "Toward a Butch/Femme Aesthetic."
14. See Gillian H. Hanscombe and Jackie Forster, *Rocking the Cradle—Lesbian Mothers: A Challenge to Family Living* (1–38).

15. See Jonathan Dollimore, "Sex and Death."
16. For reference to "the Law of the Father" which dominates the symbolic order, see Toril Moi, *Sexual/Textual Politics* (11).
17. For reference to queer social and sexual formations see Eve Sedgwick, "Queer and Now." Gelder discusses Rice's *Vampire Chronicles* in the light of queer theory in *Reading the Vampire* (112–119).
18. For a discussion of the lesbian political fiction of the 1970s and early 1980s, see Palmer, *Contemporary Lesbian Writing: Dreams, Desire, Difference* (37–62).
19. Jody Scott, *I, Vampire* (51, 54).
20. Scott's humorous analysis of the vampire image and the changes it has undergone furnishes her with a vehicle to interrogate essentialist concepts of identity and, by introducing allusions to classic works such as Stoker's *Dracula*, to highlight the fictionality of her own text. It also enables her to parody the syndromes of self-oppression in which women who identify as lesbian can become entrapped. Sterling's attitude towards her vampire/lesbian identity fluctuates wildly according to her mood. The exaggerated sense of pride she feels when in a positive frame of mind resembles the politically right-on views expressed by the 1970s Gay Liberation Movement; she enthusiastically proclaims, "I adore being a vampire. I love the lore, history, rich tradition and sense of fabulous majesty it confers" (5). On other occasions, however, she experiences bouts of severe self-doubt, pathetically confessing that she is tired of the stigma and would "love to be 'cured'" (5). While taking refuge in the essentialist cliché "I was born this way" (13), she expresses resentment at the prejudice that vampires frequently encounter and determines, as a result, to keep her identity secret. In her case, however, concealment is by no means easy. As she ruefully confesses, alluding to the longevity that vampires allegedly enjoy, "It's tough to keep a secret for seven hundred years" (12). The stresses and strains of a lesbian lifestyle are amusingly parodied in her admission that vampiric immortality is a mixed blessing, since "It's demonic to outlive fifty-two lovers!" (33). Further references to the construction of lesbian identity, this time on a literary plane, are provided by Scott's intertextual references to Radclyffe Hall's *The Well of Loneliness* (1928). Echoing the self-justificatory assertions voiced by Hall's protagonist Stephen, Sterling insists that she "is not a bit guilty" about her lesbian orientation since "God has made me this way" (3). Like Stephen, she finds religion a comfort in times of crisis; she nostalgically recalls that, on being thrown out of her home by her outraged parents, "I bowed my head and commended my soul to Saint Jude, the patron saint of vampires" (3). She also emulates Stephen's warm response to the animal world. Whereas Hall portrays her upper-class protagonist communing with her horse in moments of depression, the socially inferior Sterling admits, on a humbler level, to "crying myself to sleep between two warm, friendly cows"(3). These references to shifting constructs of vampirism/lesbianism, combined with the critical asides Sterling makes when she steps beyond the parameters of the conventional vampire role to ridicule hetero-patriarchal values and attack the oppressive nature of the scripts assigned to women through the ages, foreground the artifice of the vampire narrative itself. They also highlight its problematic aspects. They draw attention to its intellectual and ideological limitations—in particular, the prejudiced and deficient images of femininity and homosexuality that it has produced.
21. Shari Benstock discusses Vivien's life and writing in *Women of the Left Bank: Paris 1900–1940* (215–90).
22. It also develops and parodies the vampiric allusions that characterize the treatment of lesbianism in nineteenth century *fin-de-siècle* culture. Baudelaire and Swinburne portray the lesbian as a vampiric figure whose unnatural desires, though fascinating to the male voyeur, are morally corrupt and threaten to undermine the fabric of society. See Faderman, *Odd Girls* (252–70), and Healey, *Lesbian Sex Wars* (61–155). Vivien herself was strongly influenced by this cult of decadence and reworks in her writing the sadistic image of the lesbian popularized by the male writers of the period. Critics disagree about the precise significance of her appropriation of it. Lil-

lian Faderman disapproves, regarding it as oppressive (*Surpassing the Love* 362), while Susan Gubar interprets it in a more sympathetic light. She argues that Vivien, in reworking decadent aesthetic conventions, reclaimed them for women, transforming the lesbian into the prototype of the artist. See Susan Gubar, "Sapphistries." Livia's portrayal of Vivien interelates these contrary viewpoints. Minnie is irritated rather than impressed by Vivien's anorexic appearance and pose of world-weary sulleness; she privately refers to her by the unflattering epithet of "the thin pout." However, her friend Nea, who hails from California, finds Vivien immensely attractive. In fact, she is so captivated that she accepts her invitation to embark on a love affair. The New Age construct of lesbianism, Livia mischievously implies, is not only compatible with the *fin-de-siècle* decadent image but also reveals affinities with it. Nea and Vivien discover to their surprise that despite the significant age gap between them they have interests in common. Both enjoy enacting models of femininity from earlier periods and revel in displays of role-play and pseudo-religious ritual. Nea, who regards herself as "a reincarnation of an Inca priestess" (152), is delighted by Vivien's description of herself as "an altar maid of an Eastern temple" (153).

23. Another issue of topical interest in the late 1980s and early 1990s that *Minimax* explores is role-play, lesbian as well as Gothic. As the relationships between the two couples around whom the narrative revolves develop, the novel becomes a veritable masquerade of shifting roles and identities. In a Gothic context, the reader is treated to the ludicrous picture of Barney entertaining Minnie in her cabin by offering her a glass of freshly squeezed orange juice, while she herself enjoys a glass of rhesus positive from the icebox. From a lesbian point of view, the novel addresses the topic of butch-femme role-play. This was of particular interest to readers at the time of the novel's publication, since the late 1980s and the 1990s saw the attempt on the part of the lesbian sexual radicals to re-evaluate the practice and, in some cases, revive it. The controversy that this provoked was, of course, a contributory factor in the lesbian "Sex Wars." For reference to butch-femme roles and the controversies the issue has generated see Faderman, *Odd Girls and Twilight Lovers: A History of Lesbian Life in Twentieth-Century America* (260–70), and Emma Healey, *Lesbian Sex Wars* (118–55). Livia treats the debate about role-play in an irreverently frivolous manner. The emphasis she places on the performative aspect of identity looks forward to the concept of "gender as performance" promoted by Judith Butler. Gender, Butler maintains, rather than reflecting an essence, is constituted through a set of "discursively constrained acts that produce the body through and within the categories of sex" (*Gender Trouble* x). She argues that butch-femme and gay roles do not, as people generally assume, mirror original heterosexual identities. Instead, they have the effect of exposing and "bringing into relief the utterly constructed status of the so-called heterosexual original" (31). *Minimax* similarly foregrounds the constructed aspect of role and identity, heterosexual as well as gay. A significant source of the humor in the novel is the arbitrary nature of roles along with the social and sexual confusions that can occur if the semiotics of behavior and dress are misread. Californian Nea, who identities as femme and favors brightly colored clothes, mistakenly assumes that Minnie, who wears dark sweaters and jeans, identifies as butch. In actual fact Minnie identifies as lesbian feminist and has no use for role-play. Episodes of this kind illustrate the novel's satiric scope.

24. See Faderman, *Odd Girls* (252–70), and Healey, *Lesbian Sex Wars* (61–155).

25. For reference to the "lesbian sexual radicals," see Faderman, *Odd Girls* (253–7), and Palmer, *Contemporary Lesbian Writing* (22–30).

26. See Jessica Benjamin, "Master and Slave: The Fantasy of Erotic Domination," and Myra Goldberg, "Issues and Answers."

27. Connections are also apparent between Forrest's and Scott's two vampire protagonists. Captain Drake resembles Scott's Sterling O'Blivion in both her intelligence and her articulateness. Like Sterling, she utilizes these attributes to interrogate the myths and fallacies of male-supremacist culture. Whereas Sterling ridicules contemporary vampire romances, dismissing them as mindless rubbish which fail to do jus-

tice to the complexities of vampire existence, Drake—ironically considering the fact that her name is indebted to its protagonist—comments disparagingly on Stoker's *Dracula* (1897). In fact, she regards Stoker not as a writer of fiction at all but, as she scornfully remarks, "a historian—and a most limited one at that" (215). Other features of classic vampire lore also provoke Drake's contempt. She demolishes the idea that vampire sexual practice is necessarily injurious to human beings and explodes the myth that vampires always sleep in coffins. In exposing the popular image of the vampire as inaccurate and prejudiced and correcting misconceptions by reference to personal experience, both Sterling and Drake advertise the deconstructive aims of the texts in which they appear. They also emulate the role of the writers who created them, acting in this respect as their doubles. They dismantle outdated myths about vampires just as Scott and Forrest dismantle erroneous images of lesbianism.

28. Harper's feelings for Drake, a complex mingling of infatuation and disquiet, resemble the response of Le Fanu's Laura to her vampire lover Carmilla.
29. See Califia, *Sapphistry: The Book of Lesbian Sexuality*.
30. For reference to S&M practice and theory, see Healey, *Lesbian Sex Wars* (89–112), and Palmer, *Contemporary Lesbian Writing* (26–7).
31. See Rosemary Jackson, *Fantasy: The Literature of Subversion* (1–37).
32. See Christine Holmlund, "The Lesbian, the Mother and the Heterosexual Lover: Irigaray's Recodings of Difference."
33. See Christine Holmlund.
34. See Elizabeth Grosz, *Jacques Lacan: A Feminist Introduction* (82–114).

Works Cited

Auerbach, Nina. *Our Vampires Ourselves*. Chicago: University of Chicago Press, 1995.
Baudelaire, Charles. *Les Fleurs du Mal*, 126–30, trans. Richard Howard. Brighton: Harvester, 1992.
Benjamin, Jessica. "Master and Slave: The Fantasy of Erotic Domination." In *Desire: The Politics of Sexuality*, ed. Ann Snitow, Christine Stansell and Sharon Thompson, 292–311. London: Virago, 1984.
Benstock, Shari. *Women of the Left Bank: Paris 1900–1940*. London: Virago, 1987.
Brownworth, Victoria A., ed. *Night Bites: Vampire Stories by Women*. Seattle: Seal Press, 1996.
Butler, Judith. *Gender Trouble: Feminism and the Subversion of Identity*. London: Routledge, 1990.
Byron, Lord George Gordon. "Fragment of a Novel." In *The Penguin Book of Vampire Stories*, ed. Alan Ryan, 1–6. Harmondsworth: Penguin, 1988.
Califia, Pat. *Sapphistry: The Book of Lesbian Sexuality*. Tallahassee: Naiad, 1980.
_____. "The Vampire." *Macho Sluts*. Los Angeles: Alyson Publications, 1988.
Case, Sue-Ellen. "Toward a Butch/Femme Aesthetic." In *Making a Spectacle: Feminist Essays on Contemporary Women's Theater*, ed. Lynda Hart, 282–97. Ann Arbor, MI: University of Michigan Press, 1989.
_____. "Tracking the Vampire." *Differences: A Journal of Feminist Cultural Studies* 3.2 (1991): 9.
Creed, Barbara. *The Monstrous Feminine: Film, Feminism and Psychoanalysis*. London: Routledge, 1993.
Dijkstra, Bram. *Idols of Perversity: Fantasies of Feminine Evil in Fin-de-Siècle Culture*. Oxford: Oxford University Press, 1986.
Dollimore, Jonathan. "Sex and Death." *Textual Practice* 9.1 (1995): 27.
Faderman, Lillian. *Odd Girls and Twilight Lovers: A History of Lesbian Life in Twentieth-Century America*. Harmondsworth: Penguin, 1992.
_____. *Surpassing the Love of Men: Romantic Friendship and Love between Women from the Renaissance to the Present*. London: The Women's Press, 1985.

Forrest, Katherine V. "O, Captain My Captain." In *Daughters of Darkness,* ed. Pam Keesey, 208–9. Pittsburgh: Cleis, 1993.
Frayling, Christopher. *Vampyres: Lord Byron to Count Dracula.* Faber and Faber, 1991.
Garber, Eric, ed. *Embracing the Dark.* Boston: Alyson Publications, 1991.
Gelder, Ken. *Reading the Vampire.* London: Routledge, 1994.
Goldberg, Myra. "Issues and Answers." In *Desire: The Politics of Sexuality,* ed. Ann Snitow, Christine Stansell and Sharon Thompson, 276–81. London: Virago, 1984.
Gomez, Jewelle. *The Gilda Stories.* London: Sheba Feminist Publishers, 1991.
_____. "White Flowers." In *Serious Pleasure: Lesbian Erotic Stories and Poetry,* 49–59. London: Sheba Feminist Publishers, 1989.
Grosz, Elizabeth. *Jacques Lacan: A Feminist Introduction.* London: Routledge, 1990.
Gubar, Susan. "Sapphistries." *Signs* 10.1 (1984*)*: 43–62.
Hall, Radclyffe. *The Well of Loneliness.* London: Jonathan Cape, 1928.
Hanrahan, Barbara. *The Albatross Muff.* London: The Women's Press, 1978.
Hanscombe, Gillian H., and Jackie Forster. *Rocking the Cradle—Lesbian Mothers: A Challenge to Family Living.* London: Peter Owen, 1981.
Healey, Emma. *Lesbian Sex Wars.* London: Virago, 1996.
Holmlund, Christine. "The Lesbian, the Mother and the Heterosexual Lover: Irigaray's Recodings of Difference." *Feminist Studies* 17.2 (1991): 283–308.
Jackson, Rosemary. *Fantasy: The Literature of Subversion.* London: Methuen, 1981.
Juicy Lucy. "If I Ask You to Tie Me up, Will You Still Love Me?" In *Coming to Power: Writing and Graphics on Lesbian S&M,* by SAMOIS, 31. Boston: Alyson Publications, 1982.
Keesey, Pam, ed. *Dark Angels.* Pittsburgh: Cleis, 1995.
_____, ed. *Daughters of Darkness.* Pittsburgh: Cleis, 1993.
Kristeva, Julia. *Powers of Horror: An Essay on Abjection,* trans. Leon S. Roudiez. Hemel Hempstead: Harvester Wheatsheaf, 1991.
Lawrence, D.H. *The Rainbow.* Harmondsworth: Penguin, 1949.
Livia, Anna. *Minimax.* Portland: Eighth Mountain Press, 1991.
Martinac, Paula. *Out of Time.* Seattle: Seal Press, 1990.
Modkeski, Tania. *Feminism Without Women: Culture and Criticism in a "Postfeminist" Age.* London: Routledge, 1991.
Moi, Toril. *Sexual/Textual Politics.* London and New York: Methuen, 1985.
Palmer, Paulina. *Contemporary Lesbian Writing: Dreams, Desire, Difference.* Buckingham: Pen University Press, 1993.
_____. *Lesbian Gothic: Transgressive Fictions.* London: Cassell, 1999.
Polidori, John. "The Vampyre." 1819. Rpt. in *The Penguin Book of Vampire Stories,* ed. Alan Ryan. New York: Penguin, 1989.
Ryan, Joanna. "Psychoanalysis and Women Loving Women." In *Sex and Love: New Thoughts on Old Contradictions,* ed. Sue Cartledge and Joanna Ryan, 196–209. London: The Women's Press, 1983.
Scott, Jody. *I, Vampire.* New York: Ace Science Fiction Books, 1984. London: The Women's Press, 1986.
Sedgwick, Eve. "Queer and Now." In *Tendencies,* 1–20. London: Routledge, 1994.
Swinburne, Algernon Charles. "Faustine." In *Selected Poems,* ed. Humphrey Hare, 67–71. London: William Heinemann, 1950.
Tennant, Emma. *The Bad Sister.* London: Gollancz, 1978; Picador, 1979.
Weiss, Andrea. *Vampires and Violets: Lesbians in the Cinema.* London: Jonathan Cape, 1992.
Williams, Linda Ruth. *Critical Desire: Psychoanalysis and the Literary Subject.* London: Edward Arnold, 1995.
Zanger, Molleen. *Gardenias Where There Are None.* Talahassee: Naiad, 1984.
Zimmerman, Bonnie. "Daughters of Darkness: The Lesbian Vampire on Film." In *Planks of Reason: Essays on Horror Film,* ed. Barry Keith Grant, 157–62. Metuchen, NY: Scarecrow Press, 1984.

15
Another "Gendered Other"?: The Female Monster-Hero[1]
JULIE MIESS

> *Pejorative otherness, or "monstrous others," helps to illuminate the paradoxical and dissymmetrical power relations within Western theories of subjectivity.*
> —Rosi Braidotti, "Teratologies"

Norms, Monsters, Differences

Every contemporary horror text carries the blueprint of the eighteenth century English Gothic novel and thus carries visible traces of genre conventions. In addition to the haunted castle and the secret manuscript, a certain formula of male and female figures—heroes, villains, victims, and monsters—has lasted from Ann Radcliffe's Gothic novel *The Mysteries of Udolpho* (1794) to Tobe Hooper's artful slasher film *The Texas Chainsaw Massacre* (1974) and beyond. The genre of Gothic horror constantly interlocks with our monstrous collective imagination, where fears and nightmares circulate. Thus our collective imagination is still saturated with traditional constructions of "male" and "female."

The masterplot of the horror text begins when the male culprit is set in the "predatory position," as Carmilla Griggers puts it in "Phantom and Reel Projections" (1995): "Well into the twentieth century, the predatory position itself was historically thought of as always ultimately male" (163). There are several versions of the male predator. A male Gothic villain may function as dangerous seducer, disturbing and fascinating at the same time, or he may appear as a fully repulsive monstrous male predator. In either case, the woman is set in the victim position in relation to the male. Although the male predatory monster as figure of sexual Otherness once represented a break in the convention of supernatural monsters of the past, such human monsters have now become conventional themselves: the horrifying male is a staple of horror fiction. While the supernatural monster continues to lead a parallel existence in the genre, the roles of male monster/culprit and female victim have flourished; frequently the supernatural monster is actually figured as sexually male: the vampire, the werewolf.

The monster formula of aggressive male and passive female strangely corresponds to the position of male and female writers within the Gothic. Although the Gothic genre as we know it today was substantially influenced by Ann Radcliffe and Mary Shelley, there is a strain of Gothic fiction that is more closely associated with Radcliffe's male successors: horror fiction. While Radcliffe's *Mysteries of Udolpho* is terrifying, Matthew Lewis's *The Monk* is horrifying.[2] Radcliffe herself sets up the dichotomous idea of a male school of explicit horror and a female school of subtle terror. In "On the Supernatural in Poetry," she establishes a strong distinction between her own female, or terror, Gothic writing, which leaves room for imaginative speculation, and the much more explicit male or horror tradition of Gothic literature pursued by her competitor, Lewis. This distinction endures into the twentieth century. As Lisa Tuttle writes, women writers are still identified as writers of a more "soft and subtle" horror: "I don't know how many times I have heard it suggested that although there are a few women writing horror, they write gentler or less visceral or more subtle or softer horror than their male colleagues.... What it comes down to is just another way of saying women don't write horror" (3).

The gendering of horror/terror becomes problematic as these distinctions start to generate hierarchies as suggested by Tuttle. This gendering also moves toward a dangerous naturalization by suggesting essentialist ideas: man is aggressive and active by nature; woman is emotional and passive. The possibilities for the woman thus become constricted. She may be the passive victim or, if she chooses not to inhabit that role, she is figured as the inhuman mythological female monster. The conventional representation of the female monster, like the Medusa and the *femme fatale*, are more than anything male fantasies, expressing male anxiety regarding powerful women. As Creed asserts in her introduction to *The Monstrous Feminine*, "The presence of the monstrous feminine in the popular horror film speaks to us more about male fears than about female desire or feminine subjectivity" (7).[3] Thus the conventional code of the monster as female Other, as source of fear and danger, is created from a hegemonic perspective of the male who fears female power. One way contemporary writers oppose the positioning of female as victim is by recovering and celebrating the figure of the female monster, creating the female monster-hero.[4] This figure interrogates the situation of the male predatory position as the cultural norm, and posits that the position of the male predator as source of aggression, activity and power is generated from a hegemonic perspective. This figure also revisits the conventional depiction of the inhuman female monster, discovering within this figure positive models for female action and power. Such reworkings represent the frightening monster as female, and celebrate activity and power when located in a female figure.

Celebrating the Female Monster: Undead Housewife and Likeable Lamia

Contemporary feminist writers who present the powerful female monster as positive and joyous thus invert this representation. To think of the female monster from the female, non-hegemonic perspective is as an act of rethinking the Other. Although this perspective is not strictly bound to the female writer, it does depend on a focus upon feminine subjectivity, on seeing the female monster from within. This radical inversion of perspective functions to challenge dominant norms. The female monster described from within is transformed from a code of hegemonic anxiety to a signifier of cultural change. As Derrida says, "Faced with a monster, one may become aware of what the norm is and when this norm has a history—which is the case with discursive norms, philosophical norms, socio-cultural norms, they have a history—any appearance of monstrosity in this domain allows an analysis of the history of the norms" (385). The shift to a focus on the subjectivity of the monster, in fact, results in a re-evaluation of difference, and an embracing, rather than rejecting, of the Other. Instances of the new mode of female monstrosity are taking shape in recent (re)works of femininist Gothic horror. The play *Krankheit oder moderne Frauen* (1984), by the Austrian Nobel Prize winner Elfriede Jelinek, features Carmilla, the re-presentation of the *femme fatale*/female vampire as undead vampiric housewife. The short story "Immunity" (1996), by African-American writer Toni Brown, features Celeste, a likeable lamia.

Conventionally, the female vampire is doubly abject (presented as a figure to be cast off): as an objectified body, a corpse without a soul[5] and, because of its connection to the *femme fatale*, the classic powerful object of male fear and desire. Yet the conventional representation provides an opportunity for radical feminist revision. As Gina Wisker puts it in her essay "Love Bites: Contemporary Women's Vampire Fictions,"

> In conventional fictions, women vampires connote unlicensed sexuality and excess, and as such, in conventional times, their invocation of both desire and terror leads to a stake in the heart—death as exorcism of all they represent.... Contemporary women writers, however, have found in the figure of the vampire marvellous potential for radical reappropriation [167].

A thoroughly radical reappropriation of the conventional figure of the female vampire is presented in Elfriede Jelinek's grotesque play *Krankheit oder Moderne Frauen (Disease, or, Modern Women)* (1984).[6]

The two main characters in Jelinek's drama, the women vampires Carmilla and Emily, seem to be paradigms of pure Otherness, as presented from the patriarchal perspective. We know the name Carmilla from Le Fanu's famous tale, where the female vampire is depicted as a lesbian *femme fatale*, an embodiment of the monstrous feminine as male fantasy. In Jelinek's play, Carmilla is part of a figure constellation that forms a rigid patriarchal hierarchy. As a passive housewife, Carmilla dies during childbirth in the medical practice of Dr. Heidkliff,[7] who is simultaneously an orthodontist and gynecologist. Carmilla's husband, Mr. Hundekoffer, a tax adviser, attends the birth (and death) scene. He and the doctor watch without emotion as Carmilla dies in labor. Hundekoffer is the quintessential monster/patriarch; he cares only for the son and heir his wife has given birth to. Considering these power relations, Jelinek's choice of names is more than a vague allusion to the history of the genre. Her Carmilla relates to the original figure like a negative to a photograph. Seen from a patriarchal perspective, Jelinek's Carmilla is the prototypical dream of a perfect woman, passive and absent, in contrast to the nightmarish fantasy of the sexually active, lesbian *femme fatale* created by Le Fanu. But as it is performed in the play, the dream seen from the traditional male perspective transforms into a nightmare from the female perspective.

The fourth character in the hierarchical constellation is Emily, Heidkliff's unruly wife: nurse, writer, lesbian, and vampire. She enters the scene and soon turns the dead Carmilla into her vampiric companion. When the two vampires describe themselves in their dialogue, each line can be read both as a description of the female vampire as monster, from the male perspective, or as sympathetic representation of the abject woman, from the female perspective. Emily says: "I am the Other. It does exist, too" (9); "I am neither half nor whole. I'm in between" (14).[8] Carmilla replies: "I am godless. I am an amateur of existence. It's a miracle that I speak" (15); "Yes, unfortunately, I'm dead now" (19). In Emily's words, we can also witness the will to disrupt conventions: "Unfortunately, I'm lesbian.[9] I'm different from you. I don't give birth. I want you" (21); "I am really a writer. I run after the flesh. I am not only Ariadne, assistant to a hero" (21); "I want these two important teeth to be made extendible. I need a similar device as you men" (33, translation mine). Jelinek thus deploys the conventional figure of the female vampire as a metaphor for women's existence, but also reveals the anxious misogynist core within the conventional female vampire.[10]

Jelinek deploys a second subversive, inverting, strategy. The stereotypical, patriarchal gaze—the invisible, norm-inducing perspective which informs conventional vampire fiction such as the classic Carmilla narrative—is made visible onstage by the male characters' performances. The brutality of the patriarchal perspective is explicitly displayed to the audience: Hundekoffer cares only for his newborn son and heir; Carmilla is reduced to the function of a birth machine. Doctor Heidkliff's profession, orthodontist *and* gynecologist, is emblematized by a medical device that dominates the stage setting of the first act: a monstrous combination of gynecologist's and dentist's chair, as if made to pull the teeth from a *vagina dentata*. Thus it not only refers to an icon of monstrous femininity, but also reveals the equally monstrous male aggression that leads to the construction of such icons.

Toni Brown's story "Immunity" (1996) also invites readers to identify with a creature who is a revised version of classic female monsters: the Medusa and the Lamia. Here too the typical female monster is reworked as the female monster-hero who, re-presented from within, no longer appears as dangerously monstrous. Traditionally, the Medusan myth represents the monstrous feminine as the classic object of male fear. The legendary ugliness of the Medusa, which immediately sets her off from the norm of female beauty, derives from the snakes that grow instead of hair from her head. The Medusa thus represents to the male a frightening appropriation by the female of male phallic power. The Medusa also appropriates and inverts the power of the male gaze: she turns to stone anyone who looks at her. As Creed states, "We can see that the medusan myth is mediated by a narrative about the difference of female sexuality as a difference which is grounded in monstrousness and which invokes castration anxiety in the male spectator" (2).[11]

Brown's use of the motif is a development of the strategy of the wave of feminism that "reappropriated" the Medusa as metaphor, as exemplified by Hélène Cixous in "The Laugh of the Medusa" (1975). Like Cixous, Brown inverts the myth of female monstrosity to show the beauty of the powerful and active woman. Celeste first appears as a sympathetic African-American mother, soothing her daughter who is afraid of vampires at night, explaining why African people are immune to vampire bites: "'Long ago when our ancestors still lived in Africa, another people came to visit us.... The Lamia were a people similar in some ways to the ones they now call vampires.... We made an agreement with these Lamia.... All African people are protected by that agreement'" (76). At the end of the story, the reader learns that the sympathetically portrayed Celeste is herself a vampire with the looks of the ancient Medusa: "her kinky, corded hair began to move, transformed into pencil-thin snakes that writhed sinuously. Her skin deepened to a shiny black. Her fingernails also blackened and grew long and pointed.... She opened her mouth to accommodate the sharp row of teeth that grew there" (78–79). Thus the Medusa—from the conventional, patriarchal perspective a creature to be feared and destroyed—becomes a figure with whom the reader can sympathize or even relate. Although the monster is always ambiguous—partly disgusting and partly fascinating—this female monster is aestheticized in a new way, with attributes of glamour: the shiny black skin and the sinuously writhing, elegant snakes.

Not only is Celeste a vampire with the looks of a Medusa, she is also part Lamia. The Lamia of ancient demonology has inspired works from Philostratus's *De Vita Apollonii* (170) to John Keats's poem "Lamia"[12] (1819). She is a monster with the body of a woman, who preys upon human beings and sucks the blood of children. The Lamia is also often described as witch and she-demon, as the ancient *femme fatale*. Although Celeste is a Lamia, the narration does not cast her in the position of the object of desire or fear. In a comical twist, she is a devoted single mother. Brown thus responds to Julia Kristeva's assertion in *Powers of Horror* that the maternal is abjected by the patriarchal culture because it does not respect boundaries: "Rituals of defilement, based on the feeling of abjection and all converging on the maternal, attempt to symbolize the other threat to the subject: that of being swamped by the dual relationship" (64) between mother and child. The abject and horrifying mother of horror films from *Psycho* to the *Alien* series is thus the final convention Brown overcomes through Celeste. Although Celeste's Lamian nature drives her to suck blood from her daughter Nia's wrists now and then, thus seemingly corresponding to the concept of the transgressive, threatening mother that Kristeva observes, she is not a dangerous mother: Nia "would not be harmed by the tiny sips of blood Celeste sometimes took from her wrist" (Brown 78). Given the biology of maternity, the few sips of blood Celeste takes seems fair exchange for all the biological matter Nia has received from her. Even when Celeste dons a Medusan shape in the end, she remains a loving (and comfortingly powerful) mother: "She murmured 'Good night, Nia,' as she disappeared into the night" (79). Brown thus doubly subverts stereotypical representations of the maternal: the mother is not dutifully and self-effacingly protective towards her daughter—she bites her daughter to sustain herself; nor is the mother fully monstrous—she soothes and comforts her daughter. Both mother and daughter benefit from the power the mother derives from her monstrosity. Brown thus inverts the traditional models of the female monster and the monstrous mother, embracing the female Other and revealing her power as a source of joy rather than fear. Monstrosity is embraced and the mother is no longer the Other.

I Was a Teenage Girlwolf: Feminizing Male Monsters

Jelinek and Brown invert the model of the female monster by showing that the conventional female monster is not an object to be feared, but a subject to be celebrated. Contemporary feminists who rework the werewolf myth take an even more radical approach: they feminize a monster who is typically represented as male, and in doing so show that casting the monster as female makes the monster less monstrous. In *Baby Bitches from Hell*, Creed writes, "Males do become monsters at puberty, but their transformations into rough beasts (as in *I Was a Teenage Werewolf*, 1957) are perfectly in keeping with the male role of sexual predator" (2). It is true that the *femme fatale* as female monster could also be understood as a "sexual predator," but because she remains a stereotypical, continuously paradoxical object of desire and abjection, there is always a certain passivity to be found in her—the active status of rough beast is rarely attained by female monsters. This is a disadvantage, if we consider H.R. Brittnacher's definition in *Ästhetik des Horrors* (1994): "Monster stories tell about the yearning for an archaic force that allows one to take what one desires. ... they symbolize the desire for not having to take social conflicts and compromises any more, but to resolve them by brute force" (219, translation mine). The legendary werewolf thus seems to be an ideal, self-gratifying monster, as Brittnacher describes it:

> The existence of the werewolf—that is, roaming around freely, with the power over life and death—is also experienced as precious, at least, as a relief. The werewolf myth does not only express specific fears but also secret promises: the yearning for an atavistic existence without the burdens of individuation; the wish for a life led by unalienable instincts [211–212 translation mine].

Ingeborg Vetter offers an interesting explanation of why there are so few texts about female werewolves: they are unsuitable to serve as objects of desire and lack the necessary allure that contributes to the ambiguity of other conventional female monsters: "On the one hand, the delicate and exquisite cruelty of the *femme fatale* terrified the reader, on the other hand, it contributed to male fantasies of submission. A furry female monster as an object of desire—be it obscure—was nearly unthinkable as a topic for literary depiction" (18, translation mine). Thus women conventionally appear only as victims in werewolf tales: "The image of women impregnated by werewolves is a condensed version of the image of innocent suffering" (209).

The Canadian feature film *Ginger Snaps* (2000) offers several different perspectives.[13] Although the film is inspired by Suzy Charnas's short story "Boobs" (1989), it differs from the story in displaying a conflict between following and subverting conventions, while the story is more explicitly subversive. Both werewolf texts have a similar plot dealing with the onset of first menstruation and the association of puberty with the werewolf myth.[14] The film capitalizes on the colloquial association between menstruation and curse: "B, I just got the curse," Ginger says desperately to her sister Brigitte. The two girls stand on a dark, deserted playground at night, when they suddenly witness blood trickling down Ginger's thighs. The girls have come to the playground to prepare for playing a trick on the hated high school queen, but the scene ends with Ginger bitten by a strange creature that rushes out of the woods. "It is said that bears come after girls 'on the rag' cause of the smell," Brigitte incorrectly explains shortly after, but we as spectators know that the creature from the wood was not a bear. The film literalizes the metaphor of menstruation as curse. For Ginger's menstruation does result in the curse of becoming a werewolf.

As Ginger turns into a werewolf she actually goes through all the stages of female monstrosity available in the genre. At the first stage of her transformation, her sexual appetite increases. From nerdish, innocent girl in baggy black clothes, she turns into a *femme fatale*, a vamp in the true sense of the word. Day after day she looks more like a conventionally seductive female vampire. Then, as the transformation proceeds, she becomes the monstrous mother: a row of teats like a she-wolf's appears on her belly. But the *femme fatale* stage as well as the monstrous mother stage are only momentary: in the end, she turns into an unfeminine rough beast, a predator lacking female features. Apart from a few more hairs on the beastly head and a hint of breasts, she looks similar to the male-identified creature that tore from the bushes in the playground scene.

Yet this film lacks any of the celebration of female monstrous power that we see in Jelinek's and Brown's texts: after Ginger has killed several people, even the likeable male protagonist Sam, Brigitte desperately kills her. Therein lies the film's conflict. On the one hand, the conclusion of the film presents the conventional male viewpoint: the monster, namely the female monster, is truly monstrous and must be destroyed. On the other hand, by framing the monster as female, the film does break the convention of the male predatory position. Moreover, the film does offer a positive alternative to the notion of menstruation as curse, when, for example, Brigitte stands comically confused in front of a gigantic shelf full of tampons and pads in the supermarket, or in another comic scene, when the sisters seek advice from the school nurse, who awkwardly untangles the mysteries of menstruation in a few rough words.

Most significantly, menstruation as teen trouble is addressed seriously by the film. Significantly, then, adolescent girls are directly addressed as spectators of the film. This is a truly subversive move, since the genre of horror films is typically addressed to boys. Even critics tend to dismiss the presence of the female audience. Carol Clover's *Men, Women, and Chainsaws*, for example, a highly gender-conscious work in horror theory, tends to focus on the adolescent boy viewer. Yet, although *Ginger Snaps* is subversive in imagining a female monster observed by a female audience, on-screen *Ginger Snaps* ultimately mirrors the status quo of contemporary culture: reinforcing the patriarchal notion of the female monster who is a threat and who must be destroyed.

This is surprising since the inspiration for the film, the short girl-into-wolf story "Boobs" (1989) by the American writer Suzy McKee Charnas, works to subvert the traditional paradigm. In the story, Charnas reinvents the female werewolf as female monster-hero. Unlike Ginger, Kelsey, the protagonist of "Boobs," survives and celebrates her monstrosity. Charnas refuses to punish female sexuality as truly monstrous deviance. In "Boobs," monstrosity is a reward, a liberating removal from the constrictions of society, and becoming a monster is a valuable strategy to someone who might otherwise be powerless. "Boobs" challenges the association of menstrual blood with dangerous monstrosity; blood and monstrosity become positive signifiers of power.

Unlike Ginger, who is transformed into a werewolf against her will, Kelsey controls her transformations. Kelsey, the first girl in her class to get "female curves," is harassed by her classmate Billy, who taunts her with the title epithet and with a hit that breaks her nose. Kelsey's stepmother Hilda gives her daughter the following advice: "I'm sorry about this, honey, but really, you have to learn it sometime. You're all growing up and the boys are getting stronger than you'll ever be. If you fight with boys, you're bound to get hurt. You have to find other ways to handle them" (19). Since Hilda describes being a girl as a devalued difference —they're stronger than you'll ever be—the story begins with performing, in a laconic, non-sentimental fashion, the naturalized construction of female inferiority.

Yet, Charnas refutes the notion of female disempowerment. The morning after the incident with Billy, Kelsey has her first menstruation, again the curse. As in *Ginger Snaps*, the clichéd association "full moon/menstruation/femininity" is transformed into the association "full moon/the curse/werewolf." Yet Kelsey's first menstruation puts an end to her victimhood right away. The curse—which to the conventional tragic figure like Stephen King's Carrie[15] remains a symbol of the Biblical curse of Eve, a symbol of female abjection—is reinterpreted in "Boobs." The curse of the werewolf is no longer a curse that denotes female sexuality as devalued monstrosity, but is a blessing that initiates Kelsey's resistance to the structures that equate female sexuality with monstrous ugliness. For Kelsey, first menstruation is a moment of epiphany. Unlike Ginger, who is taken by surprise not only by the curse of menstruation but also by the curse of the werewolf, Kelsey's becoming a werewolf is a positive, almost voluntary process: "It felt—interesting. Like something I was doing, instead of just another dumb body-mess happening to me because some brainless hormones said so" (24). Kelsey's act of defense is thus not merely monstrous but is an act of self-empowerment, suggesting a positive association with female power. The monstrous and aggressive woman who defends herself, often associated with the cliché of the grim feminist in everyday life, is revalued as glamorous and her status as desirable.

Through Kelsey's transformation, Charnas changes the image of innocent female suffering: "I realized all of a sudden, with this big blossom of surprise, that I didn't have to be scared of ... anybody. I was strong, my wolf-body was strong" (25).[16] Kelsey's empowerment is rapidly visible at the next full moon. After another series of humiliations, Kelsey lures Billy to a park at night and tears him apart. This killing inverts the conventional paradigm of rape by male agent of female victim. Kelsey reports: "I tore through the bushes and leaped for him, flying. ... [H]e was just sucking in a big breath to yell with when I hit him like a demo-derby truck. I jammed my nose past his feeble claws and chomped down hard on his face" (36). Although we may pity Billy, the narrative strategy of the text—it is told from Kelsey's perspective—helps us to understand the subjectivity of the monster. We have witnessed the source of her rage and are likely to end up feeling empathy for her.

In a short epilogue to her story, Charnas writes about readers' reactions to "Boobs." Gardner Dozois, the male editor of the science fiction magazine *Asimov's*, who bought the story,

> found our heroine a bit too "unsympathetic." ... My stepdaughter had reacted in a similar fashion, objecting that Kelsey is too cold-blooded about wolfish violence.... It may be of interest ... that the people at the word processing center ... where I did my final edit of this story ... had a very different reaction. These are (for the most part) working women in their twenties and thirties.... They said they liked the story very much, but several of them objected to the killings of the dogs [38].

It becomes obvious that character and narrative perspective invite female readers to identify and empathize with Kelsey and perhaps to envy her wolfish transformation and empowerment. In this, the story appeals to adult women, quite a different target group from the average adolescent male horror fan. Thus, Charnas's text, like *Ginger Snaps* (despite its limitations), challenges the norm of the Other not only on the level of content. These texts also challenge the norms of reader expectations and of the definition of the intended reader of the horror genre.

Kelsey is, then, an ideal version of the female monster-hero, the female monster who is presented as subject rather than as object, who is thus not all that monstrous, not the mysterious and unknowable Other. In "Boobs," Charnas transforms the female monster into a positive cultural image of power and independence. Kelsey freely roams around in the park at night, fearlessly scaring others, fulfilling female (rather than male) fantasies of power. Kelsey, who enjoys her monstrosity, subverts a number of conventions. Not only is the male character no longer the subject fantasizing about the monstrous female object; the female reader is addressed as the subject by being encouraged to empathize with the female monster. "Boobs" is an ideal example of the text of the new female monster which challenges the norm by addressing the female subject and female fantasies.

Gendered Figures of Transgression

In their introduction to *Athena's Daughters*, Early and Kennedy describe a "rigidly bounded system of representation" (2) that determines the situation of the male and female in narrative paradigms, in which the male is typically the active force. This accurately describes the conventional position of the woman in the monstrous universe of Gothic horror, a distinction that still seems to be influenced by the once-established distinction between a male world of Gothic horror and a female world of Gothic terror: "[M]odifying the dominant male story has proven difficult because [the male protagonist's story] precludes women's agency, but also defines woman as an object of desire or as a boundary figure, often in the form of a monstrous mother 'other' that the male hero must overcome." Yet, the contributors to *Athena's Daughters* argue that a disruption of narrative traditions is possible. Early and Kennedy quote from Marilyn Farwell: "The space occupied by the male hero is only conditionally male defined by the result of history, tradition, symbolic connections, and reader's expectations" (3). This comment may be translated to the situation of the male and the female monster. As the female monsters discussed above show, the space occupied by the male monster, desirable because it signifies choice and agency, is also only conditionally male-defined.

In *Images of Women in Peace and War* (1987), Sharon McDonald writes on the power of symbols to effect alterations in the way we conceptualize female agency and subjectivity: "In contrast to closed images that can be likened to stereotypes, open images have the capacity to be interpreted, read, and to an extent repopulated" (22–23). The likeable Lamia, Medusa and *femme fatale* vampire, the girl werewolf in teen trouble, are such "open images." These monsters indicate that closed images are somewhat arbitrarily determined by narrative traditions of the male horror genre. The transformation in the representation of the monstrous exposes and interrogates the norms that are the effect of cultural processes, revealing that monstrosity defines the norm. Thus the monster that is positively female interrogates and destabilizes the norm that dictates that the female be passive and virtuous and also disrupts the concept that the female Other is essentially different and therefore unknowable and to be abjected.

Because gender still matters, qualities like aggressiveness and activity are still so closely identified with the male that a monster with these qualities, depicted as genderless, would automatically be read as male. Recovering the abject female monster, to claim power and agency for women, aligns with the project of feminism. Because gender still matters, Celeste and Kelsey are creatures in a transitional phase, females who subvert the binary of male-monster/female-victim, without entirely erasing it. Perhaps they point towards a utopian future world of creatures whose gender does not matter. More significantly, Celeste and Kelsey represent a shift from the icons of distressed female victim and abjected *femme fatale* towards a new generation of she-monsters, woman warriors and heroines. The creation of the open image of the female monster-hero serves as a strategy to close the gap "between new subject-positions women have begun to develop and the forms of representation of their subjectivity which their culture makes available to them" (Braidotti 171). Narratives of the female monster-hero, in which the norms of monstrous Otherness are evolving, resist the conventional demonization of the female Other, presenting instead the subjectivity of the female Other. As a significant side-effect, they resist the erasure of women writers and readers from the definitions of the horror genre, expanding the definition of the Female Gothic to include Lewis's horror as well as Radcliffe's terror. The most significant effect of the new narratives is the production of the powerful and sexual female figure, a transformation that benefits all readers. As Braidotti says: "We need to learn to think of the anomalous, the monstrously different not as a sign of pejoration but as the unfolding of virtual possibilities that point to positive alternatives for us all" (172). The female monster-hero directs the reader in this hopeful, utopian direction.

Notes

1. I would like to thank Dr. Ruth Anolik, Dr. Renate Hof, my fellow graduate students and Jens Friebe, as well as the Berliner Pogramm zur Förderung der Chancengleichheit für Frauen in Forschung und Lehre and the Berliner Graduiertenförderung (NaFöG).
2. For the erasure of Mary Shelley as author and authority in the horror tradition, see Randi Gunzenhäuser.

3. The complexity of this phenomenon is illustrated in Barbara Creed's work *The Monstrous Feminine* (1993), which refers to Julia Kristeva's psychoanalytic work *Powers of Horror: An Essay on Abjection*. Creed's text critiques the conventional conceptualizations of women in horror films. Yet the monsters Creed describes are limned from the patriarchal perspective: "the amoral primeval mother (*Aliens*, 1986); vampire (*The Hunger*, 1983); witch (*Carrie*, 1976); woman as monstrous womb (*The Brood*, 1979); woman as bleeding wound (*Dressed to Kill*, 1980)" (1). Seen from the male perspective, these powerful female monsters are sources of fear and horror.

4. The term "female monster-hero" refers to Carol Clover's term "female victim-hero" in *Men, Women, and Chainsaws* (4). The female victim-hero or "final girl," also a term coined by Clover, is the "damsel in distress" of contemporary horror texts.

5. The corpse is described as a major object of abjection in Kristeva's *Powers of Horror*.

6. Elfriede Jelinek describes her strong affinity to the Gothic novel when she talks about her next work of prose to come: "It will be a ghost story again ... a gothic novel, with which I have found my form" (qtd. in Diez, 23).

7. This is a reference to the character "Heathcliff" in Emily Brontë's *Wuthering Heights*; the name of the vampire Emily is an allusion to Brontë herself.

8. In *Skin Shows*, Judith Halberstam describes "in-betweenness" as a main characteristic of the Gothic monster. "The monster dwells at the gates of difference" (7), states thesis four of Jeffrey Cohen's seven theses on monster culture. Its in-betweenness seems to predestine the monster to be cast in the position of Otherness. Jelinek comments on her work: "The vampires in *Krankheit oder Moderne Frauen* are paradigmatic for woman's existence, which is neither wholly there nor wholly gone" (qtd. in Carp 91).

9. In this, Jenlinek makes explicit what is only implied by Le Fanu's text.

10. Regine Friedrich writes in the epilogue to the print edition: "Jelinek creates her figures, like Frankenstein creates his monster, as prototypes.... The woman vampire is a creature that doesn't leave any traces in the mirror of culture and history.... Woman can always be brought back to her natural place by male power and order" (87–89, translation mine).

11. Creed also refers to Sigmund Freud's essay "Medusa's Head," in which Medusa's head is described as a symbol of the female genitalia (Creed 2).

12. Keats's poem anticipates Brown's depiction. His Lamia is not merely monstrous; she is a loving woman in the first place, not an immoral beast. But she is also created in relation to the perspective of the male characters in the poem, Hermes and Lycius, and thus remains a seductress, taking shape and dissolving under the male gaze.

13. *Ginger Snaps* has become a cult film, with a sequel, *Ginger Snaps: Unleashed* (2003), and a prequel, *Ginger Snaps: The Beginning* (2004).

14. Of course, menstruation is not only teen trouble. It also signifies an old hegemonic excuse for abjecting the female as dangerously monstrous. According to Kristeva's *Powers of Horror*, to the patriarchy, menstruation is a major "type of defilement": "Menstrual blood ... stands for the danger issuing from within the identity (social or sexual); it threatens the relationship between the sexes within a social aggregate and, through internalization, the identity of each sex in the face of sexual difference" (71).

15. *Carrie*, made into a film by Brian de Palma (1976), also starts with the protagonist's first menstruation and ends with an act of killing as a kind of revenge-scenario. In the first scene in the film, Carrie stands under the shower in the girls' changing room and does not know why there is suddenly blood between her legs; her religiously fanatic mother did not tell her the facts of life. Carrie screams for help, and her classmates bombard her with tampons and pads.

16. This acceptance of a girl's wild and wolfish side is anticipated in Angela Carter's 1977 "The Company of Wolves," where the female protagonist embraces the wolfish

Other in a literal sense: "[S]ince her fear did her no good, she ceased to be afraid.... she freely gave the wolf the kiss she owed him ... she knew she was nobody's meat" (219).

Works Cited

Braidotti, Rosi. "Teratologies." In *Deleuze and Feminist Theory,* ed. Ian Buchanan and Claire Colebrook, 156–172. Edinburgh: Edinburgh University Press, 2000.
Brittnacher, Hans Richard. *Ästhetik des Horrors.* Frankfurt/Main: Suhrkamp, 1994.
Brown, Toni. "Immunity." In *Night Bites: Vampire Stories by Women,* ed. Victoria Brownworth and Judith Redding, 71–79. Seattle: Seal Press, 1996.
Carp, Stefanie. "Das Katastrophale Ereignis der Zweiten Republik" ("The Second Republic as Catastrophic Occurrence"). Interview with Elfriede Jelinek. *Theater der Zeit* 3 (May/June 1996): 90–91.
Carrie. Dir. Brian de Palma. Perf. Sissy Spacek, John Travolta, Piper Laurie, William Katt, Amy Irving, Betty Buckley. United Artists, 1976.
Carter, Angela. "The Company of Wolves." In *Burning Your Boats. Collected Short Stories,* 212–219. London: Vintage, 1996.
Charnas, Suzy McKee. "Boobs." In *Skin of the Soul: New Horror Stories by Women,* ed. Lisa Tuttle. London: Women's Press, 1990.
Clover, Carol. *Men, Women, and Chainsaws: Gender in the Modern Horror Film.* Princeton: Princeton University Press, 1992.
Cohen, Jeffrey. "Monster Culture (Seven Theses)." In *Monster Theory: Reading Culture,* ed. Jeffrey Cohen, 3–25. Minneapolis: University of Minnesota Press, 1996.
Creed, Barbara. *The Monstrous Feminine: Film, Feminism, Psychoanalysis.* London: Routledge, 1993.
_____. "Baby Bitches from Hell: Monstrous Little Women in Film." *Scary Women.* March 2003. http://www.cinema.ucla.edu/women. 2000.
Derrida, Jacques. *Points: Interviews, 1974–1994.* Trans. Peggy Kamuf, et al. Stanford: Stanford University Press, 1995.
Diez, Georg. "Die Nobelpreis-Erträgerin" ("Bearing the Nobel Prize"). Interview with Elfriede Jellinek. *Frankfurter Allgemeine Sonntagszeitung,* 10 October 2004, 23.
Early, Frances, and Kathleen Kennedy, eds. *Athena's Daughters. Television's New Woman Warriors.* Syracuse: Syracuse University Press, 2003.
Ginger Snaps. Dir. John Fawcett. Perf. Emily Perkins, Katherine Isabelle, Kris Lemche, Mimi Rogers. Concorde, 2000.
Griggers, Carmilla. "Phantom and Reel Projections: Lesbians and the (Serial) Killing Machine." In *Posthuman Bodies,* ed. Judith Halberstam, 162–176. Bloomington/Indianapolis: Indiana University Press, 1995.
Gunzenhäuser, Randi. "Frankenstein: Geburt des Helden—Tod der Autorin" ("A Hero's Birth—Death of the Woman Writer"). In *Horror at Home: Genre, Gender und das Gothic Sublime.* Essen: Die Blaue Eule, 1993.
Halberstam, Judith. "Bodies That Splatter: Queers and Chainsaws." *Skin Shows: Gothic Horror.* Judith Halberstam. Durham, NC: Duke University Press, 1995.
Jelinek, Elfriede. *Krankheit oder Moderne Frauen (Disease, or, Modern Women).* Köln: Prometh, 1984.
Kristeva, Julia. *Powers of Horror: An Essay on Abjection.* New York: Columbia University Press, 1982.
McDonald, Sharon. *Images of Women in Peace and War: Cross-cultural and Historical Perspectives,* ed. Sharon McDonald, Pat Holden and Shirley Ardener. Madison: University of Wisconsin Press, 1987.
Radcliffe, Ann. "On the Supernatural in Poetry." *New Monthly Magazine* 16 (1826): 145–152.
Tuttle, Lisa. Introduction to *Skin of the Soul,* 9–17, ed. Lisa Tuttle. London: Women's Press Ltd, 1990.

Vetter, Ingeborg. "Lykanthropismus in einigen deutschen Horrorgeschichten um 1900" ("Lycanthropy in the 1900 German Horror Story"). *Quarber Merkur* 49 (1978): 17–22.
Wisker, Gina. "Love Bites: Contemporary Women's Vampire Fictions." In *A Companion to the Gothic,* ed. David Punter, 167–179. Oxford: Blackwell, 2000.

16
Imagineer: Clive Barker's Queering of the Conservative Bent of Horror Literature
K. A. Laity

In the late 1980s Clive Barker hit the publishing world with a palpable slap, simultaneously releasing three collections of short stories, ominously called *The Books of Blood*, at a time when short stories were seen as unmarketable. Stephen King, then reigning king of the genre, most memorably declared Barker to be the "future of horror" (King xiv). Two of the stories were quickly—and lamentably—turned into awful films, but the phenomenal success of the books gave Barker sufficient cachet to direct a film himself and get it right.[1] Clive Barker was a man with a difference. But just what constituted that "difference"? It may have been his art school training; it may also have been his background in fringe theater, both of which color the subject matter and narrative voice of his writing; however, the fact that he is a gay man also significantly shapes the stories he tells and the point of view from which he writes.

There has long been a conservative thrust to horror narratives, which tend to impose and reinforce norms. Critics from Freud onward have recognized the pattern: something uncanny which threatens normality must be destroyed to restore the norm. Long before it was a recognizable genre, the tropes of the Gothic were used in medieval texts for the rhetorical purposes of warning the faithful away from trouble. Indeed, telling a scary story to keep the listeners from harm may be a technique as old as the cave paintings. In the Middle Ages, it was raised to an art form. Travelogues of hell, like the *Visio Pauli*, were designed to keep the faithful from straying off the straight and narrow path of righteousness before them by demonstrating with gory details the penalties of hell for each specific sin, in which, as in Gilbert and Sullivan's *Mikado*, "the punishment fit the crime." For instance: "angels with a blazing razor [who] lacerate the lips and tongue of another man, a reader who read the commandments to the people, but did not himself keep them" (Bernstein 298). Perhaps the most famous rendition of this phenomenon is Dante's *Inferno*, in which the fates of famous historical figures are detailed in the elaborate travelogue of hell. If people could not be tempted to do good in order to achieve the reward of heaven, the thinking of the medieval patriarchs seemed to go, they could perhaps be frightened into avoiding evil by vivid descriptions of rivers of fire, painful torture and unbearable punishments, each tailored specifically to the selected sin.

Little has changed since that time: horror still works to keep readers on the straight path by warning them of the consequence of the detours. In his introduction to the 1988 collection *Prime Evil*, Doug Winter notes:

> a glance into the dark mirror of modern horror reveals no less reactionary trends. Conventional horror has always been rich with Puritan subtext: if there is a single certainty, it is that teenagers who have sex in cars or in the woods will die. Most books and films of the eighties offer a message as conservative as their morality: conform ... it is proper behavior, not crucifixes or silver bullets, that tends to ward off the monsters of our times [4].

We can recognize the codification—even fossilization—of that conservative message in modern horror texts. This code is assimilated by the knowing teens in the *Scream* and *Scary Movie* franchises, both of which promote that old school norm, while subverting the other genre conventions. We can certainly see this in the works of America's most famous horror writer, Stephen King, whose plucky everyday people must battle everything from vampires to the apocalypse in small town America. Time after time, ordinary people—whose normalcy is their greatest strength— succeed against monsters of every stripe. Today the norm remains a force in horror, whether we look at the latest Dean Koontz thriller or a bigbudget film like *Constantine*; the horror, the monstrous, is out there and we (the representatives of the norm) are in danger. The monster is the "Other" who must be extinguished.

In *The Philosophy of Horror* Noël Carroll writes of this concept of the Other in the horror text: "the objects of art-horror are essentially threatening and impure" (42). Freud argued that we feel horror for anything "*unheimlich*" (usually rendered "uncanny"), particularly when there is any doubt that we can surmount it. Much of horror literature invites the desire to overcome or dissipate the "threatening or impure," whether the monster is alien or human. The norm must be restored at all costs. This conservative trend in horror has held sway for centuries, asking readers to fight vicariously for the death and destruction of the *unheimlich* because it disrupts society.

One aspect of the norm that contemporary horror tends to reinforce is the heterosexual norm, as delineated by male heterosexual writers.[2]

Winter himself continues the trend of testosterone-fueled status-quo-reinforcing narratives with his novel, *Run* an account of homosocial gun culture and violence (Guran). As Harry M. Benshoff writes in *Monsters in the Closet*, "both movie monsters and homosexuals have existed chiefly in shadowy closets. ... [T]o create a broad analogy, monster is to 'normality' as homosexual is to heterosexual" (1–2). In *Epistemology of the Closet*, Eve Kosofsky Sedgwick clarifies the slipperiness of the category of homosexual: "sexual desire is an unpredictably powerful solvent of stable identities" (85). Through the genre of horror, then, the heterosexual majority promotes an anxious (but variable) desire to demarcate and control the homosexual minority.

In this, Clive Barker explicitly veers from the norm set by contemporary horror. In fact, for Barker, the monster—whether or not we identify it as homosexuality—not surprisingly, proves seductive, powerful and transformative. Although Barker[3] was once publicly coy about his sexuality, he has never shied away from the more outré facets of life in his writing. *The Books of Blood*, from the first volume of stories, presents positive depictions of homosexuality. He deals with AIDS in his novels *Imajica* and *Sacrament*. The release of the latter novel was accompanied by a series of interviews trumpeting his gay identity, but Barker considered it a non-issue:

> I have done readings at gay bookstores throughout the world since my first book was published. And I never considered my homosexuality an issue. Not until last year however did I get myself a publicist, which is when the "gay thing happened." I appeared in *The Advocate, OUT, 10%* and *Genre* all practically at the same time, which kind of made the whole issue noteworthy.

Before that exposé, Barker remembers "interviews where people would come to my house, and see my boyfriend, pictures of male nudes hanging on the walls and gay paraphernalia lying about" (qtd. in Nasson). It is not just his gay identity which sets Barker apart from the mainstream horror creators, however. Much of his work suggests not a return to the norm, but rather a desire for the unknown, for what "normal" society considers "the monstrous."

As Linda Badley writes in *Writing Horror and the Body*, Barker made horror "a vehicle for ideas, forcing a 'reactionary' genre to take on taboos and open up to controversial issues" and "turned 'splatter' into an iconography of confrontation and paradox" (74). Barker's works explore the "threatening and impure" but rather than seeking to destroy or overcome the monster, his narratives invite awe, respect and even love for the *unheimlich*, the monstrous. While the monstrous Other may provoke alarm for conventional writers, for Barker it proves to exert an attraction. For Barker, the "threatening and impure" need not be stamped out; instead it should be embraced, loved, admired, envied, and desired. Moreover, the final aim may in fact be to *become* the *unheimlich*, removing forever its separation from the self. Thus Barker reverses the conservative assumption that deviations from the norm must be destroyed.

The introduction to the first of the *Books of Blood* is written by Ramsey Campbell, who recognizes a kindred spirit in Barker, as well as the tendency toward "reactionary" tropes in horror fiction. Campbell avers that many writers and publishers seem to believe that "horror fiction is fundamentally concerned with reminding us what is normal," and he breathes a sigh of relief that "thank heaven nobody convinced Poe of that, thank heaven for writers as radical as Clive Barker" (xi–xii). Barker's stories are not tales that frighten children around the campfire to safely restore the norm; Barker's *Books* explode our notions of safety, undoing even our sense of the integrity of our flesh with the playful yet chilling opening epigraph: "Everybody is a book of blood. Wherever we're opened, we're red."[4]

The opening narrative, "The Book of Blood," frames the other stories in the collection. This narrative thrusts us into the life of a scientist who wishes to explore forbidden pathways. The highways of the dead, Barker reveals, run "behind our lives ... in the broken places of the world ... [and] can be glimpsed when the heart is close to bursting, and sights that should be hidden come plainly into view" (5). This "forbidden highway" retains much of the shadowed life of the closet, "behind" and "hidden."

In this story, we can see Barker's re-presentation of the sexual terms of contemporary horror. Barker lingers over the physical description of the young man, McNeal, the supposed medium who pretends to commune with the dead.[5] McNeal is aware of his effect on the researcher, Mary Florescu, who voyeuristically pries into the secret world. She "liked it when she looked at his nakedness" (9). But Barker de-emphasizes McNeal's heterosexuality. While McNeal's thoughts focus on his own attractiveness, he is unaware that Dr. Florescu sees his body as "like a girl really—the roundness of him, the sweet clarity of him—the innocence" (10). Barker develops the trope of homosexual invasion in his description of the moment when McNeal actually does accomplish communion with the dead. While it is the doctor who opens the "crack" to the other world, it is the boy the dead seek, "pressing at his lying back, hungry and irrevocable" (13). Barker seems to relish the pun on "lying," indicating both the supine position and the boy's cheating. Florescu shares with the boy the pain of the dead's entry and declares it "not so terrible," but McNeal writhes and fights his attackers. The dead "didn't want her up there" but she fights against their tide to reach the upper story and finds the boy "sprawled, surrounded by his attackers. His briefs were around his ankles: the scene looked like a kind of rape" (16). Thus Barker shows the invasion of the dead as a transgression of the sexual norm. It is the horror of this transgression that kills Florescu's more conservative, unimaginative colleague, who dies immediately from the shock of discovering that the hidden world of the dead exists.

The intrusion of Florescu appears to restore the norm; the arrival of the woman signals the defeat of the dead, "their voices becoming wistful" (18) as the normative sexual order appears to be restored. Yet Barker resists the conventional restoration of the norm. The boy's lies and Florescue's transgressions have tapped into an unexpected Other. The boy has been transformed into a narrative of the dead:

> a map of that dark highway that leads out of life towards unknown destinations. Few will have to take it.... But for a few, a chosen few, the horrors will come, skipping to fetch them off to the highway of the damned. So read. Read and learn [20].

In fact, Florescu, too, chooses the non-normative path. The boy who was mildly interesting as a mere human becomes an obsession for Florescu once he has been transformed. And while the non-normative path may be the "highway of the damned" to the mainstream, Barker's description suggests it is also sublime. If we have any doubts about the allure of the highway, they are dismissed by the fascination Florescu feels for the stories left by the dead, the assurance that "she would read them all, report them all, every last syllable that glistened and seeped beneath her adoring fingers" (20). Covered with the texts of the dead, the boy's body is irresistible to her as a site for *ecriture*, for which she was "his sole translator." For the man who cannot speak his desire for other men, the woman must provide "translation," in taking on the task of reading his flesh. Florescu is thus masculinized by claiming of the physical discourse actually written upon the boy's body as McNeal is feminized by his submission to the dead. Barker thus takes a page from the broader context of queer theory by complicating the supposed dichotomy of heterosexual/homosexual or norm/Other. Queering thus destabilizes the traditional dichotomies which scholars like Eve Kosofsky Sedgwick identify as "secrecy/disclosure, private/public, masculine/feminine, majority/minority, innocence/initiation, natural/artificial, growth/decadence" (217). To the list Barker may well add a queering subversion of the dichotomy of normal/monstrous.

The construction of the monstrosity of the norm and normality of the monstrous is amplified in the first story of the collection, "Midnight Meat Train," in which Barker suggests that the hegemonic norm itself is monstrous. In the opening situation of this story, the protagonist Kaufman represents the conventional, heterosexual norm: his love for New

York, which is represented as a female, is figured as heterosexual love. Yet, Kaufman, who was once in love with her, now regards her with disgust and revulsion: "He had seen her wake in the morning like a slut, and pick murdered men from between her teeth, and suicides from the tangles of her hair" (22). Kaufman had been in love "from afar" but the view up close of his lady love horrifies him. Yet, despite his disgust with the object of his heterosexual desire, he finds it difficult to let go of this "love affair" (22). Kaufman seems to find it difficult to get beyond his gender disappointments and betrays a fastidious distaste for the "decadence" surrounding him. He is thus ripe for the discovery of the secret life below Manhattan's surface.

In contrast to Kaufman, Mahogany appears to represent the conventionally deviant monster. Kaufman encounters him in the subterranean world of the subway, when Kaufman dozes off. Jerking awake, he realizes that a spaced-out youth he had previously noticed has left the car even though the train has not stopped and he imagines the youth "probably between the driver's legs even now," regarding this with a magnanimous tolerance: "after all, everyone had their right to a little love in the dark" (36). Standing up, Kaufman slips in blood, but rather than seeking escape, he is compelled to follow the source of the blood. The insistence on seeing the forbidden, the terrible, marks Kaufman's transition to his new awakening, his movement beyond the conservative norm. He looks into the car to the rear through "a tiny hole" and sees a sight that "couldn't be real, but his flesh knew it was" and "his body became rigid with terror" (37). The scene easily reads as a coded sexual encounter. Although he succumbs to a faint in a vaguely feminized moment, Kaufman quickly regains his masculine strength and the power of the gaze as he watches Mahogany, the butcher; his senses fill with the spectacle. Yet he is overtaken by curiosity rather than by revulsion at the work of the monstrous Mahogany. The first body Kaufman examines is, of course, the youth's; its opened flesh, lolling tongue and flapping penis draw his fascinated gaze.

Yet our expectations of the norms of horror fiction are almost immediately subverted; represented subjectively, from the inside, Mahogany the serial killer is a sympathetic figure. Like a closeted homosexual, he lives a secret life; however, "Mahogany longed to announce his identity to the world, but he had responsibilities" (28). He chafes at the closeted life. Pride, not shame, creates that yearning to break free of his secret life, to proclaim it to the world, particularly as he grew older and recognized the need "to think about training a younger man for his duties" (28). The multileveled reading—pride and secrecy, glamour and horror—reveal the anxieties of the closet, but it seems significant that while the text is horror, the subtext of homosexuality offers the real key, particularly given the ending of the tale.

When he inadvertently alerts the butcher to his presence, Kaufman looks eagerly to the confrontation and arms himself with the trusty phallic substitute beloved of horror films, the straightforward knife. Facing at last the terrifying butcher Mahogany, Kaufman smirks to find an overweight, balding man whose "mouth was rather small and delicately lipped. In fact he had a woman's mouth" (44), but his arrogance fades when he realizes that his knife "looked a little small beside the Butcher's paraphernalia" (45). Mahogany's own confidence in his dominance withers as he attacks first with an anti-Semitic insult then with a too broad stroke of his mighty cleaver. Kaufman easily dodges his blow and penetrates the butcher's neck with his blade. The wound further feminizes Mahogany as "blood issued from his lips, painting them, like lipstick" and he drops his weapon (46). Kaufman removes the knife to produce a spurting arc of blood as a final orgasm of death.

What Barker ultimately reveals is that it is not Mahogany, the pathetic closeted butcher, who is the monster, but his masters; yet these monsters too are presented with a kind of sympathy for their hideousness. When the train arrives at its destination Kaufman recognizes the beneficiaries of the butcher's feast. Rather than the slobbering monsters he expects, these creatures possess a "distressing vulnerability" (48). His fear of the monstrous gradually transforms to a kind of sympathy. While the horror is apparent, Kaufman also focuses on other aspects of their behavior:

> gracile hands were laid upon the shanks of meat, and were running up and down the shaved flesh in a manner that suggested sensual pleasure.... The eyes of the monsters were flickering back and forth with hunger and excitement [49].

The blending of sexuality and horror suggests an erosion of the clear cut lines between society's definitions that seems to call into question all the classifications. Kaufman's revulsion at the cannibalism he sees is slowly superceded by a protective feeling. While he produces disgust while watching as the creatures begin their feast, he eventually acquiesces to the demand that since he has killed Mahogany, he must now get the food for the monsters.

In a final inversion of the paradigm, these monsters are revealed as the city fathers who represent the truly monstrous heterosexual patriarchy and the state. Asked to meet the most ancient among them, Kaufman falls to his knees before the "Father of Fathers." The monster is awe-inspiring, unimaginable but also compelling. In a sign of submission to the request that he serve them, Kaufman allows the little father's fingers down his throat but mistakes the intention; he has joined the secret society, but due to the anxieties of the dominant culture, silence must be enforced. The creature removes his tongue and eats it before him. Returned to the surface world, become himself monstrous, and feminized by the loss of his tongue, he finds a new appreciation for the female Palace of Delights he had come to despise and "kisse[s] the dirty concrete with his bloodied [and perhaps feminized] lips, silently swearing his eternal loyalty to its continuance" (56).

Thus Kaufman himself is transformed from normative heterosexual to monstrous homosexual, and yet this transformation is figured as a positive one. Like the closeted homosexual who finally discovers the camaraderie of the gay bar, Kaufman recovers his joy and sees the world with new eyes even though the closeting strictly enforces its silence; but as in the case of Mahogany, we can see that the secret also leads not to shame but to pride. The monstrous, initially terrifying, becomes a source of pleasure, providing Kaufman with a new mission and a new outlook.

These themes continue in the other stories of the first volume.[6] The undercurrent of homoeroticism and the explicit inversion of the conventional representation of the monstrous comes to the foreground in the last story of the volume, "In the Hills, the Cities." In this story, Barker inverts the assumptions of horror fiction—that homoeroticism signals monstrousness—by transforming the desire of the Other into a complicated norm. This story begins with the assumption of homosexuality as norm, with the typical problems of any relationship. The protagonist of the story is a gay man who has decided his current relationship is not working: "it wasn't until the first week of the Yugoslavian trip that Mick discovered what a political bigot he'd chosen as a lover" (175). We see also Judd's point of view, also realizing what a mistake he has made. It's all matter of fact; there's no real point to making the characters gay— they simply are the soon-to-be-ex-lovers, bickering. Apart from an offhand classification of the church as a place of "lies" and the gloating observation that Judd's face "made women weep with frustration that he was gay" (179), homosexuality is irrelevant to the story line—until it comes to sex. It is on the brink of sex that both Barker and his characters pause. Judd recognizes that "it was a dangerous game ... this wasn't San Francisco or even Hampstead Heath" (180), locations long (in)famous for tolerance of gay encounters. The experienced reader might cringe, thinking here comes the monster, evoked by something monstrous—oh my! Sex between men!—but instead, the lovers enjoy one another, the golden summer day, and reconcile sweetly, if only temporarily.

Because there *is* a monster in this story: a giant is heading down upon them. The monster consists of the population of the village of Popolac, all strapped together into a gargantuan walking figure, ready to do battle *en masse* with their rival village, Podujevo. It is the epitome of the unified conforming society: "every single citizen, however young or infirm, the blind, the crippled, babes in arms, pregnant women" is there, for "the confrontation had to be total, city against city" (187). Thus the ultimate figure of the monster in this concluding story is the figure of the norm: of social harmony and uniformity, the normative monstrosity that excludes the sexual Other. Podujevo falls due to a weakness in its citizens' uniformity as the victorious Popolac strides on in a kind of "numbness, a sheep-like acceptance of the world as it was" (199). Its citizens are literally locked into position, "one mind, one thought, one ambition" (200), in a monomaniacal social order. "It is the body of the state" (203), the lone survivor of Podujevo whispers before dying.

Even in death, the gay man, who becomes a victim of the monstrously normal, takes joy in Otherness, in monstrosity. While Judd is killed by the approaching figure, Mick screams and runs toward it, "longing to embrace the monster" and "screaming his sheer ecstasy" when he takes his place on the giant's leg and becomes "a hitchhiker with a god" (212). Embracing the monster brings ecstasy, power and a new life for Mick, and he is raised to heights unimaginable. Mick's joyful embrace of the monster remains troubling; the monster is, after all, the monolithic body politic. Certainly there the horror lies, particularly at present, perhaps more so in the past. The ending may be ambivalent, but Barker himself suggests that there is another view:

> both protagonists die, but they gain meaning, extraordinary meaning. Perhaps not a meaning that one would want to celebrate.... It's ambiguous. But when they see the beasts in the hills, some new vision is presented to them which hitherto they wouldn't even have been capable of imagining.... I very much like the ambiguity or the ambivalence of a moment which can be terrible and significant simultaneously, the way that many of the pivotal moments in our lives are very often rites of passage moments in which things are lost which can never be claimed again. Yet the territory ahead is, by virtue of the fact that it is new, also exciting and extraordinary [qtd. in Floyd].

That new territory is the payoff; the adventure of the further realms of experience may be the reason to go on, to embrace the monster if only to achieve a moment of communion with something extraordinary. The queering of the categories of "norm" and "monstrous" throw us onto shifting grounds that avoid easy answers. The norm may reject the monster, but once it becomes monstrous itself, it too can become a figure of desire to those outside the norm when it moves from the banal to the extraordinary.

In the end, it is this queering of categories and the embrace of the unknown that has made Barker's work appealing not only to other gay readers but to all who identify as Other, as outsiders. As his novella

Cabal—later the film *Nightbreed*—suggests, the state may hate the monsters, but monsters are what we dream. The monstrous cities in the hills suggest that even the state may dream of becoming the awesome monster. As one character in the film says: "To be able to fly? To be smoke, or a wolf ... to know the night, and live in it forever? That's not so bad. You call us monsters. But when you dream it's of flying, and changing, and living without death." As Clive Barker suggests, for many, access to the secret world of monsters is the sanctuary we seek.

Notes

1. That film, *Hellraiser*, brought an icon to the screen, in the shape of the lead Cenobite, "Pinhead"; it also brought cult status to actor Doug Bradley, who portrayed the scarred, pierced and fetish-ware clad "explorer into the further regions of experience." Before Bradley appeared, with his headful of pins, his gashed chest and similarly decorated companions, the now omnipresent tattoos and piercings were seen only among the fringes of society.
2. Few female authors write in this genre.
3. Although making a name first as a writer of extreme horror stories, Barker has refused to be pigeonholed by genre or even medium, continuing to write while directing, painting and performing. As Dennis Cooper writes:
> His effect on the contemporary horror novel and film is self-evident. But when you consider that such artists and entities as *Buffy the Vampire Slayer*, Marilyn Manson, Chris Carter, goth culture, the "edgy" rock video, and virtually all original programming on the Sci-Fi Channel would not exist in their current forms without Barker's groundbreaking work, his impact becomes astonishing.

4. The original editions in the United Kingdom also included Barker's distinctive artwork on the covers, a phantasmagoria of wild skin, teeth, tongues and torture. The first volume prominently features a sculpted young man, naked, poised between revealing and shielding his figure, on his face a look as enigmatic as the Mona Lisa's. In place of a fig leaf we find Barker's drawing of a torn photograph of himself. The placement makes the observer wonder whether his photo stands as censor or voyeur.
5. In his own words he is "a cheat" who finally must give up the charade and admit to his real truth.
6. In "The Yattering and Jack" there is an offhand mention of Jack's daughter as a lesbian. Pointedly, it is she who is the first of the two women to notice the monstrous presence of the Yattering: "she knew, oh yes, she knew" (67). "Pig Blood Blues" and "Sex, Death and Starshine" take place in spaces often coded by gay narrative: the boy's school and the theater. Both also deal frankly with the erotic. "Pig Blood Blues" deals directly with ex-cop Redman's gradual realization of homosexual desire: "Was there something in him that wanted Thomas Lacey naked beside him?" (115).

Works Cited

Badley, Linda. *Writing Horror and the Body*. Westport, CT: Greenwood, 1996.
Barker, Clive. *The Books of Blood*. Vol. 1. London: Sphere Books, 1984.
Benshoff, Harry M. *Monsters in the Closet: Homosexuality and the Horror Film*. Manchester: Manchester University Press, 1997.
Bernstein, Alan E. *The Formation of Hell: Death and Retribution in the Ancient and Early Christian Worlds*. Ithaca: Cornell University Press, 1993.

Carroll, Noël. *The Philosophy of Horror or Paradoxes of the Heart*. New York, Routledge, 1990.
Cooper, Dennis. "Fuck the Canon." *L.A. Weekly: Literary Supplement,* 31 August—6 September 2001. http://www.laweekly.com/ink/01/41/weekly-cooper.php.
Floyd, Nigel. "Clive Barker." In *Clive Barker: Revelations*, ed. Phil and Sarah Stokes. 21 March 2005. http://www.clivebarker.info/bloodbarker.html.
Guran, Paula. "Douglas E. Winter: Offering Revelation." In *Dark Echo*. April 2000. http://www.darkecho.com/darkecho/horroronline/winter.html (accessed 21 March 2005).
King, Stephen. "Introduction: 'You are Here Because You Want the Real Thing.'" In *Clive Barker's Shadows in Eden,* ed. Stephen Jones, xiii–xv. Lancaster, PA: Underwood-Miller, 1991.
Nasson, Timothy. "Clive Barker." *In Step Magazine* 14.13 (25 July—6 August 1996). http://www.clivebarker.com/html/visions/confess/nonls/instep/instep.htm.
Nightbreed. Dir. Clive Barker. Perf. Craig Sheffer, Anne Bobby, David Cronenberg. WB/Morgan Creek, 1990.
Sedgwick, Eve Kosofsky. *Epistemology of the Closet*. Los Angeles: University of California Press, 1990.
Winter, Douglas, ed. *Prime Evil*. New York: New American Library, 1988.

Contributors

Michael Ackerman is a Ph.D. candidate at Wilfrid Laurier University. He is currently finishing a dissertation on the Gothic elements within Victorian dramatic verse with an emphasis on Alfred Tennyson and Robert Browning.

Victoria Anderson is based in London. She gained her doctorate from the University of Leeds in 2006, and currently teaches part-time in the cultural studies department at Leeds. She specializes in the sociohistorical analysis of folklore and fairy tales, tracking the development of certain leitmotifs through the oral tradition and into literature. Her dissertation on the appearance and reappearance of "Bluebeard" motifs throughout literary history, insofar as it pertains to writing by women, is currently being expanded for publication.

Ruth Bienstock Anolik teaches at Villanova University. She has published essays in *Modern Language Studies, Legal Studies Forum, Partial Answers* and *Studies in American Jewish Literature*. She has co-edited a collection of essays with Douglas L. Howard, *The Gothic Other: Racial and Social Constructions in the Literary Imagination* (McFarland, 2004). She is currently working on a book-length study of the concept of possession in the Gothic mode, and on a collection of essays that considers the representation of illness and disability in the Gothic.

Damion Clark is currently a Ph.D. candidate at the University of Maryland, College Park.

Octavia Davis received her Ph.D. in comparative literature from the University of California, San Diego. She lives in New York City, where she works as editor and production assistant for Factory School, a learning and production collective.

Dawn Fulton is an assistant professor in the Department of French Studies at Smith College. She has published articles on French Caribbean literature in *Romanic Review, Callaloo,* and *French Forum*, and she recently completed a book manuscript on the novels of Guadeloupean writer Maryse Condé. Currently she is at work on a project on Francophone literature of urban migration.

Contributors

Elizabeth Harlan is a Ph.D. candidate at George Washington University, with a focus on eighteenth and nineteenth century British novels. She is currently working on a new edition of the works of Juliana Horatia Ewing.

Tamar Heller, associate professor of English and comparative literature at the University of Cincinnati, is the author of *Dead Secrets: Wilkie Collins and the Female Gothic*, and co-editor of both *Approaches to Teaching Gothic Fiction* and *Scenes of the Apple: Food and the Female Body in Nineteenth- and Twentieth-Century Women's Writing*. She has also edited Rhoda Broughton's *Cometh Up as a Flower* for Pickering and Chatto's *Varieties of Women's Sensation Fiction* and is at work on a book-length study of Broughton's fiction.

Katherine Henry earned her Ph.D. from Rutgers University and is an assistant professor of English at Temple University, Philadelphia, specializing in nineteenth century American literature. She has published articles on American citizenship and the rhetoric of the anti-slavery movement, and is currently completing *Liberalism and the Culture of Security: Readings in the Nineteenth-Century Rhetoric of Reform*, a study of the persistent tendency in liberal thought to figure citizenship as protected space.

K.A. Laity is an assistant professor of English at the College of St. Rose, where she teaches medieval literature and popular culture. She is completing a study of women as witches in Anglo-Saxon England while co-editing with R. Scott Nokes a collection of essays on Old English charms. Laity received a 2006 Finlandia Foundation grant and the 2005 Eureka Short Story Fellowship to work on *Unikirja* (Dreambook), a collection of short stories based on Finnish mythology and the *Kalevala*. She has published a novel, *Pelzmantel: A Medieval Tale* (2003), and publishes and presents papers on medieval studies, fantasy, horror, comics, film and writing, including two encyclopedia entries on Clive Barker.

Adrienne Antrim Major is an associate professor of English at Landmark College in Putney, Vermont. She is currently working on a biography of the playwright Susanna Centlivre.

Julie Miess has an M.A. in North American studies, German literature, and linguistics. She is currently working on her dissertation, "Reworking the Monstrous: Horror, Gender, Woman Writer," at Humboldt University (Berlin, Germany) supervised by Dr. Renate Hof. She has contributed the essay "Warning from space" to *Japan—die Monsterinsel [Japan: Monster Island]*, edited by Jörg Buttgereit (2006). She also plays bass in the Berliner band Britta and has recorded "Monster" on the album *Das schöne Leben [Beautiful Life]* by Britta Flittchen (2006).

Bernice M. Murphy completed her Ph.D. thesis on Shirley Jackson at Trinity College, Dublin, in 2003. She has edited the collection *Shirley Jackson: Essays on the Literary Legacy* (McFarland, 2005) and written a series of articles on modern American horror writers for the online Literary Encyclopaedia (www.litencyc.com). She is currently a Government of Ireland post-doctoral research fellow based at TCD and is beginning a major new research project which examines depictions of American suburbia in Gothic and horror-themed films, literature and television.

Paulina Palmer has retired from the post of senior lecturer in the English department at the University of Warwick, U.K., and now teaches part-time for the M.A./M.Sc. in gender, culture, politics at Birkbeck College, University of London. Her publications include *Contemporary Women's Fiction: Narrative Practice and Feminist Theory* (1989); *Contemporary Lesbian Writing: Dreams, Desire, Difference* (1993); and *Lesbian Gothic: Transgressive Fictions* (1999). She is a member of the steering committee of the Contemporary Women Writers' Network and is currently co-editing the proceedings of the network's inaugural conference. She has recently completed two essays on the fiction of Sarah Waters for publication, and is now embarking on a study of the concept of "the lesbian uncanny."

Andrew Scahill is a Ph.D. student in the department of radio-television-film at the University of Texas at Austin, where he specializes in 1950s Cold War era films, particularly B-cinema. His work frequently engages issues of queer spectatorship, camp, and star image to uncover alternative reading subjectivities for cinematic texts. He is currently completing his dissertation on the recurring figure of the monstrous child in horror cinema.

Brian Whaley earned a Ph.D. at the University of Oregon and works as an assistant professor of English and literature at Utah Valley State College in Orem, Utah. He teaches twentieth century and contemporary British literature and directs the college's writing program. He lives in Salt Lake City.

Index

Against Our Will 107
aliens 9, 16, 19, 181, 185; *see also Aliens*; *I Married a Monster from Outer Space*; *I, Vampire*; Scott, Jody
Aliens (film) 9, 18, 27–32, 238
"Amorous Bondage" 38n.10–11
Anolik, Ruth Bienstock, ed., *The Gothic Other* 3, 199
anorexia 56, 61, 64
The Apparitional Lesbian 15, 151–152
aristocrats and aristocracy *see* Gothic tropes and conventions
Ästhetik des Horrors 239
Auerbach, Nina, *Woman and the Demon* 29, 37n.7, 38n.12
Austen, Jane, *Northanger Abbey* 113
Ayesha: The Return of She 64

Barker, Clive 18, 248–257; *The Books of Blood* 250–258
Barney, Natalie 211–214
Beauvoir, Simone de, *The Second Sex* 4, 8–10, 19, 30–33, 35
La Belle Créole 78n.1
Benjamin, Jessica, *The Bonds of Love* 17
Benshoff, Henry M., *Monsters in the Closet* 191, 194, 250
Between Men 14
binary categories 208, 224; citizen-foreigner 167, 190; homosexual-heterosexual 6, 172, 189, 194, 197, 252; known-unknown 76; life-death 27, 30, 68; male-female 5–6, 8, 15, 41, 45, 72, 193, 234; realism-fantasy 74; self-Other 35–37
The Bird's Nest 135–136, 138–140
The Blood of the Vampire 9–10, 40–54
Bluebeard stories 13, 111–112, 115–116, 118–119

The Bonds of Love 17
"Boobs" 18, 239–243
The Books of Blood 250–258
Botting, Fred, "Power in the Darkness" 37n.5
Brantlinger, Patrick: *The Reading Lesson* 2, 14; *Rule of Darkness* 55
Brittnacher, H.R., *Ästhetik des Horrors* 239
Brontë, Charlotte, *Jane Eyre* 13, 43, 111, 113–121
Brontë, Emily, *Wuthering Heights* 67, 245n.7
Brown, Marshall, *The Gothic Text* 1
Brown, Toni, "Immunity" 235, 237–238
Browning, Robert: "My Last Duchess" 122, 128; *The Ring and the Book* 13, 122–134
Brownmiller, Susan, *Against Our Will* 107

Califia, Pat, "The Vampire" 205, 214, 217–221
cannibalism 52, 119n.2, 254
Carmilla 15, 18, 151–166, 204, 218, 228n.6, 236
Case, Sue-Ellen, "Tracking the Vampire" 206, 208
Castle, Terry: *The Apparitional Lesbian* 15, 151–152; *The Female Thermometer* 1–2, 6–7
The Castle of Otranto 4–5, 7, 11, 14, 16, 86
castration and emasculation 31, 56, 60, 62–64, 65n.11, 69, 123, 128–129, 131, 181, 189, 237
categories, conceptual, construction and transgression of 5, 178; contesting 201–258; racial/cultural 58–

60, 72, 77, 190; *see also* binary categories
Catholic Church 4–5, 12–13, 87–88, 102–106, 127–128, 130–132
Célanire cou-coupé 10, 67–79
Charnas, Suzy, "Boobs" 18, 239–243
Christabel 204
Cinderella stories 13, 116–117
The City of Dreadful Delight 41
Cixous, Hélène, "The Laugh of the Medusa" 17, 237
Clark, Anna, *Women's Silence* 107–108
Coherence of Gothic Conventions 28
Coleridge, Samuel Taylor: *Christabel* 204; *The Rime of the Ancient Mariner*, 27
colonialism *see* empire, anxieties of
Communism 16; see also *I Married a Monster from Outer Space*
Condé, Maryse: *La Belle Créole* 78n.1; *Célanire cou-coupé* 10, 67–79; *La Migration des coeurs* 67; *Moi, Tituba sorcière . . . noire de Salem* 78n.1
Culture and Imperialism 120n.6, 167

Darwinism 42, 25, 63
Daughters 43, 47–49, 87, 89, 107–108, 117–118, 135–148, 153, 238- 239; *see also* Jackson, Shirley
"Death, Femininity and Identification: A Recourse to 'Ligeia'" 38n.9
Derrida, Jacques 235; *see also* "Derrida and Gender"; Kamuf, Peggy
"Derrida and Gender" 7, 21n.5
Devil 2, 20n.3, 21n11, 94
domestic violence *see* marriage; wives and fiancées
Dracula *see Dracula*; Stoker, Bram
Dracula 15, 167–176, 179, 204, 215, 217, 221
DuBois, Page, *Torture and Truth* 36
dynasty *see* patriarchs and patriarchy; sons
Dyson, Joan, "Amorous Bondage" 38n.10–11

emasculation *see* castration and emasculation
empire, anxieties of 10, 35, 41, 43–44, 53n.4, 70, 77, 77n.11, 167, 169, 174n.2; *see also* Haggard, Rider; *She*
enclosure and imprisonment *see* Gothic tropes and conventions

Enlightenment 1–2, 5–7, 15; *see also* scientists and science
Epistemology of the Closet 170, 250, 252
Evil Incarnate 2–3
The Evolution of Sex 45–47
"explained supernatural" 87, 102, 109, 113

fairy tales 112–115; *see also* Bluebeard stories; Cinderella stories
fantastic 10, 67, 72–77
The Fantastic see fantastic
fathers 12–13, 83–101, 117–118, 192, 197; *see also* Jackson, Shirley; Law of the Father; patriarchs and patriarchy
Female Gothic 11, 13, 15, 151, 162, 164, 168, 234
The Female Thermometer 1–2, 6–7
Festinger, Leon, *When Prophecy Fails* 147n.3
Fiedler, Leslie, *Love and Death in the American Novel* 29, 37n.7
film 18–19, 20n.3, 204, 209, 245n.15; *see also* Aliens; Ginger Snaps; *I Married a Monster from Outer Space*
Forrest, Katherine V., "O, Captain, My Captain" 205, 214–217
Francophone Caribbean *see* Condé, Maryse
Frankenstein 19, 139–140, 186n.10
Frankenstein's monster *see Frankenstein*; Shelley, Mary
Frankfurter, David, *Evil Incarnate* 2–3
Freud, Sigmund 30, 83: *Totem and Taboo* 20n.4; "The Uncanny" 132, 249

Geddes, Patrick, *The Evolution of Sex* 45–47
Gilbert, Sandra, *No Man's Land* 65
The Gilda Stories 205, 221–226
Ginger Snaps (film) 239–242
Goddu, Teresa, *Gothic America* 96, 190
Gomez, Jewelle, *The Gilda Stories* 205, 221–226
Goodbye to Berlin 184
Gothic America 96, 190
Gothic (Re)Visions 36
The Gothic Other 3, 199
The Gothic Text 1
Gothic tropes and conventions 1, 29, 112, 125, 133n.4, 140–141, 143,

154–155, 178, 233; (*see also* Female Gothic); aristocrats and aristocracy 47, 83–91, 177–180, 185 (*see also* Browning, Robert; *The Italian*; Radcliffe, Ann); dark villains 12–13, 92, 103; distancing, cultural and geographic 115–116, 154 (*see also* Other); double 190, 193, 196–197; enclosure and imprisonment 13, 27, 29, 31, 34, 43, 83, 87–93, 97n.3,103–105, 108, 111–112, 114, 118, 138, 141; forbidden chamber 112, 119; house, destruction of 112–113, 119, 131, 146–147; house, haunted 2, 11, 13, 29, 89–90, 92–93, 96 (*see also The Haunting of Hill House*; Jackson, Shirley); invasion motif 251 (*see also The Blood of the Vampire*; *Carmilla*; *Dracula*; Le Fanu, Sheridan; *I Married a Monster from Outer Space*; Marryat, Florence; Stoker, Bram); labyrinth 1, 9, 133n.1 (*see also Aliens*); madness 43, 92, 118, 135–138, 143–148, 172; rape 4, 11–14, 20n.3, 88, 127–129, 135, 148n.7, 242, 252 (*see also The Italian*; Radcliffe, Ann); supernatural 1–2, 4–5, 13, 19, 20n.4, 73, 76, 83–87, 89–96, 116, 136, 139, 142, 144–146, 168, 179, 233–234 (*see also Carmilla*; *The Italian*; Le Fanu, Sheridan; Radcliffe, Ann); textual ambiguity, hermeneutic and generic 10–11; textual flexibility 20, 37, 64
government *see* laws, marriage and inheritance; state
Gregory, James: "Vegetarians in the 'Kingdom'" 61; *The Vegetarian Movement* 61–62
Gubar, Susan, *No Man's Land* 65

Haggard, Rider: *Ayesha: The Return of She* 64; *King Solomon's Mines* 57, 63; *She* 10, 55–66
Hall, Radclyffe, *The Well of Loneliness* 229n.20
Halberstam, Judith, *Skin Shows* 9, 12, 128–129, 177–178, 185, 245n.8
Hangsaman 135–138
The Haunting of Hill House 135–136, 142–145
Hogarth, William 107
homosexuals and homosexuality 5, 15, 149–200; male 4, 14–15, 18; *see also* Barker, Clive; binary categories, homosexual-heterosexual; lesbians
homosocial groups and spaces 63, 130, 132, 174, 193, 195–198
Horace Walpole 14
house, haunted; destruction of *see* Gothic tropes and conventions
How the Poor Live 41
Howard, Douglas L., *see* Anolik, Ruth Bienstock, *The Dark Unknown*
humor in the Gothic 208–217, 240
husbands and fiancés 12–13, 83–101, 112–121, 236; *see also* Browning, Robert; *I Married a Monster from Outer Space*; marriage, patriarchs and patriarchy, wives and fiancées

I Married a Monster from Outer Space (film) 16, 188–200
I, Vampire 205, 209–212
"The Imagination of Disaster" 190
"Immunity" 235, 237–238
Invasion of the Body Snatchers (film) 190–191,193, 199n.9
incest 4, 20n.3, 104, 117–118, 155–156
Innes, Sherrie, "It's a Girl Thing" 37
Isherwood, Christopher: *Goodbye to Berlin* 184; juvenalia 184–185; *Mr. Norris Changes Trains* 15–16, 177–187
The Island of Dr. Moreau 53n6
The Italian 12–13, 102–110
"It's a Girl Thing" 37

Jackson, Shirley 13; *The Bird's Nest* 135–136, 138–140; *Hangsaman* 135–138; *The Haunting of Hill House* 135–136, 142–145; *The Sundial* 135–136, 140–142; *We Have Always Lived in the Castle* 135–136, 145–147
Jane Eyre 13, 43, 111, 113–121
Jelinek, Elfriede, *Krankheit oder moderne Frauen* 18, 235–237

Kahane, Claire, "The Maternal Legacy" 30
Kamuf, Peggy, "Derrida and Gender" 7, 21n.5
Keats, John, "Lamia" 245n.12
King, Stephen 245n.15, 249
King Solomon's Mines 57, 63
Krankheit oder moderne Frauen 18, 235–237

Kristeva, Julia, *Powers of Horror* 8, 9, 17, 238, 245n.14

labyrinth *see* Gothic tropes and conventions
The Lair of the White Worm 29–31
Lamia 17, 204, 237–238, 245n.12; *see also* Keats, John; "Lamia"
Laquer, Thomas, *Making Sex* 5–8
"The Laugh of the Medusa" 17, 237
Law of the Father 96, 143, 208, 224, 229n.16
laws, marriage and inheritance 11–13, 16, 88–91, 93, 95–96, 116, 124–125, 127–132; *see also* patriarchs and patriarchy
Le Fanu, Sheridan, *Carmilla* 15, 18, 151–166, 204, 218, 228n.6, 236
Lesbian Gothic 205, 208, 227; *see also* vampires, lesbian
lesbians 4, 15, 17, 71, 203–232; *see also Carmilla*; Le Fanu, Sheridan
Lewis, Matthew, *The Monk* 4–5, 14, 99n.22
"Ligeia" 9, 32–36, 190
Linden Hills 12, 91–97
Livia, Anna, *Minimax* 211–214
Love and Death in the American Novel 29, 37n.7
"Love Bites" 235
"Lykanthropismus in einigen deutschen Horrorgeschichten um 1900" (Lycanthropy in the 1900 German Horror Story) 239

madness *see* Gothic tropes and conventions
Making Sex 5–8
Maria 113–114
marriage 13, 83–101, 111–121, 136–137, 143, 156; lesbian challenge to 204–205, 207; *see also* Browning, Robert; husbands and fiancés; *I Married a Monster from Outer Space*; wives and fiancées
Marryat, Florence: *The Blood of the Vampire* 9–10, 40–54; *The Spirit World* 49; *There Is No Death* 48, 50
masculinity, anxieties of 10, 56, 60, 85; *see also* Browning, Robert; *I Married a Monster from Outer Space*; *The Ring and the Book*
"The Maternal Legacy" 30

Maturin, Charles, *Melmoth the Wanderer* 4–5
McFie, Sean, "'They Suck Us Dry'" 52
medieval literature 248–249
Medusa 17, 20n.3, 21n11, 69, 234, 237–238; *see also* Cixous, Hélène, "The Laugh of the Medusa"
Melmoth the Wanderer 4–5
men 4, 5, 10–13, 81–148, 233; *see also* fathers; husbands and fiancés; masculinity; patriarchs and patriarchy; sons
menstruation 5, 9, 18, 46, 207, 240–242
midwives 84–85
La Migration des coeurs 67
Minimax 211–214
miscegenation 42–43, 47, 49, 52, 57–60, 63–64, 67, 70–72, 77–78, 175n.6
Mr. Norris Changes Trains 15–16, 177–187
mob 146, 153, 197, 256
Moi, Tituba sorcière . . . noire de Salem 78n.1
The Monk 4–5, 14, 99n.22
Monsters in the Closet 191, 194, 250
mothers and motherhood 7, 9, 10, 21n7, 77–78, 83–101, 109n.5, 117, 137, 142, 145, 152–156, 197, 236–238; lesbian discourse of 206, 208, 219–220, 224–226; *see also* Aliens; *The Blood of the Vampire*; Marryat, Florence; miscegenation
Mowl, Tim, *Horace Walpole* 14
"My Last Duchess" 122, 128
The Mysteries of Udolpho 11, 108

Naylor, Gloria, *Linden Hills* 12, 91–97
Nazism 15–16, 182–183
New Woman 47–48, 56, 60, 62, 204
No Man's Land 65
Northanger Abbey 113

"O, Captain, My Captain" 205, 214–217
"On the Supernatural in Poetry" 6, 86, 234
Orientalism 115
Other, destruction of 42, 51, 59, 63, 77, 95, 124, 130–132, 145, 152–53, 159, 161, 173–174, 180–181, 197, 240–241, 249, 256; racial, religious, social 2, 3,

10, 15, 19, 43–47, 49, 52, 96, 114–115, 199n.4, 199n.5, 199n.8, 237–238; spectralization of 2–3, 6–8, 14–16, 88–93, 96–97, 152, 205; *see also Célanire cou-coupé*; Condé, Maryse; dark villains; *Dracula*; Gothic tropes and conventions; Haggard, Rider; *She*; Stoker, Bram

patriarchs and patriarchy 8–9, 11, 13, 15–16, 84–86, 89, 92–93, 96, 151–152, 155, 160–162, 164, 174, 205, 236, 254; challenge of homosexuality to 207–208; *see also* Browning, Robert; *Carmilla*; fathers, husbands and fiancés; Jackson, Shirley; Law of the Father; Le Fanu, Sheridan
physicians *see* scientists and science
Poe, Edgar Allan, "Ligeia" 9, 32–36, 190
Politics 248–250; *see also* laws, marriage and inheritance; state
"Popular Perceptions of Rape as a Capital Crime in Eighteenth-Century England" 107
"Power in the Darkness" 37n.5
Powers of Horror 8, 9, 17, 238, 245n.14
Puberty 46, 239–243
Punter, David, "Death, Femininity and Identification: A Recourse to 'Ligeia'" 38n.9

Queer and Now 229n.17
queer culture and queer theory 18, 191, 205–206, 224, 226, 252, 256

Radcliffe, Ann: "explained supernatural" 87, 102, 109, 113; *The Italian* 12–13, 102–110; *The Mysteries of Udolpho* 11, 108; *A Sicilian Romance* 12, 86–92, 94–6; "On the Supernatural in Poetry" 6, 86, 234
rape *see* Gothic tropes and conventions
The Reading Lesson 2, 14
Reading the Other 3
Realism, relationship to the Gothic 20n.4, 87, 113, 183–184
Rifelj, Carol de Dobay, *Reading the Other* 3
The Rime of the Ancient Mariner 27
The Ring and the Book 13, 122–134
"A Room of One's Own" 13

Rule of Darkness 55
Russ, Joanna, "Somebody's Trying to Kill Me and I Think It's My Husband" 11

Sade, Marquis de 22n11
Said, Edward: *Culture and Imperialism* 120n.6, 167; *Orientalism* 115
Satan *see* Devil
science fiction *see Aliens*; Forrest, Katherine V.; *I Married a Monster from Outer Space*; *I, Vampire*; "O, Captain, My Captain"; Scott, Jody
scientists and science 9, 41–7, 49–52, 67–69, 72, 74, 135, 139–140, 153, 154–155, 161–162, 165n.16, 175n.6, 236–237, 251; *see also* Darwinism
Scott, Jody, *I, Vampire* 205, 209–212
The Second Sex 4, 8–10, 19, 30–33, 35
Sedgwick, Eve Kosofsky: *Between Men* 14; *Coherence of Gothic Conventions* 28; *Epistemology of the Closet* 170, 250, 252; *Queer and Now* 229n.17
Sexual Anarchy 6, 8, 19, 172
Shakespeare, William, *The Winter's Tale* 12, 83–85, 92–96
She 10, 55–66
Shelley, Mary, *Frankenstein* 19, 139–140, 186n.10; see also *Célanire cou-coupé*; Condé, Maryse
Showalter, Elaine, *Sexual Anarchy* 6, 8, 19, 172
A Sicilian Romance 12, 86–92, 94–6
Simpson, Antony E., "Popular Perceptions of Rape as a Capital Crime in Eighteenth-Century England" 107
Sims, George, *How the Poor Live* 41
Skin Shows 9, 12, 128–129, 177–178, 185, 245n.8
"Somebody's Trying to Kill Me and I Think It's My Husband" 11
sons 47, 51, 83, 87, 89, 92–94, 105, 174, 236–237
Sontag, Susan, "The Imagination of Disaster" 190
The Spirit World 49
state 255–257; *see also* laws, marriage and inheritance; Nazism
Stoker, Bram: *Dracula* 15, 167–176, 179, 204, 215, 217, 221; *The Lair of the White Worm* 29–31
The Sundial 135–136, 140–142

supernatural *see* Gothic tropes and conventions

There Is No Death 48, 50
"'They Suck Us Dry'" 52
Thomsom. J. Arthur, *The Evolution of Sex* 45–47
Todorov, Tzvetan, *The Fantastic see* fantastic
Torture and Truth 36
Totem and Taboo 20n.4
"Tracking the Vampire" 206, 208

"The Uncanny" 132, 249

"The Vampire" 205, 214, 217–221
vampires 9, 10, 15, 17, 19, 20n.3, 179, 181, 203; female, 203–204, 235–238; lesbian 204–208, 227–228; *see also The Blood of the Vampire*; Califia, Pat; *Carmilla*; *Dracula*; Forrest, Katherine V.; *The Gilda Stories*; Gomez, Jewelle; *I, Vampire*; Jelinek, Elfriede; *Krankheit oder moderne Frauen*; Le Fanu, Sheridan; Livia, Anna; Marryat, Florence; *Minimax*; "O, Captain, My Captain"; Scott, Jody Scott; Stoker, Bram; "The Vampire"
The Vegetarian Movement 61–62
vegetarianism 61–62
"Vegetarians in the 'Kingdom'" 61
Vetter, Ingeborg, "Lykanthropismus in einigen deutschen Horrorgeschichten um 1900" (Lycanthropy in the 1900 German Horror Story) 239
Vivien, Renee 211–214

Walkowitz, Judith, *The City of Dreadful Delight* 41

Walpole, Horace, *The Castle of Otranto* 4–5, 7, 11, 14, 16, 86
We Have Always Lived in the Castle 135–136, 145–147
Weimar Republic *see* Isherwood, Christopher, *Mr. Norris Changes Trains*
The Well of Loneliness 229n.20
Wells, H.G., *The Island of Dr. Moreau* 53n6
werewolves 18, 125–126, 239–243
When Prophecy Fails 147n.3
Wilde, Oscar 15, 169–171, 228n.3
The Winter's Tale 12, 83–85, 92–96
Wisker, Gena, "Love Bites" 235
witches 2, 84–85, 87, 94, 147, 205, 228n.9, 238
wives and fiancées 83–101, 111–121, 125–134, 235–237; *see also* husbands and fiancés; *I Married a Monster from Outer Space*; marriage
Wollstonecraft, Mary, *Maria* 113–114
Wolstenholme, Susan, *Gothic (Re)Visions* 36
Woman and the Demon, 29, 37n.7, 38n.12
women 4–5, 8–10, 25–79, 105; celebration of, 234–235, 243–244; *see also* daughters; menstruation; midwives; mothers and motherhood; New Woman; witches; wives and fiancées
Women's Silence 107–108
Woolf, Virginia 5, 86, 96, 98n.12, 210–212; "A Room of One's Own" 13
Wuthering Heights 67, 245n.7

www.ingramcontent.com/pod-product-compliance
Lightning Source LLC
Chambersburg PA
CBHW051213300426
44116CB00006B/553